Phonology and Syntax

Current Studies in Linguistics Series
Samuel Jay Keyser, general editor

Phonology and Syntax:
The Relation between
Sound and Structure

Elisabeth O. Selkirk

The MIT Press
Cambridge, Massachusetts
London, England

First MIT Press paperback edition, 1986

This book was set in VIP Times Roman by Village Typographers, Inc.,
and printed and bound by The Murray Company in the United States
of America.

Library of Congress Cataloging in Publication Data

Selkirk, Elisabeth O., 1945–
  Phonology and syntax.

  (Current studies in linguistics series; 10)
  Bibliography: p.
  Includes index.
  1. Grammar, Comparative and general—Phonology.
  2. Grammar, Comparative and general—Syntax.   I. Title.
  II. Series.
P217.3.S44   1984   414   83-17453
ISBN 0-262-19226-8 (hard)
        0-262-69098-5 (paper)

This book is dedicated in loving memory
to my father George H. Selkirk

Contents

Contents

Series Foreword

We are pleased to present this book as the tenth volume in the series Current Studies in Linguistics.

As we have defined it, the series will offer book-length studies in linguistics and neighboring fields that further the exploration of man's ability to manipulate symbols. It will pursue the same editorial goals as its companion journal, *Linguistic Inquiry,* and will complement it by providing a format for in-depth studies beyond the scope of the professional article.

By publishing such studies, we hope the series will answer the need for intensive and detailed research that sheds new light on current theoretical issues and provides a new dimension for their resolution. Toward this end it will present books dealing with the widest range of languages and addressing the widest range of theoretical topics. From time to time and with the same ends in view, the series will include collections of significant articles covering single and selected subject areas and works primarily for use as textbooks.

Like *Linguistic Inquiry,* Current Studies in Linguistics will seek to present work of theoretical interest and excellence.

Samuel Jay Keyser

Preface

This book was largely written in 1981–1982, though it has been much longer in the making. It was erroneously dubbed "forthcoming" (as it indeed in some sense was) when only parts were written, and now it turns out that those pieces that earlier circulated and were referred to as part of this book do not even have a place here. My conception of the book has changed over time. Of a chapter on English word structure and the theory of word syntax that was written in 1977, part was revised and expanded in early 1981 and then published separately as *The Syntax of Words* in the Linguistic Inquiry monograph series. Another part was published as "English Compounding and the Theory of Word Structure" in *The Scope of Lexical Rules,* ed. by T. Hoekstra, H. van der Hulst, and M. Moortgat. A chapter on the syllable, in English and in general, was written in 1978, found not to fit in 1982, and given to be published in *The Structure of Phonological Representations (Part II),* ed. by H. van der Hulst and N. Smith. I had thought that there would be far more in the book on syllables and on other (putatively) higher-order units of prosodic structure like the foot, the prosodic word, and the phonological phrase. As the reader will soon see, I am no longer an exponent of a theory of phonological representation that gives the last three a central place, if any place at all, and so in the end I have devoted little space to them here. There were less principled reasons for leaving out any consideration of syllabification and its relation to syntactic representation. To treat these questions seriously would simply have required more time in research and writing and would have made this book too long. But I hope the reader will agree that the book, and the theory of the relation between syntactic and phonological representation developed here, survive this omission.

The book began as a revision of my doctoral dissertation, *The Phrase Phonology of English and French,* written in 1972. I sometimes ask myself why it has taken so long, but I suppose it isn't that much of a mystery. Phonological theory has undergone dramatic changes in the last ten years, my own views have changed, and each change has required a rethinking of the book. What I thought to be the topic of the book has also expanded considerably in some ways, and has been retracted in others. It began as a study of junctural phenomena in English and French. Now it covers far more than juncture, but it does not deal with French in any serious way. (When it became clear that this book was not a revision of the dissertation, the dissertation was published unrevised.) To live up to the title I gave the book long ago, before it was even forthcoming, I also felt it necessary to take on the study of stress, in both the word and the sentence, and intonation. This has taken a certain time. Yet the labors of research and thought do not entirely explain why so many years have gone by with the book still forthcoming. Some of us feel ambivalence about our work—do we like it or not, does it live up to our own expectations, do we really want to let it go? I am no exception. And, though since that earlier writing I have continued in this scholarly business, I still feel the ambivalence I expressed when I dedicated my dissertation to Antonio Gramsci, "who chose not to continue his promising career in linguistics."

During the last ten years, I have been lucky to have colleagues and friends with whom I have had very fruitful intellectual exchange. Jean-Roger Vergnaud, Morris Halle, Alan Prince, Janet Pierrehumbert, Mark Liberman, and François Dell have been very important interlocutors on matters phonological and otherwise. Getting started was made less difficult by Joan Bresnan, who nurtured with me a preoccupation with the organization of the grammar, and Jay Keyser, who supported my work and gave me hope. Colleagues and friends at the University of Massachusetts at Amherst then and now have provided an extremely stimulating atmosphere for the study of both phonology and syntax, in classes, discussions, and casual remarks. I am very grateful to Emmon Bach, Edwin Williams, Irene Heim, Roger Higgins, Lyn Frazier, and Tom Roeper. I am also deeply grateful to friends in the Pioneer Valley and beyond who have given me support, as well as respite from that stimulating linguistic atmosphere. Over the years a number of people have given me much-needed help in preparing this book for publication, and I thank them all for making the task easier. Lynne Ballard typed most of the manuscript, beautifully, and gave me encouragement. Janet Pierrehumbert very kindly arranged to have drafted versions of figures from her dissertation provided to me, courtesy of AT&T Bell Laboratories. Jan Wager, Toni Borowsky, Lori Taft, Jan Bing, Judith Katz, Kathy Adamczyk, Barbie Dick, and especially Shinsho Miyara aided in other aspects of preparation. I would also like to express my gratitude to those who have provided me with a roof and a welcome workplace at various points in past years when this work was still ongoing: Maurice Gross, for his hospitality at the Université de Paris VII; Mario Rossi, Albert di Cristo, Daniel Hirst, and Thamy Benkirane, for my time spent at the Institut de Phonétique in Aix-en-Provence; and especially Jay Keyser and members of the speech group at MIT, for hosting me during the last year when, as a postdoctoral fellow at the Center for Cognitive Science, I brought this work very near to completion. Finally, I want to thank Anne Mark, who did an impeccable job of editing the manuscript, and Armin Mester and Jun Ko Ito for producing the index.

Lisa Selkirk
Northampton, Massachusetts

The Author to Her Book

Thou ill-form'd offspring of my feeble brain,
Who after birth didst by my side remain
Till snatcht from thence by friends less wise than true
Who thee abroad expos'd to publick view,
Made thee in raggs, halting to th' press to trudge
Where errors were not lessened (all may judge)
At thy return my blushing was not small,
My rambling brat (in print) should mother call.
I cast thee by as one unfit for light,
Thy Visage was so irksome in my sight;
Yet being mine own, at length affection would
Thy blemishes amend, if so I could:
I wash'd thy face, but more defects I saw
And rubbing off a spot, still made a flaw.
I stretcht thy joints to make thee even feet,
Yet still thou run'st more hobling than is meet;
In better dress to trim thee was my mind,
But nought save home-spun Cloth i'th'house I find.
In this array 'mongst Vulgars mayst thou roam,
In criticks hands beware thou dost not come,
And take thy way where yet thou art not known.
If for thy Father askt, say, thou hadst none:
And for thy Mother, she alas is poor,
Which caus'd her thus to send thee out of door.

Anne Bradstreet
1612–1672

Phonology and Syntax

Chapter 1
The Relation between Syntax and Phonology

1.1 An Overview of the Issues

A sentence of a language, uttered, is but a stream of sound, and that stream of sound has associated with it a certain meaning, or meanings. A grammar of a language is a characterization of the relation between sound and meaning for the sentences of that language. This relation between sound (phonetic representation) and meaning (semantic representation) is not a direct one. It is mediated by structure, or syntax, the arrangement of a sentence into parts. The meaning of a sentence is a function of the meaning of its (syntactic) parts, and, too, the sound of a sentence is a function of the sound of its parts. In both instances the function is rather complex. The purpose of this book is to contribute to our understanding of the ways in which the phonology of a sentence may be determined by its syntax, to attempt to characterize the relation between sound and structure in language.

A theory of grammar has the task of characterizing the set of possible relations between sound and meaning (the set of possible grammars) for language in general. The theory of grammar adopted here has developed within the framework of generative grammar—in the works laying the foundation of the so-called standard theory, notably Chomsky 1965 and Chomsky and Halle 1968, and in works that have since contributed to revisions of it. Basic to this theory (in its revised extended form; see Chomsky 1980, 1981) is the assumption that the linguistic description of a sentence involves assigning to it a set of phonological representations $P_1 \ldots P_n$, a set of syntactic representations $S_1 \ldots S_n$, and a logical form, LF. (The logical form of a sentence is not in fact a representation of its meaning, but only a representation serving as a crucial link between the syntactic representation and the semantic rep-

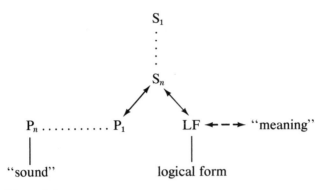

Figure 1.1

resentation (see Chomsky 1981, for example). Since that distinction is for the most part immaterial to our concerns, however, we will in general ignore it.)[1] The representation of the pronunciation or sound of a sentence, P_n, is seen to relate to its logical form via a system of intermediate representations, where the syntactic representation, the surface structure S_n, is pivotal (figure 1.1).[2]

Thus the linguistic description of a sentence involves a *representation* of that sentence by three different components of the grammar: the phonological, the syntactic, and the "syntacticosemantic." A theory of grammar must specify the nature of the representation by each of these components and what types of rules, if any, define these representations (the *representation question*). It must also specify whether more than one representation by each of these components is relevant to linguistic description and, if so, specify the nature of the set of rules that relate these representations within a component (the *derivation question*). Finally, it must specify the relations between the components, i.e., between the representations defined by the different components (the *interpretation question*).

It is a fundamental assumption of the generative theory of phonology and syntax that only the *surface* syntactic representation, S_n, has a place in characterizing the sound-meaning relation for a language. We believe this assumption to be well founded and will, where appropriate, defend it against evidence (such as that offered by Bierwisch 1968 or Bresnan 1971a, 1972) that might seem to indicate that other, nonsurface representations of the syntax impinge in some way on the phonology. (See chapters 5 and 7.) It is also a fundamental assumption of the standard theory, one that we adopt in somewhat modified form here, that characterizing the relation between the surface syntactic representation S_n and the surface phonological (or phonetic) representation P_n involves (a) a set of rules defining the mapping between S_n and an underlying phonological representation P_1 and (b) a set of rules mapping P_1 into P_n. The first are rules that *interpret* the syntactic representation as a phonological representation—that is, translate one sort of representation into another. We will call these the *rules of the syntax-phonology mapping*. The second are rules that *derive* one phonological representation from another. These might appropriately be called the *phonological rules* of the grammar. In this book, we will advance and defend a particular theory of that relation between (surface) syntactic representation and (underlying) phonological representation (the syntax-phonology mapping) and will explore the implications of this theory for the theory of phonological derivation.

The conception of the syntactic level, or syntactic component, that doubtless prevails in the current context is the one born with the so-called *standard theory* (Chomsky 1965) and retained, in its most general lines, in the various extensions and revisions of this theory (see, for example, Chomsky 1981 and references therein). This *revised extended standard theory* specifies, as do other syntactic theories, that a syntactic representation S_i is a well-formed labeled bracketing, or tree. It specifies further, and here parts company with some, that a set of syntactic representations $S_1 \ldots S_n$ is associated with any particular sentence. It claims that S_1, the deep structure, can be characterized in terms of (or generated by) a set of context-free rewriting rules (the phrase structure rules) and a lexicon (Chomsky 1965).[3] Finally, it claims that S_1 is related to S_n, the surface structure, by a set of transformational rules. According to the revised extended standard theory, then, there is a transformational derivation within the syntactic level. In the present articulations of the theory, it should be noted, the surface syntactic representation S_n, which is phonologically interpreted (put in direct relation to P_1), is not identified with the only near-surface syntactic representation S-structure, which is put in relation to logical form (Chomsky and Lasnik 1977). The status of this distinction is a matter of debate at present, and we will for the most part ignore it, understanding "surface structure" in the standard sense, as the syntactic representation wherein the full transformational derivation is complete. In recent years, alternative theories of syntax have been proposed that entirely eliminate the transformational derivation, i.e., the positing of a distinction between deep and surface syntactic representations. (See, for example, Bresnan 1982 and the works cited therein, and Gazdar 1981.) According to such theories, there is but one syntactic tree representation, the surface structure.

In what follows, the term *syntactic representation* will refer not only to the representation of phrase structure, or syntactic structure, but also to the representation of word structure, or morphological structure. The two share essential formal properties (see Selkirk 1982). Yet it will prove useful to maintain a distinction between sentence grammar, on the one hand, and word grammar, on the other, the first characterizing the sound-meaning relation of the sentences of a language and the second the sound-meaning relation of its words (see Bach 1983). In this we depart somewhat from the standard theory. A word grammar might consist of a word-syntactic component, characterizing the possible word structures of the language (see Selkirk 1982, for example), a phonological component interpreting these word structures phonologically, and a semantic component. The rules and principles of these components, and their interaction, could conceivably be rather different from those of sentence grammar. While it is our contention that word grammar and sentence grammar are in fact parallel in many important ways (see the discussion in sections 3.1, 3.4, 8.3), establishing that parallelism is not a primary concern of this book. Rather, we seek to investigate questions primarily involving sentence grammar and the syntax-phonology interaction within it.

To make the focus on sentence grammar entirely clear, we will simply construe the syntactic surface structure of a sentence as consisting of a sequence of words, defined by a separate word grammar. The aspects of these words that are relevant to sentence grammar are (i) their (surface) word structure, (ii) their (derived) phonological representation (i.e., the output of the phonological rules of word grammar), which we will call the *word-level phonological representation,* and (iii) their semantic representation. The second, of course—and perhaps the first as well—is directly relevant to our main concern, which is the phonological interpretation of syntactic structure.

Whereas the answer to the representation question in syntax has remained more or less the same in the successive articulations of syntactic theory within the generative framework, this is not true of the answer to the representation question in phonology. The last decade has seen fundamental changes in the theory of phonological representation, changes whose implications are perhaps not fully understood, but that clearly require radically different answers to the derivation question and the interpretation question (the relation between syntax and phonology) than the standard theory offered, especially as articulated in *The Sound Pattern of English* (Chomsky and Halle 1968; hereafter SPE).

Common to most approaches to the linguistic representation of the sound of sentences is the notion that the sound continuum must be analyzed as a sequence of discrete sound *segments*. Generative phonology has characterized a sound segment as a complex of distinctive features, and thus has construed the sequence of sound segments making up an utterance as a *distinctive feature matrix*. Within the standard theory, all phonological properties of an utterance, even those termed "suprasegmental," such as tonal contours and stress patterns, are held to be "segmental," in the sense that they can be reduced to a representation in terms of the distinctive feature complexes forming part of the unilinear sequence. A sequence of segments, then, is taken to be the representation of what is properly phonological—of what, ultimately, is pronounced. Yet, as has long been recognized, a sequence of phonological segments alone cannot permit an insightful description of the significant phonological properties of an utterance, for it can be shown that there exist different sorts of relations between the segments in sequence, relations that may be thought of as varying "degrees of connectedness." Standard generative theory, following in the steps of American structuralist linguistics, represents some of these relations between segments as "juncture" elements, or *boundaries,* proposing that these boundaries are themselves segments, occupying a place between the truly phonological segments in the strictly linear arrangement of phonological representation. Moreover, according to standard generative phonology, characterizing the relations between segments in a phonological representation of a sentence also involves the full range of information represented in the labeled bracketing or tree of its syntactic representation. A major contribution of SPE and other early works in the generative tradition was the demonstration that certain phonological properties of sentences, in particular their stress patterns, are determined in a rather direct way by their (surface) syntactic structure. Thus, in the standard framework, phonological rules were seen to apply to the segments of phonological representation in virtue of the syntactic constituent structure relations obtaining between the segments (or subsequences of them). For the standard theory, a phonological representation is a syntactic labeled tree or bracketing of a terminal string consisting of a sequence of sound segments and boundaries.

Surface structure, in the standard theory, is a labeled bracketing of sound segments. The relation between surface structure and underlying phonological representation is defined by rules of a "readjustment component." On this theory the underlying phonological representation of a sentence differs little from surface structure: it contains the same sequence of segments (with some possible additions, made by readjustment rules that "spell out" "empty" morphemes),[4] and it has more or less the same labeled bracketing (though this may be modified somewhat by readjustment rules, in ways never made explicit). The essential difference between the two is the presence of boundaries in phonological representation. These grammatical formatives are said to be introduced by a set of conventions forming part of the readjustment component, which insert boundaries in the phonological representation on the basis of the surface structure (SPE; Stanley 1973; Selkirk 1972, 1974). The boundaries of the standard phonological representation constitute a very rough translation, into linear terms, of the hierarchical syntactic structure of the sentence. Whereas some rules of the phonological component apply directly in terms of the syntactic labeled bracketing of the sentences, others, according to the standard theory, appeal only to the relational information encoded in boundaries.

It is now more than a decade since what came to be called the standard theory of generative phonology was propounded in *The Sound Pattern of English*. And it is by now well established that a phonological representation is more than a mere string of segments (sound segments and boundaries) with an associated syntactic structure. It is known that a phonological representation consists of a sequence of *syllables,* and that the syllable has an internal constituent structure, its "terminal" positions coinciding in general with what we know as segments.[5] It is also known that there may be more than one *autosegmental tier* in a phonological representation, and that on each of these independent tiers phonological features or feature bundles are arranged (as segments, or "autosegments," to use Goldsmith's term) in linear fashion.[6] Following recent work on this topic (see, for example, Halle and Vergnaud 1980), we will view the sequence of syllables (or, perhaps, their terminal positions) as the *core,* or *axis,* of a three-dimensional object in which the autosegmental tiers are parallel to the axis, the (auto-)segments of the tiers being "connected" to one or more consecutive positions in the axis by "association lines." (See especially Halle and

Vergnaud 1979, McCarthy 1979a, Clements and Keyser 1981, Selkirk 1984.) Moreover, it is known that the syllables of phonological representation are arranged in some kind of hierarchical organization. By "hierarchical organization" we do not mean the complex of autosegmental tiers; the elements of the various tiers appear not to be related to each other hierarchically or in any direct fashion whatsoever, but to be directly related only to the syllable axis. (On one autosegmental tier will be represented the tonal segments consisting of the tonal or intonational contours, on another the features involved in vowel harmony, and so on.) By "hierarchical organization" we mean, very roughly speaking, the organization of the units of phonological analysis into layers, vertically arranged on the same plane. Just what the nature of that hierarchical phonological representation is will be a major focus of this book.

There are in fact two distinct sorts of hierarchical organization that form part of a phonological representation. One is what may be called *prosodic constituent structure* (a term that includes *metrical trees;* see section 1.2). It is a structure of the same general sort that is familiar from syntactic description, one in which linguistic units are grouped into yet larger units, constituting a well-formed labeled bracketing or tree. The syllables (and their internal constituents) are clearly units of this hierarchy, as are, above them, intonational phrases. What units, if any, may intervene between syllables and intonational phrases in this prosodic constituent structure is a matter of some debate (section 1.2). The other sort of hierarchical organization within the phonological representation of a sentence is a representation of its *rhythmic structure*. Rhythmic structure per se can be represented as a *metrical grid* (Liberman 1975). A metrical grid is a representation of a hierarchy of temporal periodicities. It consists of a hierarchy of metrical levels, each level in turn consisting of a sequence of positions (beats) that stand for points in (abstract) time and define the recurring periodicities of rhythm; it is not a tree. The rhythmic structure of a sentence is the alignment of its syllables with a metrical grid.

Why these hierarchical aspects of "nonlinear" phonological representation deserve special attention here should be obvious. This conception of phonological representation as having its own hierarchical structure(s) demands a radical rethinking of the relation between syntax and phonology. Phonological representation can no longer be seen simply as a "readjusted" surface structure. It has its own defining properties. Thus the interpretation question—the question of the mapping between phonological representation and syntactic representation—takes on a much greater importance than in the standard theory, and has an entirely different quality to it. It must be viewed as a characterization of the relation between the syntactic hierarchy, on the one hand, and the phonological hierarchy (or hierarchies), on the other.[7]

This emerging richer conception of a phonological representation has further implications for the theory of the relation between syntax and phonology. We believe that it is in terms of the hierarchical organization(s) of phonological representation that the "juncture" or the "degrees of connectedness" between the segments of phonological representation that may affect the application of phonological rules should be represented. Over the years, it has been argued (in a number of different ways) that the junctural properties of sentences should somehow be represented "suprasegmentally" rather than as the segmental boundaries of the standard theory (see, for example, McCawley 1968, Pyle 1972, Selkirk 1981a, Rotenberg 1978, Basbøll 1978). Here we take that line of thinking one step further and propose that these junctural properties be characterized in terms of the already independently motivated hierarchical structures of the representation. Thus the theory of phonological representation that we will advocate here eliminates segmental boundary elements altogether. (See chapters 3, 6, and 7 for discussion of the role of the phonological hierarchies in supplanting boundaries.)

In sum, the "revised theory" of the phonological representation is that it consists of (a) a *prosodic constituent structure* (including a sequence of syllables), (b) a set of *autosegmental tiers,* (c) a rhythmic structure, the *metrical grid,* and (d) a specification of the *associations or alignments* between these various aspects of the representation. The "revised theory" of the relation between syntax and phonology is that it is a mapping from a syntactic representation into a fully specified phonological representation with these properties.

Our theory departs from the standard theory of the syntax-phonology relation in another way as well. As mentioned earlier, we will assume that a grammar consists of a word grammar and a sentence grammar, and that the syntax-phonology relation must be characterized for both. Given our assumption that syntactic surface structure consists of a sequence of words (the outputs of word grammar), with their individual word-level phonological representations,[8] our goal of characterizing the syntax-phonology relation for sentence grammar strictly speaking commits us only to investigating the phonological properties of the sentence that are governed by the rules and principles of sentence grammar. (Though, of course, since there is significant overlap in the rules and principles of the two subgrammars, there will be occasion to examine the syntax-phonology mapping in word grammar as well.)

As we will show, the properly syntactic aspects of the surface syntactic representation play a crucial role in determining just how the phonological representation of the sentence is hierarchically organized—in governing how the phonological representation is, in essence, "constructed." Whether the surface syntactic labeled bracketing has any greater role in phonological description—that is, whether or not it actually governs the application of phonological rules of sentence grammar (and thus has a direct role in a phonological derivation)—is debatable. We will argue that in the unmarked case, phonological rules of sentence grammar are affected by syntactic structure only indirectly, through the influence of syntactic structure on the hierarchical structure of phonological representation. (See especially chapter 6.) It is the latter sort of structure that appears to govern the application of the vast majority of phonological rules. Note that an important conceptual distinction is being made here between *phonological rules,* which apply in a derivation in terms of a phonological representation, hierarchically arranged, and *rules for constructing or defining the representation* (e.g., rules of syllabification and resyllabification (see section 1.2.3), rules of intonational phrasing, rules aligning syllables with the metrical grid, and so on), which apply (partly) in terms of surface syntactic representation. The latter rules define the mapping between syntactic and phonological representation, and will be the focus of concern in this book.[9]

1.2 Hierarchical Structures in Phonology

1.2.1 Rhythmic Structure

Liberman 1975 proposes a formal representation of rhythmic structure for language that embodies the claim that the rhythmic organization of speech is quite analogous to that of music. This representation is called the *metrical grid.* We will argue here that the metrical grid forms an integral part of the phonological representation of the sentence, that it is in terms of the grid that patterns of stress or prominence are to be represented, and that it is in terms of the grid that a theory of stress patterns in language must be couched. Prince 1981, 1983 argues convincingly that a theory that views stress patterns as resulting from a set of rules for defining directly the alignment of the syllables of the sentence with the rhythmic structure of the metrical grid is not only possible, but highly desirable, and preferable to other approaches to the analysis of stress patterns. We view Prince's position as essentially correct and will elaborate on it here.

Before introducing the metrical grid, we will review the general characteristics of musical rhythm that any formalized system must represent. In their discussion of the temporal organization of music, Cooper and Meyer 1960:3 define a *pulse* as "one of a series of regularly recurring, precisely equivalent stimuli," as for example the ticks of a clock (or a metronome). The existence of a regular succession of pulses is of course prerequisite to any organization into rhythmic patterns, the patterns themselves being impossible in the absence of this basic regularity. For Cooper and Meyer, the pulses of musical time are arranged into *metrical patterns:*

Meter is the measurement of the number of pulses between more or less regularly recurring accents. Therefore, in order for meter to exist, some of the pulses in a series must be accented—marked for consciousness—relative to others. When pulses are thus counted within a metric context, they are referred to as *beats*. Beats which are accented are called "strong"; those which are unaccented are called "weak." (Cooper and Meyer 1960:3)

To see this, consider the following diagram, where the x's are taken to be pulses (points in time) and the underlining indicates which pulses are "marked for consciousness."

(1.1)

x̠ x x̠ x x̠ x x̠ x x̠ x

Cooper and Meyer will call the pulses here *beats,* because those that are marked for consciousness (accented) are organized into metrical patterns; that is, they recur in regular fashion—in this case in a strictly binary alternating pattern. (For Cooper and Meyer, the underlined beats are the strong beats; the others are weak.) Keeping in mind that what Cooper and Meyer call *meter* in music is what we, in referring to speech, are calling *rhythm,*[10] we will use this musical analogy, as Liberman (1975) has done, to pursue the analysis of speech rhythm and its implications for linguistic representation. Now, in the temporal organization of music, there is a hierarchy of levels (Cooper and Meyer 1960:4–5), each with its own beats, strong and weak; that is, there are various levels of pulses, and on each level the pulses are organized into metrical patterns. In addition,

[in] the metrical schemes of Western classical music, each level of the hierarchy is periodically regular; the "pulse" at a given level is fixed (with some exceptions) at a periodicity which coincides with the periodicity of the next level up in a constant way, generally either two to one or three to one. (Liberman 1975:272)

Any representation of the rhythmic organization of music, or of any system with a rhythmic organization like that of music, must thus give representation to pulses, or beats, to the distinction between strong and weak beats, and to the various levels on which these strong-weak distinctions may obtain. The metrical grid, proposed by Liberman 1975, is just such a representation. We will outline its essential features here; for a discussion of its formal properties, see chapter 5 of Liberman 1975 and section 3.3 of Liberman and Prince 1977. It is a two-dimensional object consisting of parallel horizontal levels on which there are points, marking periodicities. Because the periodicities are hierarchically arranged, any point on a higher level will coincide (vertically speaking) with a point on a lower level (though not vice versa). (1.2) shows a well-formed metrical grid:

(1.2)
```
x                     x
x         x           x
x   x     x   x     x     x   x
x x x x x x x x x x x x x x x x x
```

The horizontal levels will be called *metrical grid levels,* or *metrical levels,* for short.[11] For reasons to be explained later, the points on the lowest metrical level will be referred to as *demibeats.* All points on the second metrical level and above will be referred to as *beats.* A beat (or demibeat) that does not coincide with a beat on the next higher metrical level will be referred to as a *weak* beat (or demibeat). A beat (or demibeat) that does coincide with a beat on a higher metrical level will be referred to as a *strong* beat (or demibeat).

Note that there is nothing in the grid representation itself that specifies the nature of the periodicities of the pulses (metrical patterns) on any metrical level. In principle, any sort of pattern "graspable by the mind"[12] could be employed in a rhythmic organization and be represented by the metrical grid. But in fact, in many sorts of rhythmically organized activity, whether it be Western classical music, dance, marching in military style, or uttering the syllables of a language, there is a noted tendency to an alternation of strong and weak beats. As a variant on this binary organization, one may encounter ternary beats (a strong accompanied by a sequence of two weaks), but quaternary groups seem to be felt as two binary. Thus there may be some quite general *Principle of Rhythmic Alternation* lying behind the patterns attested.[13] We offer a provisional formulation of this principle: that between two successive strong beats there intervenes at least one and at most two weak beats. We take this principle to be a plausible, not entirely far-fetched hypothesis about the nature of rhythmic patterns. It is an empirical question, of course, whether such a principle is really at play in the diverse realms of human activity that may be subject to rhythmic organization.[14] It may be that there is no magic about the number two and its variant three, and that the patterns attested are more heterogeneous. But we will for the time being take this Principle of Rhythmic Alternation as a working hypothesis to guide our investigation, holding onto the idea that there is more to rhythmic organization than the mere existence of patterns of beats at various levels, that there may be something important to be learned about rhythm, and human cognitive capacities, in determining the types of patterns that are involved.

1.2.2 The Role of Rhythmic Structure in Linguistic Description

Liberman's claim, which we support and for which we will present additional evidence, is that the rhythmic organization of natural language is analogous to that of music. More specifically, the claim is that it is appropriate to represent the rhythm of an utterance as the alignment of its syllables with a metrical grid, in particular a metrical grid governed by something like the Principle of Rhythmic Alternation in its provisional form. Liberman's position on the place of rhythmic organization in linguistic description can be construed as one according to which the rhythmic organization of speech is a relatively superficial phenomenon, produced as part of the phonetic implementation of a more basic phonological representation having quite different properties.. According to this theory, the metrical grid alignment of the sentence is a representation in terms of which such things as the tendency toward the isochrony of stressed syllables and, more generally, the relative durations of syllables might be expressed (see chapter 2). Liberman 1975 and Liberman and Prince 1977 also assign it a role in characterizing the conditions under which the stress shift rule of English (which gives *thírtèen mén* from *thìrtéen mén*) might apply.[15] However, they do not assign it a role in characterizing the basic patterns of stress, or prominence, in language. For Liberman 1975, the description of stress requires (first) a representation of the organizaton of the utterance into a "metrical pattern"[16] and (then) a representation of its organization with respect to the metrical grid. The former is the system of relations of relative prominence obtaining among the elements of the utterance (its syllables, words, and phrases). For Liberman, it is a representation in terms of a binary-branching tree structure whose nodes are labeled *s* (strong) and *w* (weak)—a *metrical tree*.[17] Thus Liberman 1975, Liberman and Prince 1977, and other more recent works in the "metrical" tradition posit as part of linguistic description an abstract stress pattern, which is independent of the metrical grid and which mediates between it and the syntactic structure of the sentence.[18]

Liberman and Prince propose that relations of relative prominence above the level of the word be represented merely by annotating the nodes of the surface syntactic tree of the sentence with the labels *s* and *w*.[19] Under this analysis, the English Nuclear Stress Rule becomes simply "label the right-hand node *s*" (from which it follows that its sister will be *w*). The sentence *Mary's sister adores Russian novels* is thereby assigned the metrical pattern in (1.3):

(1.3)

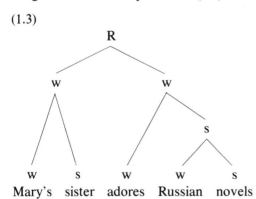

(*R* is the root of the tree.) As for patterns of word stress, Liberman and Prince do not represent them wholly as *s/w*-labeled trees, but retain the feature [stress], now merely binary, to express the distinction between stressed and unstressed syllables. The words *reconciliation, gymnast,* and *modest* are represented as follows:[20]

(1.4)

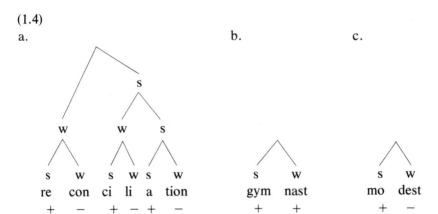

a.   b.   c.

```
              s              w   s
             /\             /\  /\
        s   w   s  w  s  w        s   w           s   w
        re  con ci li a  tion     gym nast        mo  dest
        +   -   +  - +  -         +   +           +   -
```

Thus prominence relations among stressed syllables, whether within
the word or on the phrase, are uniformly represented with metrical
trees. Liberman and Prince's proposals have given rise to an extremely
fruitful line of research, into word stress in particular. (See Prince 1976,
Halle and Vergnaud 1979, Kiparsky 1979, McCarthy 1979a, Safir 1979,
Selkirk 1980b, Prince 1980, and Hayes 1980, among others.) From this
work, most notably that of Halle, Vergnaud, and Hayes, very important insights have been gained into possible patterns of stress, and a
theory of the parameters involved in a universal theory of stress (at the
word level) has been evolving. This research has shown that a certain
enrichment of the hierarchical branching tree representation permits a
representation and characterization of word stress patterns that does
away with the feature [stress] entirely. This enrichment involves introducing units of prosodic constituent structure[21] into the description—
in particular, the units *syllable, foot,* and *(prosodic) word.* With this
elaboration, the representation of the words in (1.4) is instead seen to
be something like (1.5):

(1.5)

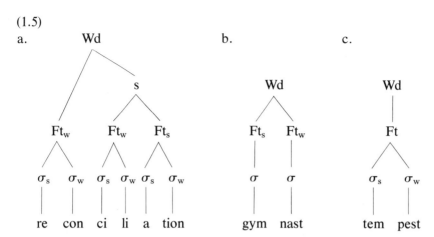

a. Wd

b. Wd

c. Wd

A stressed syllable (σ) is here represented as the strong(est) syllable of a foot (Ft). (The sole syllable of a monosyllabic foot is by convention considered strong.) A stressless syllable is one that is weak. The description of the distribution of stressed and unstressed syllables in words is no longer a matter of rules assigning the feature [±stress], but of rules that indicate (among other things) what constitutes a well-formed foot in the language, often in terms of the nature of the component syllables. On this view, the foot is a unit of phonotactic description, much like the syllable.[22] In the more recent articulations of "metrical theory," then, the abstract stress pattern of words and sentences is represented in terms of prosodic constituent structure with an s/w labeling of the nodes. Though most research in the metrical framework (with the exception of Dell (to appear)) has not attended to the place of the metrical grid in linguistic description, Liberman's theory of an abstract stress pattern that is ultimately translated into a metrical grid representation is more or less presupposed.

Prince 1981, 1983 has argued, however, that metrical trees should be eliminated in a theory of stress, and that the metrical grid must be given the fundamental role in the representation of prominence relations and in the theory of patterns of prominence. This is the position that we will develop here.[23]

The notions "stressed," "unstressed," and "degree of stress" are straightforwardly represented in the alignment of syllables with the grid. In grid terms, a stressed syllable is one that is aligned with a beat (or basic beat, or strong demibeat—all are equivalent with respect to this definition); an unstressed syllable is one that is instead aligned with a weak demibeat. As for degrees of stress, one syllable has "more stress" than another if the beat aligned with the first coincides with beats on a metrical level higher than that of the beats aligned with the second. Consider in this light the following stress patterns:

(1.6)

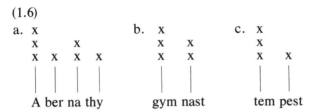

In all cases, the first syllable has the greatest stress (is the most prominent); it is the only one to be aligned with a beat on the highest metrical level. In (1.6a), the first and third syllables are stressed (associated with beats), and the others are stressless. In (1.6b), both the first and the second syllables are stressed, and there are no stressless ones. And in (1.6c), the first syllable is stressed, and the second stressless.[24] Clearly, the grid theory of stress has the means to represent the distinctions needed for an insightful analysis of stress, at the word level or higher.

In arguing, in general terms, for a "relational" representation of stress, as against the standard "numerical" representation, Liberman and Prince 1977:261–264 make the point that a relational theory of stress is to be preferred in that it makes understandable ("rationalizes") the array of special properties that characterize the stress feature and stress-assigning rules in the standard framework, e.g., the n-ary nature of the stress feature, the syntagmatic character of nonprimary stress, the nonlocal effects of the Stress Subordination Convention, and so on. We believe this is an argument of fundamental importance: with a relational theory of stress, these special characteristics "follow directly from the way the phenomenon is represented, rather than being arbitrary typological observations" (Liberman and Prince 1977:263).

In describing the advantages of a relational theory of the representation of stress, Liberman and Prince had in mind a particular theory of relational representation: metrical trees. But, we submit, their argument could just as well be taken as one in favor of representing stress with the metrical grid, for the alignment of the sentence with the metrical grid is, in part, a relational representation of stress, in Liberman and Prince's sense of the term. There is no upper limit on the number of metrical levels that contain beats aligned with syllables ("stress" is n-ary). A beat may be added, moved, or eliminated at some remove from others, but nonetheless depending on the presence of some other(s) within the same grid ("stress" is nonlocal). And, as we will show in chapter 2, whether or not a syllable bears a certain "degree of stress" is a function, in part at least, of the "degrees of stress" of syllables in the surrounding context (nonprimary "stress" is syntagmatic).

But stress is not strictly relational. It is well known that an individual syllable may be stressed (rather than stressless) regardless of whether its neighbors are stressed. Within metrical grid theory, a syllable is "stressed" only by virtue of its alignment with a basic beat in the metrical grid, and there is nothing to prevent a sequence of syllables from being aligned with basic beats. In that sense, "stress" is not relational in metrical grid theory. It should be noted that a basic-beat-aligned syllable in the present theory is the analogue of the strong (or only) syllable of a foot in the revised metrical tree theory, which includes prosodic constituents as part of the representation of stress. According to the latter theory, it is possible for monosyllabic feet to succeed each other, and thus possible for a sequence of syllables to be stressed—that is, for a syllable to be stressed without regard to its neighbors (Selkirk 1980b). There is also a second sense in which stress is not relational: a syllable with "main word stress" is always more prominent than a syllable that is merely "stressed," (section 3.2.2). This greater prominence is represented in metrical grid theory as an alignment with metrical level three or higher. To capture this "inherent" greater prominence of main word stress in metrical/prosodic tree theory, it could perhaps be stipulated that a syllable that is the strongest within a prosodic word be interpreted as more prominent than one that is merely the strongest within a foot. (In a metrical tree theory without prosodic category levels, such a relation could not be expressed at all.)[25]

The metrical grid theory of stress thus gives a uniform representation of both the relational and the nonrelational aspects of the stress patterns of words (and phrases), while a metrical/prosodic tree theory expresses relational concepts by labeling trees with *s* and *w*, and nonrelational concepts by means of the organization of the tree into prosodic constituents. We will show in the course of what follows that the homogeneous and highly restrictive representation of stress patterns offered by the metrical grid is quite adequate to the descriptive task, and moreover that it provides the basis of an explanation for many stress-related phenomena.

We ask of any theory of stress not simply that it make available an appropriate representation of stress patterns and that it permit an insightful analysis of the stress patterns of particular languages, but also that it constitute a theory of the notion "possible stress pattern in language." Actually, it is an empirical question whether there is anything of interest to be said about universals of stress at the word level or above, whether there is anything at those levels that calls for explanation. Research on word stress, which has recently become quite intensive, has led to the conclusion that there are indeed highly interesting things to be said in a theory of word stress. A first apparently universal property of word stress, one that distinguishes it from other phonological phenomena, is that there are patterns to it—there are discernable regularities in the occurrence of stressed and unstressed syllables, as well as regularities in the location of primary stress. It is not the case that the distribution of unstressed, stressed, and main-stressed syllables is random in language (see chapter 2). This observation has serious implications for any theory of stress.

Suppose that stress were a feature of vowels, as in the standard theory of generative phonology. Such a theory would have to accord the feature [±stress] a status different from that of any other feature characterizing vowels or other segments. If [±stress] were a feature just like [±high], for example, there would be no more reason to expect any particular word to contain a vowel specified [±stress] than to expect it to contain a [+high] vowel. Nor would there be any reason to expect vowels specified [+stress] to be arranged in any particular pattern with respect to each other within the word. Without additional stipulations, the standard theory can explain neither the reliable presence of stressed syllables nor their patterning. For the standard theory, the presence of stress patterns would have to be reflected in the stipulation that, universally, grammars include rules for assigning the feature [stress], rules stipulated to be of just the sort that give rise to the patterns attested. But the theory cannot explain why it should be stress, as opposed to some other phonological feature, that has this privileged status in the grammar, and it cannot explain why the word stress patterns should be as they are. For these and other reasons, the standard theory of stress has been recognized to be inadequate.[26]

The very existence of patterns as a fundamental property of stress could be taken as indicating that in the phonological representation of stress, patterns are somehow primitive. This point of view has influenced recent work on stress, which, following Liberman's lead, has viewed patterns of stress as reflecting hierarchical (patterned) arrangements of the syllables of the utterance, represented as metrical trees. But metrical tree theory is unable, without further stipulation, to provide any insight into the notion "possible pattern." There is nothing about metrical trees from which it follows that in stress-timed languages the number of stressless syllables intervening between stressed syllables is usually one and on occasion two, and that a pattern will never be based on intervals of two, or three, or more. In one articulation of the metrical tree theory of word stress, Hayes 1980 proposes that binary feet be stipulated as the only possible basic pattern, ternary feet being allowed as variants under special circumstances. Binarity *is* fundamental to patterns of stress, particularly at the lowest levels; yet in metrical tree theory this is merely stipulated. While acknowledging that such stipulations are not in principle objectionable, if part of a universal theory, we submit that a theory of stress from which it specifically follows that patterns would have this shape is to be preferred. The rhythmic theory of stress is just such a theory. If the alignment of syllables with a rhythmic structure such as the metrical grid is the representation, then these patterns are the expected ones, for rhythmic structure, be it in language or any other human activity, is governed by something like the Principle of Rhythmic Alternation (PRA). Roughly speaking, the PRA ensures that rhythmic clashes and lapses will be avoided, at all metrical levels, and that strong beats or demibeats will appear at regular intervals, two or three beats or demibeats away from a preceding or following strong. The patterns exhibited in well-documented languages appear to conform to this organization: on the third metrical level it is common for beats to be either two or three basic beats away from each other; at the basic beat level, it is even more common for beats to be two demibeats away from each other, ternary beats being allowed only in particular cases.[27] The claim, then, is that a metrical grid theory of stress is better able to explain these stress patterns.

The theory of stress patterns proposed here, to which chapter 2 provides a general introduction, is that they result from the conjoined effects of two sorts of rules: (i) *text-to-grid alignment rules* and (ii) *rules of grid euphony*. The *text* is surface structure as defined earlier, and text-to-grid alignment (TGA) rules construct a partial grid, aligning certain syllables with beats on various levels of the grid by virtue of their internal composition and/or their position within specified syntactic domains. The Nuclear Stress Rule is a rule of this sort. TGA rules establish fixed loci of prominence from which the alternations so characteristic of stress patterns emanate, introduced by the rules of grid euphony (GE). Rules of grid euphony thus complete the construction of the grid. We suggest that they are defined solely in terms of the grid and apply at all metrical levels. Their role is to ensure that the grid is truly rhythmic, to make it conform as closely as possible with the PRA. The stress shift or "Rhythm Rule" of English is a rule of this sort. In this analysis, both GE rules and TGA rules belong to the component defining the mapping between surface syntactic representation and underlying phonological representation.

Now, the rhythmic structure of an utterance is in fact more than the representation of the prominence patterns of its syllables, more than beats of the grid that are aligned with syllables. Liberman 1975 suggests that the metrical grid of an utterance may also contain *silent grid positions* — positions not aligned with syllables, whose presence is determined in some way on the basis of the syntactic structure of the utterance. (Abercrombie 1968 refers to them as *silent stresses*.) Liberman takes these silent positions to be the means by which the apparently syntactically governed phenomena of pausing and final lengthening are to be explained. We will call these positions the *syntactic timing* or *juncture* of the sentence. As the book progresses, we will elaborate to a considerable extent the idea that there are silent positions within the metrical grid with which the syllables of an utterance are aligned. In chapter 6 we will show not only that this idea allows us to explain why the phenomenon of final lengthening should exist (alongside pausing) in the first place, but also that it provides the appropriate means of representing some of the junctural properties of the sentence and thus ultimately explains differences in applicability in different locations of the sentence of grid-based rules like stress shift, as well as of phonological rules of sandhi.

In sum, the rhythmic structure of a sentence consists of a metrical grid containing grid positions with which syllables are aligned, giving representation to *patterns of prominence,* and silent grid positions, giving representation to *syntactic timing* or *juncture.* The representation of the rhythmic structure of the sentence *Abernathy gesticulated,* for example, we claim to be as follows, where the underlined positions are the silent ones.[28]

(1.7)

```
                    x
x                   x
x       x           x   x
x  x  x  x x x  x  x x x x  x x x
Abernathy       gesticulated
```

It is worth noting in this connection that the demonstration that there must exist positions of rhythmic structure that lack an alignment with syllables provides important evidence for construing rhythmic structure as independent of segments and their organization into syllables.

If it is true, as we claim, that the application of numerous phonological rules of sentence grammar is governed by the "adjacency" of syllables and segments defined with respect to the grid, then it must be concluded that the grid is present at an early point in the phonological derivation. We will assume that it is present in the (underlying) phonological representation, P_1, the output of the syntax-phonology mapping. This position, it should be noted, is the only one consistent with both the fact that (some of) the timing relations represented in the grid are determined directly by the surface constituent structure of an utterance (see chapter 6) and the interestingly restrictive assumption that syntactic structure is not available to the phonology (or phonetics), once the mapping from syntactic representation to phonological representation (via "construction rules") is complete (see section 1.3). Giving the metrical grid a place in the (underlying) representation P_1 does not force the conclusion that a metrical grid alignment is the one and only representation of the stress pattern of an utterance, however, for that representation also consists, we believe, of a prosodic constituent structure. Given this, it would be entirely possible to entertain a theory like Liberman's, according to which stress patterns are represented fundamentally in terms of the prosodic constituent structure (metrical trees), and according to which prosodic constituent structure has an immediate, simultaneous translation into a metrical grid alignment for the sentence. (This is the approach taken in very recent work by Halle and Vergnaud, for example.) Given this approach, the theory of stress— that is, the theory of the notion "possible stress pattern" in language— would be cast in terms of prosodic constituent structure. Our claim, with Prince 1981, 1983, is a different one. It is that: (i) stress patterns are represented only in terms of the metrical grid alignment, not at all in terms of prosodic constituent structure, and (ii) the theory of possible stress patterns is cast in terms of a theory of syllable-to-grid alignment. Much of this book is devoted to arguing for this position.

Chapter 2 reviews the general motivation for attributing a rhythmic structure to an utterance and outlines the proposed theory of metrical grid alignment for words and sentences. Chapter 3 sketches a theory of English word stress based on the metrical grid, drawing on insights gained by the earlier metrical framework concerning the nature of stress patterns in general and English word stress patterns in particular. Chapter 4 shows that a metrical grid approach allows an insightful characterization of all phrasal rhythmic phenomena and argues against a metrical tree approach to phrase stress. Chapters 4 and 5 also present a grid-based theory of the relation between stress and intonation. With this, we hope to make clear that only the representation of relative prominence available in the grid is needed for an adequate, insightful description of the tunes and rhythms of the sentence. Thus we maintain that the metrical grid alignment of the sentence is the one and only representation of the stress or prominence relations of the sentence, as of the word.

1.2.3 Prosodic Structure: The Syllable

The syllable had no place in standard generative phonology (represented by SPE), though most other theories of phonology have recognized its fundamental importance.[29] Studies in the last decade in the generative framework have given the syllable an ever larger place in the theory, both as a unit of phonological representation and as a unit in terms of which many generalizations about phonological representation and phonological rules are expressed. The syllable is the paradigm case of a unit of prosodic constituent structure, and so will provide a point of reference in discussing the status of other such hierarchical units in the theory.

The syllable is now understood to be a "suprasegmental" unit. Departing from earlier works in the generative tradition such as Hooper 1972, 1976, Vennemann 1972, and Hoard 1971, which defined syllables in terms of syllable boundaries, Kahn 1976 and Anderson and Jones 1974 proposed that the syllable is a separate unit "standing above" the segmental string, to which the segments are "associated." Selkirk 1978b,c, Kiparsky 1979, McCarthy 1979a,b, Halle and Vergnaud 1979, and others have argued further that the syllable has an internal constituent structure, the segments being the structure's terminal string; their work thus rejoins earlier theories of the syllable such as those of Pike and Pike 1947, Kuryłowicz 1948, and Fudge 1969. Recent studies have proposed that the terminal positions of this syllable structure hierarchy are only "placeholders" of sorts, and that segmental material is represented on (one or more) autosegmental tiers, separate from those terminal positions, and associated with them by rules having a substantive character.[30] Given this more recent articulation of the theory, which we adopt here, the syllable and its internal structure form the *core* or *axis* of phonological representation to which segments on the various autosegmental tiers are associated. What we are assuming, therefore, to use Halle and Vergnaud's 1980 term, is a theory of "three-dimensional phonology." On this theory, defining a possible syllable for a language and the possible segmental associations to it expresses basic phonotactic generalizations about the language.[31] It is in terms of the syllable structure of the language that the segmental composition of the utterance is "organized."

In this book, the particulars of the segment-to-syllable association will usually not be relevant. We will therefore often represent the syllabic and segmental content of the sentence as a sequence of syllables and (written below them in standard orthography) a sequence of segments. For example:

(1.8)

A ber na thy

It has been widely recognized that tonal phenomena require an autosegmental theory according to which tones are represented "suprasegmentally" as a sequence of elements on a tier separate from the segmental or the syllabic (see especially Goldsmith 1976a,b, Williams 1971, and Leben 1973, 1978, as well as the references in Fromkin 1978 and note 6). The tone-syllable relation may now be viewed as simply a special case of a more general set of relations between autosegmental tiers and the syllabic axis. In some languages individual morphemes or words may have their own tonal "melody"; in others the tonal melody may be defined only with respect to some larger domain, such as the intonational phrase (see sections 5.3, 5.4); in still others the pitch contours may consist of both a "tonal" and an "intonational" contribution. But in any case, it is with respect to the syllabic composition of the utterance that the autosegmental tonal units are "realized." The tone-to-syllable association is governed by universal and language-particular well-formedness conditions. Among these are language-particular conditions stating how many tones may associate with a syllable, conditions that may in so doing make crucial reference to the internal structure of the syllable (see Clements and Ford 1979 and Halle and Vergnaud (in preparation)).

The alignment of the syllables of an utterance with a metrical grid, which we take here to be the representation of the prominence patterns of the utterance, may be viewed as a special instance of the association of syllables with an autosegmental tier (though we hasten to point out that other autosegmental tiers are apparently not hierarchical structures). Strictly speaking, then, the representation of the rhythmic structure of *Abernathy gesticulated* is as follows, where the syllable sequence mediates the relation between segments and the positions of the metrical grid.

(1.9)

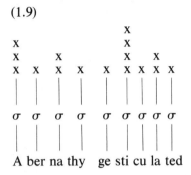

A ber na thy   ge sti cu la ted

(In discussing rhythmic structure, we will often omit the syllabic axis from the representation, for the sake of typographical simplicity, representing rhythmic structure simply as in (1.7).)

In sum, then, we see that the syllable has a crucial place in the theory of phonological representation and a crucial role in a theory defining the notion "possible phonological representation" for language in general. It is in terms of the syllable sequence of the core or axis that many rules governing the range of possible phonological representations of particular sentences are defined. In other words, the syllable has a central place in the mapping from surface syntactic representation to underlying phonological representation.

The syllable also has a major role in the phonological derivation, in governing the application of phonological rules. For example, the syllable serves as a *domain* for phonological rules; that is, it defines subsequences of the utterance within which phonological rules may be restricted to applying. It is now known that the notions "syllable-initial position," "syllable-final position," and "within the same syllable as," among others, are necessary in a theory of phonological rules, in order to express generalizations about a great number of phonological phenomena. Thus the syllabic structure of an utterance serves to define some of its junctural properties, i.e., some of the relations between segments in sequence that are ultimately relevant to pronunciation.

Given the central role of syllable structure in phonological representation, it is important to determine how that organization into syllables may be governed by the syntactic representation of the sentence. (By *syntactic representation,* we refer to both word structure and phrase structure.) We offer two related proposals in this regard. The first is that morphemes are syllabified either as lexical items or in the course of the first cycle, and that there are language-particular well-formedness conditions, which we call *rules of basic syllable composition,* that either serve as redundancy rules on these lexical representations or introduce the initial syllabification, and define the notion "possible syllable" for the language. (This position is outlined in Selkirk 1978b, 1984.) The second is that, in cyclic fashion, this original syllable structure is rearranged at the limits of morphemes and successively higher units of morphological and syntactic structure. This amounts to saying that there is a partial "resyllabification" on successively higher cyclic domains (cf. Kiparsky 1979). Two sorts of *resyllabification* probably must be distinguished: resyllabification according to the basic syllable composition (BSC) rules of the language, and resyllabification according to some sort of universal principles. In English, for example, the (recursive) category level Root of word syntax is the domain of the syllabification and resyllabification according to the BSC rules of English. (The Root in English includes the so-called nonneutral affixes (Selkirk 1982).) On higher domains within the word—specifically, on the domain of the (recursive) Word category—resyllabification does not follow the BSC rules, but only certain restricted universal principles, such as the principle that makes a coda consonant the onset of a following onsetless syllable. And on domains higher than the word, it is debatable whether any resyllabification takes place at all.[32] English would thereby seem to contrast with French, for example, for which all word-internal cyclic domains are domains of resyllabification according to the BSC rules of the language, and for which resyllabification takes place, according to universal principles, on (certain) phrasal domains (Delattre 1940, Schane 1978).

In all cases we have encountered, BSC resyllabification is restricted to word-internal domains. Moreover, it seems quite likely that the possibilities of resyllabification *between words,* in phrasal contexts, are not defined directly with respect to syntactic structure (by syntactic-prosodic correspondence rules), but rather are determined by the syntactic timing of the sentence—by the adjacency of syllables defined with respect to the grid. If this were indeed shown to be true, then phrasal resyllabification must probably be construed as a "late-level" phenomenon, applying, along with rules of external sandhi, to a phonological representation fully defined; it would not form part of the syntax-phonology mapping.

Because the limits of syllables may coincide with the limits of syntactic constituents, and because some phonological rules may have syllable structure domains, the application of phonological rules may reflect the surface constituent structure of the sentence—but only indirectly. Syllable structure thus provides one of the crucial, intermediate links between syntax and phonology. It was originally our intention to make the investigation of the syntactic structure–syllable structure relation—in particular, the study of the syntax of resyllabification—an integral part of the present work. It appears now that an adequate treatment of this extremely important question is beyond the scope of the book, in part because it would require more research than we have carried out so far. And so it is with regret that we leave a general consideration of this topic for a later time and place.

1.2.4 Prosodic Structure: Suprasyllabic Constituents

In previous work, we have assumed that a fairly rich hierarchy of prosodic constituents or prosodic categories forms part of phonological representation (see, for example, Selkirk 1978c, 1980a,b, 1981a). We have suggested that the hierarchy for English includes at least the following categories:[33]

(1.10)
intonational phrase (IP)
phonological phrase (PhP)
prosodic word (Wd)
foot (Ft)
syllable (Syl)

We have proposed that a category of level i in the hierarchy immediately dominates a (sequence of) categories of level $i-1$ (Selkirk 1981a). (Assuming *syllable* to be level 1, the others will be levels 2, ..., n.) We will call this the *strict layer hypothesis,* and will take it as a useful working hypothesis here. In earlier work, we presumed that, like the syllable, each of the suprasyllabic units in this hierarchy had the potential for playing a role in the description of the phonotactics of words and/or phrases (including their stress patterns) and in the description of tonal patterns and the domains of application of phonological rules. It is necessary now, we believe, to reassess the claims for the existence of those suprasyllabic prosodic constituents, for it is clear that some of the phonological phenomena that were thought to provide motivation for these higher units of structure are better explained in terms of the metrical grid alignment of the sentence. Some categories will disappear entirely from the prosodic structure repertoire; others will be given a much reduced role in phonological description, once the role of rhythmic structure in phonology is fully understood. For each of the units listed in (1.10), we will briefly review what is at stake.

1.2.4.1 Intonational phrase   This unit corresponds to a span of the sentence associated with a characteristic intonational contour or melody (see section 5.4). A sentence may correspond to one or more intonational phrases. An intonational phrase typically contains material belonging to a sequence of words and/or phrases, and it is not necessarily isomorphic to any constituent of syntactic structure (Selkirk 1978c). There are two possible intonational phrasings for *Abernathy gesticulated:*

(1.11)
$_{IP}$(Abernathy gesticulated)$_{IP}$
$_{IP}$(Abernathy)$_{IP}$ $_{IP}$(gesticulated)$_{IP}$

The existence of the intonational phrase is motivated primarily by the necessity of defining intonational contours with respect to some unit of representation that is both larger than the word and variable in extent. That unit cannot be a syntactic one, because the syntactic sequence with which an intonational contour is associated may not be a constituent of syntactic structure. And the metrical grid alignment of the sentence defines no such unit in the representation. In languages with characteristic intonational contours, then, we are led to posit intonational phrases as part of the prosodic constituent structure of phonological representation. (See section 5.4.)

   Studies in the generative tradition have usually held that the surface syntactic structure of a sentence determines, in some fashion or other, the division of the sentence into intonational phrases (Downing 1970, 1973, Bing 1979a,b, Selkirk 1978c, 1980b, 1981a). Here we reject this idea, in favor of one that has its roots in earlier work on the topic: the idea that the definition of what may constitute an intonational phrase is essentially semantic in character. For Halliday 1967a, for example, intonational phrases are units of "information structure."

Our specific hypothesis, defended in chapter 5, is that the immediate constituents of an intonational phrase must bear either a head-argument relation or a head–(restrictive) modifier relation to each other. This hypothesis may be seen as an attempt to spell out what it means to say that an intonational phrase is a "sense unit." As an implementation of this basic hypothesis, we suggest that the intonational phrasing of a sentence is assigned (freely) to the surface structure of the sentence, and that particular phrasings are subject to a well-formedness condition (or filter) that encodes the aforementioned constraints on the semantic relations obtaining among the constituents within the successive intonational phrases. This well-formedness condition, which we will call the *Sense Unit Condition,* may be stated either on an intonationally phrased surface structure or on (intonationally phrased) logical form, depending on where the semantically relevant information is considered to be available.[34] Thus the statement of the possible relations between syntactic constituent structure and intonational phrasing—the syntactic-prosodic correspondence rule for the intonational phrase—is quite trivial. It need merely be stated that a (highest) sentence corresponds to a sequence of one or more intonational phrases. Any general further constraints on the constituent membership of intonational phrases are claimed to follow from the semantically based Sense Unit Condition.

We will show in chapter 5 that the free assignment of intonational phrasing to a sentence and the subjecting of this phrasing to the Sense Unit Condition are entirely consistent with the approach that must be taken to assigning intonational contours to the sentence. We will argue that the tonal elements making up the pitch contour of the intonational phrase are assigned directly (and freely) to surface syntactic structure, and that it is on the basis of this assignment that the essentially semantic properties of the focus of the sentence are defined.

In our investigation of phrasal rhythm, we will show that the intonational phrase serves as a domain with respect to which patterns of rhythmic prominence are defined. It has also been thought to serve as a characteristic domain of rules of segmental phonology, especially rules of external sandhi.[35] However, caution is needed here in assessing the role of the intonational phrase with respect to phonological rules of sandhi. The limits of intonational phrases often coincide with substantial pauses, which our theory represents as silent positions in the metrical grid. Thus it may be that juncture-sensitive rules that have been thought to have the intonational phrase as their domain are simply rules whose application is governed by the adjacency of segments and/or syllables defined with respect to the metrical grid.

In general, it will be necessary to adjudicate the respective roles of the metrical grid and of prosodic constituent structure in characterizing the junctural properties that are relevant to the application of phonological rules. We will take the position that a phonological rule may be sensitive to either of the two types of junctural representation; that is, it will be sensitive either to prosodic structure domains or to adjacency defined on the grid. Because segmental phonology above the level of the word is (lamentably) still grossly underinvestigated, it is not possible at this point to know whether rules appealing to the same sorts of junctural information share other properties as well.

1.2.4.2 Phonological Phrase   Let us use the term *phonological phrase* for any level of prosodic constituent structure that may include one or more major category words.[36] In principle, the proposed analysis will allow for the possibility that language may exhibit more than one level of phonological phrase, in which case finer terminological distinctions can be made: PhP^1, PhP^2, ..., PhP^n. With this terminology then, an intonational phrase is a special case of a phonological phrase, one that is associated with a characteristic tonal contour and that has an important function in representing the "information structure" of the sentence. The unit *utterance,* if it existed, would also be a phonological phrase in this sense.

The term *phonological phrase* has been used to apply to a (putative) level of English prosodic structure falling between the intonational phrase and the prosodic word (see Selkirk 1978c, 1981a). The English phonological phrase has been thought to have a role in the timing of the utterance, with an influence both on its rhythmic properties (Selkirk 1978c) and on its division into pauses (Gee and Grosjean 1981). We now think that the existence of this unit in English is highly suspect, for syntactic timing (silent positions in the grid) gives a representation of the disjuncture or separation between syllables that is more appropriate to the description of such rhythmic phenomena (see chapters 4 and 6). Indeed, we would now explicitly deny that the existence of a level of phonological phrase below that of the intonational phrase is well motivated in English.

1.2.4.3 Prosodic Word   A variety of linguists have thought it necessary to isolate a roughly word-sized unit of phonological representation.[37] Such a unit could serve to define such phonologically relevant notions as "word-initial," "word-final," and "word-internal," and it would seem to be required particularly when the words of the sentence defined in syntactic terms fail to correspond exactly to the "words" playing a role in the phonology. In Selkirk 1980a,b we suggested that there exists a unit of prosodic constituent structure, the *prosodic word,* for English, Sanskrit, and other languages. We claimed that it was within the (prosodic) word that prominence relations particular to word-sized units were defined—that is, that the unit "(prosodic) word" played a role in metrical theory in permitting the characterization of "main word stress." (See also Halle and Vergnaud 1979 and Hayes 1980.) In addition we claimed that the unit that serves to define main word stress is the unit in terms of which the notion "word" relevant to the application of phonological rules is defined. The hypothesis was that the *domains* for both principles governing prominence relations and rules for segmental phonology systematically coincide.

Given a metrical grid approach to characterizing word stress, of course, there is no obvious motivation for a phonological constituent Word for the realm of word-internal prominence relations (see chapter 3). "Main word stress" is a metrical grid alignment at a certain level of the grid that is established within a domain characterized in syntactic terms. As for junctural notions like "word-internal," "word-initial," and "word-final," we submit that they may be expressed, and more appropriately so, either in terms of adjacency defined with respect to the grid, or directly with respect to word-syntactic structure. Our proposed theory of syntactic timing (see chapter 6) has the result that there are no silent grid positions inside the syntactic word; hence, syllables internal to the same word are strictly adjacent with respect to the metrical grid. We suggest, then, that "grid-adjacent" may substitute for at least some instances of the notion "word-internal." Between words, the theory of syntactic timing assigns varying degrees of rhythmic disjuncture—that is, varying degrees of closeness with respect to the grid—in that differing numbers of silent grid positions are assigned between words in the representation, depending on the syntactic constituent structure of the sentence. Thus one could claim that certain appeals to the notions "word-initial" and "word-final" should be supplanted by appeals to "lack of grid-adjacency to what precedes" and "lack of grid-adjacency to what follows." Other appeals to the former notions might well be appeals to syntactic structure itself. Thus we see little if any need for a prosodic word in phonological description.

1.2.4.4 Foot   The foot is a suprasyllabic unit, usually smaller in size than the word, that has played a central role in the description of stress patterns in the framework of "metrical phonology." It has rendered service in representing the distinction between stressed and stressless syllables, and as a device for computing the distribution of stressed and stressless syllables within specified domains. In this function, as Prince 1983 argues quite effectively, the foot has been supplanted by the metrical grid theory of stress. It is important to note, moreover, that there is relatively little evidence that the foot itself serves as a domain for phonological rules. Most alleged foot-sensitive rules can be easily and with no loss of generalization recast as rules sensitive to the stressed-stressless distinction.[38] In the present theory such rules would be recast as rules sensitive to the metrical grid alignment of syllables. We hypothesize, therefore, that there is no prosodic constituent *foot*.

The particular claim we are making about the prosodic constituent structure of phonological representations in English, then, is that the phonological phrase, the prosodic word, and the foot are not units in the hierarchy, but that the syllable and the intonational phrase are. With the syllable sequence as the lowest layer, the prosodic constituent structure of *Abernathy gesticulated* is then either (1.12a) or (1.12b).

(1.12)

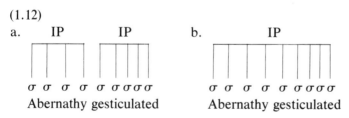

a.   IP   IP   b.   IP

σ σ σ σ σ σ σ σ   σ σ σ σ σ σ σ σ

Abernathy gesticulated   Abernathy gesticulated

1.3 The Mapping between Syntax and Phonology

According to the theory sketched thus far, there are three principal stages in the mapping from syntax to phonology. The first is *surface syntactic structure*, S_n (figure 1.1). (Recall from section 1.1 that this includes a sequence of word-level phonological representations.) The second is surface structure *cum* intonational structure, or *intonated surface structure*, S_n'. (The term *intonational structure* designates the intonational phrasing of the sentence, the (autosegmentally represented) tonal contours of the intonational phrases, and the assignment of certain of these tonal elements to particular constituents of surface structure; see chapter 5.) The third is surface structure *cum* intonational structure *cum* metrical grid, or *intonated and rhythmated surface structure*. It may be called S_n'' or, more appropriately perhaps, P_1. This is what should be thought of as the underlying phonological representation of the sentence.

S_n'', or P_1, is a representation in which the hierarchical aspects of phonological representation are essentially fully established (except, possibly, for some phrasal resyllabification). It includes as well all the segmental aspects of phonological representation, represented on the various autosegmental tiers. This representation P_1 is mapped by what we have been calling *phonological rules* of the sentence into a surface phonetic representation P_n that shares many properties with P_1 (but not all).[39] We will have little to say about the rules participating in the derivation from P_1 to P_n in what follows. But it does seem worth pointing out (again) that this class of rules appears to be defined only in terms of those aspects of the representation that are strictly phonological. In the unmarked case at least, they do not appear to be sensitive to syntactic structure. It also appears that this class of rules does not apply cyclically. Both these characteristics of phonological rules may be seen as reflections of a single general condition: that phonological rules are blind to syntactic structure. In the general case, then, phonological representation, richly structured itself, mediates between syntactic structure and the phonological rules that ultimately specify the details of the phonetic realization of the sentence. Cases where phonological rules may appear to appeal directly to surface syntactic structure are highly marked and may even be surface suppletions.

The representation S_n', the intonated surface structure, is one whose properties we are only beginning to investigate here. The mapping from surface structure S_n to S_n' is quite trivial, it seems. As mentioned earlier, we adopt the hypothesis that intonational phrasing is freely assigned to surface structure, the only structural restriction being that the entire sentence be parsed into a sequence of one or more nonoverlapping intonational phrases. (An additional, independent hypothesis is that the tonal elements constituting the intonational contours of the phrases are also freely assigned in this mapping from S_n to S_n'.) We claim that it is at the level S_n' (or a mapping of it into logical form) that certain well-formedness conditions governing the intonational structure-meaning relation are defined. These include the Sense Unit Condition, governing the semantic composition of intonational phrases. (They include as well the focus rules, which govern the relation between the intonational contour of the sentence and its focus structure.) These conditions, and this general approach to intonation, are defended in chapter 5. It may turn out to be the case that the intonated surface structure, S_n', has quite a large role in grammatical description, as the level at which generalizations concerning the relation between prosody and word order, or prosody and ellipsis, are to be expressed. Unfortunately, we cannot explore these possibilities here.

The mapping from the intonated surface structure S_n' to the intonated-and-rhythmated surface structure S_n'' (= P_1) is one of the central concerns of this work. A theory of that mapping is a theory of how the various aspects of S_n'—the syntactic labeled bracketing, the organization into syllables, the intonational phrasing, and the assignment of focus-relevant tonal elements—determine a rhythmic structure for the sentence. The theory defended here is that four components are involved in this mapping: text-to-grid alignment, grid euphony, syntactic timing, and destressing. The rules of two components, text-to-grid alignment and syntactic timing, appeal directly to the syntactic structure of the sentence, as well as to its intonational phrasing (chapters 2–6). Rules of destressing and text-to-grid alignment appeal directly to the syllable composition of the sentence (chapters 2, 3, and 7). Finally, text-to-grid alignment takes into account as well the tonal associations of the syllables (chapters 4 and 5).

A significant result of these investigations into the S_n'-P_1 mapping is the discovery that the rules involved apply in *cyclic fashion* (see sections 3.4, 4.4, 7.2.2, and 8.2). It is important to note that, given the present conceptual framework, these cyclic rules are not rules "of the phonology"; rather, they are rules that collectively *construct* a phonological representation on the basis of syntactic representation. We may speculate that, in sentence grammar at least, the cycle is a principle governing only the *interpretation* of syntactic representation *as a* phonological representation, rather than a principle governing the relation of one phonological representation (syntactically structured) to another. (Of course, restricting the cycle to the mapping constructing the underlying phonological representation P_1 would be unnecessary if syntactic structure were simply "deleted" at P_1, a possibility certainly worth considering.)

We sum up this view of the organization of the grammar in figure 1.2. Though still not complete in all details, this diagram is a fleshed-out

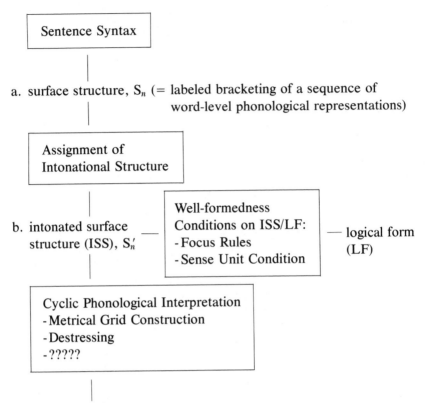

a. surface structure, S_n (= labeled bracketing of a sequence of
                        word-level phonological representations)

b. intonated surface — Well-formedness Conditions on ISS/LF: - Focus Rules - Sense Unit Condition — logical form (LF)
   structure (ISS), S'_n

c. (underlying) sentence-level phonological representation, S''_n or P_1
   (= an intonated, rhythmated surface structure)

d. phonetic representation, P_n

Figure 1.2

version of figure 1.1, constructed by adding a theory of the mapping between the surface syntactic representation S_n and the (underlying) phonological representation P_1 of the sentence. The general theory of the organization of the grammar being assumed here is therefore to be understood as a revision and extension of the standard theory of generative phonology.

It is worth mentioning again that, as should be clear from figure 1.2, our model of the syntax-phonology relation in sentence grammar is based on the assumption that the output of word grammar forms part of the surface syntactic representation to which this mapping applies. Included in this surface structure is a concatenation of the derived phonological representations of the "word level." This notion that the phonological output of a separate word grammar forms a discrete level of representation in the overall grammar (the "word level") is suggested by Kiparsky 1983a,b, Mohanan 1982, and others developing the framework of so-called lexical phonology and morphology. Although we are not committed to certain other details of that theory (see sections 3.1, 3.4, 8.2, 8.3), this assumption seems a useful one to adopt.

Chapter 2
Rhythmic Patterns
in Language

2.1 Generalities

Speech—like music, that other culturally codified production of sound—is a rhythmically organized activity. Just as the rhythmic schemes of the different musical traditions are a codification presumably reflecting both universal properties of rhythmic organization and the conventionalized choices about particulars made by the culture (from the range of choices that are available within the confines of a (universally defined) rhythmic organization), so too, we will argue, do the diverse rhythmic patterns of prominence found in language reflect both universal and particular aspects of rhythmic organization. The rhythmic patterning of every language is codified, and the linguistic description of speech rhythm, therefore, is a description of that code. A successful theory of rhythmic structure in language will involve sorting out what is language-particular and what is universal in that code.

Rhythm, as we said in chapter 1, is founded upon a recurrence of pulses, some of which emerge as accented with respect to each other, forming patterns on different levels. Various aspects of rhythmic organization inhere in the metrical grid representation. A grid position is a pulse, a point in (abstract) time. The notion of pattern requires a differentiation among the pulses, and this is provided by ascribing to them a place on different levels. Sequences of rhythmically equivalent pulses are represented as the sequence of grid positions on the different metrical levels. To every level, then, there is a patterning. Thus, claiming that speech is rhythmically organized—that in the linguistic representation of an utterance syllables are aligned with a metrical grid—amounts to claiming that (a) there are discernable pulses in speech, (b) some of these syllables emerge as accented with respect to each other, forming recurrent patterns, and (c) there may be a hierarchy of accented syllables, corresponding to patterns on the different metrical levels. It may be argued, and has been, that all these statements hold true for speech.

What does not inhere in the grid, in our conception of it, is the precise nature of the patterns themselves. An accented (strong) position could in principle be followed, or preceded, by any number of non-accented (weak) positions. This, we believe, is entirely appropriate: the grid itself simply *represents* patterns, as the organization of pulses of abstract time into levels. The patterns are *characterized* by principles or rules that govern the particulars of the metrical grid organization.

There is arguably a universal rhythmic ideal, one that favors a strict alternation of strong and weak beats. Following Sweet 1875–76, we will call this, as in chapter 1, the *Principle of Rhythmic Alternation* (PRA). That the rhythmic organization of language or music aspires to such an ideal state is indicated by a number of general tendencies that are attested in rhythmic patterning: (i) binary patterns (successions of *ws* or *sw*), at various levels, are by far the most prevalent in either domain of activity, (ii) ternary patterns (*wws* or *sww*) are not (usually) basic in the rhythmic patterning at any level, but rather exist alongside binary patterns and constitute a special departure from them, and (iii) quaternary patterns simply do not exist, inasmuch as they may be interpreted as two binary patterns. This is Sweet's point, one also implicit in Liberman 1975. In his work on rhythm in French, Dell (to appear) also argues for a universal "ideal" rhythmic organization, following *le principe d'eurythmie,* according to which an ideal metrical grid contains no adjacent strong positions and is maximally alternating.

Our position is not that the PRA plays a direct role in the linguistic description of a language's patterns of prominence, but rather that the rules of a grammar that define the possible metrical grid alignments of the sentences of that language conspire in approximating that ideal, on every level of organization. At the end of this chapter, we will outline our theory of metrical grid alignment (or theory of the notion "possible rhythmic 'score'" for language) and will show how we think the rhythmic ideal is embodied in the rules for constructing a metrical grid on the basis of a text. In the immediately following section, we will examine the evidence for viewing speech as a rhythmically organized activity, one that both respects an abstract rhythmic structure having the character of a metrical grid alignment and shows patterns reflecting the operation of the PRA.

2.2 The Rhythmic Nature of Speech

Scholars working on the phonetics of English have long recognized that rhythmic organization at what we will call the "lower levels" plays an important role in the description of speech.[1] A major insight of these investigations is that the quantities (durations) of the syllables of a sentence are determined by the sentence's rhythmic properties. According to D. Jones 1964:§886, for example,

Vowel length depends to a considerable extent [in English] on the rhythm of the sentence. There is a strong tendency in connected speech to make stressed syllables follow each other as nearly as possible at equal distances.

For D. Jones 1964:§888–890, the musical notation in (2.1a) and (2.1b) represents the fact that in (2.1a) "*ei, ai* are something like twice as long in the second sequence as they are in the first" and that in (2.1b) "the *i:* in *scene* is considerably longer than the *i:* in *scenery*."

(2.1)

a.

'eiti:n   'nainti:n 'twenti   vs.   'eit   'nain 'ten

eighteen nineteen twenty   *eight nine ten*

b.

ðə 'si:n wəz 'bju:təfl   vs.   ðə 'si:nəri wəz 'bju:təfl

The scene was beautiful   *The scenery was beautiful*

Pike 1945:34 makes a not dissimilar observation about American English. He points out that the space of time elapsing between the stressed syllables *man* and *here* is roughly the same in *The man is here* and *The manager's here,* with the result that in the latter the syllables are "crushed together" (pronounced very rapidly), in order to be "fitted in."

Building on the insights of Jones and others, Abercrombie 1964 laid the foundation for further work on the topic by positing a unit of analysis, the *foot* (not to be confused with the foot of metrical phonology), in terms of which, he argued, the rhythmic properties of syllables may be explained:

English utterances may be considered as being divided by the isochronous beat of the stress pulse into feet of (approximately) even length. Each foot starts with a stress and contains everything that follows that stress up to, but not including, the next stress. '*This is the* '*house that* '*Jack* '*built* has therefore four feet, and they can be most conveniently represented by the use of vertical lines:

This is the|house that|Jack|built

The quantity of any syllable is a proportion of the total length of the foot within which the syllable occurs, and it is relative to the quantity of any other syllable in the foot. (1964:217)

The claim being made, then, is that English utterances can be characterized in rhythmic terms, as consisting of a sequence of isochronous pulses. This claim about isochrony in English speech has engendered considerable debate (see Lehiste 1980 for a review).[2] We feel that much of this debate, and the apparent lack of resolution on the question, stems from a failure to understand rhythm, and the isochrony of its basic pulses, in sufficiently abstract terms. With Liberman, Lehiste, and others, we claim a psychological reality for rhythmic organization in both the production and the perception of speech, but acknowledge that the ideal isochronicity this organization presupposes may not always reveal itself in easily measurable terms in the acoustic signal.

We may liken the metrical grid alignment of a sentence—the linguistic representation of the sentence's rhythmic structure—to a musical score. It must be recognized that a musical score, or a metrical grid alignment, though grounded in its very conception by the rhythmic capacities of the human organism (the rules for defining possible scores or metrical grid alignments embodying, as they do, universals of rhythmic organization), is but an abstract scheme. The same score may be interpreted in many different ways by the same or different performers; though of course there are limits within which variation in interpretation is confined, if the score is to remain recognizable, that is, if the score is to be considered to have been "realized" in the performance. A distinction must therefore be made between the score and its interpretation. This is the distinction between *langue* and *parole,* or between competence and performance (using the latter term now in its technical sense). For linguistic patterns of prominence, this is the distinction between the metrical grid alignment of the sentence and its phonetic implementation. In measuring for isochrony, one is measuring only the performance of the score, and not the abstract patterning that makes it up. We give full credence, therefore, to the *impression* of isochrony—to the impression of rhythm—as revealing something about how the mind grasps the organization of speech in time.[3] It is what the mind grasps that is of interest to us here, for that is presumably what is embodied in the metrical grid alignment of a sentence. Indeed, isochrony should in no way be considered as the sine qua non of a truly rhythmic system. The notion of *pattern*, as consisting of a regular recurrence of motifs defined in strong-weak terms, may be just as important as isochrony in establishing the rhythmic character of speech.

The thrust of the observations about isochrony in English is that not all syllables are rhythmically equivalent to each other; only some are. Moreover, only some are in the relation of (ideal) isochrony with respect to each other. This means that all syllables do not qualify as pulses, in Cooper and Meyer's sense. Rather, it is only the "stressed," Abercrombian foot-initial syllables that align with the pulses, or beats, of the rhythmic organization of English speech. The others have in fact a somewhat variable realization in time, depending in part on how many of them there are between the basic pulses. What does this mean for the alignment of these syllables with the metrical grid? We could contemplate giving Pike's second example the grid alignment below, where the sequence of x's represents the lowest level of the metrical grid (and the higher levels of beats are not represented):

(2.2)

```
   x        x
The manager's here
```

Here only the syllables that coincide with a pulse, an x, are specified for an alignment. The others are in limbo, so to speak. Alternatively, we could postulate a yet lower level on the metrical grid, one with which all syllables would be aligned, but not one where the points are taken to mark out ideally isochronous pulses. Given this approach, the pulses, or beats, would be represented only on the second level and above. *The manager's here* would have the following grid alignment (still incomplete at the higher levels):

(2.3)

```
   x        x
x  x x x    x
The manager's here
```

As will become clear, it is extremely useful to assume that all syllables of the utterance are integrated into the rhythmic organization of the utterance, in the sense of having a specified alignment with the metrical grid. In particular, this assumption makes possible a straightforward treatment of patterns of word stress, a description of rather fine details of timing within feet, and a representation of subtle aspects of syntactic timing. We will therefore adopt the latter sort of metrical grid alignment for language. Within the metrical grids of speech rhythm, we will thus distinguish a *first metrical level* (the lowest), a *second metrical level,* and any number of levels (in principle, infinitely many) above that. The positions on the second metrical level and above will be referred to as *beats.* The positions on the second metrical level will be referred to more specifically as *basic beats.* Finally, the positions on the first level will be referred to as *demibeats,* this term being chosen to reflect the only quasi-pulse status of the positions on the lowest level.

It may be argued that the difference between languages that Pike 1945 has called *stress-timed,* like English, and those that are *syllable-timed* can, and indeed must, be represented at the basic beat level of rhythmic organization. A syllable-timed language is one in which it is said that there is a tendency towards isochrony of all syllables, a relative constancy in the duration of syllables in the utterance, and a (relative) lack of vowel reduction (Pike 1945:35–37, Catford 1977:85–88, Abercrombie 1967:96–98). French, Italian, and Spanish are often cited as examples of syllable-timed languages.[4] For example, in the Italian *il popolo,* the syllables are pronounced as a staccato progression of evenly spaced beats. Viewed in metrical terms, a syllable-timed language is one in which each syllable is aligned with a (basic) beat in the metrical grid. Given the assumption that beats appear only at the second metrical level, then, the minimal well-formed syllable-to-grid alignment for *il popolo* will be as follows:

(2.4)

x x x x
x x x x
il popolo

Evidence for this particular conception of the grid alignment for syllable-timed languages is presented in Selkirk (in preparation).

So far, then, we have demonstrated some reason for positing two levels of rhythmic organization in speech: the level of basic beats and a lower level of demibeats. It is around these levels that the major part of the discussion concerning isochrony in speech has revolved.[5] It is also at these levels that the most copious evidence concerning rhythmic patterning has accumulated, as, for example, in recent work on word stress, where it has been shown that in stress-timed languages the number of weak "stressless" syllables intervening between "stressed" syllables is usually one or two, when there is a pattern at all (see Halle and Vergnaud 1979, Safir 1979, Hayes 1980). In other words, in the patterns of stress that are attested in natural language, it appears that at most two weak demibeats intervene between strong ones. This sort of syllable count gives obvious support to our formulation of the Principle of Rhythmic Alternation, and more generally to the idea that speech is a rhythmically organized activity.

In studies subsequent to Abercrombie 1964 such as Catford 1966 and Halliday 1967a, the rhythmic *foot* has been seen as the central, and in fact unique, unit in the analysis of sentential rhythm.[6] Translated into the terms in which we have been discussing the problem of rhythm, this amounts to saying that only two metrical levels are involved in speech rhythm: syllables are organized into basic beats, and that's it. If this were indeed a correct assessment of the facts, the motivation for invoking the complexly hierarchized representation of rhythm that is embodied in the metrical grid would be weak. However, as we will demonstrate, speech does show a greater hierarchy of rhythmic arrangements. Indeed, the term *foot,* as defined by Abercrombie, is relevant only to these lower levels of rhythmic organization, where the difference between stress-timing and syllable-timing is represented.

What of the *degrees* of rhythmic prominence (often referred to, in the tradition of Trager and Smith 1951, as *degrees of stress*)—that is, the distinctions between strong and weak beats on various levels? It seems that these distinctions have been recognized, but that in the notational representation of rhythm they have been obscured. Catford, for example, allows the sentence *John bought two books last week* to have any of the following arrangements into *feet:*

(2.5)
| John | bought | two | books | last | week
| John | bought two | books last | week
| John bought | two books | last week
| John bought two | books last week
   etc.

But the notion "foot" employed here cannot be the same one defined by Abercrombie, for each of the monosyllabic words in these examples is stressed, and so constitutes a foot on its own. The vertical marks must in fact be taken as indicating strong-weak relations on a level above that of the foot. The point is made clear when multisyllabic words consisting of a stressed syllable followed by unstressed syllables are substituted for the monosyllables in (2.5): for example, *Mary purchased twenty pamphlets yesterday morning.* The intuition is that the same placements of vertical lines are appropriate, that is, that the same rhythmic groupings are possible for the sentence. Yet within the spans of the utterance flanked by the lines still further rhythmic distinctions are made, as shown below, where the italics indicate local rhythmic prominences (beats):

(2.6)
| *Ma*ry | *pur*chased | *twen*ty | *pam*phlets | *yes*terday | *mor*ning
| *Ma*ry | *pur*chased twenty | *pam*phlets yesterday | *mor*ning
| *Ma*ry *pur*chased | *twen*ty pamphlets | *yes*terday *mor*ning
| *Ma*ry *pur*chased twenty | *pam*phlets yesterday *mor*ning
    etc.

The intuition, then, is that rhythmic groupings are made at more than one level.[7] This, along with other evidence (to be reviewed directly) that there are degrees (or levels) of rhythmic prominence in speech, shows that a hierarchical representation of speech rhythm such as the metrical grid is necessary.

The necessity for distinguishing a minimum of two metrical levels above the basic beat level in the metrical grid with which a sentence is aligned is quite common. Consider the English sentence *Ábernàthy gestículàted.* Here some syllables are aligned with beats (they are marked with accents) and some are not; and among the beat-aligned syllables some are aligned with a strong beat (they bear acute accents). Thus, in this example a strong-weak alternation of beats is clearly perceived. Any representation of speech rhythm requires some means of denoting this strong-weak contrast. The alignment of the words of the sentence with the metrical grid would minimally involve three metrical levels:

(2.7)
```
x             x
x    x        x   x
x  x  x  x  x  x x x x
Abernathy gesticulated
```

The syllables aligned with strong beats here (coinciding with points on the third metrical level) are often referred to as syllables bearing word stress, or more specifically, main word stress. And indeed, in the words of many languages, whether they are stress-timed like English or syllable-timed like Italian, there will be a locus of rhythmic prominence, a beat reliably stronger than the others. The existence of (main) word stress, then, indicates rhythmic organization above the basic beat level.

The strong beat of main word stress does not mark the highest level of rhythmic organization in an English sentence, or in the sentences of many other languages. In the normal English sentence, there exists a strong-weak distinction between beats at more than one level: a beat that is strong on one level may coincide with a beat on a higher level that is either weak or strong. This is the case in the sentence *Abernathy gesticulated,* where the syllable *-ti-* is the most prominent of all, either in the "neutral" pronunciation of the sentence with a pitch accent only on the verb, or in the "nonneutral" pronunciation in which both words bear pitch accents. The syllable *-ti-* may be said to bear main sentence or phrase stress. The full alignment of the sentence with the grid would be as follows:

(2.8)

```
              x
x             x
x     x       x   x
x  x  x  x  x  x x x x
```
Abernathy gesticulated

Thus the existence of just one degree of sentence or phrase stress alongside main word stress shows that at least two levels of rhythmic organization must be distinguished above the level of basic beats. Again, it is quite common among languages for the main-stressed syllables of the words making up a sentence to differ in their degrees of rhythmic prominence. Partly the existence and location of phrasal rhythmic prominence are to be attributed to the operation of rules of grammar that are sensitive to syntactic structure, such as the Nuclear Stress Rule of English, and partly the appearance of rhythmic prominence on the phrase is to be attributed simply to the demands of rhythmic organization per se, and in particular to the PRA. The different contributions to phrasal prominence will be discussed in section 2.3 and in chapters 3 and 4.

One potentially very telling sort of "nonintuitional" evidence for degrees of rhythmic prominence in speech is hinted at by Pierrehumbert 1980. She shows that the phonetic values for the tones (i.e., pitch accents) composing intonational contours in English are in part a function of the relative prominence of the syllables with which they are associated, where "prominence," for Pierrehumbert, is largely (though not entirely) a matter of stress, i.e., rhythmic prominence.[8] Pierrehumbert offers a convincing case for representing intonational contours as consisting (largely) of a sequence of atomic pitch accents. She argues that these pitch accents, which associate with the main stresses of words, are to be characterized either as one of two single level tones, high (H) and low (L), or as binary combinations of these (see section 5.3). Moreover, she shows that in the same intonational contour, given a pair of pitch accents consisting, say, of one high tone each, the high tone that is associated with the rhythmically most prominent syllable will consistently have the higher frequency (when the effects of declination are factored out, of course).[9] This relation holds not only between a nuclear pitch accent and a prenuclear pitch accent, but also between two prenuclear pitch accents with different prominence values, as shown in figure 2.1. In this example, *In November, the region's weather was unusually dry,* each of the principal words bears a high tone pitch accent. The sentence has a "declarative contour." It corresponds to two intonational phrases, demarcated here with the % symbol. (For the particulars of such contours, see section 5.3.)

The English Nuclear Stress Rule determines that *weather* will be more prominent than *region's,* that *dry* will be more prominent than *unusually,* and that the most prominent element of the last phrase (i.e., *dry*) will be more prominent than any other element of the sentence. The alignment of the sentence with the metrical grid would thus be, minimally, as shown in figure 2.2.[10] A comparison of the two figures shows them to be consistent with Pierrehumbert's suggested generalization: that F_0 height is a reflection of relative rhythmic prominence. We will pursue this question of the relation between intonation and rhythm in chapters 4 and 5. For now, we seek only to point out that there exists evidence beyond intuitions about timing that points to the sort of rhythmic organization being claimed to exist.

Liberman 1975 and Liberman and Prince 1977 have offered another important sort of evidence from English for degrees of rhythmic prominence and, specifically, for representing these prominence relations in terms of levels on the metrical grid. They argue that to properly characterize the conditions under which the pervasive phenomenon of *stress shift* (often referred to as the "Rhythm Rule") takes place crucially requires making a distinction in levels of rhythmic organization. Consider, for example, the location of stress prominences in the normal pronunciation of the phrases below:[11]

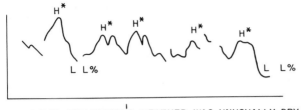

IN NOVEMBER, THE REGIONS WEATHER WAS UNUSUALLY DRY.

Figure 2.1

```
                                              X
                            X                 X
        X         X         X         X       X
        X X       X         X     X   X       X
X     X X X   X     X X X       X   X   X X X X   X   X
```

In November, the region's weather was unusually dry

Figure 2.2

(2.9)

Dúndèe mármalàde	(the) thírtèenth of Máy
Wéstmìnster Ábbey	(the) únknòwn sóldier
(a) góod-lòoking lífegùard	ánaphòric réference
thírtèen mén	áchromàtic léns

(The acute accent indicates "primary word stress" and the grave indicates "secondary word stress"; in the terms used here, strong vs. weak beats.) Of significance is the fact that main stress in the first word is not located where it would be if that word were pronounced in isolation or in other phrasal contexts: *Dùndée, thìrtéen, ànaphóric, more gòod-lóoking than you*, etc. The main stress has been "shifted backward" in the examples above. Liberman and Prince's approach to this matter is to say, roughly, that a surface representation like *áchromàtic léns* is derived by a rule of stress shift from an underlying representation in which the first word has its "normal" lexical word stress pattern, e.g., *àchromátic léns*. Liberman and Prince argue that the stress shift rule applies only when two stresses of the *same level* are *adjacent*, in the relevant sense, and hence constitute a "stress clash." The stress clash is eliminated by shifting the first of the clashing stresses backward.

Clearly, strict adjacency of stressed syllables is not required as a precondition for stress shift, for the rule applies in the phrases with *Westminster, good-looking,* and *anaphoric,* as it does in *(the) thirteenth (of May)*, where a stressless syllable intervenes between the two apparently clashing stressed syllables. Thus, as Liberman and Prince point out, the offending adjacency must be represented as occurring at a higher level; it cannot be explained purely in terms of the linear arrangement of syllables. This notion of higher level can of course be characterized, in terms of the metrical grid or in other not strictly linear representations of stress.[12]

Assume that "before" stress shift the metrical grid alignment of *achromatic lens* is as shown in (2.10a) and that stress shift converts it into (2.10b).

(2.10)

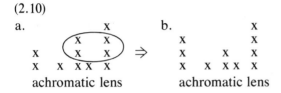

(The alignment at the first three levels in (2.10a) is determined by the principles of word stress in English, and the fourth level beat on *lens* corresponds to the effects of the Nuclear Stress Rule.) It is easy to explain in terms of the grid why the concatenation of rhythmic units in (2.10a) is ill formed and therefore subject to modification by stress shift. In general, a grid configuration of the following sort will be judged deviant, regardless of what metrical levels are involved:

(2.11)
....
...x x...
...x x...
....

This is because the grid (i.e., the rhythmic structure) fails to "alternate" in such a configuration, in the sense that two strong beats are not separated by a weak beat. This offending configuration appears in the representation (2.10a) of *achromatic lens,* where it is circled. Thus, though the stressed syllables in (2.10a) are not themselves adjacent, the strong beats with which they are aligned are, in the metrical grid, and this is what constitutes the stress clash. Thus the clash can be defined here only in terms of the second metrical level and above. Supporting this characterization of the stress clash is the fact that stress shift does not take place as readily, or at all, when the main stress is some distance away and thus not involved in a clash. We will see examples of this in section 4.3, where the "Rhythm Rule" of English is discussed in some detail.

As Liberman and Prince point out, of course, stress shift is not the only means available for avoiding a stress clash in the grid. Alternatively, the final syllable of the first word may be lengthened, or a pause may be placed between the words. It may be argued that the possibilities of lengthening and pausing are attributable to the presence of additional "silent" beats, whose appearance is governed by syntactic factors (see section 4.3 and chapter 6) and which themselves prevent stress clash from arising.

What is important to the more general point at hand is the fact that characterizing the ill-formed grid configuration referred to as a "clash" requires reference to two metrical levels. In the particular cases under discussion, it means that reference is made to both the basic beat level and one level above; and this in turn means that stress clash and its consequent stress shift provide evidence for the existence of at least three levels of rhythmic organization in English words.

In discussing rhythmic organization in speech and in particular the metrical grid, we have suggested that language exhibits a quite general *Principle of Rhythmic Alternation (PRA)*, which determines the patterns of alternation appearing in the grid. A provisional formulation of the PRA is as follows:

(2.12)
Between two successive strong beats on a metrical level n there must intervene at least one (and at most two) weak beat(s) of the metrical level n.

Note now that in (2.11) the two points on the lower metrical level are both strong beats, in that they both coincide with beats of the next metrical level up, and that because the two strong beats are adjacent, this configuration does not conform to the PRA. It seems reasonable, then, to view the PRA as in some way responsible for ruling the stress clash in (2.10a) ill formed, and this is in fact the view we will take (see section 2.3). Note that although the PRA itself does not refer to more than one metrical level (the strong and weak beats to which it refers are all of one level), the very notions of "strong beat" and "weak beat" that it invokes require reference to two metrical levels. Thus the characterization of a stress clash as a configuration ruled ill formed by the PRA does involve an appeal to more than one metrical level.

The characterization of stress clash given by Liberman 1975 and Liberman and Prince 1977:312–313 does not invoke a general principle of alternation. Instead the offending ill-formedness is defined directly, as that grid configuration in which two positions on level m are not separated by a position on the next lower level $m-1$. Either approach makes the case for higher levels of rhythmic organization, and the two are equivalent for the cases examined so far. As we will show, however, there is quite independent motivation for the PRA—it apparently operates in numerous other circumstances where the notion of stress clash is simply irrelevant. The value of characterizing the ill-formedness of a stress clash in the way advocated here, then, is that this analysis invokes a principle of some generality in the grammar, not one relevant only to the problem at hand.

Another sort of arhythmicity may arise in the derivation of the phonological representation of a word or sentence, one that, like the stress clash, is often enough done away with in the surface phonological representation of a sentence. This other sort of grid configuration is an overlong sequence of weak beats that is not punctuated by any strong, as depicted in (2.13).

(2.13)

```
. . . . . . . . . .
.... o o o ....
.... x x x ....
. . . . . . . . . .
```

(The symbol o indicates the absence of any beat at the point that o occupies in the grid.) Here, too, we find an absence of rhythmic alternation. We might call this a rhythmic *lapse,* to distinguish it from the clash. It will be desirable to (re)formulate the PRA so that it can rule out both types of nonalternating configuration.

Considerable evidence shows that the rhythmic organization of speech abhors a lapse as much as it does a stress clash. We can see this in the rhythmic organization of phrases. For example, for a normal "neutral" pronunciation of sentence (2.14), where there is a pitch accent only on the final word, which also bears main phrase stress (see sections 4.2.2 and 5.5), there must be a rhythmic prominence before the final main stress.

(2.14)
(I know quite well that) it's organized on the model of a gallon of worms.

The metrical grid alignment (2.15) is avoided in favor of some alternating pattern, be it that of (2.16) or (2.17).[13] (To simplify matters, the lowest metrical level noted here corresponds to primary word stress (i.e., the third metrical level).)

(2.15)

```
                                      x
        x               x     x       x
```
. . . it's organized on the model of a gallon of worms

(2.16)

```
            x
x           x
x   x   x   x
```

(2.17)

```
            x
    x       x
x   x   x   x
```

(2.15) is the minimal grid alignment consistent with the Nuclear Stress Rule (NSR) and the assignment of a pitch accent to the final word (see chapter 4). But consistency with the NSR and pitch accent assignment is not enough to make the metrical grid alignment well formed, if the grid does not otherwise exhibit the appropriate alternation in rhythmic organization. Something like the PRA would seem to be at work.

Another set of facts indicating that the rhythmic organization of speech avoids lapses involves secondary word stress. In both stress-timed and syllable-timed languages, the rules of the grammar will define the alignment of syllables with basic beats and often enough will also pick out which of these beats is the most prominent (main-stressed) in the word. For example, the rules for basic beat alignment and main word stress in syllable-timed Italian will give the grid alignment (2.18) for the penultimately stressed word *generativa:*

(2.18)

```
    x
x x x x x
x x x x x
```
generativa

But this alignment, which involves a lapse preceding the main stress, is not actually attested. What is found instead is a secondary stress preceding the main stress at a distance of either one or two syllables

(Malagoli 1946, Nespor and Vogel 1979, Chierchia 1982b, Vogel and Scalise 1982), as illustrated in (2.19) and (2.20).

```
(2.19)        (2.20)
        x             x
x       x     x       x
x x x x x     x x x x x
x x x x x     x x x x x
generativa    generativa
```

We will also be proposing (section 2.3 and chapter 3) that the very existence of alternation at the lowest (basic beat and demibeat) levels is to be ascribed to the PRA in some way. A sequence of syllables each of which is aligned only with a (weak) demibeat at the first metrical level is but one very long rhythmic lapse and is obviously avoided.

In general, the tendency to avoid lapses, at all levels of rhythmic organization, is overwhelming. We will reformulate the PRA to reflect this. As provisionally stated in (2.12), the PRA rules out any instance of clash, as well as those instances of lapse where strong beats (or demibeats) flank a sequence of more than two weaks. But there are other instances of rhythmic lapse where the overlong sequence of weaks is not flanked on both sides by strongs, e.g., (2.15) and (2.18). If the failure of these configurations to appear in surface phonetic representation is to be attributed to the PRA, then it must be reformulated so as not to require the presence of the flanking strongs. Suppose the PRA specified instead that any weak beat or demibeat may be preceded by at most one other weak. This says, in effect, that there may be at most two weaks in sequence. It has the effect of ruling out overlong weak sequences between strong beats or demibeats, and such sequences not flanked on both sides as well. Let us call this the *anti-lapse provision* of the PRA.

We might now consider reformulating the *anti-clash provision* of the PRA, which currently states that at least one weak beat or demibeat must intervene between two strongs. In fact, one alternative to this appeal to the flanking strongs appears to make certain correct predictions about the facts that the earlier formulation leaves unexplained. This alternative consists in specifying simply that at least one weak beat (or demibeat) must follow a strong.[14] Like the first, this formulation ensures that there will be at least one weak between two strongs; unlike the first, however, it ensures in addition that a weak beat (or demibeat) will always follow a final strong beat. (The notion "final" will be defined with respect to some domain—word, phrase, etc.—and thus is not limited to sentence-final position.) For the time being, then, let us entertain the formulation in (2.21) as an alternative to (2.12):

(2.21)
The Principle of Rhythmic Alternation

a. Every strong position on a metrical level n should be followed by at least one weak position on that level.

b. Any weak position on a metrical level n may be preceded by at most one weak position on that level.

The consequences of formulating the principle in this way will be examined more fully in the following chapters.

To sum up, then, there appears to be considerable evidence for the rhythmic organization of speech, and for representing that rhythmic organization as an alignment of the syllables of a sentence with positions in a metrical grid. Like a musical score, the alignment of a sentence with a grid represents the (ideal) isochrony of the pulses of speech, the relative durations of individual syllables, and their degrees of relative prominence. Moreover, the grid permits an understanding of the alternations in the rhythmic realizations of words in the sentence. This is an extremely important point. The metrical grid allows the generalization to be expressed that the same rhythmic ideal, the Principle of Rhythmic Alternation, governs (in a way yet to be defined) the patterns to be found *at all levels*. The PRA, formulated with respect to levels of the metrical grid, "expresses" the propensity to alternation at the lower levels in the same terms as the propensity to avoid clash, or to introduce alternation, at the higher levels. Thus, viewing stress patterns in terms of the metrical grid rationalizes the properties of stress systems even further than the metrical tree theory of stress patterns, for it rationalizes the pattern question itself (see sections 1.2.2 and 4.2). It is for this reason that we view the metrical grid as crucial to a theory of stress patterns and thereby more than worthy of supplanting the now otiose trees in this function.

2.3 Building the Grid

2.3.1 The Framework

We are interested here in developing a theory of patterns of rhythmic prominence in language, a theory of the notion "possible metrical grid alignment." We believe that that theory must incorporate universals of rhythmic organization, and must delineate the range of choices that are available to grammars of individual languages for the codification of particular rhythmic patterns. What we are aiming for is a *core theory* of rhythmic patterns (see Chomsky 1981 and references cited therein). Given such a core theory, the grammar of an individual language will specify not language-particular rules, but which among the (universally defined) rules made available by the theory are actually at play in a particular language. Following Chomsky, we will call this a language-particular specification of the *parameters* delineated by the theory.

In recent years considerable research has been done in metrical phonology with a view toward developing a core theory of word stress patterns, based on a metrical (prosodic) tree representation of prominence relations. This effort has been advanced most notably by the work of Halle and Vergnaud 1979 and developed more recently in Hayes 1980. As will become clear, many of the fundamental insights into the parameters of stress theory gained in these works, and others, are readily and perspicuously characterized in a metrical grid framework. With Prince 1981, 1983, we argue that a theory of stress patterns is *better* expressed when the metrical grid is assumed to be the basic representation of stress. Many of the basic lines of thinking pursued here find their inspiration in Prince's work, though the particular articulations of the ideas are different in certain respects, having been developed independently.

As stated earlier, we propose that the relation between the text (a syntactic representation) and its metrical grid alignment is to be expressed as a set of rules that "construct" a metrical grid alignment for the text according to the principle of the cycle. On this theory, these rules progressively build up the metrical grid alignment of a sentence (a rhythmic "score"), from the lower levels to the higher, on successively larger cyclic domains. An alternative theory is entirely conceivable, according to which the text is in one way or another "matched up" with a full-fledged grid somehow independently defined, a grid that may undergo modification once aligned with the text. This is the approach implicit in Liberman 1975, Liberman and Prince 1977, and Dell (to appear). There, the text, which includes the abstract stress pattern of the sentence, is matched up with a "preexistent" grid, without appeal to the cycle. Let us consider this alternative theory, stripped of its assumption that the text includes metrical tree patterns of stress.

Two issues must be distinguished here: whether the text-grid relation is established by "construction" or "matching," and whether the relation is established cyclically or not. We submit that the principle of the cycle is essential to the proper characterization of this relation, and we will argue for this position in several ways in this chapter and in chapters 3 and 7. The fact that the text-grid relation must be cyclically defined removes any possibility of entertaining the matching theory, we believe. Fragments of a metrical grid, corresponding to the lowest cyclic domains, could perhaps be considered to be preexistent and matched with the text. But there could no longer be a preexistent metrical grid of the entire sentence, in any interesting sense, given that the grid matched on lower cycles would be modified cyclically. And to say that the grid is only matched at the lowest levels removes any force from this proposal, making it very much like the construction theory. It will become evident that a grid construction model permits the various sorts of generalizations about patterns of rhythmic prominence that a theory must capture to emerge quite perspicuously at all levels of the grid, and it is for this reason that we adopt such a model here.

The theory of metrical grid construction has two major components. The first is a set of *text-to-grid alignment* (TGA) rules. Through these rules, the particular properties of the text may impose requirements on the rhythmic realization of the sentence. For example, it may be stated in the grammar of a language, as a TGA rule, that syllables having such and such a degree of sonority must receive rhythmic prominence, while syllables of lower sonority do not. Or it may be stated that syllables aligned with beats located at the beginnings or ends of words or phrases must receive more rhythmic prominence than others in the overall rhythmic structure of the word or phrase. Thus a number of important properties of particular stress systems follow not so much from the properties of the grid itself as from the principles in the grammar of individual languages that govern just how the syllables of their utterances (texts) are aligned with the grid. Quite certainly, one of the major descriptive tasks for a metrical grid theory of stress is to characterize the TGA rules available to language. As we will show, it seems that these rules fall into just four classes: (i) the (universal) rule of *Demibeat Alignment* (DBA), which aligns each syllable with a single grid position on the lowest metrical level, (ii) the *basic beat rules,* which align syllables with beats on the second metrical level by virtue of (a) their composition (i.e., the composition of their *rime*) and/or (b) their position with respect to a particular syntactic domain, (iii) the *domain-end prominence rules* (the End Rules of Prince 1983), which ensure the greatest prominence of syllables aligned with beats at the beginning or end of some specified syntactic domain, by promoting them to beat-hood on metrical level three or higher (e.g., the English Main (Word) Stress Rule, Compound Rule, and Nuclear Stress Rule), and (iv) the *Pitch Accent Prominence Rule* (PAR), which ensures that syllables with which the pitch accents forming an intonational contour are aligned are rhythmically prominent with respect to non-pitch-accented syllables. These rule types will be examined in later chapters.

The Principle of Rhythmic Alternation defines an ideal rhythmic organization; by requiring that a strong beat be followed by a weak and that a weak be preceded by at most one other weak, it defines an ideal metrical grid. Yet the rules of language for aligning syllables with a grid—the TGA rules—pay no heed to this ideal. From the point of view of the PRA, these rules are capable of producing chaos, or more precisely, undesirable lapses and clashes. Nonetheless, the PRA is a sort of Platonic ideal to which the rhythmic structure, grounded in syllables, tones, and syntactic structure, aspires. It is the rules of *grid euphony* (GE) that aid actual sentences in attaining this ideal, and they thus form the second major component of the core theory of prominence patterns. We will give evidence for three types of grid euphony rules: (i) Beat Addition, (ii) Beat Movement, and (iii) Beat Deletion. Rules of these types attempt to set things right; they build rhythmic order, or some semblance of it, out of the chaos that the TGA rules are capable of producing. We gather them together here:[15,16]

(2.22)
Beat Addition

```
            x
a. x x ⇒ x x   (left-dominant addition)
              x
b. x x ⇒ x x   (right-dominant addition)
```

(2.23)
Beat Movement

```
      x        x
      x x    x   x
a. x x x ⇒ x x x   (left movement)
   x        x
   x x    x   x
b. x x x ⇒ x x x   (right movement)
```

(2.24)
Beat Deletion

```
     X         X
   X X       X     c. X X        X
a. X X ⇒ X X        X X ⇒ X X

   X         X
   X X       X     d. X X        X
b. X X ⇒ X X        X X ⇒ X X
```

The interesting property of these rules is that they are defined solely in terms of the grid, make no reference to the properties of the text, and apply in principle at any metrical level. They are purely rhythmic in character. In our view, they are the "collective essence" of the PRA. One important set of parameters to be fixed in the grammar of an individual language will be the indication of whether or not one, or more, of these rule types applies on a given metrical level, and a specification of which particular rule ((a), (b), etc.) the language chooses. In other words, just how the PRA is realized in the rhythmic structure of a language, and to what extent it is, is a matter for language-particular description. The universal of rhythmic organization in language, then, is that *by means of grid euphony rules* languages "aspire," in one way or another, to meet the PRA in their metrical grid alignments.

A fundamental question now arises. How do the GE rules interact with TGA rules like the Nuclear Stress Rule, the domain-end prominence rules of word stress, and so on? More specifically, under what circumstances may the GE rules obliterate the effects of the TGA rules? The answer makes crucial use of the notion of the cycle. We will show that, within a cyclic domain, the GE rules may not undo the prominence relations that are required on that domain by TGA rules, and that there is reason to posit the following general condition on grid construction:

(2.25)
Textual Prominence Preservation Condition (TPPC)

A text-to-grid alignment rule applying on a syntactic domain d_i is necessarily satisfied on that domain.

This principle has far-reaching implications for a theory of metrical grid alignments. For example, it will ensure that on a given cyclic domain Beat Addition may not change the location of a TGA-specified greatest prominence on that domain, so that it will not undo the effects of the Main Stress Rule in words or the Nuclear Stress Rule on phrases on that domain, but only complement them. This is the correct result, as we will show.

2.3.2 The Interaction of the Two Grid Construction Components

2.3.2.1 The First Metrical Level   It seems reasonable to entertain the hypothesis that, universally, phonological representations conform to this principle: every syllable of an utterance is aligned with at least one demibeat in the metrical grid. This principle simply says that every syllable participates in the rhythmic organization of the utterance. At this point in our investigation it would be counterproductive to assume otherwise. The principle as stated is probably not restrictive enough, however, since it would allow a single syllable to be aligned with several beats at once. But such a situation does not seem to arise, except in the rather limited circumstances involving syntactic timing.[17] For example, at the limits of words and phrases, a final syllable that is aligned "underlyingly" with a single beat or demibeat may in addition be aligned in a "derived" representation with one or more silent grid positions, whose presence in the grid is attributable to the syntactically governed silent demibeat addition that gives rise to syntactic timing (see chapter 6). We propose, then, as a condition on the initial text-to-grid alignment (the first step in the construction of the metrical grid, preceding silent demibeat addition), that a syllable align with just one demibeat. Under the grid construction approach, this is stated as the following (universal) TGA rule:

(2.26)
Demibeat Alignment
Align just one demibeat with every syllable.

This rule would derive the alignment of (2.27b) from the syllable sequence (2.27a) on the lowest cyclic domain:

(2.27)

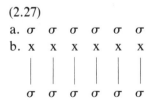

This formulation of Demibeat Alignment, coupled with the restrictive assumption that the other TGA rules do not augment the grid horizontally by adding grid positions on the first metrical level, will ensure that, except in circumstances created by the silent demibeat addition of syntactic timing, there will be one demibeat for every syllable and one syllable for every demibeat. We will call this additional assumption about TGA rules the *Minimal Demibeat Condition*. It may turn out to be too restrictive an assumption, in particular as far as the basic beat rules are concerned,[18] but we will take it as a part of our working hypothesis for the moment.

2.3.2.2 The Second Metrical Level   If the grammar of a language contained no rules other than Demibeat Alignment for governing the alignment of the syllables of the text with the grid, but if it did allow Beat Addition to apply on the second metrical level and above, then that language would be a stress-timed language, of a rather special sort. The alignment of syllables with basic beats and beats on higher levels would be determined neither by the nature of the syllables themselves, nor by their position in the word or the phrase, but simply by the rhythmic tendencies expressed in Beat Addition. The patterns of beats might vary freely in their location within words. In fact, we know of no language like this. The grammars of languages with which we are acquainted often do include additional rules that, in conjunction with Demibeat Alignment and GE rules, determine in more specific fashion how syllables are to be aligned with basic beats of the second metrical level. These are the basic beat rules.

A syllable-timed language has only one basic beat rule, which specifies that *every* syllable will have a basic beat (see Selkirk (in preparation)). We could formulate it provisionally as: align every syllable with a beat. But in stress-timed languages, at least those of the more commonplace sort, whether or not a syllable is aligned with a basic beat seems to be able to depend on its *composition,* its *position* in the domain, both of these factors, or neither (as in the hypothetical case cited above). We will suppose that universal grammar makes available the following rule schemata, and that languages may choose their basic beat rules from these:

(2.28)
Basic Beat Rules
a. Align a syllable of compositional type x with a beat.
b. Align a syllable in position y with a beat.

A syllable-timed language falls under the universal rule schema (2.28a): in such a language, *every* syllable is of "type *x*." A theory of stress-timed languages will involve a theory of (i) what distinctions in compositional type may be appealed to in basic beat rules, and (ii) what sorts of specifications of position within the cyclic domain may be made. We will not attempt to elaborate such a theory here. We repeat, however, the widely made observation that the possibilities of "stressing" a syllable seem to involve only the properties of the rime constituent of the syllable, not those of the onset (Pike and Pike 1947, Kuryłowicz 1948). The position has been taken that the relevant properties of the rime are to be expressed in "geometrical" terms—in other words, that the branching of a syllable into one or more constituents is what is crucial in determining its place within stress patterns.[19] However, there is good reason to believe that pure geometry is not the important factor. It is known that the syllable type distinctions that play a role in attested stress systems may have to do with the quantity or "weight" of a syllable (i.e., whether or not it has a long vowel, or whether or not it has a long vowel or is closed by a consonant), *or* the quality of the vowel contained in the syllable, *or* the syllable's tonal specifications.[20] Little insight is to be gained by seeing the last distinction as "geometric." Prince 1981, 1983 hypothesizes that they are all ultimately to be explained as distinctions in the sonority of the syllable.[21] As for position, the cases with which we are familiar involve domain-initial position, domain-final position, or the position before the main stress (strongest beat) of a word.[22] If these cases are representative, then the class of positions is quite narrowly circumscribed. Again, though, it is not our purpose at present to pursue the theory of word stress from the point of view of the syllable types or positions involved in "stress rules," for these issues are not crucially related to the concerns of this study.

Our interest is in understanding the patterns that result from the presence in the grammar of basic beat rules invoking these type and position distinctions. Note that these language-particular basic beat rules do not mention an alternating pattern of any sort. Our hypothesis is that the attested alternations in weak and strong demibeats are, in a sense to be made precise, largely the contribution of GE rules and, in particular, the rule(s) of Beat Addition. It is in defense of this hypothesis that we hope to establish the well-foundedness of the metrical grid theory of stress.

Given a grid construction approach, the basic beat rules are instructions for adding beats to the grid on the second metrical level. A rule of type (b) in which y stands for "at the beginning of the word" would read:

(2.29)
Align a (basic) beat with the first syllable on the domain Word.

It would derive the alignment in (2.30) from that in (2.27b), supposing that sequence to be a Word.

(2.30)

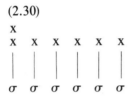

In this way, Demibeat Alignment and the language-particular basic beat rules jointly construct a partial grid. A partial grid so produced is not necessarily a well-formed rhythmic structure, however. (2.30), for example, contains a rhythmic lapse and is therefore abhorrent to the PRA. Within the grid construction framework we are proposing, that partial grid is further built up by the pattern-engendering GE rules. The main agent of this build-up, we suggest, is a rule that adds beats—the rule of Beat Addition.

For most non-syllable-timed languages, Beat Addition is obligatory at the basic beat level (see section 3.2.5), which is to say that most such languages exhibit some sort of regular alternating pattern at that level. There may possibly be some languages that have no Beat Addition on the second metrical level,[23] but more typically, it seems, languages will require that Beat Addition apply on the basic beat level. Specifically, they will require that either (2.22a) or (2.22b) apply. Adapting a term borrowed from Hayes 1980 to our own uses, we will call Beat Addition (2.22a) *left-dominant* and Beat Addition (2.22b) *right-dominant*. This, then, is one parameter the grammar of a language may set. There is yet another to be set for Beat Addition at the basic beat level. It is well known that patterns of stressed and stressless syllables may be established in directional fashion, from right to left (R–L) or from left to right (L–R) across some particular domain. In terms of the present analysis, this means that Beat Addition on the second metrical level may be directional in nature, the two values of that parameter being R–L and L–R. Notice, now, that the obligatoriness of Beat Addition and its directional character ensure that spans of the domain not disturbed by the presence of a basic beat established by TGA rules will exhibit a strictly alternating binary pattern. This is precisely what is found in stress-timed languages, and therefore confirms our general approach to the matter.

Suppose that a language has no basic beat rule(s), but does have obligatory left-dominant Beat Addition, applying from right to left. Such a specification of parameters would produce the patterns in (2.31):

(2.31)
odd   *even*

```
  x   x       x   x   x
x x x x x   x x x x x x
```

These are the patterns for odd and even syllables attested in Warao (Osborn 1916, cited in Hayes 1980). Other parameter settings in other languages will give a basic beat on the final syllable combined with alternation from right to left, and so on.

Consider in this light the hypothetical partial grid (2.30). In a language requiring no Beat Addition, it would stay as it is. But four other completions of the second level are possible when Beat Addition comes into play, which arise as a result of specifying the parameters for dominance and directionality. The language Maranungku (Tryon 1970, cited by Hayes 1980) is one in which the domain-initial basic beat rule (2.28b) is at play. In this language, the initial syllable is "stressed," as is every other odd syllable, including the final one in odd-syllabled words. Given the present framework, this indicates that Maranungku has a right-dominant rule of Beat Addition that proceeds left to right. The output of this Beat Addition is shown in (2.32):

(2.32)
odd   *even*

```
x   x   x     x   x   x
x x x x x   x x x x x x
```

Let us consider the example of a language with a basic beat rule involving the compositional syllable type, namely, "Cairene Classical" Arabic. "Cairene Classical" Arabic is the pronunciation of classical Arabic used by speakers of the Cairene dialect, as reported by Mitchell 1960. McCarthy 1979a,b offers an extremely plausible account of the stress pattern of this "dialect," drawing on Mitchell's description. Two aspects of the stress pattern are of interest here. First, heavy syllables (CVC or CVV) must be feet on their own, to use McCarthy's terms. Second, a sequence of nonheavy syllables enters into a (preferentially) binary pattern of beats, going from left to right and starting from the beginning of the word and from any heavy syllable. The first stressed syllable in a sequence of light syllables following a heavy syllable is located *immediately after* the heavy:

(2.33)

$$\text{CÝ CV CÝ ...} \qquad \text{...} \begin{Bmatrix} \text{CÝV} \\ \text{CVC} \end{Bmatrix} \text{CÝ CV CÝ ...}$$

McCarthy's analysis of Cairene Classical patterns at the foot level translates into the following analysis of basic beats in the metrical grid framework:

(2.34)

a. *Basic Beat Rule*

Every heavy syllable is aligned with a basic beat.

b. *Beat Addition*

Left-dominant

Left to right

Thus the beat patterns of the words *kaataba, inkasara,* and *ʔad-wiyatuhu* will be derived as follows:

(2.35)

	kaataba	inkasara	ʔadwiyatuhu
DBA	↓	↓	↓
	x x x	x x x x	x x x x x
	kaataba	inkasara	ʔadwiyatuhu
BBR	↓	↓	↓
	x	x	x
	x x x	x x x x	x x x x x
	kaataba	inkasara	ʔadwiyatuhu
BA	↓	↓	↓
	x x	x x	x x x
	x x x	x x x x	x x x x x
	kaataba	inkasara	ʔadwiyatuhu

The last syllable in *inkasara* is not promoted to basic beat status by the left-dominant Beat Addition, simply because its structural description is not met.[24]

With these brief examples, we do not purport to have shown the superiority of a metrical grid theory of patterns of stressed syllables such as the one we have proposed. It is beyond the scope of this book to attempt this. We refer the reader first to Prince 1983, who has made a persuasive case for a metrical grid theory of these patterns, covering the range of phenomena that has been treated in earlier metrical tree analyses, and second to chapter 3 of this volume, which will demonstrate the appeal of a metrical grid approach to English word stress. In sketching the preceding analyses, we have simply attempted to render plausible the general approach we have been advocating, which is to see these patterns as resulting from the effects of TGA rules and Beat Addition.

Note next that while it is in principle possible for the GE rules of Beat Movement and Beat Deletion to apply on the second metrical level, certain general conditions appear to limit this possibility severely. The preservation of the basic beat alignments required by a basic beat rule is guaranteed by the Textual Prominence Preservation Condition. Thus, two adjacent second-level grid positions will remain in place if both are introduced by the basic beat rules of the language. Moreover, if a clash is created by the joint effects of a basic beat rule and an application of Beat Addition, only the grid position introduced by Beat Addition is susceptible to being deleted. In general, however, clashes on the second metrical level seem to be tolerated quite well. There is thus some reason to speculate that Beat Movement and Beat Deletion are simply not applicable on the second metrical level. We will give evidence for this in subsequent chapters. (In chapter 4, we will propose a condition of Basic Beat Level Integrity, (4.49).)

The core of this particular articulation of the metrical grid theory of patterns of stressed and stressless syllables, then, is a system of rules for constructing the second level of the grid "on top of" the demibeats aligned with the sequence of syllables contained in a word. Universal grammar makes available two distinct sets of rules relevant to metrical level two: the basic beat rules (TGA rules) and the rules of grid euphony. The choices that a particular language makes from these sets of rules (including the choice of dominance and directionality for Beat Addition)—that is, the way it sets these parameters—constitute the linguistic description, or grammar, of the patterns of stressed and stressless syllables for the language.

This core theory of patterns of stressed and stressless syllables does not give expression to lexical idiosyncrasies that may be manifested in the stress patterns of languages, which is as it should be. Although it is relatively common in describing individual languages to need to consider some syllable of a particular stem or suffix to be "inherently" stressed, this fact should not lead the analyst from the main theme of the investigation, which is the understanding of the *essential* properties of stress systems, properties that we are justified in believing to be describable in terms properly phonological.

Lexical idiosyncrasies, which can often be expressed as a lexically specified alignment with a basic beat, usually occur in languages where the patterns of stress are for the most part (or in large part) the effects of principles of this universally defined core, i.e., basic beat rules and other rules of grid construction. Our approach will be to consider that the lexically specified alignments and the alignments introduced by the basic beat rules jointly specify the partial grid to which Beat Addition applies and upon which the filtering function of the PRA is felt.

2.3.2.3 The Third Metrical Level and Above   In terms of the metrical grid theory of prominence patterns, *main word stress* is the alignment of some basic beat of the word with a beat on a higher metrical level. In many languages, every word will bear a main word stress (except, often enough, for the class of function words).[25] The location of that main word stress may be governed by rule, by lexical idiosyncrasies (as is in large part the case in Russian (Halle 1973b)), or by both rule and idiosyncrasy (as, for example, in English (Liberman and Prince 1977, Hayes 1980, Selkirk 1980b)). In such languages we will say that there is a grammatically governed main word stress.

Some languages are reported to have no main word stress (e.g., Tübatulabal (Swadesh and Voegelin 1939) and Igbo (Green and Igwe 1963, Clark 1978)). But if the metrical grid and the alignment of the syllables of an utterance with it is a universal, as we have suggested, then these languages must have an organization of basic beats into beats on the third metrical level or above, at least in cases where the utterance contains more than one or two basic beats. Though we are in no position to verify it, we advance the hypothesis that the seeming lack of main word stress in these languages is to be attributed to the lack of a consistent presence of main stress in words and to the lack of a reliable location for it within a word when it is there. This would be the case if prominence on the third metrical level were not guaranteed by a TGA rule with a word-size domain. The presence of beats on the third metrical level would be required only to satisfy the PRA, which means that a word would not necessarily have a main stress, and if it did, it would be introduced by Beat Addition; but even then not necessarily, if Beat Addition were not obligatory on that level. The position of a beat of level three or higher would vary, depending on the number and location of basic beats within that word and probably on the number and location of basic beats and beats in neighboring words as well. Whether stress systems of this sort exist—assuming of course that they can and do—we leave as an open question.

The TGA rules, which determine the presence and location of main word stress, are the analogue on the third metrical level (or above) to the basic beat rules, which determine (in part) the presence and location of beats on the second metrical level. Apparently, in languages where the location of a strongest beat in the word is TGA-rule-governed (not lexically (i.e., idiosyncratically) determined), it tends to be localized toward the ends of the word—most commonly on the first syllable or on the final or penultimate syllable (see Hyman 1977a, Hayes 1980).[26] The evidence thus points to the existence in the core grammar of word stress of a relatively small number of principles determining the possible locations of main word stress. Prince 1981, 1983 proposes that there is one basic rule, along the following lines:

(2.36)
Domain-End Prominence Rule[27]

The basic beat that is $\begin{Bmatrix} \text{a. first} \\ \text{b. last} \end{Bmatrix}$ in the word is aligned with a beat on a higher metrical level.

(The (a) version will be referred to as the *Left Domain-End Prominence Rule,* the (b) version as the *Right Domain-End Prominence Rule.*) The claim is that a language may choose either version and that no other choices are available in core grammar. (It will be assumed that the Domain-End Prominence Rule applies, even where a cyclic domain has only one basic beat, and therefore that "main word stress" means the alignment of a syllable with a third metrical level at the least. Chapters 3, 4, and 7 contain explicit arguments for this assumption.)

We believe Prince's proposal that domain-end prominence rules form the core grammar of primary word stress to be essentially correct, though for reasons of space we will not evaluate it right here. What is crucial to the metrical grid theory of stress is not so much the character of the rules that define where in the word a beat on the third metrical level will reliably be located, but rather the nature of the patterns of "secondary" stress that coexist with this main stress on the third metrical level (and above). The metrical grid theory of stress, which takes the Principle of Rhythmic Alternation as fundamental, predicts the existence of a secondary prominence either two or three beats away from the rule-governed main stress. And this alternating pattern of secondary stress is indeed to be found, for instance in Italian and English. As an example, the initial syllables of the English words in (2.37) are more prominent than the other non-main-stressed beat-aligned syllables.

(2.37)

```
a.        x        b.          x     c.            x
    x        x         x        x         x            x
    x     x x         x    x    x         x       x    x
    x x   x x x x      x    x    x         x  x   x x x x
    reconciliation     chimpanzee         tintinnabulation
```

Our hypothesis is that this secondary stress is introduced by Beat Addition, which gives the rhythmically regular patterns exhibited. These examples show that the Beat Addition applying on the third metrical level is left-dominant. (Left-dominance is doubtless the unmarked case for Beat Addition.)

    Consider now the fact that Beat Addition does not undo the effects of the rule assigning main word stress in English. (The Main Stress Rule (MSR) is an instance of the Right Domain-End Prominence Rule; see chapter 3.) The basic beat rules and the MSR of English derive the following partial grids (again, see chapter 3 for details):

(2.38)

```
a.        x        b.          x     c.            x
    x     x x         x    x    x         x       x    x
    x x   x x x x      x    x    x         x  x   x x x x
    reconciliation     chimpanzee         tintinnabulation
```

Beat Addition then applies on the third metrical level. But rather than giving either (2.39a), for example, where the added beat and the (formerly) main-stressed beat are on a par, or (2.39b), where Beat Addition has applied yet a second time (its structural description being satisfied by the two beats on the third level in (2.39a)), Beat Addition is accompanied by a promotion of the main-stressed beat itself, as in (2.39c):

(2.39)

```
a.*                    b.*  x                c.              x
   x      x                 x      x             x          x
   x    x x                 x    x x             x        x x
   x x  xxx x               x x  xxx x           x x      xxx x
reconciliation          reconciliation       reconciliation
```

The evidence that the main word stress is indeed promoted as in (2.39c) is the fact that if a pitch accent falls on the word, in a non–stress shift environment, it will fall on that last beat. The general principle governing the assignment of pitch accents to words is that a pitch accent falls on the most prominent syllable of the word (see chapter 5). Thus, if the post–Beat Addition representation of *reconciliation* were (2.39a), we would expect that (in a non–stress shift environment) the pitch accent could fall on either the first or the last syllable, there being no "most prominent" one. This does not happen. If the post–Beat Addition representation were (2.39b), we would expect the pitch accent to fall on the initial beat. This does not happen either. The conclusion is that (2.39c) is the appropriate post–Beat Addition representation of *reconciliation*.

But what is the evidence that Beat Addition has applied at all? It comes from the behavior of these words under stress shift. When Beat Movement applies, it throws the most prominent beat back onto the *initial* beat: *(There was a) réconciliàtion of párties, (They heard the) tíntinnabulàtion of bélls, (You stop these) chímpanzèe híjinks!* This is what would be expected if there had been Beat Addition on that first beat (and promotion of main stress), for that makes the first beat the closest beat to the left of the main stress beat on the next level down, and thus the one onto which Beat Movement would place the fourth-level main stress beat. Had Beat Addition not applied, the second pre–main stress basic beat would have been the first one to the left of main stress on the next level down (see (2.38)). Beat Movement therefore would have derived **reconcílià tion of párties, *tintinnábulàtion of bells, *chimpánzèe híjinks,* which are ungrammatical.

We conclude that Beat Addition does apply in words (in fact necessarily so, as these examples indicate),[28] but that it does not act to override the MSR. On a higher domain, however, there is a GE rule, Beat Movement, which does override the MSR. Beat Movement deflects the main stress back to a position it would never have otherwise occupied. It is therefore not appropriate to impose the general, global condition that GE rules not override the MSR. The appropriate generalization seems to be that within the MSR's own domain of application it may not be undone by a GE rule. Thus, if we assume that these rules apply in cyclic fashion, the *Textual Preservation Prominence Condition* (2.25) can be stated and can be given the responsibility of ensuring that the correct patterns are "constructed."[29]

Beat Movement and Beat Deletion can come into play on the third metrical level. Adjacent third-level grid positions will be created in English by applications of the domain-end prominence rule creating main word stress, for example. Within the word, such a situation will arise only if there have been multiple applications of the MSR on successively embedded word-internal cyclic domains. Within the phrase, a clash between two adjacent third-level beats will arise simply when the main stresses of adjacent words are juxtaposed (with respect to the grid). In both instances, that clash may be eliminated by a rule of grid euphony.

Kiparsky 1979 argues, for example, that the stress pattern of a word like *èxpectátion* is derived from the more basic *èxpéct,* through an application of the "Rhythm Rule"—that is, stress shift (here, Beat Movement). The derivation in grid terms would be as follows:

(2.40)

$$[[\text{ex pect}] \text{ a tion}]$$

Cycle 1

```
                              x
                       x      x
DBA, BBR, MSR          x      x
```

Cycle 2

```
                                     x
                              x      x
                       x      x      x
a. DBA, BBR, MSR       x      x      x   x
                                     x
                       x             x
                       x   . x       x
b. BM                  x      x      x   x
```

Examples of Beat Movement on the phrase have already appeared in section 2.2.

In English, Beat Movement to the left takes precedence over Beat Deletion, thus guaranteeing that prominence will be preserved on that level of the grid, albeit in a location different from its original one with respect to the text. But Beat Movement in English appears to be asymmetrical. (Given the core theory approach, this means that the grammar of English chooses only the (2.23b) left movement version of Beat Movement from the universal set available.) As Liberman and Prince point out, the compound *sports contest,* with greatest prominence on *sports,* as in (2.41), does not become (2.42) by Beat Movement:

(2.41)   (2.42)
```
 x             *  x
 x   x            x       x
 x   x   x        x    x  x
 x   x   x        x    x  x
sports contest    sports contest
```

If anything, the underlying (2.41) simply undergoes Beat Deletion, to become (2.43):

(2.43)
```
 x
 x    x  x
 x    x  x
sports contest
```

And Beat Addition, not obligatory above the level of the word, will not act to restore the prominence on *con.* Thus, Beat Deletion in English applies where Beat Movement does not. We would suggest that Beat Deletion, too, is asymmetrical, in other words that the grammar of English has chosen (2.24b) from the universally available set (see section 4.2.2).

The TGA rules of English that apply on syntactic domains larger than the word are the Compound Rule and the Nuclear Stress Rule (NSR). The English Compound Rule assigns prominence on the fourth metrical level or above to the most prominent third-level beat contained within the first (or leftmost) immediate constituent of the compound. In similar fashion, the NSR assigns rhythmic prominence at the right extreme of a phrase. We are inclined to make the rather strong hypothesis that the TGA rules applying on all such syntactic domains are domain-end prominence rules, in this particular sense. (See the discussion in chapter 4.) The NSR will ensure that the text of a sentence like (2.44) will receive the partial grid alignment of (2.45) (ignoring the metrical levels below the three of main word stress):

(2.44)

[It was [organized [on [the model [of [a gallon [of worms]]]]]]]

(2.45)

```
                                              x
   x                       x         x        x
```
It was organized on the model of a gallon of worms

This is what would be derived if Beat Addition were not to apply in the course of the cyclic grid construction. It could apply, however, eliminating the rhythmic lapses. The other possible outcomes for (2.44), therefore, are (2.46) and (2.47).

(2.46)

```
                                              x
                         x                    x
   x                     x         x          x
```
It was organized on the model of a gallon of worms

(2.47)

```
                                              x
   x                                          x
   x                     x         x          x
```
It was organized on the model of a gallon of worms

Note that any application of Beat Addition requires the "promotion" of the main stress required by the domain-end prominence rule, the NSR. At the phrase level, then, as at the word level, the two sorts of grid construction rules interact in the same way, bringing about rhythmic patterns that respect the requirements of the text.

2.3.2.4 Summary   In proceeding "level by level" in the preceding exposition, we have sought to give plausibility to our claim that the patterns of rhythmic prominence in language can be insightfully characterized by a set of quite general grid-based rhythmic principles, the rules of grid euphony, in conjunction with a set of syntactic-structure-based principles, the text-to-grid alignment rules. Our argument for the necessity of viewing the metrical grid as the representation of prominence patterns in terms of which the core theory of prominence patterns is to be cast relies on showing that real generalizations are captured in this way, that none are (systematically) lost, and that no other theory can do as well. In the following chapters we will further elaborate this theory and the particular analysis of English stress patterns on which our argument is partly based. Where necessary, we will make the appropriate comparisons with alternative theories.

So far we have said nothing about the ordering of the various sorts of rules in the derivation of syllable-to-grid alignments of sentences. In fact, there is not much to be said, for we will consider most of the ordering relations to be intrinsically defined. Demibeat Alignment must precede anything else; the basic beat rules must precede Beat Addition on the second metrical level; the main stress rules must precede Beat Addition on the third metrical level; etc. Another general ordering principle that suggests itself is that the alignment should proceed level by level, from the lowest to the highest. The facts of many languages are consistent with this "level ordering." In Cairene Classical Arabic or in Italian, for example, the assignment of beats at the third metrical level, in both cases carried out by the Right Domain-End Prominence Rule, presupposes a prior assignment of basic beats on the second metrical level. Perhaps, then, there is in fact nothing to be said in the grammar of a language about ordering in the building of the syllable-to-grid alignments.

There are languages, though, such as Russian, in which alignment on the third metrical level "precedes" organization into basic beats on the second level. In Russian, the locus of main stress (third-level beat alignment) is in part lexically (morphologically) determined (Halle 1973a), and that lexically specified alignment with the third (and hence second) metrical level serves as the axis around which organization into beats on the second metrical level is defined. The pretonic (pre-main stress) syllable in Russian is always associated with a beat on the second metrical level, and the syllables preceding it appear in an alternating pattern (Karčevskij 1931). It would be interesting to know whether all divergences from "level ordering" appear in cases like Russian, where the specification of the upper level alignment is a matter of lexical idiosyncrasy. If so, then it will be possible to retain the idea that the ordering of grid construction rules by metrical level (from lower to higher) is the unmarked case, the state of affairs when all proceeds according to principles that are phonological in character.

Chapter 3
Word Stress and Word Structure in English

In this chapter we have two principal concerns. The first is to argue for a particular analysis of the patterns of English word stress within the general framework laid out in chapter 2. In so doing, we will show that the proposed core theory of metrical grid construction is eminently well suited to providing the basis for a descriptively adequate treatment of the rhythmic properties of English words. Needless to say, this new approach to English stress necessitates a serious revision in our conception of the role of prosodic or metrical tree structure in representing and characterizing these patterns. We will show that the account proposed here is as good as, and even better than, the tree-based accounts of Selkirk 1980b and Hayes 1980, 1982. With this grid-based analysis of English word stress, then, we hope to establish the plausibility of the general approach to characterizing patterns of prominence (at the lower levels) that we are arguing for in this study.

English word stress is notoriously complicated. On the basis of a study of English word stress alone, one would probably never arrive at even a rudimentary understanding of what might constitute a universal or core theory of word stress patterns. Indeed, no consensus has been reached concerning even the basic elements of a description of English word stress. The approach we will take here is to view English word stress through the eyes of a core theory of word stress. In taking this approach, we are following the pioneering work of Halle and Vergnaud 1979 and Hayes 1980. As these authors have emphasized, an adequate general theory of word stress patterns is absolutely necessary, in order to severely limit the range of possible descriptions (grammars) available, given a particular range of data, and thus to answer the projection problem. We will examine the possible grammars of English made available by the core theory defined in chapter 2, and it will become clear that one of these grammars is quite successful in characterizing the fundamentals of the English patterns. We will also examine the conditions under which deviations from the basic patterns arise, developing along the way the outlines of a theory of the rules that may modify basic patterns. In this effort, we are indebted in particular to Hayes 1980, 1982. Hayes has shown that surface divergences from the basic patterns may be more considerable than had been anticipated in earlier work (Liberman and Prince 1977, Selkirk 1980b) and has proposed a system of rules to account for them that forms the backdrop of the analysis we will present here.

Our second concern in this chapter is the relation between the syntactic constituent structure of English words and these patterns of stress. According to our theory of the syntax-phonology mapping, construction of the hierarchies of phonological representation proceeds in cyclic fashion, the particular rules governing that construction operating only within designated syntactic domains. The analysis of the syntax-phonology relation for a particular language, we suggest, involves specifying (i) which among the universally defined construction rules are at play and (ii) the syntactic domains within which they operate. We will presuppose the account of English word syntax presented in Selkirk 1982. This account gives an essentially syntactic characterization of the important distinction between the *neutral* and *nonneutral* affixes of English. As Siegel 1974 has shown, a generalization can be made about the distribution of neutral and nonneutral affixes in word structure: neutral affixes systematically fall outside of nonneutral ones in the order of affixes contained within words. The analysis defended in Selkirk 1982 is that the different affix types have different places, so to speak, in the structure of English words. Neutral affixes are sister to constituents of the category type Word, and nonneutral affixes are sister to constituents of the category type Root.[1] Because Roots (in English) are always embedded within Words (or other Roots) and Words are never embedded within Roots (but only within other Words), it follows that neutral affixes are always outside nonneutral affixes. We will show how this syntactic difference between affixes of the two classes is systematically reflected in their differing phonological properties, among them the ones relating to stress. We will propose, essentially, that the grid construction rules crucially involved in word stress have the Root category as their domain, and thus fail to incorporate the neutral affixes into canonical word stress patterns.

There are a number of respects in which the theory of the syntax-phonology relation being presented here is quite standard. A fully elaborated syntactic constituent structure tree, in this case the structure internal to words, is taken to be the representation with respect to which patterns of stress are defined, and these patterns are claimed to be defined in cyclic fashion, by rules with designated syntactic domains of operation. What is nonstandard here is, first, the conception of the stress patterns themselves as being embodied in a suprasegmental hierarchical representation (the metrical grid); second, the conception of stress rules not as phonological rules per se but as rules that construct a phonological representation; and third, the notion that the principle of the cycle governs this mapping from syntactic representation to phonological representation, but not (necessarily?) the application of "real" phonological rules (section 1.3). As for the theory of English word syntax being presupposed here, it is quite standard in its assumptions about the nature of word structure and, more generally, syntactic structure, and the nature of the rule system for generating it (see section 3.1).

The elimination of boundary elements from phonological representation is another nonstandard feature of this general theory of phonological representation and its relation to syntactic representation, and of this particular analysis of English words. Boundaries have no role in defining the domains of the grid construction rules responsible for generating patterns of English word stress: these rules have a domain defined uniquely in terms of syntactic constituent structure. Moreover, it has been shown that many other putatively boundary-sensitive rules of English phonology are in truth sensitive to syllable structure (see especially Kahn 1976) and that the limits of syllables may coincide with the limits of certain types of syntactic constituents. Boundary elements are not required to demarcate the limits of these constituents, however (contra Kahn): in the context of the present theory, (re)syllabification is simply confined to domains defined in terms of syntactic constituent structure. The implicit claim, then, is that any "work" done by boundaries in a (standard) linguistic description, as in the SPE account of the phonological distinction between neutral and nonneutral affixes, is better and more appropriately done in this framework, either by the syntactic structure itself, which directly governs the construction of phonological representation, or by one of the two hierarchies of phonological representation thus created, both of which do encode to some degree the syntactic relations of surface structure.

We must say at the outset that this chapter by no means offers an exhaustive treatment of the stress patterns of English words. Such a treatment would require more time and space than are available. Our purpose in presenting this sketch of the relation between English word structure on the one hand and the metrical grid alignments of words on the other is to provide an example, reasonably well motivated, but not fleshed out and justified in all its details, of what an analysis looks like within the general framework we have described. We hope that this example will prompt further research along the lines suggested here.

3.1 English Word Syntax

The structure of words in English is basically no different in nature from the structure of phrases or sentences. It may be represented as a labeled bracketing or tree. In Selkirk 1982 it is argued that word structures are generated by a system of context-free rewriting rules, and that lexical materials is inserted into structures thus generated, as in Chomsky 1965. One main feature of the general theory proposed in Selkirk 1982 is of special interest here: namely, the idea that the categories involved in word syntax have the same formal character as syntactic categories, which, according to the $\bar{X}$ theory of phrase structure presupposed here,[2] are decomposed into (i) a *category type* or *level* specification and (ii) a *category name* specification. The former corresponds to the number of bars of the category: the symbols X, $\bar{X}$, and $\bar{\bar{X}}$ stand for categories of different types. The latter corresponds to the "feature bundle" that specifies, among other things, that a category is nominal as opposed to verbal, for example. (The "bundle" will also include any diacritic features of the category.) The category type Word (X^0, or simply X), of which Noun (N), Adjective (A), and Verb (V) are instances, is the "lowest" in the $\bar{X}$ hierarchy to play a role in phrase structure. At the same time, we suggest, it is the highest category involved in a description of English word structure. The others are *Root* (X^{-1}, or X^r) and *Affix* (X^{af}).[3] Noun root (N^r), Verb root (V^r), etc., are instances of the former type; Noun affix (N^{af}), Verb affix (V^{af}), etc., are instances of the latter.[4] The idea, then, is simply that a description of the syntax of words has available to it an array of categories defined in $\bar{X}$ terms, and that generalizations embodied in the rewriting rules generating word structures may be formulated in terms of such category distinctions. We will make crucial use of this idea in our analysis of English affix classes.

We have shown in Selkirk 1982 that Word and Root are recursive category types, and that the word structure grammar of English contains rules like N → N N, V → P V, A → N A^{af}, A^r → N^r A^{af}, etc. Speaking very "schematically," the context-free grammar for English words contains rules of the following sort:

(3.1)
Word → Word Word

(3.2)
Word → Word Affix

Word → Affix Word

(3.3)
Word → Root

(3.4)
?Root → Root Root

(3.5)
Root → Root Affix

Root → Affix Root

Rules like (3.1) generate the native English compounds. It is not entirely clear whether the schema (3.4) is required for generating the so-called Greek compounds.[5] The others are responsible for introducing suffixes and prefixes. As should be clear from this rule system, an affix that necessarily appears as sister to a Word will appear outside an affix that requires a Root sister.

Affix morphemes, on this theory, are lexical items. The information contained in the lexical entry of such a morpheme includes a subcategorization frame, which indicates what sort of category the affix may have as its sister in word structure. The proposal of Selkirk 1982 is simply that, in addition to indicating what the category *name* of that sister constituent must be, a subcategorization frame for an affix morpheme may also indicate what its *type* (or level) must be. On this theory, neutral affixes (the Class II affixes of Siegel 1974) subcategorize for categories of type Word; nonneutral affixes (Siegel's Class I) subcategorize for categories of type Root. Table 3.1 is a sample listing of affixes with their subcategorization frames.

Table 3.2 illustrates the word structures generated by rules of the sort schematized in (3.1) through (3.5) and by lexical insertion governed by

Table 3.1

Nonneutral/Class I/Root	Neutral/Class II/Word
-ous: [N^r ___]	*-less:* [N ___]
-ity: [A^r ___]	*-ness:* [A ___]
-ive: [V^r ___]	*-er:* [V ___]
-ate: [A^r ___]	*-y:* [$\left\{\begin{matrix}N\\V\end{matrix}\right\}$ ___]
-ory: [V^r ___]	
-al: [N^r ___]	*-ize:* [N ___]
-ify: [$\left\{\begin{matrix}N^r\\A^r\end{matrix}\right\}$ ___]	*-ish:* [$\left\{\begin{matrix}N\\A\end{matrix}\right\}$ ___]
in-: [___ A^r]	*ex-:* [___ N]
de-: [___ V^r]	*non-:* [___ $\left\{\begin{matrix}N\\A\end{matrix}\right\}$]

Table 3.2

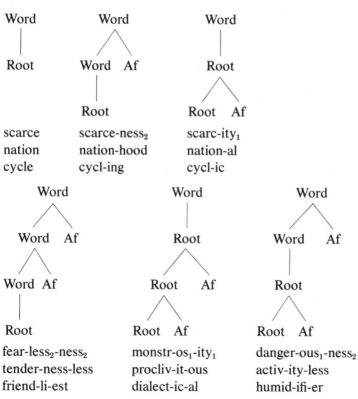

scarce	scarce-ness$_2$	scarc-ity$_1$
nation	nation-hood	nation-al
cycle	cycl-ing	cycl-ic

fear-less$_2$-ness$_2$	monstr-os$_1$-ity$_1$	danger-ous$_1$-ness$_2$
tender-ness-less	procliv-it-ous	activ-ity-less
friend-li-est	dialect-ic-al	humid-ifi-er

Table 3.2 (cont.)

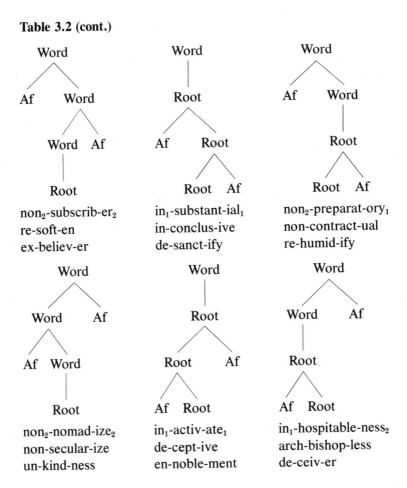

non₂-subscrib-er₂
re-soft-en
ex-believ-er

in₁-substant-ial₁
in-conclus-ive
de-sanct-ify

non₂-preparat-ory₁
non-contract-ual
re-humid-ify

non₂-nomad-ize₂
non-secular-ize
un-kind-ness

in₁-activ-ate₁
de-cept-ive
en-noble-ment

in₁-hospitable-ness₂
arch-bishop-less
de-ceiv-er

subcategorizations such as those in table 3.1. (The subscript 1 stands for *nonneutral,* Siegel's Class I affixes; the subscript 2 stands for *neutral,* Siegel's Class II affixes.) For details of this analysis, the reader is referred to Selkirk 1982.

To sum up, then, distributional considerations lead us to posit two different $\overline{X}$ levels or category types for the major (nonaffixal) categories within English words: Root and Word. Given our theory of the syntax-phonology relations, it is in principle possible for this distinction to play a role in the construction of phonological representation. For instance, the syntactic domains of rules of grid construction, resyllabification, or prosodic wording (if it existed) could be specified in terms of one or the other of these category types. And this is indeed what we claim to be the case for English: Root is the cyclic domain for those rules of word stress that have domains, such as the Main Stress Rule (see section 3.2.5). Root is also the domain of resyllabification according to the Basic Syllable Composition rules. Word, on the other hand, is the domain of a less restrictive resyllabification. Thus Root affixes are completely incorporated into the canonical patterns of stress and syllabification in English, while Word affixes are not entirely so. This is just the appropriate characterization of the phonological difference between the neutral and nonneutral affixes, as we will demonstrate.

Simply because word syntax involves two "levels," it does not necessarily follow that these "levels" will be reflected in phonological structure, as in English. Pesetsky 1979 argues, for example, that Russian word syntax has two "levels," yet he observes that there are no corresponding phonological differences.[6] For Russian, it might be suggested, the domain of "word stress" and resyllabification is simply a category of type X^n, where n stands for word-level or below in the $\overline{X}$ hierarchy. Thus in the cyclic syntax-phonology mapping in Russian words, no heed is paid to any distinction in "level." In the context of the general theory proposed here, distinctions made available by syntactic structure, whether of the word or of the phrase, are not necessarily encoded in phonological structure. The choice of the category type or level that serves as a domain for rules constructing a phonological representation is precisely one of the parameters along which languages may differ.[7]

Before we turn to the phonological representation of English words, we will briefly review two earlier approaches to English word syntax and its relation to English word phonology. In the SPE analysis, the structure of words is conceived of as a labeled bracketing or tree, as is the structure of phrases, though the system of rules involved in generating word structures is not explicitly mentioned. Rules of the phonology are divided into two classes, cyclic and noncyclic (the latter sometimes referred to as "word-level" rules). Cyclic rules, such as the English stress rules, apply in cyclic ("bottom-up") fashion on domains defined in terms of syntactic constituent structure. In the SPE analysis of English, certain stress rules apply on cyclic domains of category type *word* (i.e., "noun, verb, or adjective"), others on the phrase. No distinction in category type is made within words, where all nonaffix constituents are assumed to be of the same type as the word of the phrase structure component. This lack of distinction in category type within the word is not a matter of principle, of course, but simply one of analysis (or lack thereof). The SPE theory would countenance such distinctions.

Following Newman 1946, the SPE authors conceived of the two English affix classes as being distinguished solely on the basis of their phonological properties. It was observed about neutral affixes that (a) they did not enter into the canonical patterns of word stress (hence the term *neutral,* for "neutral with respect to stress"), (b) they failed to be analyzed (or "counted") by certain phonological rules, such as Trisyllabic Laxing, Velar Softening, and Coronal Assibilation, and (c) certain rules (putatively) restricted to word-final environments, such as Sonorant Syllabification, applied before them.[8] The phonological behavior of nonneutral affixes was seen to be quite different. It was observed that (a) they enter into the canonical patterns of word stress, (b) they are "visible" to such rules as Trisyllabic Laxing, and (c) word-final rules do not apply before them. The SPE analysis of this difference, quite an ingenious one, was that the affixes of the different classes are separated from the words (sic) to which they attach by boundary elements of different types. The proposal was that a word boundary, #, intervenes between a neutral affix and its sister constituent, while a morpheme boundary, +, intervenes between a nonneutral affix and its sister. This proposal was made in the context of a general theory of phonology that accorded systematically different properties to the two types of boundaries. Briefly, the theory held that phonological rules applying to a string of segments could ignore the presence of a morpheme boundary in that string. For English, this meant that the stress rules, and rules like Trisyllabic Laxing, would treat an affix separated from its sister by only a + as though the two formed part of the same word, honorarily monomorphemic. As for word boundary, the theory held that it would block the application of a rule that did not explicitly mention it in its structural description; this boundary could also provide a "positive" environment for rules, such as those limited to word-final position. Thus, by formulating the stress rules and rules like Trisyllabic Laxing in such a way that their structural descriptions did not include #, the SPE analysis ensured that the application of these rules to strings containing neutral affixes would be blocked,[9] and ensured as well that word-final rules would find their environments satisfied before neutral affixes. Thus, in SPE, the differences between the two affix classes lay in the property of being associated with one boundary or the other. Whether an affix took one or the other had to be specified as part of its lexical entry.

As mentioned earlier, the motivation for boundaries falls away in the theoretical framework being developed here. The SPE analysis of the affix classes was made in the context of an inadequate analysis of English morphology and an insufficiently developed understanding of the nature of phonological representation and its relation to syntactic structure. As will become clear, the phonological phenomena that the SPE analysis sought to explain have a straightforward treatment within the present theory.

Siegel 1974 was the first to observe a regularity in the distribution of the affixes of the two classes with respect to each other: namely, that the neutral affixes appear outside the nonneutral ones. We have called this the *Affix Ordering Generalization* and have provided further support for it in Selkirk 1982. Siegel, and M. Allen 1978 following her, have sought to relate the phonological properties of the affixes to these distributional properties. Their proposal departs significantly from the standard theory, in that it relies on a different conception of the relation between the various components of the grammar. Siegel's and Allen's proposal is that certain word formation rules may "apply before" certain rules of the phonology, while other word formation rules may "apply after" these rules. Specifically, they propose that the nonneutral morpheme boundary affixes be "attached before" the English stress rules apply and that the neutral word boundary affixes be "attached afterward." Rules of compounding then follow these. On this theory, then, affixation and compounding rules apply in the course of a derivation, and may be extrinsically ordered with respect to each other and with respect to phonological rules. Boundaries do not play a role in distinguishing the stress-related properties of the affix classes: this is accomplished by the ordering of the affixation rules and the stress rules. (But boundaries are assumed to be required for the role they have with respect to other phonological rules.)

A theory of word syntax according to which morphological rules may be extrinsically ordered into levels (or "blocks") does not entail, however, that word formation rules and rules that build a phonological representation (e.g., stress rules) or apply to it (i.e., phonological rules) should be interspersed. A theory of word formation such as Siegel's and Allen's is consistent with a theory of the syntax-phonology relation in which these phonology-related processes apply in cyclic fashion to the structures generated by the (ordered) rules of the word syntax, if what they generate is a labeled tree. In practice, however, advocates of Siegel's and Allen's theory of word syntax, including Kiparsky 1982 and Mohanan 1982, have wedded this morphological theory to a theory of the syntax-phonology relation holding that rules of phonology and morphology are interspersed.

Siegel, Allen, Kiparsky, and Mohanan thus take a radically different approach to both the theory of word syntax and the theory of the (word) syntax-phonology relation from the approach we are advocating here. The general model we propose, for both words and phrases, is that a fully elaborated syntactic constituent structure (of the word as of the phrase) is mapped, in cyclic fashion, into a complete phonological representation. On this model, just as there are rules in the grammar for defining a well-formed surface phrase structure, so there are rules for defining a well-formed surface word structure. It is claimed that for words, as for phrases, a set of context-free rewriting rules provides the foundations of that description. This is a "syntax-first" model, where the organization of the grammar into components imposes an ordering of constituent structure formation rules before rules constructing or modifying phonological representation. The purpose of this book is to develop this theory of the syntax-phonology relation and an analysis of the particulars of English within that framework. In this chapter and in chapter 7, we will show that an entirely satisfactory, even illuminating, account of the stress-related properties of English words can result from a syntax-first theory of the syntax-phonology relation. In the immediately following chapters, we will show that the same general framework permits an insightful characterization of the stress-related properties of phrases. We will claim, then, that a theory that views the syntax-phonology relation in the same way for words and phrases is not only possible, but desirable. This claim that a unified theory of the syntax-stress relation for words and phrases is in order relies, of course, on demonstrating that a unified approach to word syntax and phrasal syntax is both possible and appropriate. The case for viewing word syntax in terms entirely analogous to phrasal syntax was made in Selkirk 1982.

3.2 Grid Construction in English Words

3.2.1 The Second Metrical Level
For each metrical grid level relevant to the representation of English stress patterns, we ask two basic questions: What text-to-grid alignment rules are involved (if any)? and What grid euphony rules are involved? With respect to the latter rules, we also ask, What parameters

govern their application? The answers to these questions will constitute the basic grammar of word stress for English.

We begin with the patterns of stressed and stressless syllables, i.e., the alignment of syllables (or lack thereof) with positions on the basic beat level. Are there any basic beat rules at play in English? The answer, clearly, is yes. There is an overwhelming tendency for syllables with long, or tense, vowels (CVV) to be stressed in surface patterns: *dáta, rótàte, éulogìze.*[10] In contrast, open syllables with lax, or short, vowels (CV) behave quite differently. A noninitial CV will be stressed only if followed by at least one stressless syllable: *Àlabáma, América, inítial, mètricálity.* An initial CV may be stressed regardless of what follows: *sùttée, ràccóon, sátìre.*[11] These facts alone suggest (a) that there is a basic beat rule that distinguishes at the least between CVV syllables and CV syllables, aligning only the former with second-level beats, (b) that there is a basic beat rule requiring the alignment of syllables in initial position with a second-level grid position (on the Root domain, as we will show), and (c) that the Beat Addition that is responsible for the alignment of CV syllables with the second level is left-dominant. Given the core theory, no other options are available. If CVV syllables are consistently stressed in surface patterns, then they must be so in the basic (underlying) patterns; if initial syllables may be stressed regardless of what follows, then a position-sensitive basic beat rule must be at play. And so on. But note that, already, this basic analysis implies a certain concomitant analysis of divergences from the basic patterns. Because basic beat rules and Beat Addition at the second metrical level are (by hypothesis) obligatory, underlying CVV syllables that on the surface are stressless (and contain reduced vowels), as in *èxplănátion* (cf. *expláin*), must somehow be "destressed" by separate rules of the grammar, as must initial stressless CV or CVC syllables, such as those in *Ămérica* or *cŏndémn.* Such "destressing" rules, which will be discussed in section 3.3, might be called *grid transformations.* Given the core grammar approach, it is the proper characterization of these later grid transformations that requires the greater part of the analytical "work" done by the language learner or the linguist.

Assuming that this outlined analysis of the basic patterns is essentially correct, two questions still remain: what is the precise nature of the basic beat rule that differentiates between syllable types, and what is the directionality of Beat Addition? The answer to the first question requires an understanding of the facts concerning the stressing of syllables of the shape CVC, where V is a lax vowel: do these behave like

CVV syllables or CV syllables? In surface patterns, CVC syllables may be stressed in the absence of a following stressless syllable, either in final position or before another stressed syllable: *chîmpànzée, gýmnàst, cónvìct, Àgamémnòn, Àdiróndàcks, pársnìp*. This behavior is like that of CVV syllables, and completely unlike that of CV syllables. Yet CVC syllables are unlike CVV syllables in that it is quite common for them to appear stressless on the surface: *hýmnăl, cátăly̆st, àppĕndéctomy, éxpŭrgàte, Nèbuchădnézzăr*.[12] In this, they appear to resemble CV syllables. But our core theory allows no middle ground. There is no way for the CVC syllables of the earlier examples to have been made "stressed" except by a basic beat rule aligning CVC syllables with a second-level grid position. And because, by hypothesis, basic beat rules are not optional—do not have the possibility of sometimes aligning CVC syllables and sometimes not—the stressless CVCs of the latter examples must therefore be analyzed as arising in some other fashion. This is indeed the view we will seek to uphold: that surface stressless CVC syllables arise (in large part) via a grid transformation that "destresses" basic-beat-aligned CVCs in specific circumstances.[13] Our analysis of the basic beat rules of English is thus as follows:

(3.6)

English Text-to-Grid Alignment (Basic Beat Level)

a. Align a syllable of type CVV or CVC with a basic beat.[14]

b. Align a syllable in initial position in the Root domain with a basic beat.

The first we will call the *Heavy Syllable Basic Beat Rule* (HBR), and the second the *Initial Basic Beat Rule* (IBR).

To complete this analysis of the patterns at the basic beat level, we need to specify the directionality of the left-dominant GE rule of Beat Addition. It can be shown to apply right to left.[15] Given this, the stress patterns of English words consisting only of CV syllables, for example, would be as shown in (3.7b) and (3.8b):

(3.7)

a.
```
    x
    x   x   x
    CV  CV  CV
    ⇓ BA_R-L
```
b.
```
    x   x
    x   x   x
    CV  CV  CV    Ex.: váníllă
```

(3.8)

a.
```
    x
    x   x   x   x
    CV  CV  CV  CV
    ⇓ BA_R-L
```
b.
```
    x           x
    x   x   x   x
    CV  CV  CV  CV    Ex.: Míssĭssíppĭ
```

The (b) grid alignments are produced on the basis of the partial grids in the (a) examples, which themselves are the product of the universal Demibeat Alignment and the English IBR. The Main Stress Rule (MSR) of English, a domain-end prominence rule that is yet to be discussed, will align the last basic beat in the Root domain with a third-level beat. And a "destressing" rule, also yet to be discussed, will demote the initial syllable of *vanilla*. These rules will produce the surface patterns of (3.7d) and (3.8c):

(3.7)   (3.8)

```
        c.      x                   c.            x
            x   x                            x        x
            x   x   x                        x   x    x   x
MSR         CV  CV  CV                        CV  CV  CV  CV  =
                                              Mìssìssíppì

        d.      x                   d.
                x
            x   x   x
Destressing CV  CV  CV  = văníllă         inapplicable
```

Of course, these are not the only patterns exhibited by words with comparable syllabic compositions. *Pámĕlă* and *Ămérĭcă* are also attested. With Hayes 1980, 1982, we will assume that the availability of two patterns for words of these shapes reveals nothing about the basic analysis of English stress patterns in terms of the universal core theory, but instead simply attests that the grammar of English offers the possibility that the final syllable in a domain may be "ignored," as *extrametrical,* by the rules constructing the stress patterns. (See the folowing section.) The final syllables of *Pamela* and *America* are thus assumed to be extrametrical. The derivation of their stress patterns would proceed as follows:

(3.9)   (3.10)

```
             Pa me (la)em                   A me ri (ca)em
DBA          x   x   (x)                     x   x   x   (x)

             x                               x
IBR          x   x   (x)                     x   x   x   (x)

                                             x   x
BA_{R-L}     inapplicable                    x   x   x   (x)

             x                               x
             x                               x   x
MSR          x   x   (x)  = Pámĕlă           x   x   x   (x)

                                             x
                                             x
Destressing  inapplicable                    x   x   x   (x)  = Ămérĭcă
```

This, then, is the analysis of the alternative set of patterns for CVCVCV and CVCVCVCV.[16]

Notice now that if Beat Addition applied left to right, then all these patterns could not be derived, as long as the other aspects of the analysis were left unchanged (in particular, the assumption that there exists a TGA rule of IBR that is intrinsically ordered before Beat Additon). (3.11) shows the patterns that could be derived by left-to-right Beat Addition:

(3.11)

```
                x   x   x        x   x   x
DBA            CV  CV  CV       CV  CV (CV)
                x                x
IBR             x   x   x        x   x   x
                x   x
BA_L-R          x   x   x        inapplicable
                x                x
                x   x            x   x
MSR             x   x   x        x   x   x
                    x
                    x
Destressing     x   x   x        inapplicable


                x   x   x   x        x   x   x   x
DBA            CV  CV  CV  CV       CV  CV  CV (CV)
                x                    x
IBR             x   x   x   x        x   x   x   x
                x   x                x   x
BA_L-R          x   x   x   x        x   x   x   x
                    x                    x
                x   x                x   x
MSR             x   x   x   x        x   x   x   x
                    x                    x
                    x                    x
Destressing     x   x   x   x        x   x   x   x
```

Among these there is no possible derivation of *Mississippi,* though the patterns corresponding to *vanilla, Pamela,* and *America* are generated. For this reason, Beat Addition must apply right to left in English.

To sum up, then, the parameters governing the operation of Beat Addition on the second metrical level in English are set as follows:

(3.12)

English Grid Euphony (Basic Beat Level)

Beat Addition, which
a. is left-dominant and
b. applies right to left.

Together, (3.12) and (3.6) constitute the grammar of the basic patterns of stressed and stressless syllables for English.[17]

3.2.2 Extrametricality

Before we examine the grammar of the patterns found at the higher metrical levels in words, it is necessary to properly introduce the notion of *extrametricality*, which has come to play an important role in recent metrical treatments of stress. Liberman and Prince 1977 introduce the term to describe syllables, usually found at the limits of words, that are systematically ignored in the computation of stress patterns in English. Hayes 1980, 1982 has shown that the notion bears fruit in the treatment of stress patterns in a great variety of languages. As Hayes points out, it allows one to severely restrict the inventory of possible foot types and more generally the inventory of possible stress systems in language. We believe Hayes's argument for extrametricality to be convincing, and we adopt the notion here.

Specifically, Hayes proposes that the grammar of a language may stipulate that a single constituent of some designated type (e.g., segment, syllable, foot, morpheme) is extrametrical. It is also proposed by Hayes 1980, 1982 and Harris 1982 that extrametricality, an admittedly powerful device, be severely constrained, so as to characterize only constituents found at the extremes of particular domains. Hayes 1982 states that the domain of extrametricality in English is the phonological word, by which he means the syntactic word minus the neutral (= Root) affixes or the domain of the word stress rules (personal communication). We suggest that extrametricality is defined only with respect to syntactic domains, since only syntactic domains govern the applicability of grid construction rules. We propose moreover that just two sorts of constituent may be extrametrical—*syllables* and *segments*—thereby rejecting the possibility of assigning the property of extrametricality to morphological constituents[18] or to prosodic constituents higher in the prosodic hierarchy than the syllable. (Of course, since we claim that there is no prosodic constituent *foot*, feet cannot be treated as extrametrical.) This is an entirely natural restriction within our theory of stress patterns. The sort of information about a word (or phrase) to which "stress rules" have access in the construction of a metrical grid is limited to the internal structures of the syllables in sequence on a particular domain and the metrical grid that is aligned with this syllable sequence. The sorts of things that are ignored are of the same type: in the case of an extrametrical segment, an element of internal syllable structure is ignored; in the case of an extrametrical syllable, as we see it, a syllable (*and* the grid position(s) with which it may be aligned) are ignored. Why extrametricality should be confined to the limits of morphological domains, as it apparently is, and why it should be restricted to just one segment or syllable in that position are questions for which neither this theory nor Hayes's provides an answer. These are merely stipulations, ones that allow for an interestingly restrictive theory of possible perturbations in the patterns expected on the basis of a core theory of stress.

Further restrictions that we propose for extrametricality are that it is a property of lexical items, that the ascription of extrametricality to a syllable or segment will "precede" the application of any and all grid construction rules, and that any generalizations concerning the assignment of extrametricality are therefore to be expressed in the form of lexical redundancy rules. We will elaborate on this restriction below.

A final proposal concerning extrametricality is that it is not relevant to all grid construction rules, but only to those that in effect "care" whether a final (or initial) segment or syllable is within a particular cyclic domain. This restriction has important consequences. Given our theory of stress patterns, segment extrametricality will be relevant only to basic beat rules, and specifically only to those that appeal to the internal composition of syllables, for no other rules of grid construction pay heed to the segmental composition of the string. A final CVC syllable, for example, would be treated as a CV syllable by a basic beat rule like the HBR, if the final C were extrametrical. In English, Hayes argues (and we concur), a final C may be extrametrical.[19] This must be so if the grammar is to generate the stress pattern of *Nantucket* [nèntʌ́kət], for example. Were that final C not extrametrical, Demibeat Alignment and the basic beat rules of English would give the partial grid of (3.13).

(3.13)

```
  x     x
  x  x  x
```
Nantucket

There would be no room for Beat Addition to apply, and the medial syllable (a lax open one) would not be aligned with a basic beat (that is, it would not be "stressed"). As far as the syllable-structure-sensitive basic beat rules of English go, then, an English CVC at the limit of the constituent α in (3.14a) may be treated as if it had the structure in (3.14b):

(3.14)

a. $_\beta[\dots \ _\alpha[\dots \text{CVC}_{\text{em}}]_\alpha \dots]_\beta$

b. $_\beta[\dots \ _\alpha[\dots \text{CV}]_\alpha \ \text{C}_{\text{em}} \dots]_\beta$

On the cyclic domain α the final syllable would act like a CV syllable; on the higher domain β, however, that syllable would be treated like any other CVC syllable on that domain.

We propose a similar conception of syllable extrametricality. Here, too, the function of extrametricality is in essence to redefine the limits of a cyclic domain. A syllable is extrametrical with respect to a particular syntactic constituent, and by being extrametrical it is treated as if it were outside that constituent. Thus a word with a word structure representation like (3.15a) would be treated, in the cyclic application of rules, as if it had the representation (3.15b):

(3.15)
a. $_\beta[\dots \ _\alpha[\dots \sigma \ \sigma_{\text{em}}]_\alpha \dots]_\beta$
b. $_\beta[\dots \ _\alpha[\dots \sigma]_\alpha \ \sigma_{\text{em}} \dots]_\beta$

That is, on the cycle on α, the extrametrical syllable will be ignored. On the cycle on β, however, it will act like any other syllable in the sequence on β. This is a consequence both of viewing extrametricality as being defined with respect to a particular constituent and of our theory of grid construction rules, which, at the word level at least, ignore the constituency internal to a cyclic domain.[20]

This conception of syllable extrametricality has another interesting consequence in the context of our grid-based theory of stress patterns: grid construction rules for which the location of the limits of the cyclic domain is irrelevant will not be affected by extrametricality. Demibeat Alignment is such a rule. The prediction, then, is that syllables are never extrametrical with respect to Demibeat Alignment. This merely amounts to claiming that all syllables of an utterance enter into the overall rhythmic organization of the sentence, which appears to be a correct representation of the facts. Under this theory of extrametricality, the basic beat rules that appeal only to the internal composition of a syllable, but not to its position within a domain, are also not subject to syllable extrametricality (though they may be affected by segment extrametricality, as we have shown). Thus it is predicted, for example, that in a language like English, with its HBR, final syllables of the form CVV(C) and CVC(C) will always be stressed—even though extrametricality of final syllables is a possibility. This is by and large correct for English. The reason that the prediction is not entirely borne out in fact is that final consonant extrametricality is also possible in English. The more specific prediction about the application of the HBR made by the entire system of extrametricality in English is that final CVC will be basic-beat-aligned in an underlying pattern only if its final C is not extrametrical, whereas final CVCC will always be basic-beat-aligned (regardless of whether its final C is extrametrical), as will final CVV and final CVVC.[21] Of course, since a final CVCC that is basic-beat-aligned in an underlying pattern could subsequently be destressed, the failure of a final CVCC to be stressed on the surface, as in *témpĕst, pérfĕct,* etc., is not counterevidence to our claim. (As for surface final stressless CVV, as in *háppy̆, nárrŏw, móttŏ,* etc., we claim, as do most others, that these are derived from an underlying final lax CV, tensed after grid construction in final position. See note 10.)

It is important to understand that the fact that syllables may be aligned with basic beats by the HBR does not mean that they are *not* extrametrical. Our theory is that syllable extrametricality is *relevant* only to grid construction rules for which the position of a syllable with respect to the limits of a cyclic domain is relevant, or to those grid construction rules whose structural descriptions refer to sequences of grid positions (and by extension the sequences of syllables aligned with those positions). Into this category fall (i) position-sensitive basic beat rules, (ii) Beat Addition on the second metrical level, whose application is directional and requires the representation of a "starting point" (see examples (3.7)–(3.10)), and (iii) domain-end prominence rules, such as the English Main Stress Rule. Thus it is entirely possible under this theory for a syllable to have been aligned with a beat by the HBR and at the same time for it to be extrametrical with respect to one of these other rules. In the investigation of main word stress assignment to follow, we will give examples where this must be the case.

What we have proposed, then, is a theory of extrametricality that is rather restrictive and makes what seem to be the correct predictions about (i) which sorts of grid construction rules may be affected by extrametricality and which may not, and (ii) the irrelevance on a higher cyclic domain of extrametricality that is particular to a lower syntactic constituent. We will show that this theory provides the proper foundation for a full treatment of extrametricality in the English word stress system. The analysis draws heavily on the insights of Hayes 1980, 1982, but casts those insights in a somewhat different way in the grammar.[22]

Hayes observes that in English verbs and adjectives a final consonant is quite typically extrametrical; in other words, the final syllable of a verb or adjective is stressed if it consists of CVV(C) or CVCC, as in (3.16a) and (3.16b), but not if it is simply CVC, as in (3.16c). (The examples are from Hayes 1980.)

(3.16)

a. divine	b. torment	c. astonish
atone	robust	common
obey	usurp	develop
discreet	overt	illicit

Consonant extrametricality is also found in nouns, as in the case of *Nantucket,* although, as Hayes points out, the effects of syllable extrametricality, which is quite common in nouns, tends to obscure the role of consonant extrametricality in determining the stress patterns of nouns. Hayes 1980 suggests that the grammar of English contains rule (3.17), whose function is to assign extrametricality marking to final consonants:

(3.17)
$[+\text{cons}] \rightarrow [+\text{em}] / [\ldots \underline{\qquad}]_{\text{Word}}$

(We give the rule as Hayes formulates it, though its proper domain is actually the Root; see section 3.2.5.) Our alternative, presumably more desirable because it is more restrictive and at the same time consistent with the facts, is that extrametricality is a property of lexical items, in their lexical entries. This amounts to saying that English has the following lexical redundancy rule:

(3.18)

[... $C_{em}]_{Root}$ is well formed

It would also be possible to assign extrametricality by rule, as long as it were the first rule in the grammar. But because there are exceptions to consonant extrametricality, we prefer to view it as a matter of lexical representation. We suggest, then, that words like those cited in (3.16c) have the following lexical entries:

(3.19)

[a sto nish$_{em}$]   [i lli cit$_{em}$]   [Nan tu cket$_{em}$]

Whether a final consonant is extrametrical or not is, we submit, one of the important ways in which lexical items may differ, as well as an important source of apparent "irregularities" in the English stress system. (We will see that the same is true of syllable extrametricality.) Thus, for example, there are verbs and adjectives whose final syllables do *not* behave as if the final syllable is extrametrical:

(3.20)

Verbs			*Adjectives*
begin	abut	permit	debonair
attack	harass	acquiesce	parallel
regret	caress	prolong	agog
ransack	abet	caterwaul	bizarre
combat	deter	succumb	

There are nouns of this sort as well:

(3.21)

Nouns

affair	gavotte	Pequod	troubador	monad
pollywog	saccade	Berlin	pentagon	cigar
Karloff	diadem	parsnip	aileron	burlap
Peking	maniac	albatross	Agamemnon	shindig
Molotov	ocelot	Adirondack	daffodil	Ichabod
Aztec	Mamaroneck	gazelle		

(These examples, and many more, are brought together in Ross 1972.) Our analysis is that in the lexical entries of these words, the root-final consonant is not marked extrametrical.

Hayes takes a different approach. Rather than viewing the latter cases as simple exceptions to root-final consonant extrametricality, he suggests that words with final stressed CVC are *stressed* (i.e., footed or basic-beat-aligned) not by rule, but in their lexical entries. It is puzzling that Hayes should suggest this, since his stress rules (foot assignment rules) would regularly assign stress to syllables of the form CVC here— as long as neither the syllable itself nor the final consonant were extrametrical.[23] As Hayes seems to see it, syllables could be exceptionally stressed by whatever means in the lexicon. The fact that only final CVCs (but never final CVs, for example) are lexically stressed is a mere coincidence. But this approach misses what appears to be an obvious generalization: that a final CVC syllable can be stressed because, quite generally, a CVC syllable can be stressed regardless of what follows. All that it takes to allow that final CVC to be stressed by the independently motivated rules of the grammar is to *not* treat its final consonant as extrametrical.

As for the extrametricality of syllables in English, Hayes argues that it is in general found in nouns, but not in verbs and adjectives (if they are unsuffixed). We agree that final syllable extrametricality is possible in English nouns. It is necessary to assume this in order to derive the basic beat pattern of *America*. However, we do not agree that extrametricality is the rule. The basic beat patterns of *Mississippi* and *vanilla* are derived in entirely regular fashion if it is assumed that their final syllables are not extrametrical. We suggest, then, that the lexical entries of *America* and *Mississippi* differ simply in whether or not their final syllable is extrametrical, as in (3.22):[24]

(3.22)
A me ri (ca)$_{em}$ Mi ssi ssi ppi

Again, Hayes avoids using extrametricality to characterize the difference. He suggests instead that the final syllable of *Mississippi* is indeed extrametrical and that stress is assigned to the penultimate CV because it bears a diacritic marker [+H], which notes that the syllable is "honorarily heavy." The stress rules are then taken to have the power to treat a syllable so marked as if it were indeed heavy.[25] In our opinion, such an analysis is undesirable. The use of a diacritic like this opens Pandora's box. It is in the nature of this use of a diacritic that there are no principles governing its distribution. It is therefore predicted that many stress patterns might exist that are simply not attested. It would be predicted in particular that a CV syllable could be stressed regardless of what followed it. But this is false.[26] Again, the more restrictive and therefore more interesting hypothesis, one that accords with the facts, is simply that the difference between *Mississippi* and *America* lies in the extrametrical status (or lack of it) of their final syllables. We therefore suggest the following lexical redundancy rule for English:

(3.23)

$[\dots \sigma_{em}]_{Root}$ is well formed in the case of nouns.

It is not merely nouns whose final syllables may be extrametrical. Hayes demonstrates that the final syllable of suffixed adjectives and verbs is also typically extrametrical. What shows the extrametricality of the final syllable of a suffixed adjective or verb is both its failure to receive the expected final main stress when the final syllable is stressed, as in *mollúscòid* and *críticìze*, for example, and the failure of a penultimate CV to be stressed, as in *oríginăl, prímĭtĭve, magnánĭmŏus*. The generalization that the final syllable of a suffix is extrametrical extends to nouns as well: *staláctìte, pósĭtròn, neutrálĭtỹ*. The question now is how to express this generalization concerning suffixed forms. We propose the following rule:

(3.24)

$_{Xr}[\dots {}_{Af}[\dots \sigma_{em}]_{Af}]_{Xr}$ necessarily

This says simply that extrametricality within suffixes is the rule.

To sum up, we are in essence adopting Hayes's idea that extrametricality is a crucial notion in an analysis of English word stress patterns. The use to which it is put is somewhat different in our analysis, however. First, our theory of extrametricality allows only segments and syllables to be extrametrical, and it allows only rules that are in some way sensitive to domain edges to be affected by extrametricality. Second, within the context of that theory, we suggest an analysis of "exceptions" in English word stress that relies on the notion of extrametricality. It is the property of having an extrametrical final syllable or segment, or not, that is claimed to be one of the ways in which lexical items identical to each other in their syllabic composition may nonetheless differ in their behavior with respect to word stress. (The only other important way in which lexical items differ is in their susceptibility to undergoing certain rules of destressing. We will take up this matter in section 3.3.)

3.2.3 The Third Metrical Level and Above

3.2.3.1 The Main Stress Rule   According to the grid-based theory of stress outlined in chapter 2, if a text-to-grid alignment rule plays a role at the third metrical level or above in a language, it is a domain-end prominence rule. (This is the proposal made by Prince 1981, 1983.) English words do reliably contain one stressed syllable that is more prominent than the others, and it tends to be located toward the right-hand limit of the word. According to the core theory, then, there is a "Main Stress Rule" at play, which gives third-level prominence (or higher) to the *rightmost* basic beat within a domain. That domain, as we will show, is the Root, not the Word. Our analysis, then, following Prince 1981, 1983, is that the "Main Stress Rule" of English is a rule of the following sort:

(3.25)
English Main Stress Rule: Text-to-Grid Alignment, Third Metrical Level (provisional formulation)
Align the *rightmost* basic beat within a Root constituent with a grid position on the third metrical level.

Given the core theory of stress, and given English word structure, the only other alternatives would be either a rule that placed "main stress" (at least a third-level beat) on the rightmost beat within a Word domain, or a rule that placed it on the leftmost basic beat within either a Root or a Word domain. These alternatives are out of the question, and the first, as we will show in section 3.2.4, is not consonant with the facts. We are left, then, with rule (3.25). Let us examine now what support there is for this rule as the correct generalization about the locus of main word stress in the basic underlying patterns of English words. The more general question is whether there is support for Prince's proposal that, in core theory, the only options available for third-level text-to-grid alignment are domain-end prominence rules that promote either the first or the last beat within a domain.

Given our analysis of the patterns of beats on the second metrical level, along with the possibilities in English for final consonant and final syllable extrametricality, rule (3.25) predicts several loci of main word stress, which are tabulated in (3.26)–(3.28). (The symbol σ alone stands for "any sort of syllable." The symbol ! before a word means that it has more than one possible analysis.)

(3.26)

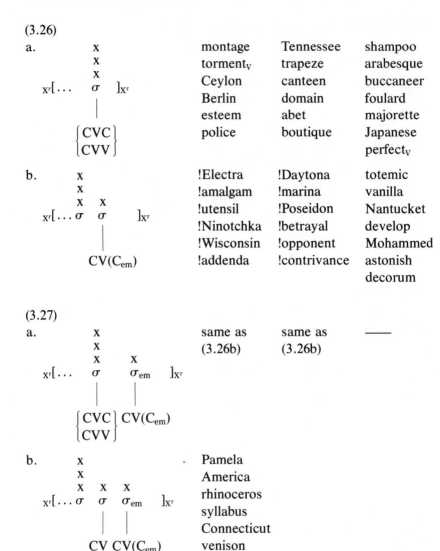

a.
```
        x
        x
        x
 xʳ[...  σ    ]xʳ
        |
       ⎡CVC⎤
       ⎣CVV⎦
```

montage	Tennessee	shampoo
torment_V	trapeze	arabesque
Ceylon	canteen	buccaneer
Berlin	domain	foulard
esteem	abet	majorette
police	boutique	Japanese
		perfect_V

b.
```
        x
        x
        x   x
 xʳ[...σ  σ      ]xʳ
           |
      CV(C_em)
```

!Electra	!Daytona	totemic
!amalgam	!marina	vanilla
!utensil	!Poseidon	Nantucket
!Ninotchka	!betrayal	develop
!Wisconsin	!opponent	Mohammed
!addenda	!contrivance	astonish
		decorum

(3.27)

a.
```
        x
        x
        x    x
 xʳ[...  σ    σ_em  ]xʳ
        |     |
      ⎡CVC⎤ CV(C_em)
      ⎣CVV⎦
```

| same as | same as | —— |
| (3.26b) | (3.26b) | |

b.
```
        x
        x
        x   x    x
 xʳ[...σ  σ  σ_em   ]xʳ
       |    |
      CV CV(C_em)
```

| Pamela |
| America |
| rhinoceros |
| syllabus |
| Connecticut |
| venison |

(3.28)

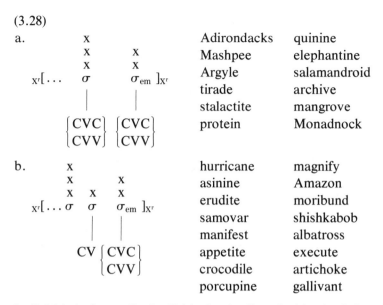

		Adirondacks	quinine
		Mashpee	elephantine
		Argyle	salamandroid
a.		tirade	archive
		stalactite	mangrove
		protein	Monadnock
		hurricane	magnify
		asinine	Amazon
		erudite	moribund
b.		samovar	shishkabob
		manifest	albatross
		appetite	execute
		crocodile	artichoke
		porcupine	gallivant

In (3.26a) the heavy final syllable that is aligned with a basic beat by the HBR is not itself extrametrical (nor, in the case of CVC, is the consonant extrametrical), and it thus receives main stress. This is the only circumstance in which final main stress is possible in English. (A final CV is never basic-beat-aligned, and is therefore never aligned with a third-level beat.) Penultimate stress, on the other hand, has a variety of sources, and for some words more than one analysis is available. The analysis of *vanilla, Nantucket,* and so on, in (3.26b) is unambiguous. These can only have been derived if the final syllable is *not* extrametrical (though the final C must be), because the only source for the basic beat on their penultimate CV is Beat Addition, which therefore must have "seen" that final syllable (cf. the discussion above). The analysis of the basic patterns of *Electra, marina,* etc., is not unambiguous, however. These patterns could have arisen either as instances of (3.26b), where the final CV(C_{em}) syllable is not extrametrical, or as instances of (3.27a), where it is. In either case, the penultimate heavy syllable would be given a basic beat and the final syllable would not. Note that yet another basic underlying pattern is available to *amalgam, Poseidon,* and the others with stressless final CVC: the pattern in (3.28a). In the examples used to illustrate (3.28a), all the final heavy (extrametrical) syllables are stressed on the surface. But if, as mentioned earlier, a rule is at work in English that may destress CVC syllables that are not aligned with third-level beats (i.e., are not "main-stressed" or "secondarily stressed"), then *amalgam, Poseidon,* etc., have a possible derivation on the basis of (3.28a) as well (see section 3.3.3). This multiplicity of sources for such words is not at all vexing, however, for each option available in the different analyses (syllable extrametricality, CVC destressing) is independently motivated in the grammar.[27]

The analysis of *Monadnock* in (3.28a), with its final stressed but not main-stressed CVC syllable, is of course not ambiguous. For the final syllable to have been basic-beat-aligned, it must be analyzed as heavy (i.e., the last C is not extrametrical); but the lack of main stress on that final syllable shows that the entire syllable must itself be extrametrical. The analysis of *Mashpee* is also unambiguous. For the final syllable to be stressed, it must be (underlyingly) a CVV syllable (note 10), but one that is extrametrical. These, then, are cases of extrametrical syllables that receive a grid alignment by one sort of grid construction rule (the HBR), but not by another (the Main Stress Rule).

As for the cases of antepenultimate main stress, the final syllable in such cases is necessarily extrametrical, and the penult is necessarily a CV syllable: if the final syllable is extrametrical, then Beat Addition cannot align the penult with a basic beat, and if the penult itself is CV, the HBR will not align it with a basic beat, either. Whether the final extrametrical syllable is heavy and basic-beat-aligned, as in (3.28b), or light (or "extrametrically" light), as in (3.27b), Beat Addition will ignore it in its right-to-left sweep and thus will place a basic beat on the antepenult, which will then be main-stressed on words where the antepenult itself is light, as in *America.* When the antepenult is itself heavy, of course, it is not Beat Addition, but the HBR, that is responsible for placing the basic beat that is promoted to "main stress."

The notion of extrametricality clearly does a considerable amount of work in this analysis of English word stress. In particular it explains the surface divergences from the domain-end prominence rule (3.25) that are exhibited in (3.28). Without syllable extrametricality, (3.25) would align a grid position of level three (or higher) with the last basic beat, which is here located on the final syllable.

From the restriction of extrametricality to single syllables, together with rule (3.25), it follows that if there is a stressed syllable following main stress in English roots, it is necessarily in final position. Given this analysis, the stress patterns of (3.29) cannot be derived.

(3.29)

a.	x	b.	x	c.	x
	x x		x x		x x x
	x x x		x x x x		x x x
	$*_{X^r}[\ldots \sigma\ \sigma\ \sigma]_{X^r}$		$*_{X^r}[\ldots \sigma\ \sigma\ \sigma\ \sigma]_{X^r}$		$*_{X^r}[\ldots \sigma\ \sigma\ \sigma]_{X^r}$
	e.g., *Wáchùsĕtt		e.g., *Mássăchùsĕtts		e.g., *chímpànzèe

As the examples show, the stress patterns in (3.29) are impossible. Rule (3.25), modulo single syllable extrametricality, therefore captures just the right sort of generalization about the placement of "main stress" in English.[28]

It would be useful to recall here how the generalizations about main word stress placement are expressed in Liberman and Prince's analysis. Liberman and Prince propose that the metrical trees that group together feet in English are right-branching and that the basic generalization governing the assignment of prominence relations (in the form of s/w labels) is roughly speaking as follows (p. 308):

(3.30)
Lexical Category Prominence Rule (LCPR)

Given two nodes, $N_1\ N_2$, N_2 is strong (s) iff it branches.

According to this analysis, the trees below would be assigned the following labels:

(3.31)

a.   b.   c.

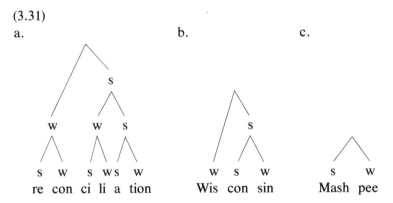

The syllable dominated only by s labels in the tree is the main-stressed syllable in the word. The overall branching pattern of the tree, together with the LCPR, guarantees that main stress will tend to fall toward the right end of the word. The requirement that the right-hand node branch has the result that the main stress will not be final. This is of course a correct result if the final syllable is stressless, but it is not always borne out in fact when the final syllable is stressed, as for example in *interséct, Tènnessée*. To account for these cases, Liberman and Prince add several provisos to the LCPR, which have the effect of allowing limited exceptions to it. Hayes 1980 adopts Liberman and Prince's account, though he offers a slightly different one in Hayes 1982 that makes fruitful use of the extrametrical property of final syllables. Our claim, which is essentially an adaptation of the one made by Prince 1981, 1983, is that trees and potentially complex labeling conventions are not required at all in order to express the appropriate generalizations about placement of main word stress in English and other languages. Prince's grid-based theory of main word stress placement is that the possibilities are either "promote the last" or "promote the first" of the basic beats within a specified domain. A domain-end prominence rule of this type, (3.25), along with a judicious appeal to extrametricality—which we know on independent grounds to be available to a grammar—predicts exactly the loci of main word stress that are attested in English.

3.2.3.2 Grid Euphony on the Third Level   So far in this section we have investigated the well-foundedness of the claim that a text-to-grid alignment rule like (3.25) provides the right analysis of the location of the most prominent beat in the metrical grid alignment of English words. Two further issues require attention. The first concerns the role of grid euphony rules in deriving the full patterns of rhythmic prominence at the third level or higher, and the second concerns the precise nature of the formulation of the Main Stress Rule.

The English Main Stress Rule is a TGA rule that is specific to a syntactic domain. It establishes the location of greatest grid prominence within that domain. In chapter 2 we suggested that the application of TGA rules is (intrinsically) ordered before the application of GE rules on any cyclic domain. This ordering expresses the generalization that the location of the beats added, deleted, or moved by GE rules on a particular level within that domain depends on the location of the beats on that level whose presence is required by TGA. There is a further generalization that the grammar of English—and, more generally, the theory of grid construction—must express. It is that, within a cyclic domain, a GE rule like Beat Addition may not undo the effects of a TGA rule like the English Main Stress Rule by introducing greatest prominence in a location not specified by the TGA rule. In chapter 2 we proposed to account for this with the Textual Prominence Preservation

Condition (TPPC), (2.25), which specified that "a TGA rule applying on a syntactic domain d_i is necessarily satisfied on that domain."

Recall the discussion of the higher-level stress patterns of *reconciliation* and *chimpanzee* (section 2.3.2.3). Each of these words contains three "stressed" (basic-beat-aligned) syllables, the last of which is the most prominent of all. And of the two stressed syllables that precede, the first is more prominent than the second. The metrical grid representation of these patterns must therefore be as follows:

(3.32)
```
a.         x          b.            x
     x     x                 x      x
     x     x x               x   x  x
     x x   xxx x             x   x  x
     reconcili ation        chimpanzee
```

We suggest that the presence of the "secondary stress" on *re-* and *chim-* is to be attributed to the (obligatory) operation of the rule of (left-dominant) Beat Addition on the third metrical level within words. The rule would take as input the representations of (3.33), which are the output of a "first" application of the Main Stress Rule:

(3.33)
```
a.         x          b.            x
     x     x x              x    x  x
     x x   xxx x            x    x  x
     reconcili ation        chimpanzee
```

The operation of Beat Addition would give as output the representations in (3.34), which are not acceptable, for the reasons given in chapter 2.

(3.34)
```
a. * x        x       b. *  x       x
     x        x x             x     x
     x x      xxx x            x  x  x
     reconcili ation        chimpanzee
```

(We argued, moreover, that a further application of Beat Addition on the fourth metrical level, giving initial main stress, was unacceptable.) What ensures that the representations in (3.34) will not be left as is, and that the TGA rule assigning main stress in roots must seemingly "reapply," is the TPPC. The TPPC will guarantee that the prominence relations required by the Main Stress Rule are "restored," as in (3.32).

Actually, it is not necessary that TGA rules and Beat Addition should be ordered. The same effect could be achieved merely by requiring that both the TGA rules and the GE rules be satisfied simultaneously on the cyclic domain. In either case, the TPPC ensures the precedence of TGA prominence over GE prominences.

Now there are certain English words with three stressed sylla-bles—for example, *Ticonderoga*—that are described as having two possible loci of secondary stress. Given the (left-dominant) Beat Addi-tion analysis, however, only one of these pronunciations can be de-rived: *Tìcònderóga*, in which secondary stress is two away from the main stress. The other (putative) location of secondary prominence is on the syllable aligned with the basic beat that is adjacent to the basic beat under main stress: *Tìcônderóga*. This prominence could not have been derived through left-dominant Beat Addition. We suggest, how-ever, that a different interpretation of the facts is in order. Specifically, we suggest that in the latter case Beat Addition has not occurred at all, and that the intuition that the syllable *-con-* has greater prominence than *Ti-* is not to be explained in terms of an alignment of *-con-* with a third-level beat. It is quite conceivable that *-con-* may be heard as more prominent when it is at the same level of rhythmic prominence as the preceding syllable because it is itself followed by a weak syllable, whereas the preceding *Ti-* is not. In what follows we will assume this interpretation of the facts and see where it leads. With this interpreta-tion, we are claiming that *Ticonderoga* may have either of the metrical grid alignments in (3.35):

(3.35)

```
a.        x        b.
    x     x                       x
    x x   x              x x       x
    x x   x x x          x x       x x x
    Ticonderoga          Ticonderoga
```

It turns out that independent evidence exists that the second pattern should be described as an (exceptional) failure of Beat Addition to apply in the word. As Liberman and Prince 1977 and Kiparsky 1979 point out, the application of the "Rhythm Rule" (= the GE rule of Beat Movement) appears to be relatively unacceptable in cases where it would create the configuration $\acute{\sigma}$ $\grave{\sigma}$ $\grave{\sigma}$. Thus compare ?*Móntàna cówbòy* (cf. *Mòntána*) to the perfectly acceptable *Càrolína cówbòy* (cf. *Càro-lína*). Liberman and Prince's claim, which is adopted and codified by

Kiparsky, is that the configuration ό ὸ ό is disfavored—in grid or tree terms, that either (3.36) or (3.37) is disfavored.

(3.36)

```
*x
 x x
 x x x
 σ σ σ
```

(3.37)

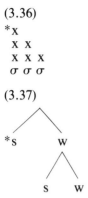

when the left-hand *s* does not branch (Kiparsky 1979)

The suggestion is that there is an output condition that rules out the offending configuration. Such an output condition enters into competition, so to speak, with the clash-eliminating Beat Movement that would derive the stress reversal in *Montana cowboy.* Since Beat Movement is only optional (see chapter 4), it does not apply. Note now that the existence of such an output condition could explain the optionality of Beat Addition in *Ticonderoga.* Beat Addition should apply obligatorily to *Ticonderoga,* in which case only (3.35a) would be derived. Our proposal is simply that it may fail to apply where it should, because of the effect of the same output condition that makes Beat Movement less likely in *Montana* than in *Carolina.* When Beat Addition fails to apply, the result is (3.35b), which is heard as prominence on -*con*-. It would seem, then, that obligatory left-dominant word-internal Beat Addition, modulo this output condition, makes just the right predictions about the presence and location of secondary word stress in English.[29]

The other GE rule needed in a description of the patterns of beats on level three or higher in English words is Beat Movement. We defer discussion of this rule, though, until we explicitly investigate the motivation for the cycle in section 3.4. There we will show that, like Beat Addition, Beat Movement contributes to defining the patterns of secondary stress that in essence "emanate from" the locus of main word stress defined by the TGA English Main Stress Rule.

Let us now consider some details of the formulation of the English Main Stress Rule. As is clear from examples with secondary stress, the Main Stress Rule must be formulated not simply to introduce a beat on the third metrical level, but to have the possibility of introducing a beat on the third metrical level *or higher,* so that the main stress introduced will be more prominent than a neighboring third-level beat introduced by Beat Addition. We must therefore revise the formulation of the Main Stress Rule in (3.25). The new formulation is (3.38), where x is a grid position and the ellipses are variables over grid positions in the vertical and horizontal dimensions.

(3.38)
English Main Stress Rule: Text-to-Grid Alignment, Third Metrical Level (revised)

$$x_j$$
$$\vdots$$

$_{\text{Root}}[\ldots x_i]_{\text{Root}} \Rightarrow {}_{\text{Root}}[\ldots x_i]_{\text{Root}}$

Conditions: (i) x_i is a second-level beat

(ii) $x_i \neq x_j$

As formulated, (3.38) could assign a fourth-level prominence to the final basic beat if there were a third-level prominence earlier in the word, as in *rêconcìliátion* or *chîmpànzée.* But what ensures that (3.38) *will* assign a fourth-level prominence there, as it must? It is conceivable to add a third condition to the rule: namely, "x_j is a beat on a metrical level n, where n is greater than the metrical grid level m of any other beat in the word." But we prefer not to do so. Such a condition would seem to duplicate the effect of the Textual Prominence Preservation Condition, and in fact a small revision of the TPPC would make the condition unnecessary as part of (3.38). Thus we propose the following revision of the TPPC:

(3.39)
Textual Prominence Preservation Condition (revised)

Within a syntactic cyclic domain d_i, a grid position assigned by a text-to-grid alignment rule on the third metrical level or higher is always (minimally) more prominent than any other prominence on that domain.

(As written, the TPPC is prevented from applying at the basic beat level. If it were to apply there, Beat Addition would be impossible in a language that had basic beat rules.) With this condition, (3.38) will assign the appropriate level of main word stress to *reconciliation.*

The revised TPPC requires that the highest grid position introduced by a rule such as (3.38) be only minimally higher than any other on the domain. Such a restriction ensures that no more grid positions will be introduced than are required either for creating a judicious alternation of strong and weak beats or for satisfying the structural description of the rule itself. Moreover, the proposed revision of the TPPC permits us to avoid including as a condition on the rule (3.38) itself the requirement that the TGA-specified prominence be greater than any other. That this is the correct approach will become obvious in chapter 4, where we will show that the TPPC so formulated guarantees just the right relative prominences in phrasal and compound stress patterns, as well as allowing the English Nuclear Stress Rule and Compound Stress Rule to be formulated without separate conditions on each to guarantee that they assign minimally greater prominence.

Note, finally, that given the formulation (3.38) (and in particular conditions (i) and (ii) combined), a third-level grid position will be aligned with a basic-beat-aligned (stressed) syllable within a root (and thus within a word) regardless of whether or not the word contains another stressed syllable. According to this proposal, then, "main word stress" is not a strictly relational concept.[30] There are a number of reasons for imputing an inherent third-level grid alignment to some stressed syllable of a root, regardless of context. First, there is the intuition that monosyllabic words are reliably more prominent than ordinary stressed syllables in words: *circumstance* ≠ *circle dance*.[31] Second, the TGA rules assigning prominence within compounds and phrases, to be discussed in chapter 4, "seek out" a third-level prominence (but ignore second-level ones), and they treat the stressed syllable of a monosyllabic word like other syllables having a third-level prominence. The third reason, to be elaborated in chapter 7, is that by assuming that normal lexical items have a third-level prominence (at the least), it is possible to distinguish between these and the so-called function words simply by assuming that the latter do *not* necessarily have such a prominence. The basic phonological property of function words—the ability of monosyllabic ones to destress—can be explained by assuming that they have only a second-level prominence. For these reasons, then, we consider it necessary for the Main Stress Rule of English to assign third-level prominence at the least.

This completes our analysis of the basic patterns of English word stress.

3.2.4 The Question of Domain

Of the grid construction rules that we have examined so far, only two specifically mention a characteristic domain of application. These are the Initial Basic Beat Rule and the Main Stress Rule. We need to explicitly examine the motivation for the characterization of the domains that has been given. We must also reflect on the role of domains for rules like Beat Addition, which make no mention of them.

As it is formulated, it is only within constituents of the category type Root that the English Main Stress Rule seeks out a domain-final basic beat to which to assign greatest prominence. It is predicted, then, that material outside the (cyclic) Root domain will have no effect on the location of main stress in English words. This is exactly the case. As can be seen from examining the "derivations" in table 3.3, a Root suffix such as -*al* will bring about a change in the locus of main stress, but a Word suffix such as -*less* will not.

The derivation of the stress pattern of the Noun root *instrument* is straightforward. The HBR aligns *in-* and -*ment* with basic beats, but since -*ment* is extrametrical with respect to N^r, it is the preceding basic beat, aligned with *in-*, that is promoted to a third-level beat by the Main Stress Rule. When that N^r *is a* Noun (nominal word), as in examples (a) and (c) in table 3.3, all that remains in the derivation is the destressing of the final nonsecondarily stressed CVCC syllable. (Destressing, and the assumption that it is "postcyclic," will be discussed in section 3.3 and in chapter 7.) When the N^r *instrument* is embedded within another root constituent in word structure, as in *instrumental,* its basic stress pattern is susceptible to modification.

On the A^r cycle in example (b), the Root suffix may or may not be basic-beat-aligned by the HBR, depending on whether or not the final C is extrametrical.[32] (If it is basic-beat-aligned, it will later be destressed.) In any case, that entire syllable -*(t)al* is final in the Root domain, and it is extrametrical. The Main Stress Rule seeks the (honorarily) final basic beat -*men-* in the A^r domain, which here is the penult, and promotes it to main stress status. The former main stress on *in-* now has the status of a secondary stress. (Probably some extension of the minimality convention imposed by the TPPC will then minimize the derived grid in (b), reducing *in-* to second-level and -*ment* to third-level.) The important point is that the stress pattern derived for *instrumental* differs significantly from that of *instrumentless*. This difference can be attributed simply to the fact that the English Main Stress Rule has a Root domain.

Table 3.3

	(a) $_N[_{N^r}[\text{instrument}]_{N^r}]_N$	(b) $_A[_{A^r}[_{N^r}[\text{instrument}]_{N^r}\text{-al}]_{A^r}]_A$	(c) $_A[_N[_{N^r}[\text{instrument}]_{N^r}]_N\text{-less}]_A$
N^r cycle DBA, HBR, MSR	x x x x x x x x instru(ment)$_{em}$	x x x x x x x x instru(ment)$_{em}$	x x x x x x x x instru(ment)$_{em}$
A^r cycle DBA, (HBR)	———	x x ——— -tal	———
MSR	———	x x x x x x x x instrumental	
N cycle	———	———	——— ———
A cycle DBA, (HBR)	———	———	x x ——— -less
MSR	———	———	———
Postcycle Destressing	x x x x x instrument [ínstrəmənt]	x x x x x x x x instrumental [ìnstrəméntl]	x x x x x x instrumentless [ínstrəmṇtlĭs]
Output			

In (c) of table 3.3, the pattern of the N^r is retained on the N cycle. On the following A cycle, there is some grid construction activity, but none that affects the basic pattern of *instrument*. The suffix *-less* is aligned with a demibeat; it may or may not be aligned with a basic beat by the HBR, depending on whether or not consonant extrametricality is defined on words. In either case, the syllable would be destressed. What is significant is that the MSR does not apply on this domain. Were it to be applicable on the Word domain, it would find a basic beat farther to the right than *in-* here—*-ment* (which is no longer extrametrical) and/or *-less* (if it is not extrametrical)—and would thus align the rightmost one found with main word stress. Since this does not happen, we conclude that the English MSR is confined to constituents of type Root.

The Initial Basic Beat Rule is the other "stress rule" of English that is specific to a domain. We have suggested that it takes categories of type Root as its domain. This of course will guarantee word-initial stress, since a Root *is a* word in syntactic structure.[33]

The GE rule of Beat Addition strictly speaking has no domain of its own. As a GE rule, rather than a TGA rule, it makes no explicit reference to the syntactic structure of the text (the syllabified surface structure of the sentence). Of course, given that GE rules apply cyclically alongside TGA rules in the construction of phonological representation, when they apply they have only the fragment of metrical grid available to them that is contained within the bounds of the current cyclic domain. This is why a GE rule like Beat Addition may appear to have a syntactic domain. More specifically, there are two ways in which Beat Addition may appear to have a syntactic domain *of its own*. First, on the second metrical level it is directional, and the starting point of its directional sweep in English is the right end of what appears to be the Root domain. An equivalent characterization, however, is that it begins its right-to-left sweep from the end of the (partial) grid that is in place. This characterization is consistent with our view that GE rules like Beat Addition are sensitive only to the grid, not to the text. Second, Beat Addition might be thought to have its own syntactic domain because it is obligatory on some domains, but not on others. As mentioned in chapter 2, Beat Addition is obligatory "within the word," but not, apparently, on the phrase. Actually, it is the root within which it is obligatory. This is shown by the lack of alternation that is possible when there is a longish sequence of Word suffixes (outside the root), as in *cólŏrlĕssnĕss, mándràkelìke,* and so on. It is shown as well by the fact that sequences of two or more stressless function words are possible on the phrase (see chapter 7). Does not the obligatoriness of Beat Addition with respect to a particular domain show that it *has* a domain? We think not. Rather than viewing the obligatoriness of Beat Addition as a property of that individual role, defined with respect to a particular domain, we could view it as part of a more global "output condition" or "filter" on the metrical grid, a condition which itself has a domain.

What it means for Beat Addition to be obligatory within the root in English is that the basic patterns contain no rhythmic *lapses,* no sequences of two weak beats on any metrical level (unless the lapses arise through extrametricality, or as in the *Ticonderoga* case, or, as we will show, through destressing). Alternation is maximized in roots (while a respect for the grid alignments required by the TGA rules is maintained). We might posit a general filter on grids, specific to a particular domain, that guarantees this absence of lapses, rather than proposing that Beat Addition is obligatory within some domain. We will formulate that condition as follows for English:

(3.40)
The Anti-Lapse Filter (English)
Within the domain of a root, there may be no lapses.[34]

(Such a condition may have a different domain for other languages, or it may not be applicable at all.) Note that this formulation guarantees that it is within the *same* domain (in English, the Root) that Beat Addition on both the second and the third metrical levels is obligatory; this requirement appears to be correct.

This alternative characterization of the obligatoriness of Beat Addition – introduced alternation in roots has the advantage of keeping GE rules like Beat Addition in check, not allowing them to have syntactic domains of their own, and thus narrows considerably the range of grammars made available by the theory. Of course some theory of the notion "possible domain of Anti-Lapse Filter" will now have to be developed, if we are to meet the goal of providing a sufficiently restrictive theory. We suggest that the domain of an anti-lapse output condition or filter like (3.40) will be identical to the domain of the TGA rule that assigns "main word stress" in the language. The idea behind this proposal is that there will be a tightly organized rhythmic organization at the lower levels of the grid, but only on the domains where that lower level organization is *defined.* And this is the domain of main word stress assignment. This correlation in domains is attested in English. It remains to be seen whether it holds up in other languages as well. The Anti-

Lapse Filter will be adopted here, and we will assume that it takes effect cyclically.

3.2.5 Summary

Thus far, we have presented an analysis of what we have referred to as the *basic patterns* of English word stress. It is an analysis couched in terms of the grid-based core theory of stress patterns presented in chapter 2, which is inspired in large part by Prince's 1981, 1983 work. We have relied crucially on Hayes's insight that consonant and syllable extrametricality give a good account of divergences from the basic patterns that are to be found at the limits of the stressing domain. Our first specific claim about English is that the patterns of stressed and stressless syllables, which in a grid-based theory are understood in terms of patterns at the basic beat level, result from the presence in the grammar of English of (a) two TGA rules, drawn from the universal repertoire: the Initial Basic Beat Rule (IBR) and the Heavy Syllable Basic Beat Rule (HBR), which treats CVV and CVC alike, and (b) a GE rule of Beat Addition, which on the basic beat level in English is left-dominant and right-to-left directional. Our second claim is that the patterns of prominence among stressed syllables (on the third metrical level or higher) result from the combined effects of (a) a TGA rule of the domain-end prominence type, the Main Stress Rule, and (b) GE rules, in particular (left-dominant) Beat Addition. Given the facts of English and the possibilities of analysis made available by the core theory we have proposed, we are in effect forced to this analysis of the basic patterns of word stress in English. This is a highly desirable state of affairs—when the descriptive options are so radically constrained that only one or a small number of grammars are available on the basis of the data.

As we have mentioned, surface stress patterns diverge in various ways from the basic patterns, and it must be shown that a grammar of the sort outlined here can adequately explain this behavior. We will do so in the next section.

We have not undertaken a critique of foot-based accounts of the basic English word stress patterns, but have instead focused on empirical generalizations that these earlier accounts sought to express[35] and on the particular analysis of these patterns made available by the metrical grid theory of stress. Within a metrical tree (and foot) theory of stress patterns it is indeed possible to capture many of the same generalizations about basic patterns in English that are captured with a metrical grid theory, and for that reason a point-by-point comparison is not particularly useful. It is in assessing the different theories for their ability to make sense of a whole host of phenomena—including the basic word stress patterns of other languages, destressing rules that may modify these patterns, phrase stress patterns, and rhythmically related syntactic timing—that we may decide which is the more explanatory and the more desirable.

3.3 Destressing

3.3.1 General Properties of Destressing Rules

Divergences from the predicted basic patterns of English word stress that are found in actual pronunciations all consist of stressless (non-basic-beat-aligned) syllables that ought to have been stressed (basic-beat-aligned) by the text-to-grid alignment and grid euphony rules of the proposed basic grammar. Our account of these surface divergences involves a small number of *destressing rules,* which eliminate a grid position on the basic beat level when certain conditions are met.

All destressing rules that we have encountered have the following property: their structural descriptions appeal to the nature of the rime of the syllable whose grid alignment is to be affected. In our rule typology, then, they do not qualify as GE rules, whose structural descriptions are formulated solely in terms of the metrical grid. In other words, destressing is not an instance of the GE rule of Beat Deletion. Destressing rules are also clearly not TGA rules, which all have the property of *creating* grid positions in alignment with the text. Thus destressing does not belong to either class of rules that contribute to defining the well-formed (basic) syllable-to-grid alignment for a sentence of a given language.

All destressing rules of English appear to eliminate only basic beats that are *not* also aligned with a position on a higher metrical level. That is, they affect syllables that are stressed, but not main-stressed or secondarily stressed. Hayes observes this, and puts the generalization in these terms (1982:257): "No foot that is in strong metrical position may be deleted." In our theory, we will express the condition in grid terms:

(3.41)
Higher Prominence Preservation Condition (HPPC)
No strong basic beat may be deleted.

(Recall that a beat is *strong* if it is aligned with a beat on a higher metrical level.) For destressing rules to respect such a condition, of course, it must be the case that they follow the operation of the grid construction rules that are responsible for establishing alignments with beats on the third metrical level or above. In the present section we will show that destressing rules in English indeed follow all grid construction rules within words; that is, they apply only after the word cycle is complete.

Note now that there is a principle from which it would follow that all destressing rules applicable in the word follow all grid construction rules within the word. This is the principle that only rules that construct (define) phonological representation operate cyclically, and that other rules are postcyclic, confined to applying to the *complete* phonological representation that is the output of the cyclic syntax-to-phonology mapping. (Recall the discussion in section 1.3.) The ordering of destressing rules and grid construction rules in English words therefore might be seen to support this general principle of grammar. Alternatively, it might simply be the case that destressing *is* cyclic, but that it has constituents of level Word (and perhaps higher) as its domain. Since the basic stress patterns are defined on the earlier Root domain, it would follow from this specification of domain that "destressing" followed "stressing." According to this analysis, it would simply be an accident of English that these processes are ordered as they appear to be. This alternative is not to be dismissed easily, and in chapter 7 we will argue in its favor. In this chapter, we will not attempt to decide the issue. Which of the alternatives correctly describes the "postcyclicity" of destressing will not affect our results here.

If destressing rules follow (cyclic) grid construction rules, and if they are limited to modifying the grid alignments of syllables whose basic beats are not strong, then it is clear that they are extremely limited in their ability to distort the stress patterns defined by the basic grammar of TGA and GE rules. A destressing rule will eliminate a basic beat already in a "trough" in the metrical grid, creating an even greater "trough," as for example in (3.42).

(3.42)

```
a.          x              b.              x
        x   x                      x       x
        x   x x      ⇒             x       x
        x x x x                    x x x x
     ...σ σ σ σ ...             ...σ σ σ σ ...
```

Given this restriction, it is understandable that the language learner could arrive at an analysis of basic patterns in terms of the core theory without too much difficulty.

We take destressing to be responsible for the presence in the surface patterns of English of any stressless CVC whose stresslessness cannot be attributed to final consonant extrametricality. Thus stressless final CVCC and any nonfinal stressless CVC must have been destressed by such a rule. If destressing rules follow all the basic grid construction rules, as suggested, then an important prediction about the distribution of stressless CVC syllables is made—namely, that these syllables will occur only in positions where in the basic patterns CVC would *not* receive main stress or secondary stress. We will show that this prediction is borne out. We also take destressing to be responsible for the presence of nonfinal ternary feet (i.e., sequences of σ́ σ̆ σ̆), as in *àbrăcădábră*. In this we follow Hayes 1980, 1982, who argues convincingly that nonfinal ternary feet arise from a more basic σ́ σ́ σ̆ sequence.

3.3.2 The Abracadabra Rule: A Source for Ternary Feet

In our treatment of stress in English and in our core theory of stress, we adopt Hayes's claim that there are no ternary "feet" in the basic patterns of stressed and stressless syllables, except at the limits of a domain (a position where extrametricality might in effect add a second syllable to the pattern). Hayes makes a good case for this claim for English; we will present his argument in its essentials below, though translated into metrical grid terms.

The important observation made by Hayes is that the distribution and composition of nonfinal ternary feet are quite restricted. They appear in surface patterns before a main-stressed syllable, when no other syllable precedes in the word, and only if the middle syllable in the sequence is CV, as in (3.43). (The following examples are from Hayes 1982:257.)[36]

(3.43)
àbracadábra
Lùxipalílla
Pèmigewássett
Òkefenókee
Wìnnipesáukee

When four syllables precede the main stress, what one finds is the sequence of binary "feet" predicted by the basic analysis, as in (3.44) (examples from Hayes 1982:260).

(3.44)

Âpalàchicóla	Ôkalòacóochee
ónomàtopóeia	hâmamèliánthum
îpecàcuána	Hânimènióa
Pôpocàtepétl	Ântanànarívo
Ânuràdhapúra	

That words of the shape in (3.44) should have only a succession of binary "feet" is particularly significant. If ternary "feet" were allowed as part of the basic patterns, then there is no reason why the words (or some of them) should not have the pattern [σ̆ σ̀ σ̆ σ̆ σ́ ...], composed of a monosyllabic "foot" (or stressless syllable) followed by a ternary "foot." The fact that they do not have this pattern therefore supports the conclusion that ternary "feet" arise only in special circumstances, and not in the patterns generated by the basic grammar of stress.

Given our theory of English stress (and its counterpart in Hayes's system), the basic pattern assigned to *Âpalàchicóla* is as follows.

(3.45)

```
          [æ pV læ cV kō lV]
DBA        x  x  x  x  x  x

           x           x
IBR, HBR   x  x  x  x  x  x

           x     x     x
BA         x  x  x  x  x  x

                       x
           x           x
           x     x     x
MSR, BA    x  x  x  x  x  x
```

This is the pattern that we see on the surface. However, the basic pattern derived for *àbracadábra* (3.46a), is not the same as the surface pattern (3.46b).

(3.46)

a.   [æ brV kV dæ brV]

  DBA   x x x x x

        x

  IBR, HBR x x x x x

        x x x

  BA   x x x x x

            x

        x x x

  MSR   x x x x x

b.   x

       x x

       x x x x

       abracadabra

We claim, following in the spirit of Hayes, that the grammar of English contains a destressing rule that maps the output of (3.46a) into (3.46b).

A word needs to be said about the basic pattern in (3.46a). Unlike (3.45), (3.46a) has no secondary stresses: the only third-level or higher grid alignment in (3.46a) is that of the main stress. We are presuming, clearly, that Beat Addition has not applied on the third metrical level to produce an initial secondary stress. Recall from the discussion of the *Ticonderoga* examples that there is an output condition disfavoring the creation, by GE rules, of the configuration σ́ σ̀ σ̆. We are suggesting here that that output condition brooks no exceptions when that first syllable is CV, as in *abracadabra*—in other words, that the output condition always overrides the Anti-Lapse Filter and prevents Beat Addition from applying in these circumstances. There is good reason to think that this analysis, and hence the representation in (3.46a), is correct. Observe that when there is a heavy syllable in the middle of a sequence of three preceding the main stress, and when the first syllable is CV, that first CV is typically destressed and stress falls on the second, as in (3.47).

(3.47)

Mŏnòngahéla

Ătàscadéro

With the assumption that Beat Addition does not apply on the third metrical level here—because of the (absolute) negative filter *CÝ σ̀ σ̆—the derivation of the correct surface patterns is absolutely straightforward. The basic grammar of stress gives (3.48), and the basic-beat-aligned initial CV syllable *Mo-* is then destressed (by Monosyllabic Destressing; see the next section) to give (3.49), which is the appropriate surface representation for examples such as those in (3.47).

(3.48)

[mV nan ga hī lV]

DBA	x x x x x
	x x x
IBR, HBR	x x x x x
BA	——
	x
	x x x
MSR	x x x x x
BA	blocked

(3.49)

```
              x
       x      x
     x x   x x x
       Monongahela
```

Note that if third-level Beat Addition had been allowed to apply to *Monongahela,* it would have produced the grid alignment in (3.50), which is not attested on the surface.

(3.50)

```
        x
  x     x
  x x   x
  x x  x x x
Monongahela
```

To avoid this undesirable consequence of third-level Beat Addition, some additional rule of grammar would have to be posited to modify the representation in (3.50) (or rule it out). In contrast, by assuming that there is no Beat Addition at all in such cases, we have an immediate explanation (in the form of the derivation of (3.48) from (3.49)) for the stresslessness of the initial syllable of *Monongahela* and other such words. We assume, then, that no third-level Beat Addition has taken place here; and we simply make the same assumption for *abracadabra.*

We suggest the following formulation for the destressing rule creating ternary "feet," which we dub the *Abracadabra Rule:*[37]

(3.51)

Abracadabra Rule

```
x   x        x
x   x   ⇒   x   x
σ CV         σ CV
```

A medial syllable loses its basic beat alignment, and a ternary "foot" is thereby created. We repeat the derivation of the surface pattern of *abracadabra* here:

(3.52)

```
      x                    x
x   x   x       ⇒      x        x
x  x x x  x            x  x x x  x
abracadabra           abracadabra
```

The raison d'être for this rule is probably that it eliminates a clash on the basic beat level of the metrical grid. From the point of view of the Principle of Rhythmic Alternation, the representation derived by the Abracadabra Rule is more euphonious (or eurhythmic) than the representation to which it applies. (Recall that the PRA disallows clashes, and allows lapses consisting of at most two adjacent weak beats.) Note, however, that the Abracadabra Rule creates a configuration that would be ruled out by the Anti-Lapse Filter, if that filter were applicable at this point. This is one reason for considering the Anti-Lapse Filter to be cyclic (and not surface true), limited in operation to its (prior) Root domain.

Note also that the impulse to eliminate second-level clashes is not without its limits. The Abracadabra Rule does not eliminate a clash when the medial syllable is heavy. It does not apply to the *Monongahela* cases, nor does it apply to the *Ticonderoga* cases, of which we list more in (3.53):

(3.53)

Tìcònderóga

Dòdècanésian

Òmpòmpanóosuc

Srìràngapátnam

There is a notable absence of ternary "feet" here.[38]

We agree with Hayes, then, that ternary "feet" are not basic in the repertoire of English stress patterns and that they are produced in just the circumstances specified by the destressing rule. Where we part company with Hayes is in the characterization of the process and in the sort of rationale that can be offered for its existence. Given a metrical grid theory of the representation of stress, the Abracadabra Rule has both a simple structural description and a simple structural change: a basic beat in a particular position in the metrical grid is identified and deleted. Moreover, the rule can be understood as one that creates a more optimal grid, where optimality is defined in terms of the PRA. A tree-based treatment of the phenomenon, such as the one offered by Hayes, does not share these advantages.

The rule that Hayes proposes is formulated as follows (1982:258):

(3.54)

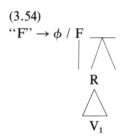

It states that a branching foot dominating two syllables, the first of which is open,[39] is deleted if it is preceded by a nonbranching foot. (A quite general condition, mentioned above, ensures that a deleted foot must be in weak position in the metrical tree.) Rule (3.54) applies to the basic tree structure (3.55a) to produce (3.55b); following this, a rule of Stray Syllable Adjunction (SSA) is required in order to produce the fully ramified surface tree structure in (3.55c).

(3.55)

a.   b.   c.

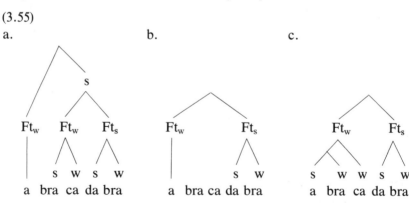

Visibly, given a tree theory of the representation of stress, powerful operations are required. Rule (3.54) eliminates tree structure, leaving an ill-formed tree. SSA builds it back up again. Even if SSA is more generally motivated, as Hayes argues,[40] a rather unconstrained general theory of tree transformations is required. In a grid-based theory of stress, on the other hand, there is no constituency, and thus no issue of derived constituent structure. Moreover, the class of destressing rules seems to be limited to those that delete a single grid position. A metrical grid theory of stress therefore provides the basis for a far more restrictive theory of possible destressing rules than does the tree-based theory. It also provides some basis for explaining why such rules as destressing should exist in the first place, whereas a tree-based theory does not. In a tree-based theory, the output representation (3.55c) is no more optimal than the underlying representation from which it is derived. (In some cases, as when the first syllable is heavy, the basic pattern is clearly more optimal than the surface one.)[41] It is for this reason, and others to be made explicit below, that we believe the metrical grid theory of the representation of stress is to be preferred.[42]

3.3.3 Monosyllabic Destressing: Stressless CVC and Related Matters

The other primary agent of destressing in English is a rule we call *Monosyllabic Destressing*. Given our basic analysis of English stress patterns, all CVC syllables are aligned with basic beats by the Heavy Syllable Basic Beat Rule (HBR) in the basic (underlying) pattern, except those whose final consonant is extrametrical. It is Monosyllabic Destressing, we claim, that is (largely) responsible for the lack of stress (basic beat alignment) exhibited by certain CVC syllables in the surface patterns of English words. It is this rule, too, that destresses CV syllables that have been promoted to a basic beat alignment by the Initial Basic Beat Rule (IBR).[43] The role that we are claiming for Monosyllabic Destressing is a big one. It replaces the rule of Initial Destressing, as well as Medial Destressing and the so-called Arab Rule.[44] In earlier analyses these rules all shared the property that they demoted (destressed, defooted) a syllable only when it satisfied three conditions: (i) it was not main-stressed or secondarily stressed, (ii) it was immediately followed by another stressed syllable or was word-final, and (iii) it was constituted of a CV and sometimes a CVC. Our proposal is that these rules are just one, and we formulate it, provisionally, as follows:

(3.56)

Monosyllabic Destressing

$$\begin{array}{ccc} x & & \\ x & \Rightarrow & x \\ \sigma_i & & \sigma_i \end{array}$$

Conditions (provisional):

a. If σ_i = CV, then obligatory.

b. If σ_i = CV $\begin{bmatrix} +\text{cons} \\ +\text{son} \end{bmatrix}$, then optionally and "often."

c. If σ_i = CV $\begin{bmatrix} +\text{cons} \\ -\text{son} \end{bmatrix}$, then optionally and "seldom."

Note that we needn't state that there is no third-level or higher grid position above σ_i. We are claiming, as does Hayes, that it is a general fact about destressing rules that they apply only in the absence of main or secondary stress. The conditions, very awkwardly put here, are an attempt to state that the rule operates virtually always when the syllable in question is a CV, and with decreasing likelihood in CVC_1 syllables, depending on whether the closing consonant is a sonorant or an obstruent. The fact that the rule does not mention CVCC and CVV should be taken to mean that it virtually never (or rarely) applies with syllables of this type.[45] It is not obvious that these conditions have to be built into the statement of the rule, but we do so here for the sake of explicitness.

What is not stated is the condition that the rule *not* apply if the syllable to be destressed is followed by a weak syllable: *Mississíppǐ* does not undergo destressing to become *Mǐssǐssíppǐ*. Monosyllabic Destressing applies only to basic-beat-aligned syllables that either precede other stressed syllables or are word-final. It would be highly desirable if that condition (that no weak syllable follow) were to result from some other, more general principle of grammar. Were this the case, it would not be necessary to add another condition to (3.56) stating that "σ_i is not followed by $\overset{x}{\sigma_j}$ (a weak syllable)."

The impermissible derivation is one mapping grid configuration (3.57a) into (3.57b):

(3.57)

a. x   *   b.
    x x   ⇒   x x
    σ σ   σ σ

In (3.57) an "alternation" is lost (and a lapse produced). We will hypothesize that it is precisely the loss of an alternation that is avoided, on general grounds, and that there is a principle of grammar, indeed a (universal) condition on the application of grid transformations, that blocks a rule from applying if an alternation will be lost. We will call this the *Alternation Maintenance Condition* (AMC) and formulate it as already shown in (3.57).[46]

But what about the Abracadabra Rule? It performs just the sort of operation that the AMC precludes, mapping grid (3.58a) into (3.58b):

(3.58)

a. x x   b. x
    x x x   ⇒   x x x

Suppose we take the AMC to govern only destressing rules that are in some sense contextless. This property would distinguish Monosyllabic Destressing from the Abracadabra Rule. The former looks neither to the right nor to the left, but the latter has a crucial environment on the left. We speculate that it is the more detailed formulation of the latter rule that allows it in effect to override the AMC. Obviously, the status of such a condition can only be assessed when destressing rules from other languages are examined; but for the time being we will assume it as a working hypothesis. Its presence in the grammar (as part of universal grammar) makes it unnecessary to include the additional condition mentioned in the statement of Monosyllabic Destressing.

The function of Monosyllabic Destressing, like that of the Abracadabra Rule, is to create a yet more euphonious grid alignment for a word. It eliminates clashes at the basic beat level, but it does so only when the syllable to be demoted is light enough. Let us look at some examples (many drawn from Ross 1972).

(3.59)

a. ăllý$_V$	pŏtáto	*Exceptions:*	ràccóon
Mălóne	băssóon		sùttée
Mŏnòngahéla	ĭnítial		Ròckétte
vănílla	dĕvélop		àugúst
Ămérica	Dĕcámeron		bàssóon[47]
măjólica			

b. Wĭscónsin[48]	ĭndícative	*Exceptions:*	hàrmónica
cŏndítion	ĕxíst		bàndána
pĕrmít	bŭrsítis		ètcétera
Bĕrlín	fĕrtílity		àndrógynous
			tèmpéstuous

(3.60)

a. állỳ$_N$	Hárvàrd
sátìre	bíngò
Wábàsh	

b. Àlabáma	Àthabáskan
Mìssissíppi	èxecútion

c. Tỳróne	Òdéssa
Pèkíng	cìtátion
Sàigón	pùgnácious
fàctítious	

The examples in (3.59) and (3.60) show that Monosyllabic Destressing can do the work of Initial Destressing. (3.59) lists words that have undergone destressing. The (a) cases contain CV syllables, and the (b) cases CVC syllables of various types. There are exceptions to the rule in both cases. The examples in (3.60) are not exceptions, however. They simply do not satisfy the rule's structural description. The initial syllables of the (a) cases have main or secondary stress, those of (b) are followed by a weak syllable, and those of (c) do not have the correct syllable composition. Actually, the status of some (c) examples, such as *factitious* and *pugnacious,* is doubtful; they may be either exceptions to the rule or examples where it should not apply. It all depends on the precise characterization of the conditions in the rule.

Consider next some cases of stressless CVC(C) in final position.

(3.61)

a.
pérfĕct	Máynărd
témpĕst	Éverĕst
éffŏrt	inhéritănce
stándărd	présidĕnt
móllŭsk	bóllĭx
módĕst	méndicănt

b.
prógràm/prógrăm	óbjèct/óbjĕct
póetèss/póetĕss	cárdamòm/cárdamŏm
ánalỳst/ánalỹst	párallèl/párallĕl
lábyrìnth/lábyrĭnth	Éndicòtt/Éndicŏtt
Decámeròn/Decámerŏn	mónàrch/mónărch

c.
áprŏn	márjorăm
vínegăr	Wachúsĕtt
gránĭte	spínăch
scávĕnge	jéttisŏn
wórshĭp	Jácŏb
ídiŏm	pícnĭc

d.
gýmnàst	Mílibànd	prócèss
Lómbàrd	póllywòg	húbbùb
ínsèct	nárthèx	Yúgoslàv
prótòn	sámovàr	cúlvèrt
hándicàp	shíshkabòb	pálimpsèst

For the examples of (3.61a–c), it must be assumed that the stressless final syllable has been destressed by Monosyllabic Destressing. In the cases of (3.61a) the syllable ends in a consonant cluster; therefore, regardless of whether the last C is extrametrical or not, the HBR would view the syllable as heavy and align it with a basic beat. The words in (3.61b) end in a CVC whose stress may vary in the pronunciation of some individual speakers. We take this to indicate optionality in the application of Monosyllabic Destressing, rather than variability in the lexical entry of the words, where the final C might be extrametrical one moment and not the next. The examples in (3.61c), whose final CVC is always stressless, have two possible derivations: if their final C is extrametrical, they would never have been stressed in the first place; but if their final C is not extrametrical, they must be seen as instances of an obligatory application of Monosyllabic Destressing. As for the examples in (3.61d), whose final CVC is never destressed, some are clearly exceptions to the rule, in that CVCs of the same type are destressed in other words. Compare *gýmnàst* with *témpĕst* or *Lómbàrd* with *stán-dărd*. But for some CVCs, such as those ending in nondental conso-nants, it may simply be that the rule should not apply—that the conditions should be formulated so as not to allow them to be de-stressed. We leave this question open here, referring the reader to Ross 1972, where several generalizations regarding CVC stress and its rela-tion to consonant type emerge.

Finally, consider cases of medial destressing. In these cases, a sylla-ble (usually immediately preceding the main stress of a word) is de-moted from the basic beat alignment that it would have as a result of the HBR.

(3.62)

a. Mòzămbíque   *Exceptions:*   chîmpànzée
   Nèbŭchădnézzar   Hâlicàrnássus
   pàrăphĕrnália   rôdomòntáde
   Kìlĭmănjáro

b. cònvĕrsátion   *Exceptions:*   êxpèctátion
   cònfrŏntátion   rêlàxátion
   pèrtŭrbátion   rêtàrdátion
   àffĕctátion   înfèstátion
   dìspĕnsátion
   dòmĕstícity
   còllĕctívity
   ìnfŏrmátion
   ànnĕxátion
   còndĕnsátion/côndènsátion
   èmĕndátion/êmèndátion
   àuthĕntícity/âuthèntícity
   Jàpănése
   spècĭfícity

The examples of (3.62a) are monomorphemes where the HBR would have given rise to a basic beat alignment on the syllable immediately preceding the main-stressed syllable. The examples of (3.62b) are mor-phologically complex ones where the pronunciation of the embedded words (*condense, collective, inform, domestic, Japan, specific,* etc.) shows that there is some stressing to be undone in the derived word. Note that the facts belie the claim, made in SPE and elsewhere, that the absence of stress on the medial syllable is a sign that the word does *not* have a cyclic history wherein that syllable was stressed on an earlier cycle. In all of the words in (3.62b), the earlier cyclically assigned stress has been removed from the medial syllable. Notice, too, that even when there is no apparent cyclic history, that medial syllable may have stress (exceptionally), as in *dèlèctátion*. Words like *rèlàxátion*, which have both a cyclic history and a medial stress, we treat like *delectation*, as exceptions to Monosyllabic Destressing.

Whether or not a word is an exception to Monosyllabic Destressing is an important source of idiosyncrasy in the grammar of English. This and whether or not the final consonant of a word is extrametrical account for almost all the idiosyncrasies in the stressing of CVC in English words.

Our basic analysis of English stress patterns, our assumptions about extrametricality, and the rule of Monosyllabic Destressing constitute what we believe to be the correct theory of the distribution of stressed and stressless CVC in English. According to this grammar, CVC syllables are always stressed in the basic patterns (unless the final C is extrametrical), and the specific prediction is made that a stressless CVC arises only in positions where (as an underlying stressed CVC) it would not have received main or secondary stress. This is very different from the claim made by Selkirk 1980b or by Hayes 1980, 1982. Selkirk 1980b puts no restrictions on the distribution of stressless CVC, treating CVC either like CV or like CVC in the basic patterns. Hayes 1980, 1982 refutes this position, citing the impossibility of assigning stress patterns to words like *Nìnótchkă* that fail to stress the penultimate CVC (and that fail, moreover, to give it main stress): **Nínŏtchkă*. The present theory overcomes this deficiency. As for Hayes's own analysis, it has the peculiar property of stressing (footing) only CVC syllables that are (speaking roughly) at the right extreme of the word (though not in the final position). His analysis thus cannot account for the medial stressed syllable in *Halicarnassus* or *chimpanzee;* significantly, it must consider them exceptional in *having* stress. On our theory they are only exceptional in not *losing* it, by Monosyllabic Destressing. Hayes also treats final stressed CVC as exceptional, a position we have already contested in section 3.2.2 on extrametricality.

We will not provide any further critique of the particulars of Hayes's analysis of CVC. We observe simply that our theory, which is that CVC must everywhere be treated the same in the basic patterns, is more restrictive and therefore, everything else being equal, to be desired—if it accords with the facts. We submit that the theory does accord with the facts, when one takes into account the rule of Monosyllabic Destressing and final consonant extrametricality. Since Hayes's analysis also requires the notion of extrametricality, as well as a rule or rules that are the analogue of Monosyllabic Destressing, then everything else is equal, and the "stress CVC everywhere" theory should presumably be adopted.

Before proceeding, we should discuss one set of cases that are apparently problematic for our theory of CVC (as they are for Hayes's theory)—those in (3.63):

(3.63)

Háckĕnsàck	Hóttĕntòt	mísănthròpe
Álgĕrnòn	ámpĕrsànd	báldĕrdàsh
cávălcàde	pálïndròme	mérchăndìse
Ábĕrdèen	Áppĕlbàum	Árkănsàs

Given our analysis, there is no way to avoid assigning stress (a basic beat alignment) to the penultimate CVC syllable of such words. Then either that syllable or the final (stressed) one would receive "main stress." The final syllable here, in avoiding main stress, must be extrametrical. Thus medial main stress should have been derived, as in (3.64):

(3.64)

```
          [hæ kVn sæk]
DBA        x   x   x

           x   x   x
HBR, IBR   x   x   x   (final C not extrametrical)

               x
           x   x   x
MSR        x   x   x
          *Hàckénsàck
```

Yet this is incorrect.

Hayes's analysis faces a similar problem. His solution is to destress the medial stressed (footed) syllable before the assignment of main stress to the word. This solution presupposes a theory of grammar that allows stressing rules and destressing rules to mingle freely. Earlier we advanced the general hypothesis that destressing rules are postcyclic and thus that they follow all rules of grid construction. If this hypothesis is correct, then Hayes's analysis cannot be.

Interestingly, there is an alternative analysis of these forms that appears to be just as illuminating, which presupposes that the basic stress rules apply before any grid transformation. Our proposal is that a grid transformation retracts the main stress (third-level beat) that was assigned to the medial stressed syllable of (3.64) and places it on the preceding basic beat. We call this rule *Sonorant Retraction,* for reasons that will soon become clear, and formulate it as follows:[49]

(3.65)
Sonorant Retraction

$$(R = \begin{bmatrix} +son \\ +cons \end{bmatrix})$$

From (3.64) this rule will derive (3.66a), which by Monosyllabic Destressing becomes (3.66b), the correct surface pattern:

(3.66)

The formulation of the rule reflects in large part the empirical generalizations brought to light by Hayes—that in words of the troublesome *Hackensack* variety the medial CVC that must be made to lose its stress (in one way or another) is closed by a sonorant (cf. *phlògístòn,* not *phlógìstòn*), that the rule does not operate if two syllables precede the CVC syllable (cf. *Àdiróndàcks*), and that it does not operate if the following syllable is stressless.

Note that this rule accounts in a similar way for morphologically complex examples discussed by Kiparsky 1979 and Hayes 1980, 1982. The observation made by Kiparsky (attributed to Gill Gane) is that in words with the suffixes *-ary* and *-ory* main stress would fall on a CVR preceding the suffixes, if the CVR were preceded by two syllables, as in (3.67a), or if it ended in an obstruent, as in (3.67b). Otherwise that CVC would be stressless, and the main stress would appear earlier in the word, as in (3.67c).

(3.67)

a.		b.		c.	
èleméntăry		trajéctŏry		légĕndàry	
còmpliméntăry		perfúnctŏry		mómĕntàry	
rùdiméntăry		reféctŏry		frágmĕntàry	
		phyláctĕry		cómmĕntàry	
				vólŭntàry	
				ínvĕntòry	
				répĕrtòry	
				prómŏntòry	

Kiparsky and Hayes observe similar behavior in front of other stressed suffixes:

(3.68)

a.	b.	c.
adamantine	ulexine	saturnine
archimandrite	stalactite	gilbertite
salamandroid	molluscoid	helminthoid

The rule of Sonorant Retraction accounts for these facts without putting the destressing rule in the cycle, unlike the account of Kiparsky and Hayes. Representative derivations are given in (3.69), where we assume with Hayes that these stressed adjective suffixes (even the surface bisyllables *-ary* and *-ory*) are extrametrical:

(3.69)

	[[element](ary)$_{em}$]	[perfunctory]	[[legend](ary)$_{em}$]
Cycle 1	x	x	x
	x x	x x x	x x
	x x x	x x x	x x
	element	perfunctory	legend
Cycle 2	x		x
	x x x		x
	x x x x		x x x
	elementary	——	legendary
Postcycle			x
			x x x
			x x x
Sonorant Retraction	——	——	legendary

(The rules of destressing complete the derivation.)[50]

The last facts to be discussed concern the destressing and laxing of medial CVV found in *explanation* (cf. *explain*), *provocation* (cf. *pro-*

voke), etc. Many have claimed (e.g., Liberman and Prince 1977, Selkirk 1980b, Hayes 1980, 1982) that this is an instance of the destressing of CVV, with consequent laxing of the vowel. We believe now that it is incorrect to view the laxing of the tense vowels here as having anything to do with destressing. First, as shown by words like *explánatory* and *provócative,* a vowel may be laxed but still stressed, so that some independent account of laxing is necessary. Second, if CVV were to be destressed by the general rule of Monosyllabic Destressing, it would be predicted that destressed laxed CVV should be found in initial and final positions as well; and, except for a few specially marked prefixes (note 45), this turns out not to be the case. Thus we have another reason for disassociating laxing from destressing in *explanation* and not allowing Monosyllabic Destressing to demote CVV.

The rule that accomplishes the laxing is none other than a modified version of what has been called *Trisyllabic Laxing.* According to SPE, for example, Trisyllabic Laxing produces *serenity*[ɛ] on the basis of a tense vowel in *serene,* and so on. We will retain the name Trisyllabic Laxing, but point out that it obscures the essentially morphological character of the rule. In our view, the rule modifies vowel quality in syllables preceding a certain diacritically marked class of suffixes; it may be construed as a rule of allomorphy.[51] The triggering suffixes are the Latinate ones: *-ic* (*isotopic* vs. *isotope*), *-ance* (*sustenance* vs. *sustain*), *-ize* (*satirize* vs. *satire*), *-ation* (*explanation* vs. *explain*), *-atory* (*declamatory* vs. *declaim*), *-ative* (*provocative* vs. *provoke*), *-ity* (*sanity* vs. *sane*), *-ent* (*president* vs. *preside*), *-al* (*vaginal* vs. *vagina*), *-ify* (*codify* vs. *code*), *-ive* (*iterative* vs. *iterate*), *-ism* (*Semitism* vs. *Semite*). In this we are following a suggestion of Ross 1972, one adopted by Kiparsky 1979 as well. By no means is the affected vowel necessarily located three syllables from the end (and by no means is it merely laxed). It is also not the case that boundaries do the trick of distinguishing the relevant class of suffixes here: not all Root suffixes trigger the rule. *Detainee, retiree, pipette,* etc., all retain their tensed vowels before the suffix, whose Root status is shown by its ability to bear main stress. The triggering suffixes must simply be marked with a diacritic distinguishing them from suffixes that do not cause the alternation. (See Dell and Selkirk 1978, who present a similar treatment of a morphologically governed vowel alternation in French, and Strauss 1979a,b, who shows that rules of English such as Velar Softening and Coronal Assibilation are morphologically governed as well.)

Viewing Trisyllabic Laxing as a morphologically governed rule (in effect, a rule of allomorphy) has a number of important consequences. One is that the rule will precede destressing and any other postcyclic rules of the grammar. It is consistent with our view of the organization of the grammar that morphologically governed rules be precyclic (restricted to applying either in the course of "word formation" or "in the lexicon") or cyclic (interspersed among the rules constructing phonological representation). The latter possibility exists because the domains of such rules are defined crucially in terms of syntactic structure (of which morphological structure is a special case).

In either case, the input to destressing, which may still be presumed to apply to *explanation,* will not include a medial CVV in an environment in which it would have been affected by Trisyllabic Laxing. With the assumption that Trisyllabic Laxing is cyclic, the derivation of stressless medial CV in *èxplănátion* proceeds as in (3.70a). The derivation is in many respects comparable to that of *Jàpănése* (cf. *Jăpán*), which we include for comparison.

(3.70)

a.   [[ex plain] a tion]   b. [[Ja pan] ese]

```
Cycle 1                      x                          x
                          x  x                       x  x
                          x  x                       x  x
                          ex plain                    Ja pan

Cycle 2                      x
                             x
                             x

Trisyllabic Laxing        ... plan a tion_em            ——
                             x                          x
                          x  x                       x  x
                          x  x                       x  x

Resyllabification         ex pla na tion_em           Ja pa nese
                             x                          x
                          x  x x x                   x  x x
                          x  x x x                   x  x x

DBA, HBR                  ex pla na tion_em           Ja pa nese
                             x                          x
                            x x                        x x
                          x  x x x                   x  x x
                          x  x x x                   x  x x

MSR                       ex pla na tion_em           Ja pa nese
```

```
                       x                        x
             x         x              x         x
             x   x x x                x   x   x
             x   x x x                x   x   x
BM                    ex pla na tion_em        Ja pa nese
Postcycle              x                        x
             x         x              x         x
             x         x              x         x
             x   x x x                x   x   x
Monosyllabic Destressing  ex pla na tion       Ja pa nese
                       x                        x
             x         x              x         x
             x   x x x                x   x   x
Output^52             explanation              Japanese
```

This completes our examination of the role of Monosyllabic Destressing in deriving the surface stress patterns of English.

3.4 The Cycle

Having shown that the English Main Stress Rule has a specific syntactic domain, we now want to show that rules of grid construction like the MSR apply in cyclic fashion. From the fact that a rule may have a characteristic syntactic domain of application, it by no means necessarily follows that this rule must apply cyclically. It could be that the rule is governed by something like the A-over-A Condition (see Ross 1967, for example), so that when constituents of its domain type are embedded within each other, it applies only on the highest instance of its domain. Or it could be that the rule applies simultaneously on all constituents that are its domain, or that it applies only each time a new constituent of its domain type is generated by the rules of the morphology. Each of these theories would allow for grid construction rules to have a characteristic syntactic domain, but would not require that those rules proceed from the most deeply embedded upward in cyclic fashion.

In what follows, we will present several arguments (one due to Kiparsky 1979) that an A-over-A application of stress rules (grid construction) is impossible. To show this, it is enough to show that morphologically complex words of type A have a stress pattern that is different from that of monomorphemic words of type A in just those ways that would be predicted if the stress rules had had access to information about the internal composition of the former in terms of categories of type A. We will also present arguments (one due essentially to Kiparsky 1979) that a simultaneous application of stress rules (grid construction) is impossible. None of these arguments appears to distinguish crucially between a theory in which the principle of the cycle governs the way in which rules apply in the course of the syntax-phonology mapping and a theory in which there is no cycle, but rather an application of rules each time a new word is "generated." There are reasons for adopting the cyclic theory, however, to which we will turn later.

It turns out that the only grid construction rules of English that have the potential for providing evidence of a cyclic (non-A-over-A, non-simultaneous) construction of the grid are those applying at the third metrical level and above. The analogous state of affairs obtains in a metrical tree theory. As shown by Kiparsky 1979 and Hayes 1980, 1982, it is the assignment of the metrical tree structure involved in the representation of main and secondary word stress that gives crucial evidence for the cycle. For lack of space, we will not explore why this should be so; but we note that the reasons are partly accidental and partly principled.

One of Kiparsky's arguments for the cycle turns on the fact that monomorphemic words like *Ticonderoga* and its fellows (supposedly) have two possible patterns of "secondary stress" before the main stress of the word (cf. (3.35a) and (3.35b)), while morphologically complex words like those in (3.71) have only one pattern.

(3.71)

sènsâtionálity	*sênsàtionálity
ìcônoclástic	*îcònoclástic
àntîcipátion	*ântìcipátion
tòtâlitárian	*tôtàlitárian
sùpêrióarity	*sûpèrióarity
thèâtricálity	*thêâtricálity

Words like *Ticonderoga* and *sensationality* are otherwise identical in the relevant respects: they contain a sequence of three syllables before the main stress, where the syllables are of the type heavy-heavy-light. Kiparsky claims that the availability of only one pattern for *sensationality* but two for *Ticonderoga* is to be attributed to cyclic assignment of main stress in the former. We agree with Kiparsky in this claim, while taking issue with the details of his tree-based analysis. The derivation of *sensationality,* given the grid-based theory and the cycle, would be as follows:

(3.72)

$$[[[\text{sensation}]\ (\text{al})_{em}]\ i(\text{ty})_{em}]$$

Cycle 1	x
	x x
	x x x
	sensation
Cycle 2	x
	x x
	x x x x
	sensational
Cycle 3	x
	x x x
	x x x x xx
DBA, BA	sensationality
	x
	x x
	x x x
	x x x x xx
MSR	sensationality
BA	inapplicable
BM	blocked (by the *Montana* Filter)

Here the earlier (cyclic) assignment of a third-level main stress to *-at-* is carried over on the higher cycle. Because that third-level position is present on *-at-*, Beat Addition cannot apply to promote the initial syllable *sen-* to third-level prominence. And because the *Montana*-motivated output filter (3.36) is at play here, Beat Movement does not dislodge that grid position and move it to the left. Thus the difference between *sensationality* and *Ticonderoga* is explained. Note that this explanation requires us to assume that the *Montana* Filter is absolute with respect to Beat Movement in words, but not so with respect to Beat Addition. Recall that on our account the initial secondary stress of *Ticonderóga* is produced by Beat Addition, in violation of the filter, whereas the pattern *Ticònderóga* is claimed to be what is derived (or rather, left untouched) when Beat Addition, discouraged by the filter, does not apply (cf. (3.35a), (3.35b), and (3.36)). Perhaps the reason that Beat Movement is entirely blocked by the filter, whereas Beat Addition is not, is that the latter exhibits a much stronger tendency to apply, at all metrical levels, than the former. (Within words, this is in particular because of the Anti-Lapse Filter.) The point of the contrast, in any event, is that it indicates the presence of a third-level grid position introduced on an earlier (or embedded) cyclic domain in *sensationality*.

Hayes 1982 points out that a similar sort of argument can be made on the basis of the contrast between monomorphemic and morphologically complex words having the shape of *abracadabra*. Complex words like those in (3.72a)

(3.72)
a. sŭblìminálity   b. *sùbliminálity
   cŏllàterálity   *còllaterálity

do not contain the ternary feet that would be produced by the Abracadabra Rule if they were treated like monomorphemes (see (3.72b)). Rather, they have a secondary stress on the second syllable, not on the first. This is what would be produced if grid construction were cyclic, as in (3.73).

(3.73)
                    [[subliminal] i(ty)$_{em}$]
Cycle 1   x
                    x x
                    x x x x
                    subliminal
Cycle 2   x
                    x x   x
                    x x x x xx
DBA, BA   subliminality
                        x
                    x   x
                    x x   x
                    x x x x xx
MSR   subliminality
BA   inapplicable
BM   blocked (by the *Montana* Filter)
Postcycle
Abracadabra   inapplicable (blocked by the third-level position
                    on -*lim*-)

These cases show that grid construction rules need to apply on successively embedded syntactic constituents, not just on the highest one.

Note also that such examples give additional evidence for the role of the Textual Prominence Preservation Condition in the grammar. The general statement of the TPPC is that within a cyclic domain, a grid position assigned by a TGA rule on the third metrical level or above is (minimally) more prominent than any other grid position within that particular cyclic domain. It has so far been motivated as a condition guaranteeing that a beat introduced by the MSR will be more prominent than any introduced by the GE rule of Beat Addition. In these examples it ensures that a beat introduced by the MSR on the current cycle is more prominent than a beat introduced by the MSR on an earlier cycle. The TPPC is therefore quite general in effect, not restricted to adjudicating the relation between a TGA rule on the one hand and a GE rule on the other.

Next we must consider the possibility that instead of applying cyclically, grid construction rules apply on all relevant syntactic domains simultaneously. There are two possible versions of a simultaneous theory. According to one, both TGA rules and GE rules are met simultaneously on all appropriate domains. This particular version is not tenable because it does not predict the patterns attested. A GE rule may move or eliminate a prominence required by a TGA rule (on a lower domain). This is what happens in *èxpectátion,* for example, where the final prominence appropriate to the verb *expéct* is deflected by Beat Movement. A theory with simultaneous TGA and GE on all domains is therefore not possible. According to a second possible version of a simultaneous theory, all TGA rules might be said to be met simultaneously on all relevant domains, and the partial patterns established on this basis might then be submitted to the GE rules. But this is not possible as an account of the TGA – Beat Addition relation, for example. If the appropriate textual prominence is to be maintained, Beat Addition must not undo the effects of a TGA rule, which it could if ordered afterward and if the TGA rule were prohibited from reapplying. (Recall the discussion of the MSR – Beat Addition relation in sections 2.2.2 and 3.2.2.) This version is therefore not tenable either. Our analysis, instead, is that there is a cycle and that TGA and GE rules like Beat Addition are met simultaneously on each successive cyclic domain, in a manner governed by the TPPC.

Another argument in favor of the cycle comes from Kiparsky 1979. Kiparsky seeks to explain the pronunciation of a complex form like *expect* when it is found in isolation ($\overset{0}{e}\overset{1}{xpect}$), with an affix like *-ation* ($\overset{2}{e}\overset{3}{xpec}\overset{1}{tation}$), and on the phrase ($\overset{0}{e}\overset{1}{xpect}\overset{1}{rain}$). (For convenience, we use integers here to indicate stress levels: 0 = stressless, 1 = main word stress, 2 = "secondary" stress, 3 = stressed.) The pronunciation of $\overset{0}{e}\overset{1}{xpect}$ arises from an application of destressing to $\overset{3}{e}\overset{1}{xpect}$; the lack of initial destressing in $\overset{2\ \ \ 3\ \ \ 1}{expectation}$ is attributed to the operation of the "Rhythm Rule" (Beat Movement), which is said to throw a secondary stress back onto *ex-* (from *-pect-*, in a clash with *-ation*) and thus to render it impervious to destressing. To derive *expectation,* then, the Rhythm Rule (Beat Movement) must precede destressing. But the pronunciation $\overset{0\ \ \ \ 1\ \ \ 1}{expect\ rain}$ shows that the Rhythm Rule must follow destressing. If destressing had not already taken place, the Rhythm Rule, applying now on a phrasal domain, would derive $\overset{1\ \ \ 3\ \ \ 1}{expect\ rain}$ (just as it derives $\overset{1\ \ \ 3\ \ 1}{abstract\ art}$ (from $\overset{3\ \ \ 1\ \ 1}{abstract\ art}$)). Thus this evidence does show that the Rhythm Rule (Beat Movement) cannot be said to apply simultaneously on both the word and the phrase domain (because of the intervening application of destressing).

This may appear to be an instance of the classic sort of argument for the cycle. Seemingly, one can explain these facts by assuming that there is a cycle, that both Beat Movement and destressing are cyclic, and that Beat Movement is ordered before destressing. But in fact this is not a classic argument of that sort, for, as Kiparsky 1979 points out, destressing is not a cyclic rule. It is instead postcyclic. Thus we are seemingly confronted with a paradox: a cyclic rule that is both preceded and followed by a postcyclic rule. What could it mean for a rule to be "postcyclic" in such cases? We have an answer to this question, and a solution to the apparent paradox, but we will postpone presenting it until chapter 7, where we will examine the role of Monosyllabic Destressing in the phrase and the sentence in some detail.

To conclude, we have presented arguments weighing against both a one-time A-over-A application of grid construction rules and a simultaneous on-every-domain-at-once application. With Kiparsky 1979 and Hayes 1980, 1982, we believe that these arguments establish the possibility of a cyclic mode of application of "stress rules" within words, a possibility that becomes a necessity once more evidence is in.

As suggested earlier, one might entertain two different sorts of explanation for the correlation noticed by Kiparsky and Hayes between secondary stress placement and presence of internal morphological structure. One comes from the theory of the cycle, the other from a theory like the one proposed by Siegel and Allen, whereby the stress rules apply "in the course of word formation." As Kiparsky 1982a points out, such a theory allows for eliminating the cycle as a mode of application within words. Kiparsky considers this a desirable consequence, assuming (following Liberman and Prince 1977) that there is no cycle above the level of the word. His point is that, in the absence of a phrasal cycle, eliminating the cycle from the level of the word would mean eliminating it from the grammar entirely, providing a certain consistency at least.

Leaving aside for the moment the issue of the (non)existence of the phrasal cycle, note that eliminating the cycle as a mode of application within the word crucially depends on the correctness of Siegel and Allen's theory of word formation. If our 1982 approach to word syntax is correct, *and* if words may be generated "on the spot" that have more than one affix, then the notion of the cycle as a mode of application is required.

In Selkirk 1980b we proposed a particular noncyclic approach within the general framework of our 1982 theory of word syntax. This approach was incorrect, for the following reasons. We suggested that the stress pattern of a lexical item be listed as part of its lexical entry (in which case the stress rules of the language constitute a set of redundancy rules over the phonological representation of lexical items). Moreover, we suggested that when a new word is generated (by affixation, for example) on the basis of an existing one, the existing word brings its stress pattern with it when it is "inserted" into the newly generated abstract word structure tree. A "new" application of the stress rules, introducing only "minimal changes" in the old lexical item, was considered to follow lexical insertion as an automatic consequence, if the newly created word structure contained the affix and the old lexical item within the appropriate syntactic domain. (So far, it seems to be merely a notational variant of Siegel and Allen's approach.) That "new" application of the stress rules was not considered to be an instance of cyclic application. Our mistake was in not understanding that the model sketched, which allows for the lexical representation of stress, is consistent with cyclic application. It is simply the case that if this model is correct, then *most* evidence for the cycle disappears, but not all of it. What is crucial to proving the existence of the cycle is an application of the stress rules on (at least) two successive domains, that is, a derivation in which a new word structure generated by the rewriting rules contains two "new" Root affixes, and hence two embedded Root domains.

Let us invent an example. Suppose that the word *probationality* is concocted (by some bureaucrat concerned with criminal affairs) and that *probational* is not a lexical item of the language. According to Selkirk 1982, the word is generated in the following way. The rewriting rules of word syntax generate the abstract word structure (3.74a), and the lexical items *probation* (with its internal structure, if any), *-al,* and *-ity* are lexically inserted, as in (3.74b).

(3.74)

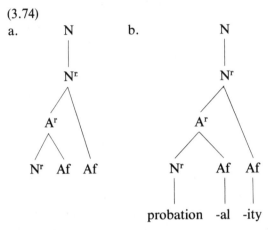

Recall that, as a lexical item, *probation is a* Noun and a Noun root. It is its Root status that allows it to be inserted into (3.74a) here. (We are ignoring its internal structure, if it has any.) Given such a structure, even if *probation* comes into the tree from the lexicon with its stress pattern assigned, the stress rules must apply cyclically, for *probation-ality* has a stress pattern reflecting its internal structure, just as *sensationality* does. The general point, then, is that given a rewriting grammar of word structure (a "syntax-first" theory), wherein complex new words are generated as illustrated here, rules must apply cyclically.

Our theory treats words no differently from phrases in characterizing their structure and in characterizing the structure-dependency of the rules that define phonological representation on the basis of syntactic representation. The rules of the syntax-phonology mapping that construct the metrical grid have syntactic domains and apply in cyclic fashion. If it is not so obvious that the principle of the cycle is required for words, it is because lexical items may be listed with their stress patterns in the lexicon. But the possibility of generating new multi-layered word structure is there, and the proper phonological interpretation of these structures requires that the cycle have a role in the mapping of word structure into phonological representation, if the rewriting grammar for word syntax of Selkirk 1982 is correct.

3.5 Summary of Rules and Conditions

The following rules and conditions have played a role in our description of English word stress patterns.

Text-to-Grid Alignment
Basic beat rules
    Heavy Syllable Basic Beat Rule   (3.6a)
    (parameters = CVV, CVC)
    Initial Basic Beat Rule   (3.6b)
    (parameters = left, Root)
Domain-end prominence rule
    Main Stress Rule   (3.38)
    (parameters = right, Root)

Grid Euphony
Beat Addition   (3.12)
    Second level
    (parameters = left-dominant, right-to-left)
    Levels above second
    (parameter = left-dominant)
Beat Movement
    Levels above second
    (parameter = left)

Grid Transformations
Abracadabra Rule   (3.51)
Monosyllabic Destressing   (3.56)
Sonorant Retraction   (3.65)

Universal Conditions
Textual Prominence Preservation Condition   (3.39)
Anti-Lapse Filter   (3.40)
    (parameter = Root)
Higher Prominence Preservation Condition   (3.41)
Alternation Maintenance Condition   (3.57)
?*Montana* Filter   (3.36)

3.6 The Role of Prosodic Categories in English Word Stress

The analysis of English word stress offered in the preceding sections makes crucial appeal to one sort of prosodic constituent—the syllable.

The internal structure of syllables and the number occurring within a particular syntactic domain are reflected in the rhythmic patterns of English words. The syllable sequence provides the anchor, so to speak, of that rhythmic patterning: the representation of the stress pattern of an utterance on our theory is the alignment of the syllables of the utterance with a metrical grid. The syllable, then, has a solid place in the theory of the phonological representation of English words. A characterization of the notion "possible stress pattern" of English depends on it, as do a theory of English phonotactics and a theory of phonological rule domains (cf. chapter 1).

The status of other prosodic constituents in the phonological representations of English words, and in phonological theory as a whole, is debatable. We would claim that no prosodic constituent other than the syllable has a role in the representation and characterization of English word stress patterns. Here we take issue with Selkirk 1980b and Hayes 1980, 1982 regarding English and with Halle and Vergnaud 1979, Hayes 1980, and others regarding the general theory of word stress. Yet other prosodic constituents could nonetheless have a place in the theory of phonological representation if a theory of phonotactics or of phonological rule domains required them. We will claim that there is no motivation for the foot (in English, and more generally), either as a unit of phonotactic description or as a unit serving as the characteristic domain of phonological rules.

Phonotactic arguments for the foot have been based essentially on the view that stress patterns are a matter of phonotactic description—that characterizing the notion "possible stress pattern" is quite analogous to characterizing the notion "possible syllable" and "possible sequence of syllables." It is claimed that characterizing the notion "possible foot" and "possible sequence of feet" provides an analysis of patterns of stressed and stressless syllables. This is the position taken for English word stress in Selkirk 1980b, for example. But as we have shown, this position is misconceived. Stress patterns are a matter not of phonotactics, but of the alignment of a syllable sequence with a rhythmic structure, represented as a grid. Thus there is no motivation for the foot as a unit of phonotactic description. The only remaining motivation for the foot, therefore, would come from a theory of phonological rule domains. Kiparsky 1979 has argued that the foot is the domain for certain allophonic rules in English, a characterization accepted in Selkirk 1980b. Selkirk 1978b, however, offers a quite satisfactory account of the same phenomena that does not appeal to foot structure. The debate is therefore open for English; and it remains to be seen whether there is evidence from other languages as well pointing to the necessity of the foot as a domain for rules.

Earlier studies (Liberman and Prince 1977, Selkirk 1980b) have argued that there is a roughly word-sized constituent of prosodic structure that has a place in the phonological representation of English utterances. That constituent has been referred to as the *mot*, the *prosodic word*, the *word*, the *phonological word*, and so on. One primary motivation for the prosodic word (Liberman and Prince's *mot*) was its role in indicating when a subpart of a metrical tree belonged to a single word and when it belonged to a compound or a phrasal constituent. Specifically, Liberman and Prince's Compound Rule was claimed to "see" branching structure, but not word-internal branching structure (see Liberman and Prince 1977 and Selkirk 1980b for discussion). The *mot* was a level below which the Compound Rule could not look. It will be clear from the treatment of compounds to be given in chapter 4 that this characterization of the Compound Rule is incorrect, and the primary motivation for a prosodic word in the representation of stress patterns thereby disappears. As for the contribution of the prosodic word as a means of representing the difference between "stress" and "main word stress," it is supplanted by the metrical grid and the third-level beat. It remains to be seen whether the prosodic word is at all motivated as a domain of phonological rules; but, as mentioned in chapter 1, we believe that it is not, and that it is either the rhythmic disjuncture of syntactic timing or the syntactic structure itself that gives the appropriate representation of "word" for rules of the phonology.

Chapter 4
Phrasal Rhythmic Prominences

The principal topic of this chapter is the representation and characterization of patterns of rhythmic prominence above the level of the word. With Chomsky and Halle 1968, Liberman 1975, Liberman and Prince 1977, and others, we assert that the rhythmic structure of the utterance does not reduce to the concatenation of the rhythmic structures of its component words, but rather that it reflects as well the arrangement of words into syntactic constituents, which is to say that there is a rhythmic organization proper to the phrasal level. With Prince 1981, 1983, we contend that the metrical grid is the *only* available representation for prominence relations; in this we depart from the approach taken in Liberman 1975, Liberman and Prince 1977, and subsequent works in metrical theory.[1] In those works, the fundamental representation of prominence relations is in terms of metrical trees, binary-branching structures whose nodes are labeled strong or weak. It is in terms of metrical trees that the syntactic contribution to patterns of prominence must be characterized; the grid is only a "later-level" representation into which the metrical tree representation of the sentence is mapped and in terms of which its rhythmic, temporal organization is expressed. Yet, as Liberman and Prince point out, it is only with the grid that certain aspects of the rhythmic patterning of the sentence can be insightfully described: the notion of stress clash requires the grid, as does the tendency toward recurrent patterns of alternating prominences at the higher levels, patterns that are not required by syntactic constituency. Metrical trees are inadequate to this descriptive task. Our point here, with Prince 1981, 1983, is that if *all* contributions to the rhythmic patterning of an utterance—both syntax-based and "rhythm-based"—can be represented, with no loss of generalization, directly in terms of the grid, then, by Occam's razor, the theory of prominence relations must be cast solely in terms of the metrical grid. Note that to say that trees form no part of the *representation* of phrase stress is not to say that trees are irrelevant to its *characterization* or description. Indeed, we will propose that patterns of phrase stress, represented in terms of the metrical grid, are defined crucially *with respect to* the surface syntactic structure of a sentence, a representation in terms of trees.

Our general approach to the description of patterns of phrasal prominence will mirror the description outlined for patterns of prominence within the word: they will be understood as resulting from the combined effects of (a) text-to-grid alignment rules, principles of grammar that specify (for example) that a prominence in a particular location within a (syntactic) domain must be the most prominent within that domain, and (b) principles of *grid euphony,* which ensure that the metrical grid of the sentence conforms (more or less) to the Principle of Rhythmic Alternation. As with words, we will view the principles governing prominence in phrases as principles for constructing the grid, on the basis of its syllabic composition and its constituent structure. The Nuclear Stress Rule (NSR) of English is a principle of type (a). Roughly speaking, it guarantees that the greatest word prominence within the rightmost constituent of a syntactic phrase is the most prominent of all the prominences in that phrase. (In this, it is more than reminiscent of the SPE Nuclear Stress Rule.) Seen in general terms, a principle of this type specifies a "reliable" location of (greatest) prominence within the sentence. The rule of Beat Addition is a principle of type (b). Usually, its effect will complement that of the NSR: while the latter specifies the reliable location of (greatest) prominence within the phrase, the former guarantees that an alternating pattern emanates from that point. There are instances, however, when the effects of the NSR are obliterated by principles of grid euphony. This is the case when "stress shift" undoes the right prominence demanded by the NSR. One theme of this chapter will be to properly formulate the various principles of prominence and to investigate their interaction. We will argue, among other things, that their operation is governed by the principle of the cycle.

The elimination of metrical trees from a description of patterns of phrase stress, then, is one departure we make here from the general theory of stress and rhythm proposed by Liberman 1975 and Liberman and Prince 1977. There is another. Liberman and Prince claim, with others in the generative tradition, that the rhythmic organization of an utterance can be characterized without regard to its intonational properties. Indeed, the approach taken by Liberman 1975, Bing 1979a,b, Ladd 1980, Pierrehumbert 1980, and Del (to appear), who have investigated the relation between phrase stress and intonation in the framework of a generative grammar, has been to view the patterns of phrase stress of an utterance as logically prior, determining the possibilities of realization of its intonational contour. A widely shared assumption has been that certain of the tonal elements constituting the intonational contour[2] are associated with the (main stress of the) words of a sentence as a function of the place those words occupy within the phrase stress patterns of the sentence. More specifically, these tonal elements are taken to be tropic to the local rhythmic prominences defined by principles of phrase stress. We believe that this theory of what Liberman calls the "tune-text relation" is misconceived, and that a radically different theory of the relation between intonation and phrase stress is required.

Our claim is that the "choices" made by the grammar with respect to the intonational properties of an utterance in fact circumscribe the range of possible patterns of rhythmic prominence within the utterance, so that the latter are in effect partly determined by the former. We will argue, for example, that the stress-relevant tonal elements (which, following Pierrehumbert 1980, we take to be the *pitch accents* of the intonational contour; see chapter 5), are assigned to words in surface structure regardless of (and indeed prior to the establishment of) phrase stress patterns, and that phrase stress patterns are defined partly as a function of the location of pitch-accent-bearing words in the sentence. (In this our approach may be taken to resemble somewhat that of Bolinger 1958b, 1981.)[3] Specifically, we will show that the presence of a pitch accent on a word in a constituent entails that the word has greater rhythmic prominence than any word within the constituent that does not bear a pitch accent. This principle we call the *Pitch Accent Prominence Rule* (PAR). The PAR may override the NSR in effect, but in the absence of pitch accents, the claim goes, the NSR will prevail. Thus the NSR and the PAR together pick out the loci of (greatest) phrasal prominence within the sentence. A sketch of a "pitch-accent-first" theory like this was suggested to us by Pierrehumbert (personal communication), though the idea was not pursued in Pierrehumbert 1980.

This "pitch-accent-first" theory of the tune-text relation will be defended for the most part in the next chapter. We believe that it can be shown to allow a more insightful characterization of the relation between pitch accents and phrasal rhythmic prominence than the "stress-first" theory. We believe also that it allows a better understanding of the way in which the suprasegmental phonological attributes of a sentence relate to its "intonational meaning," especially that involving its focus structure.[4] We claim that phrase stress is irrelevant to meaning or pragmatics, that it is simply the presence or absence of a pitch accent on a word that is taken into account in interpreting a sentence for semantic or pragmatic purposes, and thus that principles like the NSR are, in a sense to be made precise, "exceptionless" and truly "phonological."

Another advantage of the "pitch-accent-first" theory, which will be explored in this chapter and the next, is that it allows fresh insights into the principles governing the placement of prominence in English compounds. Although we will argue, with SPE, Halle and Keyser 1971, Liberman and Prince 1977, and others, that there is a Compound Stress Rule assigning left prominence to compound words in English, we will show as well that quite general principles of pitch accent assignment (i.e., focus) are ultimately (via the PAR) the source of most of the apparently exceptional patterns of prominence seen in compounds. Our proposal builds on the contributions of Bolinger 1958b, 1981 and Ladd 1981.

The main purpose of this chapter, however, is not to investigate the implications of this theory of pitch accent assignment and the PAR. It is instead to present the metrical grid-only theory of phrasal prominence and its advantages over the other theories of phrasal prominence that have been proposed. In section 4.1 we present the grid-based Nuclear Stress Rule and Compound Rule, along with the Pitch Accent Prominence Rule. In section 4.2 we describe two theories of phrase stress: the feature theory of SPE, and Liberman and Prince's metrical theory. We review Liberman and Prince's arguments in favor of a *relational* metrical tree representation of phrase stress and against the SPE's feature-based representation, and we show that the metrical grid theory is equally satisfactory in capturing the relational character of stress. We also review the arguments that more than a relational representation of stress is required, that there must be a representation in terms of which generalizations concerning *levels* and *patterns* of prominence may be expressed. Neither the SPE theory nor the metrical tree theory provides such a representation; we will claim that the metrical grid, however, does. Sections 4.2.2 (on levels and patterns) and 4.3 (on the

"Rhythm Rule") contribute to substantiating this claim. We are thus led inexorably toward the conclusion that the metrical grid is the one and only representation of phrasal rhythmic prominence.

4.1 Phrase Stress and Pitch Accents

4.1.1 The Nuclear Stress Rule and the Compound Rule

The various theories of phrase stress propounded in the generative tradition have sought to give expression to the generalization mentioned above, that the greatest word prominence of the rightmost constituent within a phrase is the most prominent on that phrase. According to this generalization, in the sentence *The mayor of Chicago won their support*, for example, the main-stressed syllable of *Chicago* is more prominent than that of *mayor,* the main-stressed syllable of *support* is more prominent than *won*, and the main-stressed syllable of *support* is the most prominent in the sentence as a whole. Let us first examine how this generalization might be expressed in a metrical grid framework. The grid representation of the prominence patterns described above would be as follows:

(4.1)

```
                              x
              x               x
x             x     x         x
```
The mayor of Chicago won their support

(For the sake of graphic simplicity we will not represent the first and second levels of the grid, unless they are relevant to the point at hand; the lowest level in (4.1) is thus the main word stress level, which we assume to be the third metrical level, for the reasons given in section 3.2.4.)

Pursuing the "grid construction" approach of chapter 3, we will view the representation (4.1) as having been derived, via the NSR, from an "earlier" representation consisting of the concatenation of words and their individual syllable-to-grid alignments. Seen in these grid terms, the NSR produces the prominences by adding beats in the appropriate positions on the appropriate levels. In doing so, of course, it makes crucial reference to the (surface) syntactic structure into which the words are organized (as does the NSR couched in any other theory of stress).[5] We suggest the following (informal) statement of the NSR.

(4.2)

Nuclear Stress Rule (informal version)

Within a given phrase, the beat of the metrical grid aligned with the rightmost immediate (daughter) constituent of the phrase that is (a) the most prominent beat of (that part of) the grid and (b) on at least the third metrical level is made the most prominent beat of the metrical grid aligned with the entire phrase.

This rule guarantees that the grid relations in (4.4) will be established on the basis of the grid relations and phrase structure in (4.3) and that the grid relations in (4.5) (= (4.1)) will be established on the basis of (4.4):

(4.3)

```
         x            x        x            x
s[NP[The mayor of Chicago]NP V[won their support]VP]S
```

(4.4)

```
                      x                     x
         x            x        x            x
s[NP[The mayor of Chicago]NP VP[won their support]VP]S
```

(4.5)

```
                                            x
                      x                     x
         x            x        x            x
s[NP[The mayor of Chicago]NP V[won their support]VP]S
```

The way in which the rule applies to derive (4.4) from (4.3) and (4.5) from (4.4) is quite straightforward. The rule will also generate the appropriate phrase stress pattern for the sentence *The mayor of Chicago won*.

(4.6)

```
                   x
     x             x        x
[The mayor of Chicago] [won]]
```

(4.7)

```
                           x
                   x       x
     x             x       x
[The mayor of Chicago] [won]]
```

Note that in this case, though *won* is less prominent than *Chicago* in (4.6) (the output of the NSR on the first cycle), it is nonetheless rendered most prominent when the NSR applies on the next cycle, as shown in (4.7). This is because the NSR requires that the greatest grid prominence within the domain upon which it is applying be localized within (i.e., coincide with the greatest grid prominence of) the part of the grid that is aligned with the rightmost immediate constituent in that domain, which in this case is the VP containing *won*.

There is one case in English where the NSR must not assign prominence to the rightmost constituent of a syntactic phrase: namely, in a sentence whose rightmost constituent is a personal pronoun, as in *The mayor of Chicago won it*. We will assume here that personal pronouns (and other function words) may fail to receive third-level word stress. (This position will be defended in chapter 7.) This assumption, coupled with the proviso in (4.2) that the NSR make more prominent only those beats that are at least on metrical level three, guarantees the correct derivation of the stress pattern in (4.10):

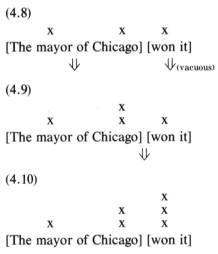

(4.8)

```
       x              x      x
[The mayor of Chicago] [won it]
       ⇓                  ⇓(vacuous)
```

(4.9)

```
                       x
       x              x      x
[The mayor of Chicago] [won it]
                       ⇓
```

(4.10)

```
                       x
                x      x
       x        x      x
[The mayor of Chicago] [won it]
```

Implied in these derivations is the assumption that the NSR applies cyclically, first on the lowest phrasal domain(s) and then on higher ones. We believe that it is indeed necessary to think of the metrical grid alignment of the utterance as being built up according to the principle of the cycle, a claim we will substantiate in section 4.4. These particular examples do not show the necessity of the cycle, however. In these cases, the NSR could equally well be viewed as a well-formedness condition on the entire metrical grid alignment of the sentence that is met simultaneously on every phrasal domain.[6]

There is one particularly interesting alternative formulation of the NSR within the framework of a metrical grid theory of stress that would also produce the stress patterns of (4.5), (4.7), and (4.10):

(4.2′)
Within a given syntactic phrase, the rightmost beat of the metrical grid (fragment) aligned with the (entire) phrase that is on at least the third metrical level is made the most prominent beat of that metrical grid (fragment).

We leave it to the reader to determine that (4.2′) gives the same results for the examples discussed.

The formulation (4.2′) is appealing as an alternative to (4.2) in that it makes no reference to the constituent structure inside the syntactic phrase upon which it is cycling and is thus consistent with a more restrictive theory of the relation between syntactic structure and the phonological structure that is the syllable-to-grid alignment than is possible with (4.2). However, there is one type of example that poses a problem for (4.2′), though not for (4.2). The example involves a phrase whose rightmost immediate constituent is itself a compound word, where the compound contains (at least) two words, each of which has a greatest prominence on at least the third metrical level. Within a compound, the Compound Rule (which we will formulate below) assigns greatest prominence to the left-hand constituent; however, on the next cycle up (4.2′) would modify those prominence relations, as shown in the (partial) derivation (4.11)–(4.13).

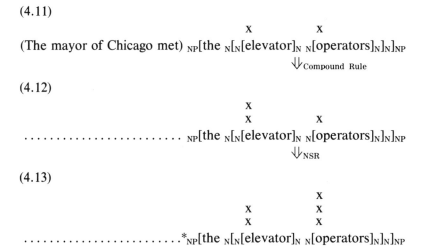

(4.11)

                 X   X

(The mayor of Chicago met) $_{NP}$[the $_N$[$_N$[elevator]$_N$ $_N$[operators]$_N$]$_N$]$_{NP}$

                     ⇓ Compound Rule

(4.12)

            X

            X   X

. . . . $_{NP}$[the $_N$[$_N$[elevator]$_N$ $_N$[operators]$_N$]$_N$]$_{NP}$

                    ⇓ NSR

(4.13)

                     X

            X   X

            X   X

. . . . $^*_{NP}$[the $_N$[$_N$[elevator]$_N$ $_N$[operators]$_N$]$_N$]$_{NP}$

The problem is that, within the domain of the NP *the elevator operators,* analyzed by the NSR in (4.12), the rightmost third-level prominence is the one on *operator*; therefore, unless otherwise constrained, (4.2′) will promote *operator* to the status of most prominent, as in (4.13). The formulation (4.2) encounters no such problems, restricted as it is to adjusting the relative prominences of the *immediate constituents* of the phrase to which it is applying. Since *operators* is not an immediate constituent of the NP *the elevator operators,* its own prominence will not be augmented by (4.2); rather, the relative prominence within the compound will be preserved. We are led, then, to retain the more elaborate version of the NSR in (4.2).

By comparing (4.2) to the more streamlined but inadequate (4.2′), we do not intend to imply that the theory of the relation between syntactic structure and phonological structure that (4.2) must presuppose is an undesirable one. The NSR formulated as (4.2) requires only the power to identify the immediate constituents of a phrase, more specifically, the immediate constituent at one extreme of the phrase (in this case the right one). It requires no other information about the structure of the phrase or the names of the categories involved.

The Compound Rule has similar properties. We express it informally as (4.14):

(4.14)
Compound Stress Rule
Within a given word, the beat of the metrical grid fragment aligned with the leftmost immediate constituent of the word that is both
(a) the most prominent beat of that fragment and (b) on at least the third metrical level is made the most prominent beat of the metrical grid (fragment) aligned with the entire word.

The NSR, expressed informally as (4.2), could be formalized in a variety of ways. We will suggest one possibility, both to facilitate comparison with formalizations made in other theoretical frameworks and to show how formally simple it in fact is. We could spell it out as in (4.15), where x_n is a metrical grid position and the ellipses are variables over sequences of grid positions in both the horizontal and the vertical dimensions.

(4.15)
Nuclear Stress Rule

$$x_j$$
$$\vdots$$

$_\alpha[\ldots\ _\beta[\ldots\ x_i\ \ldots]_\beta]_\alpha \Rightarrow\ _\alpha[\ldots\ _\beta[\ldots\ x_i\ \ldots]_\beta]_\alpha$

where α is a Phrase or S

Conditions: (a) x_i is first and last on its level
(b) x_i is on metrical level three or higher

This rule says just what (4.2) says. Operating on a cyclic domain α (a Phrase or S), it picks out the beat x_i in the rightmost immediate constituent β that is (i) most prominent within β (only a most prominent beat could be alone on its own metrical level in β) and (ii) on at least the third metrical level, and it adds positions to the grid in alignment with x_i, of which x_j is the topmost. What is not included in the rule is any condition ensuring that the highest grid position introduced will be greater than any other in the domain α. Nor is there one ensuring that such a position will be only minimally greater than the others. We do indeed want the rule to respect these conditions, but it is not necessary to make them part of the rule itself, since another quite general condition in the grammar already has the same effect—namely, the Textual Prominence Preservation Condition (3.39). This condition monitors the application of all text-to-grid alignment rules, ensuring that they produce greatest prominence on their respective cyclic domains and at the same time that the prominence is only the minimum required for satisfying the rule on the particular domain. With the TPPC, we are committing ourselves, following Prince 1981, to the claim that metrical grids are constrained in the vertical dimension, lacking superfluities in prominence.

Pursuing this impulse to formalization, we will write the Compound Rule as (4.16):

(4.16)
Compound Stress Rule

$$x_j$$
$$\vdots$$

$_\alpha[_\beta[\ldots\ x_i\ \ldots]_\beta\ \ldots]_\alpha \Rightarrow\ _\alpha[_\beta[\ldots\ x_i\ \ldots]_\beta\ \ldots]_\alpha$

where α is a category of type Word

Conditions: Same as for the NSR (4.15)

Both the Compound Rule and the NSR use the same type of conditions in the structural description of the metrical grid and the structural changes in the grid. They also appeal to the same general limited set of properties of syntactic structure: the category type (i.e., Word or Phrase) of the cyclic domain, and the analysis in terms of the immediate constituents at one limit or the other of the domain. We offer the hypothesis that this is the only information required for text-to-grid alignment rules like the NSR and the Compound Rule, which constitute one of the two components defining the mapping between syntactic structure and phonological structure.

4.1.2 The Pitch Accent Prominence Rule

The NSR and the Compound Rule are not the sole principles of the grammar responsible for specifying the location of the greatest rhythmic prominence within sentences. They are in fact principles whose effects are felt only when "all else is equal." And all else may fail to be equal when pitch accents are associated with the words in the domain on which the NSR is applying. We will leave the defense of the pre-NSR pitch accent association theory to the next chapter. Our purpose here is to describe the consequences of that theory for the NSR and the Compound Rule. In particular, we claim that the presence of a pitch accent within a given domain may in effect override the NSR or the Compound Rule on that domain. We put this claim in the form of a rule, (4.17). (The rule will be modified in section 5.3.)

(4.17)
Pitch Accent Prominence Rule (PAR)

A syllable associated with a pitch accent is more prominent (on the grid) than any syllable that is not associated with a pitch accent.

We will think of the PAR as "adding" one or more higher-level beats in the appropriate circumstances (cf. section 5.3). Through the offices of the PAR, a property of the text (the association of a pitch accent with a syllable) is reflected in the metrical grid alignment of the text. The PAR is thus a text-to-grid alignment rule. The important fact about the PAR is that it overrides all other rules of grid construction: no prominence, whether introduced by a text-to-grid assignment rule like the NSR or by a grid euphony rule like Beat Addition, will be more prominent than that of a pitch-accent-bearing syllable. The TPPC could guarantee the absolute precedence of the PAR over grid euphony rules. Because the

PAR has no syntactic domain (it is not a domain-end prominence rule), it can apply on every syntactic domain and thus by the TPPC will ensure greater prominence. The TPPC would not guarantee that the PAR will override the NSR and the Compound Rule, however. We must understand it to be in the nature of the rule itself that its requirements override the others'.

Consider now the two sentences in (4.18), which carry pitch accents. Following the PAR, they would have the metrical grid representations (4.19a) and (4.19b) (see section 5.2).

(4.18)

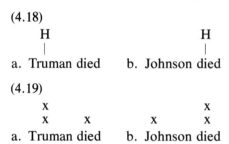

(4.19)
```
       X                     X
  X         X           X         X
a. Truman died      b. Johnson died
```

As Schmerling 1976 points out, the normal way of uttering *Truman died* would be as in (4.18a) if Truman, aged and forgotten, were not part of the previous discourse, either explicitly or implicitly.[7] (4.18b) would be natural if uttered during a period in which Johnson was widely known to be ill. Thus the presence of a pitch accent reflects in some way the "salience" of the accented element in the discourse (see chapter 5). And we are saying, with the PAR, that it entails some rhythmic prominence as well.

In fact, then, the effect of the NSR is only felt when everything *is* equal, that is, when it is the case that there are either two (or more) pitch-accented elements within a domain, or none. Consider, for example, the sentence with the pitch accent assignments in (4.20). The NSR will ensure the prominence of the second pitch accent, as indicated in (4.21).

(4.20)

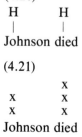

(4.21)
```
            X
   X        X
   X        X
Johnson died
```

With this analysis, then, it is the NSR that is responsible for the generalization that in English the nuclear pitch accent is always the most prominent. The nuclear pitch accent on our theory is simply the last pitch accent, and with the NSR last is greatest.

This theory of the NSR is essentially the one proposed by Newman 1946, if we take Newman's "heavy stresses" to be pitch-accent-bearing syllables. Newman's analysis was that the last heavy stress in a series of heavy stresses is the most prominent. Because not all words bear heavy stresses, this analysis does not automatically give rise to a nuclear stress on the final word in the sentence, for example. The main differences between this theory and Newman's are the claim that the NSR applies within phrases, not just on the highest domain, and the claim that it applies in the absence of pitch accents (heavy stresses) as well.[8]

Consider in this regard examples (4.22a,b). Through the combined effects of the NSR and the PAR, they translate into (4.23a,b).

(4.22)

$$H$$
$$|$$

a. [[The Queen of England] has expired]

$$H$$
$$|$$

b. [They love [the Queen of England]]

(4.23)

$$
\begin{array}{ccc}
 & & X_{PAR} \\
 & X_{NSR} & X_{PAR} \\
X & X & X
\end{array}
$$

a. The Queen of England has expired

$$
\begin{array}{ccc}
X_{PAR} & & \\
X_{PAR} & & X_{NSR} \\
X & X & X
\end{array}
$$

b. They love the Queen of England

In both (4.22) and (4.23), the noun phrase *the Queen of England* does not contain a pitch accent. There is a reliably greater rhythmic prominence on *England,* which is introduced by the NSR and noted with the subscript NSR. The positions subscripted PAR are those introduced by the PAR.

Our general claim is that in either pre- or postnuclear position, a non-pitch-accent-bearing syllable will be locally and reliably prominent if it is the last main-stressed syllable on a cyclic domain containing another stress word (but no pitch accents). This of course is the standard claim, though one denied by Bolinger 1958b, 1981 (see section 4.3.2).[9]

Our general approach to the rhythmic prominence relations exhibited within compound words is entirely analogous. It involves the claim that they reflect both the operation of a syntax-sensitive Compound Rule and, via the PAR, the operation of principles for assigning pitch accents to constituents of syntactic structure (on which, see sections 5.1 and 5.2). As such this proposal resembles in certain regards those of Ladd 1981 and Bolinger 1981, who note that prominence relations in compounds often reflect more about "information structure" than about syntactic structure. Thus the factual claim is this: a compound's greatest rhythmic prominence will occur within its left immediate (daughter) constituent when (i) neither, (ii) both, or (iii) only the left constituent contains a pitch accent, and its greatest rhythmic prominence will occur within its right daughter constituent when only that constituent (and not the left one) contains a pitch accent.[10] These claims will be investigated in sections 5.2 and 5.3. For the time being, we will focus on the NSR.

As we compare the various recent generative approaches to the representation of phrase stress, it is necessary to keep in mind that pitch accents are present in the normal pronunciations of the sentences to be investigated. We will try to use examples where pitch accent assignment and the results of the consequent application of the PAR are consistent with what the NSR would produce on its own.

4.2 Trees and/or the Grid?

4.2.1 Phrase Stress with Trees

Let us first review the standard SPE theory of the representation of phrase stress and of the characterization by rules of its regularities. Recall that in the standard theory degrees of stress (prominence) are represented by integer specifications of the distinctive feature [stress] (e.g., [1 stress], [2 stress], ... [n stress]) and that [1 stress] is the most prominent. Thus the standard theory representation corresponding to (4.1) is (4.24):

(4.24)

$$\overset{3}{\text{The}}\ \overset{}{\text{mayor}}\ \text{of}\ \overset{2}{\text{Chi}}\text{ca}\overset{3}{\text{go}}\ \overset{}{\text{won}}\ \text{their}\ \overset{1}{\text{sup}}\text{port.}$$

The mayor of Chicago won their support.

The standard theory analogue to the pre-NSR underlying representation (4.3) is (4.25), where each 1 designates a main word stress:

(4.25)

$_S[_{NP}$[The $\overset{1}{\text{mayor}}$ of $\overset{1}{\text{Chicago}}]_{NP}$ $_{VP}$[$\overset{1}{\text{won}}$ their $\overset{1}{\text{support}}]_{VP}]_{NP}$

And the NSR is formulated something like (4.26):

(4.26)
NSR (Standard Theory)

$$\overset{1}{V} \to \overset{1}{V} \, / \, _\alpha[P \underline{\quad\quad} Q]_\alpha$$

where α is a phrasal constituent or S

Condition: $Q \neq \ldots \overset{1}{V} \ldots$

In order to derive the appropriate relative degrees of stress, Chomsky and Halle propose that the NSR applies cyclically and that each operation of the rule (i.e., each (re)assignment of [1 stress] to the rightmost $\overset{1}{V}$ on the domain) is accompanied by the Stress Subordination Convention (SSC), which automatically reduces by one degree all other stresses on that same phrasal domain. Thus (4.25) gives rise to the following (cyclic) derivation:

(4.27)

$_S[_{NP}$[The $\overset{2}{\text{mayor}}$ of $\overset{1}{\text{Chicago}}]_{NP}$ $_{VP}$[$\overset{2}{\text{won}}$ their $\overset{1}{\text{support}}]_{VP}]_S$

$\Downarrow$

(4.28)

$_S[_{NP}$[The $\overset{3}{\text{mayor}}$ of $\overset{2}{\text{Chicago}}]_{NP}$ $_{VP}$[$\overset{3}{\text{won}}$ their $\overset{1}{\text{support}}]_{VP}]_S$

Consider next Liberman and Prince's metrical tree theory of phrasal prominence relations and the Nuclear Stress Rule. The insight captured in metrical theory is that stress is relational and thus to be distinguished from other, segment-bound phonological properties of an utterance. Liberman's 1975 proposal, elaborated in Liberman and Prince 1977, is that these prominence relations have their fundamental expressions in terms of a binary-branching tree whose nodes are labeled *s*(trong) or *w*(eak). Thus metrical tree theory represents the example sentence as follows:

(4.29)

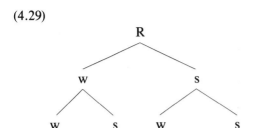

The mayor of Chicago won their support

(R is the *root* of the tree.) The simple principle that "strong is stronger than weak" guarantees the appropriate interpretation of this tree: *Chicago* and *support* are stronger than their respective weak sisters *mayor* and *won*, and the *s*-label on the node dominating *support* means that *support* is stronger than *Chicago*, the strong member of the sister weak constituent.

The metrical tree (4.29) mirrors the syntactic constituency of the sentence. For Liberman and Prince, this is no coincidence. They claim that relative prominence is a relation defined on syntactic constituent structure—that the metrical tree *is* the syntactic tree, with *s/w* labels supplied. Thus on their analysis principles of phrase stress like the NSR do not build trees, but merely label them. They state the NSR as follows:

(4.30)
NSR (Liberman and Prince)

In a configuration $_c[AB]_c$, if c is a phrasal category (or S),
B is strong.

(Since labeling one sister node *s* entails labeling the other *w*, (4.30) does ensure the full labeling of the tree.)

Liberman and Prince remark that many of the notions required in the standard phonological theory for a descriptively adequate treatment of stress are artifacts of the theory of stress as a segmental feature, and that these happily disappear once stress is understood in relational terms. They argue, then, that a metrical tree approach to stress is to be preferred, in that it rationalizes, or makes understandable, the various idiosyncratic properties of stress systems and is in that sense a more explanatory theory. We would like to show that Liberman and Prince's argument against standard stress theory and for a relational theory of stress, although certainly well taken in its general form, does not distinguish between a metrical tree theory of stress and the NSR and a metrical grid theory of stress and the NSR, both of which are relational in character.

As Liberman and Prince point out, the representation of stress itself is anomalous within the standard theory. Whereas all other distinctive features have binary specifications, the stress feature is crucially *n*-ary. Moreover, the nonprimary specifications of the stress feature have the peculiar property of being syntagmatic, defined only with respect to the presence of a primary stress somewhere else in the utterance. In this way, stress is unlike any other phonological property represented in terms of distinctive features. The standard theory simply encodes this difference, while giving no insight into the phenomenon. Once stress is understood in terms of a suprasegmental relational representation, however, its *n*-ary and syntagmatic characteristics simply follow. Given metrical grid theory, stress is *n*-ary because there is no principled limit to the number of metrical levels on which a beat may appear, and syntagmatic in the sense that a beat on a particular level is more or less prominent only with respect to the presence in the grid of beats on other lower or higher levels. Similarly, a metrical tree has built into it the notions that there are potentially infinitely many degrees of prominence and that degree of prominence is defined only with respect to the rest of the tree.

Liberman and Prince point out as well that the rules of the standard theory that embody generalizations about patterns of stress require certain conventions and formal devices that have no motivation in the grammar outside their role in describing stress. For example, the Stress Subordination Convention is a necessary concomitant of prominence-assigning rules in the standard theory, and it has, in a sense, long-distance effects: it demotes by one every other nonmain stress within the current (cyclic) domain. No convention with these general attributes plays a role in describing other sorts of phonological phenomena. The SSC need not play a role in the description of stress, either, if stress is understood in relational terms. With the metrical grid approach, the effect of subordination on the phrase is achieved by the NSR itself, which adds beats. In the representation produced by the NSR, the element whose prominence has been promoted to a higher metrical level by the rule is more prominent than any others on the same domain; the latter are in that sense subordinate to the former. With the metrical tree approach, the assignment of *s* to one node by the NSR entails the subordination of (assignment of *w* to) the sister node.

Liberman and Prince also assert that the crucial use of variables is peculiar to rules for describing stress in segmental terms. Actually, this assertion is only in part true. Abbreviatory variables of the sort commonly written with ellipses, or not written at all, are required in the rules describing many phonological phenomena, as long as these rules are thought of as applying on particular domains. For example, it seems correct to think of a rule of the form $A \rightarrow B / C \_\_\_\_ D$ as in fact being of the form $A \rightarrow B /\ _\alpha[\ldots C \_\_\_\_ D \ldots]_\alpha$, where α may be either a syntactic or a prosodic constituent.[11] What Liberman and Prince appear to have in mind is that the standard theory NSR makes crucial use of a variable with a negative condition, and that the use of this particular sort of variable seems to be peculiar to stress rules. Recall the standard statement of the NSR, repeated here:

(4.26)

$$\overset{1}{V} \rightarrow \overset{1}{V} /\ _\alpha[P \_\_\_\_ Q]_\alpha$$

Condition: $Q \neq \ldots \overset{1}{V} \ldots$

Given a segmental theory of stress, the condition on the Q variable is necessary in order that the *last* $\overset{1}{V}$ (which is not necessarily the final segment on the domain α) be picked out by the rule. The metrical grid theory does not require such a use of negative conditions on variables. The grid-based NSR simply identifies (and promotes) the greatest prominence of level three or higher within the last daughter constituent of the cyclic domain; hence, no "Q-variables" are required. As for the NSR of metrical tree theory, it obviously eliminates variables of any kind, since prominence relations are established locally, on adjacent nodes, at higher levels in the tree.

The principle of the cycle in phonology is another construct of the standard approach to stress that Liberman and Prince seek to eliminate with a relational theory of stress. To be sure, the metrical tree theory NSR requires no cyclic application; it can be satisfied simultaneously at all levels of the metrical tree. It would also be possible in principle for a grid-based NSR to be noncyclic and hence satisfied simultaneously for all constituents. However, we do not agree that it is either desirable or possible to eliminate the cycle from phonology in general. Liberman and Prince assert that the cycle is particular to stress-related phenomena in phonology. This point, it seems to us, is moot (see Kiparsky's 1982a work on the cycle, for instance); but even supposing it to be true, we are not led to view the cycle as an artifact of the representation of stress in segmental terms. The cycle does play a role elsewhere in the grammar, in the characterization of phenomena that have nothing to do with stress. The principle of the cycle says merely that if a rule of grammar has a syntactic domain, then it applies (or *may* apply) to a syntactic representation in cyclic fashion. Thus the existence of "cyclic effects" in phonology cannot be considered to reflect anything about the phonological representation itself. Rather, it would seem to reflect only the fact that (some) rules of grammar relevant to phonology—be they phonological rules or rules for building phonological representation (sections 1.3, 8.1)—have domains defined in terms of syntactic structure. For the cycle to be limited to stress rules would reveal nothing more than that only stress rules have syntactic domains.[12] Thus we see no a priori theoretical desirability in excluding the cycle from phonology.

It is important to realize that both relational theories of stress are consistent with the cycle. Earlier we sketched a cyclic derivation of a metrical grid representation of phrase stress. A cyclic derivation of a metrical tree representation is also possible. This is important because there is evidence that "stress rules" are indeed cyclic. Kiparsky 1979 and Hayes 1980 have argued that, within a metrical tree approach, English word stress must be cyclically assigned. We have argued the same in a metrical grid framework, and in section 4.4 we will offer evidence that certain aspects of phrase stress must be cyclically established as well. Thus we will consider the issue of the cycle irrelevant to evaluating the theories of stress that are under consideration.

So far, it seems that the metrical grid and metrical tree theories of stress score evenly, as theories of stress able to provide a more explanatory account than the standard nonrelational theory of the properties of prominence relations in general and the English Nuclear Stress Rule in particular. But is this equivalence real or only apparent? For metrical grid theory the descriptive task is to characterize the relation between the alignment of the syllables of an utterance with a metrical grid, on the one hand, and the organization of those syllables into a syntactic constituent structure, on the other. Our specific articulation of that relation is this: a set of principles that build up the grid, operating with respect to domains defined in terms of syntactic structure, in cyclic fashion. The NSR is one of this set of principles. For metrical tree theory, as espoused by Liberman and Prince, the descriptive task is taken to be somewhat different: the binary-branching tree of the representation *is* the syntactic structure tree, and thus all that is needed to characterize prominence relations is a set of rules for labeling the nodes *s/w*.

On the face of it, the metrical tree theory would seem to be the more desirable. It offers an extremely simple characterization of possible prominence patterns: the tree is independently given, and the rules for labeling trees would be very restricted in type. If the patterns of phrasal prominence attested in language are just those permitted in the metrical tree approach, it would seem that this theory should be preferred. But the picture is not quite so bright for metrical tree theory. As Liberman and Prince point out, not all prominence relations can be represented in terms of trees independently motivated on syntactic grounds. For example, prominence relations within words do not reflect in any systematic fashion the morphological structure of words.[13] Indeed, treatments of word stress in a metrical framework have typically included rules for *building* metrical trees on the basis of the syllables contained in the words, rules that refer to morphological structure but whose output does not necessarily mirror it. Thus in its treatment of word stress, a metrical tree theory, in its general form, parallels the metrical grid theory. In fact, the same sort of observation can be made about a metrical tree theory of phrase stress. The elegance and simplicity of Liberman and Prince's treatment of phrase stress relies on the claim that surface syntactic structure is appropriate as the shape of metrical tree, that syntactic structure and metrical structure are isomorphic. But it is not necessarily true that the constituency of syntax is reflected in the constituency of phonological representation (see Selkirk 1978c). Consider the fact that a single sentence may have several different intonational phrasings, and that it is within these intonational phrases that prominence relations are established (see chapter 5). The representations in (4.31) are all possible intonational phrasings of our familiar example, where parentheses demarcate the phrases and N marks the nuclear pitch accent.

(4.31)

a. (The mayor of Chicago won their suppᴺort)

b. (The mayor of Chicᴺago) (won their suppᴺort)

c. (The mayor of Chicago wᴺon) (their suppᴺort)

Such facts show that Liberman and Prince's contention that the syntactic structure of a sentence *is* its phonological structure is simply wrong, and that if a metrical tree theory of prominence relations is to be maintained, the metrical tree must be seen as independent of, though defined in relation to, the syntactic structure of a sentence. Given this, the metrical tree theory enjoys no particular advantage over the metrical grid theory in terms of simplicity or restrictiveness. (In this chapter, we will ignore the role of intonational phrasing with respect to rhythmic structure, however, and will assume that all the sentences discussed consist of only one intonational phrase. We return to the question of intonational phrasing in section 5.4.)

4.2.2 Levels and Patterns of Phrasal Prominence

Liberman and Prince's critique of the standard theory of stress is not confined to the point that, because it does not view stress in relational terms, it is clumsy and unilluminating. They also show that it is inadequate to describe even the most commonplace facts of phrase stress in English. The recalcitrant facts are of two basic types: they concern the proper treatment of *levels* and *patterns* of prominence. The important point, from our perspective, is that the metrical tree theory of stress, on its own, also cannot adequately handle these facts. It is for this reason that Liberman and Prince introduce the metrical grid. And it is for this reason that the status of the metrical tree representation in the theory is in question. If the metrical grid is needed to represent the essentially rhythmic level-and-pattern aspects of phrasal prominence, and if the relational aspects of phrasal prominence that metrical trees are taken to represent can be equally well (or even better) represented in terms of the metrical grid, as we have argued, then trees are obviously superfluous and should have no place in a theory of stress.

Consider for example the problem raised by Bierwisch 1968 and others for the standard theory of phrase stress: that in a multiply right-branching structure such as (4.32) the multiple (cyclic) applications of the standard NSR and its companion SSC would produce more differentiations in degree of stress, as in (4.33), than it is reasonable to suppose exist.

(4.32)
[Mary [tried [to begin [to fathom [the force [of Sara's [last remarks]]

(4.33)

$$\overset{2}{\text{Mary}} \; \overset{3}{\text{tried}} \; \text{to} \; \overset{4}{\text{begin}} \; \text{to} \; \overset{5}{\text{fathom}} \; \text{the} \; \overset{6}{\text{force}} \; \text{of} \; \overset{7}{\text{Sara's}} \; \overset{8}{\text{last}} \; \overset{1}{\text{remarks.}}$$

This great a number of stress levels has no basis in what speakers either perceive or produce. Further provisions would thus be required in the standard analysis to right the wrongs of the NSR plus the SSC.[14] A related problem is that a pattern of evenly descending prominences such as (4.33) exhibits before the main stress is simply not attested. In fact, the pattern of rhythmic prominences that a sentence like (4.32) does exhibit is one that the standard theory would be hard put to describe: there is rhythmic differentiation among the prenuclear elements (some are more prominent than others); differences in degree (or level) are not marked; and less prominent elements succeed more prominent ones in fairly regular fashion.[15] It is not at all clear what the character of the rules in the standard theory might be that would describe this sort of alternation. At the very least, they would involve some complex operation on successive integer values (thereby increasing the theory's power), where the notion "sameness of level" relevant to establishing the patterns would have to be arbitrarily specified.

As Liberman and Prince point out, the metrical tree theory displays the same sort of shortcomings as the standard theory with regard to representing and characterizing the levels and patterns of phrasal prominence in sentences like (4.32). The metrical tree for (4.32) would be (4.34):

(4.34)

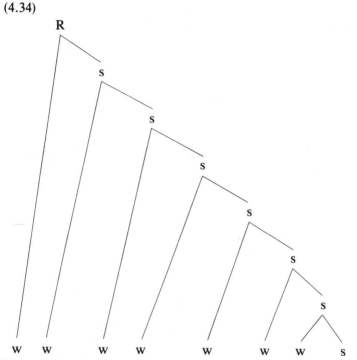

Mary tried to begin to fathom the force of Sara's last remarks

Such a tree is both too rich and too impoverished as a representation of
phrasal prominence—too rich because it in principle allows for all the
distinctions in level (degree) of stress found in the standard description,[16] too impoverished because it does not represent the patterns of
recurrent alternating prominence within the sentence. It is because
metrical trees are inadequate in this regard that Liberman and Prince
appeal to the metrical grid.

In Liberman and Prince's theory, the metrical grid is, in a sense, a
theory of the *interpretation* of metrical trees. Their idea is that a metrical tree maps onto a metrical grid representation according to the following convention (1977:316):

(4.35)

Relative Prominence Projection Rule (RPPR)

In any constituent on which the strong-weak relation is defined,
the designated terminal element of its strong subconstituent is
metrically stronger than the designated terminal element of its weak

subconstituent [where metrical strength is measured in terms of the height of a beat in the metrical grid].

The main thrust of the RPPR is to guarantee the appropriate characterization of *levels* of prominence.[17] The minimal grid configuration that conforms to the tree (4.34), following the RPPR, is (4.36).

(4.36)

```
                                                      x
    x   x         x   x         x       x   x       x
```
Mary tried to begin to fathom the force of Sara's last remarks.

Notice that the levels of prenuclear prominence are entirely flattened out here. As for the appearance of earlier prenuclear prominences, these would also be permitted by the RPPR, as long as they did not exceed the "nuclear" prominence. The grids of (4.37) are also (among the) possible realizations (interpretations) of (4.37) according to the RPPR:

(4.37)

```
                    x
     x      x   x   x
a.   x x x x x x x x

                    x
     x      x   x   x
b.   x x x x x x x x

                    x
     x      x       x
c.   x x x x x x x x
     etc.
```

Thus for Liberman and Prince the patterns and levels of phrase stress attested for a sentence like (4.32) are primarily a matter of the syllable-to-grid alignment of the sentence, where that alignment is determined by the organization of the sentence into a metrical tree and by the RPPR.

With Prince 1981, 1983, we claim that *all* aspects of the system of prominence relations of the sentence can, and should, be represented in terms of the metrical grid alone, without appeal to metrical trees. Note that, as Prince 1981, 1983 has observed, a grid-based NSR gives as its output the (minimal) representation (4.36), on the basis of the sentence structure (4.32). This is because the grid-based NSR simply requires that the greatest prominence of any constituent that is the rightmost daughter constituent in the domain be most prominent, minimally so, and this is in fact the case in (4.36). As for the tendency to an alternation in degrees of prominence before the final, nuclear prominence, this too is understandable. With the partial grid (4.36) as a base and with the essential (NSR) relations kept constant, additional prominences such as those in (4.37) are the predicted outputs of the grid euphony rule of Beat Addition, which acts to produce just those patterns of differentiation in prominence that are motivated by the PRA. (In section 4.4 we will examine phrasal Beat Addition and in particular its NSR-respecting character.)

The point that only the metrical grid appropriately represents and characterizes levels and patterns of phrasal prominence can be made on the basis of other sorts of examples, in particular ones involving left-branching structures. Consider the locutions of (4.38):

(4.38)

[[cross country] skiing]	[[ten feet] long]
[[brick chimney] red]	[[next door] neighbor]
[[clear blue] sky]	the [[U Mass] campus]

The standard theory NSR-plus-SSC would assign an ascending pattern of prominence to these expressions, as for example in (4.39).

(4.39)

$$\overset{1}{[[}\text{next }\overset{1}{\text{door}}]\ \overset{1}{\text{neighbor}}] \rightarrow \text{(Cycle 1)}$$

$$\overset{2}{[[}\text{next }\overset{1}{\text{door}}]]\ \overset{1}{\text{neighbor}}] \rightarrow \text{(Cycle 2)}$$

$$\overset{3}{[[}\text{next }\overset{2}{\text{door}}]\ \overset{1}{\text{neighbor}}]$$

But this is not the attested stress pattern. Instead, the second strongest stress is shifted back to an earlier position in the phrase: *nèxt door néighbor, cròss country skíing, clèar blue ský*, etc. As Liberman and Prince point out, the standard theory cannot explain why such a stress shift should occur, nor can it perspicuously define the operation of the stress shift rule or the circumstances under which it applies. (See the elaboration of this point in Liberman 1975:234ff. and Liberman and Prince 1977:311ff.) The phenomenon of stress shift, Liberman and Prince argue, requires that prominence relations be represented in terms of the metrical grid.

The grid representation of *next door neighbor* that would be the output either of the grid-based NSR or of the metrical tree-plus-RPPR approach would be (4.40).

(4.40)

next door neighbor

(Recall that we are only noting metrical level three and above, for the moment.) (4.40) is clearly an ill-formed grid, if grids are understood to be well formed only if they conform to the PRA. The circled configuration is what Liberman and Prince have dubbed a *stress clash*. A stress clash is a grid configuration in which two strong positions are not separated by a weak. It is when a stress clash arises, Liberman and Prince assert, that a stress shift ensues. Their point, then, is that the metrical grid is necessary to properly characterize the circumstances under which stress shift occurs. The grid also explains why there should be a rule of stress shift at all: the rule's function is to restore well-formedness to the grid.

For reasons that will become clear below, Liberman and Prince cling to characterizing the *mechanism* of stress shift in metrical tree terms. Their rule, which they call *Iambic Reversal,* is formulated as follows (1977:319):

(4.41)
Iambic Reversal (optional)

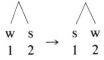

Conditions: 1. Constituent 2 does not contain the designated terminal element of an intonational phrase.
2. Constituent 1 is not an unstressed syllable.

The rule is understood to operate only in contexts where a "pressure" for change is manifested in the metrical grid. Thus Liberman and Prince's theory construes the tree-plus-grid representation (4.42) as being the object upon which stress shift operates:

(4.42)

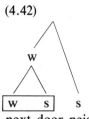

next door neighbor

```
          x
     x    x
x    x    x
```

The rule reverses the boxed *ws* labels, and the RPPR automatically reinterprets the grid, so that the full output of the rule is as follows:

(4.43)

next door neighbor

```
          x
x         x
x    x    x
```

We maintain, however, that a tree-based formulation of the "Rhythm Rule" expresses no generalization whatsoever that cannot be expressed by a rule formulated purely in terms of the metrical grid, and we will uphold this claim in the following section.

The stress shift rule to be used in our demonstration is formulated as follows:[18]

(4.44)
Beat Movement

$$\begin{array}{c} x_i \ x \\ x \ x \ x \end{array} \Rightarrow \begin{array}{c} x_i \ \ \ x \\ x \ x \ x \end{array}$$

Condition: x_i is a weak beat

(Recall the definition of strong and weak beats from chapter 2: a strong beat is aligned with a beat on the next higher metrical level, a weak beat is not. Recall also our speculation that it may be unnecessary to include this condition in the rule itself, since the condition that, of two clashing beats, it is the weak(er) one that moves (or deletes) may be quite general.) The rule would take as input a representation like (4.40) and give as output the representation (4.45).

(4.45)

```
            x
x           x
x     x     x
```
next door neighbor

Our grid-based "rhythm rule" is cast as a "movement" rule, following the suggestion by Prince 1981, 1983. A clashing beat is displaced to the left, landing on the next beat over of the next metrical level down. In section 4.3 we will show that this simple rule is a perfectly adequate characterization of the *mechanism* of stress shift, and in particular that the various features of the metrical tree rule (4.41) are unnecessary. We will show as well that the structural description of rule (4.44) adequately characterizes the *conditions* under which stress shift takes place (that is, the *pressure* for change). Given this, the fate of metrical trees would seem to be sealed: banishment to the archives of the history of ideas.

We have claimed that the "Rhythm Rule," our Beat Movement, is asymmetrical, only shifting prominence to the left. Reasons for considering this to be true were given in chapter 2. In presenting the general theory of grid euphony rules in chapter 2, we allowed in principle for Beat Movement in the opposite direction, so that what must be specified in the grammar of English, given our framework, is (a) the presence of Beat Movement (in the language) and (b) its left-moving character. There is some indication that right-deleting Beat Deletion operates in English, taking the place of right-moving Beat Movement in the grammar. In a clash where the strong beat precedes the weak, as in compounds like *sports contest,* the weaker beat may simply disappear, creating even stresses in *contest.* (Gimson 1970:230 distinguishes between two sorts of prominence of the second element of a compound, speaking of a loss of rhythmic beat in cases where the prominences of the component words are too close.) So quite possibly right-deleting Beat Deletion operates in English. There is a sense in which Beat Movement and Beat Deletion are the same rule. The function of both is to eliminate clashes by moving/deleting the weaker beat in the clash. It is perhaps because they are the same rule that they are, apparently, in complementary distribution. Conceivably, the theory makes available only one subpart of its clash-resolving strategy for either direction. In English, Beat Movement is for the left, and Beat Deletion is for the right.

4.3 The "Rhythm Rule"

4.3.1 The Superfluousness of Trees

The considerations that lead Liberman and Prince to a tree-bound formulation of the "Rhythm Rule" are not compelling, as we will show. Yet we believe it will be useful to look at them in detail, for the discussion will raise some points of central interest to the overall study.

The first argument Liberman and Prince present concerns the derivation of *Ténnessèe áir* from *Tènnessée áir*. The pre-shift representation they assume for the phrase is shown in (4.46).

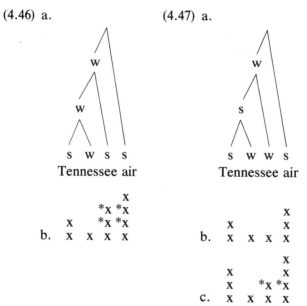

The tree of *Tennessee air* in (4.46) is constructed according to the principles of word stress, the relative prominence of the two words in the phrase is obtained through Liberman and Prince's (syntactic) tree-labeling NSR, and the grid with which the tree is associated is dictated by the RPPR. The asterisks mark the clash configuration produced in the grid. Liberman and Prince claim that the representation that results from applying stress shift to (4.46) is the tree of (4.47a) with the accompanying grid (4.47b), not the grid (4.47c). They point out that the derivation of (4.47a,b) is just what would be predicted given a tree-based stress shift rule like (4.41). The rule would invert the *s* involved in the clash and its sister *w*; as an automatic consequence the RPPR would reapply, giving the grid (4.47b). Liberman and Prince do not explore any alternative formulations in terms of the grid, but assert that if there were a grid-based rule, it could eliminate the upper clash but not the lower one, and hence would derive (4.47c). They claim that this is the wrong result and conclude that stress shift must be formulated in terms of trees.

Their argument has three crucial weaknesses. The first is the claim that the appropriate grid representation of the output of stress shift to *Tennessee air* is (4.47b), not (4.47c); the second is that the representation (4.47c) is in principle unacceptable; and the third is that, assuming (4.47b) to be correct, a grid-based analysis would be unable to derive it in as straightforward and illuminating a way. If any of these claims can be shown to be false, then the argument does not go through. We will focus on the untenability of the first claim, because it reflects a more general problem in Liberman and Prince's analysis, which concerns the difficulty of assigning the appropriate metrical strengths (levels of grid alignment) to syllables on the basis of the *s/w*-labeled metrical tree alone. In the course of the discussion, it will become clear that the second and the third claims are false as well.

The evidence Liberman and Prince offer for representation (4.47b) is the fact that stress-shifted *Ténnessèe* has the same stress pattern as *ínstitùte*. Given their analysis of English word stress, *institute* has the prominence relations represented by the tree (4.48a) and hence, by the RPPR, a grid alignment like (4.48b).

(4.48)

a.

s ww
institute

b. x   x
    x xx   c. x xx

Thus, their argument goes, applying stress shift to (4.46) must give the same representation for *Tennessee*; hence, the rule must be tree-based.

Note that both *institute* and stress-shifted *Tennessee* have a final stressed syllable and thereby contrast with *Pamela,* which does not. For Liberman and Prince, this is a contrast that has no place in the metrical tree and hence none in the metrical grid. It is represented solely in the assignment of the feature [+stress] to the last syllable of the former two words and of [−stress] to the last syllable of the third. Their general position is that the RPPR takes into account nothing but the strong-weak relations represented in metrical trees. Yet even they acknowledge that this position is overly strong, that the RPPR cannot be the sole principle determining the grid alignment of syllables. They suggest, for example, that if an *s*-labeled syllable is a Word, it must be given more metrical strength on the grid than if it is less than a Word (p. 322). This is needed to account for a difference in the likelihood of stress shift between *good-looking lifeguard* and *Montana cowboy,* which we will discuss in the next section. In a way, this particular proposal by Liberman and Prince anticipates our more general analysis of main word stress as being an alignment with at least the third level of the metrical grid. And it moves toward the idea that we have been promoting here that stress is not strictly relational, that some inherent *level* of stress is to be ascribed to such notions as "main word stress," "stressed" (vs. "stressless"), etc. Suppose now, pursuing this line within Liberman and Prince's framework, that a [+stress] syllable were always aligned with a greater grid prominence than a [−stress] syllable. If this were true, then the grid alignment of *institute* would be (4.48c), and the surface grid alignment of *Tennessee air* wherein *Tennessee* is claimed to be the same as *institute* would be (4.47c). (This is of course what we believe it should be, given our theory that a "stressed" sylla- ble is simply one aligned with a basic beat on the second metrical level (chapter 3).) But if (4.47c) is appropriate, then Liberman and Prince's argument that stress shift is a tree rule falls through (and they could just as well adopt Beat Movement (4.44)). For Liberman and Prince to pre- serve the argument, then, they would have to argue that it was not possible, for empirical reasons, to assign [+stress] syllables to a higher prominence. They would be hard put to do so.

In sum, Liberman and Prince's argument for stating the "Rhythm Rule" in terms of the tree relies on an assumption about the translation of metrical trees into metrical grids that is hardly inviolable in their own theory. Loosening this assumption—that the tree-grid relation is defined uniquely by the RPPR—means giving up the argument. On our theory, stressed syllables are aligned with a second-level grid position, main-word-stressed syllables with a third-level position at the least, and "phrase-stressed" syllables (usually) with at least a fourth-level position. Thus the pre-shift representation of *Tennessee air* is (4.47b) alone, without (4.47a), and (4.47b) is mapped into (4.47c) by Beat Movement.

What, then, of the stress clash that remains in the lower levels of (4.47c), the grid that Liberman and Prince reject? The question for our analysis is why Beat Movement does not apply to remove the clash. Our answer is simply this: Beat Movement does not apply at the lowest levels of the grid. The rationale behind this restriction is that it allows the basic beat alignments of syllables to remain intact and allows rules of grid euphony such as Beat Movement to manipulate only the relative prominences of the stressed syllables, not the patterns of stressed and unstressed syllables. We could reformulate our rule to reflect this restriction, but we will not. Instead we will attribute it to a quite general condition, (4.49). (Dell (to appear) observes that something very like this operates in French as well.)

(4.49)
Basic Beat Level Integrity (BBI)
Rules of grid euphony may not move or delete basic beats.

Thus we accept in effect that a clash is present at the lowest levels, suggesting that it is tolerated because the language resists altering the original alignment of syllables into basic beats.[19]

In Liberman and Prince's treatment the work of this condition is done, in a sense, by condition 2 on Iambic Reversal, (4.41). Condition 2 stipulates that an unstressed syllable may not receive a prominence shifted by the rule. It reflects the fact that while *àbstráct árt* becomes *ábstràct árt, cŏntént cóws,* with a stressless initial *cŏn-,* cannot turn into *cóntent cóws.* Because on Liberman and Prince's account both prenominal adjectives have the same prominence relations, [w s], the rule requires an additional condition appealing to the feature [stress]. Given the grid-based approach, of course, there is no such mixing of apples and oranges. All generalizations about stress shift are cast strictly in grid terms.

Let us consider now another possible argument for using metrical trees in the formulation of the "Rhythm Rule." Note that condition 1 of rule (4.41) states that reversal may not take place if the *s* is dominated by the *designated terminal element* (DTE) of an intonational phrase. Liberman and Prince define the notion DTE in terms of metrical trees: the DTE of an intonational phrase (or any smaller subtree) is the *s*-labeled syllable of the intonational phrase (or subtree) that is dominated by no *w*-labeled node. Put simply, it is the most prominent syllable of a constituent. Presuming that it were true that the stress shift rule, or any other, needed to refer to the DTE, in order to sustain an argument for stress shift in terms of metrical trees instead of the grid, it would have to be the case that no analogue to the DTE of a phrase could be defined in grid terms. But this is not the case. Indeed, the greatest prominence of the grid (within a phrase) can easily be defined—it is simply the beat that stands alone on a metrical level (within that phrase); by the very nature of the grid, any beat that stands alone on a level must be at the highest level. The syllable aligned with that beat is, of course, the most prominent syllable (within that phrase). Thus, were the notion DTE to be required, it would not reflect a need for metrical trees.

As it turns out, there is no need for the notion DTE or its grid equivalent in the "Rhythm Rule." We submit that the rule as we have formulated it gives exactly, and only, the information about relative prominence that is relevant to stress shift phenomena in English. It says "Move the beat that is less prominent." (It also says, like Liberman and Prince's formulation, that the movement goes only leftward.) Some indication of relative prominence is required in Liberman and Prince's rule, in order to account for the different possibilities of stress shift in pairs that would seem to contrast only in the relative prominence of their clashing elements. (We have put it in the form of a general condition.) Liberman and Prince note, for example, that in the compound $_N$[Chinése èxpert]$_N$ 'expert on Chinese' the greatest prominence on *Chinese* remains on the final syllable, whereas in $_{NP}$[Chìnese éxpert]$_{NP}$ 'an expert who is Chinese', greatest prominence shifts to the first syllable of the word. The difference is attributable to a difference in prominence relations at the supraword level: left prominence in the compound, right prominence in the phrasal collocation. In grid terms the difference would be represented as follows:

(4.50)

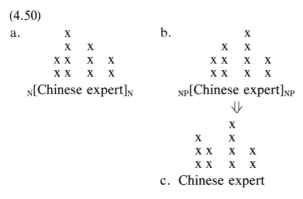

c. Chinese expert

Only (4.50b) satisfies the structural condition of Beat Movement, which changes it to (4.50c). Similar pairs are numerous: $_N$[plate gláss fàctory]$_N$ 'a factory making plate glass' vs. $_{NP}$[plàte glass fáctory]$_{NP}$ 'a factory made of plate glass' (cf. *plàte gláss*), $_N$[Indian súmmer lòver]$_N$ 'a lover of Indian summer' vs. $_{NP}$[Ìndian summer lóver]$_{NP}$ 'a lover in Indian summer' (cf. Ìndian súmmer), $_N$[kangaróo rìder]$_N$ vs. $_{NP}$[kàngaroo cóurt]$_{NP}$ (cf. *kàngaróo*). (It is worth pointing out in this connection Bolinger's 1981 observation that when each element of a compound bears a pitch accent, the greatest prominence falls on the right-hand one,[20] as a consequence of which stress shift may apply. Thus $_N$[Chínese éxpert]$_N$, when both elements bear a pitch accent.) The conclusion, of course, is that the rule must somehow take account of relative prominence.

Our formulation makes different predictions than a rule stating instead that the DTE of an intonational phrase cannot move, whether that rule is cast in tree terms, like Liberman and Prince's, or in grid terms. According to Liberman and Prince's rule, a prominence that is stronger than the one it clashes with *can* move, to the left, so long as it is not a DTE. Our formulation excludes such a movement. The evidence that Liberman and Prince give in support of their particular formulation is disputable, however. They observe that in the normal isolation pronunciation of *kangaroo rider* the greatest prominence is on *-roo,* and stays there. With this observation we concur. They then say that, when *kangaroo rider* is embedded in a phrase where greatest prominence (the DTE) is no longer on *-roo* but on some later syllable in the phrase, the expression has two pronunciations, one in which the prominence stays on *-roo,* as above, and one in which greater prominence falls on *kan-.* The latter prominence cannot be derived by our rule (though it can by Liberman and Prince's), but we would claim that our rule is quite right in not deriving it. Cast in grid terms, the pre-shift representation of Liberman and Prince's *kangaroo rider's saddle* would be (4.51) (assuming the presence of a pitch accent on both *kangaroo* and *saddle*):

(4.51)

```
                  x
        x         x
        x   x     x
  x     x   x     x
  x    x x  x x   x    x
kangaroo rider's saddle
```

The Pitch Accent Prominence Rule (PAR) (or the Compound Rule) gives prominence to *kangaroo* over *rider,* and the NSR gives prominence to *saddle* over *kangaroo.* With respect to our Beat Movement rule, this configuration is quite stable—the structural description of the rule is simply not met. But for Liberman and Prince's Iambic Reversal, since *-roo* is not the DTE, it may (optionally) lose its prominence to *kanga-.* The factual claim requires careful examination. It seems that in general in a configuration like (4.51) stress shift does *not* take place. Compare the examples in (4.52) to *kangaroo rider's saddle:*

(4.52)

[public lòo] workers' báttle, *not* *[pùblic loo] workers' báttle
[Asian làw] experts' árticle, *not* *[Àsian law] experts' árticle
[Tennessèe] lovers' convéntion, *not* *[Tènnessee] lovers' convéntion
etc.

These examples have the same basic properties as Liberman and Prince's example, yet a leftmost locus of secondary prominence is highly disfavored, if not impossible. The ungrammaticality of the shift in examples like the first two is all the more telling, since, as Liberman and Prince point out in discussing another point, stress shift is generally more likely with compounds than with simple words (compare *good-looking lifeguard* and *Montana cowboy*). Thus it would not seem to be generally true that, once liberated from the weight of the DTE, a locally strong prominence is free to move to avoid a clash. We can speculate, then, that the *kanga-* prominence that Liberman and Prince find acceptable reveals some idiosyncratic property of *kangaroo,* but nothing about principles of the rhythmic organization of English phrases. Thus we will retain our more constraining formulation, (4.44). As for Liberman and Prince's rule of Iambic Reversal, these facts suggest discarding condition 1 and substituting a different one, to the effect that the syllable dominated by *s* must be metrically weaker than the other syllable entering into the clash. This change would make the rule nearly equivalent to Beat Movement, accompanied by the general condition that only the weak move.

Instead of taking such a tack, Kiparsky 1979 has proposed a tree-based formulation of the "Rhythm Rule," shown in (4.53), that builds in the restriction that only the weaker prominence in the clash will move.

(4.53)

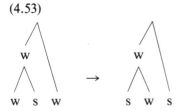

However, this rule and Beat Movement do not describe the same array of facts. Indeed, the formulation in (4.53) is too restrictive, not allowing for instances of stress shift that do in fact occur. The problem arises with examples like those in (4.53). (See Dell's (to appear) discussion of these cases.)

(4.54)
a. rather lìly white hánds   (lìly whíte)[21]
b. a really rìght on rádio show   (rìght ón)
c. a post-Kàfkaesque nóvel   (Kàfkaésque)
d. fourteen tòo many tíckets   (tòo mány)
e. a slightly ùnderripe péar   (ùnderrípe)

These examples have the syntactic constituent structure shown in (4.55a), and thus would presumably have the pre-shift metrical tree structure (4.55b):

(4.55)

a.   b.   c.

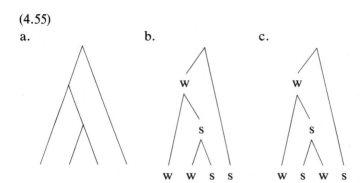

In isolation, all the medial constituents are pronounced with final prominence; given stress shift as formulated by Kiparsky, this prominence should remain final, since the constituent is not sister to the strong on the right. Yet a very natural pronunciation in these cases is one where the prominence shifts to the first element of the medial constituent, as indicated in (4.54). In metrical tree terms, the representation of the derived pattern of (4.54a–e) would be (4.55c). Since rule (4.53) cannot derive this pattern, Kiparsky's formulation must be incorrect.

On the other hand, the grid-based formulation derives these examples perfectly straightforwardly. (4.56) shows a (cyclic) derivation of the pre-shift pattern, and (4.57) gives the output of applying Beat Movement to that representation:

(4.56)

$$_3[_2[\text{rather }_1[\text{lily white}]_1]_2 \text{ [hands]}]_3$$

	x	x	x	x
	x	x	x	x
"word stress"	x x	xx	x	x
Cycle 1			x	
		x	x	
		x	x	
		xx	x	
Cycle 2			x	
	x	x	x	
	x	x	x	
	x x	xx	x	

Cycle 3

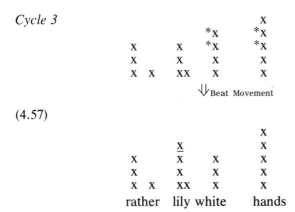

(4.57)

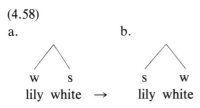

On cycle 1, the NSR promotes by one the prominence of *white* (or a pitch accent on *white* ensures its prominence, by the PAR). On cycle 2, no further modification is required: *rather* and *lily* are both less prominent than *white* and may stay equivalent in prominence to each other. On cycle 3, the relevant clash is created, and Beat Movement steps in to move the offending beat one to the left, placing it on *lily,* as in (4.57).

Note, too, that Liberman and Prince's formulation (revised as we have suggested) is unhampered by the extra branch in the structural description of (4.53) and therefore does not encounter its problems. With this formulation, the reversal of (4.58a) to (4.58b), extracted from the larger (4.55), is possible:

(4.58)

a.   b.

```
      /\                      /\
     w   s                   s   w
   lily white    →         lily white
```

There is an alternative pronunciation of the phrases in (4.54) wherein the second greatest prominence is at the far left, as in *ràther lily-white hánds, fòurteen too many tíckets, a rèally right on rádio show, pòst-Kafkaesque nóvel, a slìghtly underripe péar.*[22] In this case, the two parts of the medial constituent may be equally prominent, or one may be more prominent than the other. Let us see how such pronunciations are derived for *rather lily white hands:*

(4.59)

$_3[_2[$rather $_1[$lily white$]_1]_2$ [hands]$]_3$

```
                      x        x     x       x
                      x        x     x       x
"word stress"         x   x    xx    x       x
Cycle 1                              x
                               x     x
                               x     x
                               xx    x
Cycle 2                              x
NSR, BA               x̲              x
                      x        x     x
                      x        x     x
                      x   x    xx    x
Cycle 3                                      x
                                     *x      *x
                      x              *x      *x
                      x        x     x       x
                      x        x     x       x
                      x   x    xx    x       x
```

(4.60)

```
                                             x
                      x̲                      x
                      x      (x) or (x)      x
                      x        x     x       x
  ⇒                   x        x     x       x
                      x   x    xx    x       x
                    rather   lily white    hands
```

The crucial difference between this derivation and the earlier one is in cycle 2. In (4.56), Beat Addition did not apply; we are assuming that it is optional on the phrase. In (4.59), however, Beat Addition does apply, creating a greater prominence on *rather* (the underlined x̲), with the consequence that *white* is promoted one more, in order to preserve the NSR-dictated greatest prominence, in accord with the TPPC. On the next cyclic domain in (4.59), then, there is a clash at two levels. The one at the highest level is resolved by moving the offending beat to the closest beat on the next level down (the underlined x̲ in (4.60)), thus deriving the secondary prominence on *rather*.

What about the clashing beat on the next level down in the last cyclic domain of (4.59)? In (4.60) that beat is represented as being optionally present in either of two places. Suppose that the lower clashing beat had not undergone Beat Movement. Then it would remain there. (We are claiming that Beat Deletion in English does not operate when the weak is followed by a strong.) Suppose instead that it had undergone Beat Movement. Then the moved beat, now adjacent to the stronger beat on *rather,* is in position to undergo Beat Deletion. It might not, since Beat Deletion is optional. But if it did, the result would be even stress on *lily white.* There are thus three options for relative prominence on *lily white* when it is flanked by greater prominence on both *rather* and *hands:* greater prominence to the right or the left, or equal prominence on both members. And this seems to correctly predict the facts.

Although Liberman and Prince's stress shift rule can derive the appropriate prominence on the leftmost constituent in these cases, it cannot derive the evenly stressed alternative for the medial constituent. From (4.55b), Iambic Reversal can derive either (4.61a) or (4.61b), both with *s* on the leftmost constituent:

(4.61)

a.   b.

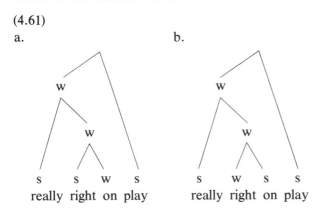

really right on play   really right on play

But there is no way to derive even stress, on the basis of the tree alone. In general, even stress on sister constituents is a problem for Liberman and Prince's theory, since according to the RPPR, a strong must be stronger than its weak sister in a metrical tree.[23] Thus if the facts are as we have described—if even stress is indeed a possibility—then the metrical tree theory of stress, with the RPPR, appears to create a problem for itself that it cannot avoid.

Summing up, then, we have shown so far that a metrical tree approach to stress shift expresses no generalizations that cannot be expressed in the simple grid-based rule of Beat Movement. We have compared Beat Movement (Prince's Move *x*) to Liberman and Prince's Iambic Reversal and Kiparsky's Rhythm Rule. It has emerged that Kiparsky's version of the tree-based rule does not cover all the data. Liberman and Prince's rule does not suffer from this defect. Thus the central comparison is between Liberman and Prince's tree-based version of stress shift and the grid-based Beat Movement. We have shown that our system of grid euphony rules (including Beat Movement and Beat Addition), applying cyclically on successively higher syntactic domains, is able to generate exactly the same set of shifted patterns as Liberman and Prince's Iambic Reversal rule. Though we have taken issue with certain facts analyzed by Liberman and Prince (concerning *kangaroo rider's saddle*), arguing that *any* local prominence, whether a DTE or not, must not be moved, these facts are not central to the comparison, since either a tree-based or a grid-based rhythm rule can express the appropriate constraint. The point, then, is that our grid theory of the rhythm rule and Liberman and Prince's tree theory of the rhythm rule cover the same facts. This simply means that trees are superfluous, since an appeal to the grid is needed to characterize the "pressure" for the shift in the first place.

We have also shown that the underpinnings of the tree-based theory of stress shift have serious defects. The RPPR, which translates the metrical tree into a metrical grid appropriate for the characterization of stress clash, appears to make wrong predictions about relative prominence in the pronunciation of certain sentences. Not only is it too strong, predicting the existence of relative prominences where there actually are none (as in the cases of even stress); it is also too weak, as indicated earlier in the discussion of *Tennessee air,* failing to consistently give great enough prominence to both stressed syllables and main word stress. The metrical grid theory has no such drawbacks. We conclude, therefore, that we should dispense entirely with trees and limit ourselves to the grid, the representation by which all the true generalizations about rhythmic organization may be simply and satisfactorily expressed.

4.3.2 The Need for the Grid
Two fundamental facts about the "Rhythm Rule" (our Beat Movement) have not yet been mentioned. First, it does not always apply, even when the prominence relations of the elements involved would seem to indicate a clash. Second, when Beat Movement does not apply, the unshifted syllable is longer than it would have been had a shift occurred. Liberman and Prince consider the rule to be optional, and they argue that it is in terms of the metrical grid—and only in terms of it—that the "variability" in its application can be explained. We agree that the rule is optional, and in this section we will investigate, in a prelimi-

nary fashion, the factors that determine whether it is more or less likely to apply. We will also seek to explain the above-mentioned correlation between syllable length and (lack of) Beat Movement. Liberman and Prince do not really take a position on the latter topic, though they suggest in passing (p. 320) that the rule is impeded if the syllable has undergone phrase-final lengthening. The explanation we will offer for the "blocking" of Beat Movement develops this suggestion along slightly different lines and in more explicit terms. We will also allow for the possibility that in a situation where Beat Movement is (for some reason independent of final lengthening) either impossible or simply not chosen to apply, another sort of "phonetic" lengthening is consequently introduced.

It seems worthwhile to extend as far as possible this claim that the grid itself provides the only information relevant to determining whether stress shift will occur and thus the claim that Beat Movement has simply the formulation (4.44). These ideas turn out to be remarkably valuable, in conjunction with three additional and very useful assumptions. The first is that syntactic "constituent breaks" are translated into grid terms by Silent Demibeat Addition (SDA) (chapters 1 and 6). Clearly SDA will be responsible for a fair amount of the variability in Beat Movement, both because it distinguishes between syntactic environments and because (in some contexts at least) it may be optional. The second assumption is that factors concerning the "stress-timed" realization of the grid may push in favor of avoiding the clash. And the third is that, because it may favor clash avoidance, the presence of a pitch accent is to be viewed as translating into an extra level of rhythmic prominence in the grid. It is these additional, rather natural assumptions that make it possible to continue to construe the "Rhythm Rule" in entirely grid terms. We thus disagree with Bolinger 1981, who sees the prominence shift phenomenon not in terms of an elaborated multilayer rhythmic structure, but rather in terms of an impulse to arrive at an optimal pitch contour. At the end of this section we will examine Bolinger's proposal, explaining why we believe it to be incorrect.

Factors other than the strictly syntactic contribute as well to setting off one word from another in time. For instance, the unfamiliarity of a word or of its appearance in a certain phrasal collocation or a certain discourse apparently may influence its timing and in particular may give rise to a pause before it.[24] Compare for example the pronunciation of a proper name used when a person is being introduced in unfamiliar company to the one used when acquaintances are referring to the person among themselves: "This is Alice O'Brian" vs. "How is Alice O'Brian these days?" In the first case there is a pause before the (unfamiliar) proper name. These subtle differences in rhythmic realization also have their place in the grid, we believe, as silent beats. One indication of this (noted by Bolinger 1981) is their ability to influence the "Rhythm Rule."

One specific suggestion we make is that the silent beats introduced by SDA may in effect "undo" a clash that might have otherwise been present if the underlying metrical grid alignment of the sentence were simply the alignment of its syllables with the grid according to the prominence principles outlined here. For example, word stress and the NSR will give (4.62) for both *Marcel Proust* and *Marcel proved (it)*.

(4.62)

```
                x
        x       x
    x   x       x
    x   x       x
Marcel ⎡Proust     ⎤
       ⎣proved (it)⎦
```

But suppose that the rules of syntactic timing are as follows:

(4.63)
a. Optionally, place a demibeat at the end of a word.
b. Place a demibeat at the end of a branching constituent.
c. Place a demibeat at the end of a daughter of the sentence node.

Rules not unlike these will be argued for in chapter 6. They would jointly give rise to the differing syllable-to-grid alignments (4.64a) and (4.64b).

(4.64)

```
a.            x          b.                x
        x     x                  x         x
    x   x     x              x   x         x
    x  x(x)   x .....        x  x(x)xx     x .....
   Marcel   Proust          Marcel      proved
```

It is this sort of difference in the metrical grid that we believe ultimately explains the fact that in *Marcel Proust* the shift in stress is virtually de rigueur (if he is being referred to as a familiar) whereas in *Marcel proved* it is highly disfavored.[25] In (4.64a), Beat Movement will operate to produce (4.65a). As for (4.64b), we would argue that it is not left untouched. Beat Addition applies to it to give a (silent) beat on the second metrical level, shown in (4.65b); it is the added beat that undoes the clash and thereby blocks Beat Movement.

(4.65)

```
a.              x        b.                       x
       x        x                   x             x
       x  x     x                   x  x    x     x
       x  x(x)  x .....              x  x(x)x x    x .....
     Marcel   Proust              Marcel      proved
```

This is by far the simplest solution. In fact, Beat Addition would have to be reformulated if it were *not* to apply. Given the long rhythmic lapse created by the rules of syntactic timing in (4.65b), the representation would be ill formed, by the PRA, if Beat Addition were not to step in at some point. That Beat Addition can step in here where the grid positions are silent follows from the nature of the rule itself. Recall its formulation:

(4.66)
Beat Addition

```
          x
x x   →   x x
```

In this, its simplest formulation, Beat Addition knows nothing of the individual alignments of the grid positions—it is an operation defined strictly on the grid, and hence will apply to silent and syllable-aligned positions alike. Thus we will assume it is the second-level beat in (4.65b) that blocks Beat Movement, by eliminating the prerequisite clash. The additional advantage of this analysis, of course, is that the rule of Beat Movement may be left intact and need not be made sensitive to the number of intervening demibeats, at the lowest level. Indeed, such a revision would deprive the theory of the well-founded generalization, which was discussed in chapter 2 and to which we return below, that the "Rhythm Rule" ignores the lowest level in the grid, paying no attention to the "real" adjacency of syllables and instead heeding only the beats with which they are aligned at the higher levels.

As a final point in favor of the silent beat explanation of the varying probability of stress shift in such cases, note that the difference in the number of demibeats in the two cases will explain why *-cel* is longer in the second than in the first—if we assume that in surface phonetic representation a syllable becomes aligned (through an autosegmental

left-to-right association) with at least some of the silent demibeats on its
right. (This assumption will be defended in chapter 6.) Thus the idea
that there are different numbers of silent demibeats in the two cases
explains both the *lack* of Beat Movement and the *presence* of (substantial) final lengthening in the one case and the opposite state of affairs in
the other. What more could one ask?

If Beat Movement is considered to be optional, it may fail to apply
where it could, as with *Marcel Proust,* leaving a clash intact. This
seems to be a correct view of the facts. Clashes do seem to persist, even
in the face of the PRA. Indeed, in some cases they are unavoidable, as
with *cŏntént cóws.* But what now of our explanation that greater (final)
lengthening in the absence of Beat Movement is to be attributed to
silent positions in the grid? By saying that Beat Movement is optional,
we are implicitly claiming that a lack of stress shift in *Marcel Proust* is
not due to extra silent grid positions provided by syntactic timing or by
the "unfamiliarity principle," for example. The extra lengthening of
-*cel* in *Marcel Proust* would thus have to have some other source. Of
course, one could imagine that extra grid positions are introduced, just
in case there is an unalleviated clash. This would amount to saying that
some additional principle of grammar is at work, introducing demibeats
and beats between others already there, in an environment defined in
terms of the grid. As such, the principle would be distinct in type from
others we have encountered, according to which the presence of demibeats is determined either by the composition of the utterance in terms
of syllables (the universal Demibeat Alignment rule of chapters 2 and 3)
or by the syntactic constituent structure of the utterance (the syntactic
silent demibeat insertion rules of chapter 6). An alternative, one that
does not require introducing this new sort of grid construction principle
into the theory, would be to view the extra length of -*cel* as being a
matter of the "phonetic realization" of the grid and, in particular, as a
manifestation of the tendency toward isochrony of beats on the various
levels.

Recall that the very notion of a stress-timed language (section 2.2)
requires the assumption that there is no fixed amount of time accorded
to any particular demibeat, on the first metrical level. This is because it
is basic beats, on the second metrical level, that tend to be isochronous
(i.e., appear at (ideally) equal intervals of time), and they are claimed to
do this despite the differing numbers of demibeats following them. The
theory of stress-timing, then, is a theory of the "phonetic realization"
of the grid, and we are suggesting that it may be extended to the present

case. The explanation for the length of the non-stress-shifted -*cel* would be this: The -*cel* of *Marcel* is a third-level beat. Because it is immediately followed by another third-level beat, it must fill the entire span of time that ideal isochrony accords a third-level beat, and it stretches out to do so.[26] In general, of course, the language "tries to avoid" this sort of circumstance, where a higher level beat must be realized in time by too small an amount of phonetic material. This is why maintaining the clash is so disfavored in *Marcel Proust,* where it can be avoided. We do not mean to imply by this that there is any absolute time value assigned to a third-level beat. Presumably it must simply be longer than a second-level beat, like the one on the preceding *Mar-.* But that is bad enough. Here, then, is a "stress-timing" account of the length of -*cel* in this case, one that does not rely on the presence of additional demibeats.[27]

In sum, then, we have been continuing to assume that a clash in the grid is necessary for the application of Beat Movement, but not sufficient. Some of the variability in the occurrence of Beat Movement is due to this simple fact—that the rule is optional. However, viewing the rule as optional does not go very far in describing the facts related to stress shift. The likelihood of taking the option to apply Beat Movement, or the possibility of taking it at all, seems to depend on other factors, including the syntactic relations of the seemingly clashing elements. We hypothesize that all these other factors find their appropriate expression either in the grid or in the principles for phonetically interpreting the grid, as outlined above.

There is a fact that would seem to go contrary to our claim that, given an (apparent) clash, the more deeply the left-hand constituent is embedded, the less likely Beat Movement is to take place (this, because of the greater possibilities of SDA). As Liberman and Prince point out, the fact is that a shift is more likely to take place when the first constituent is a compound than when it is a simple word. The pair they contrast is *[good-looking] lifeguard* and *[Montana] cowboy.*[28] Supposing that SDA, the PAR, and the NSR apply as they can in both cases, (4.67a,b) would be the two pre–Beat Movement representations.

(4.67)

a.
```
                   x
     x₁            x₂
   x   x         x   x   x
   x   x       x x   x   x
   x  xx   x  xx   x   x .....
   good-looking   lifeguard
```

b.
```
                             x
                    x₁    x₂   x
                  x  x      x   x
                  x  x  xx  x    x .....
                  Montana   cowboy
```

The underlined positions are those added by SDA (and the consequent Beat Addition on level two). In each case, then, there is but one clash, subscripted $x_1 \ x_2$. Why then should there be any difference in the likelihood of Beat Movement? Possibly the answer lies in the fact that the clashes are on different metrical levels. Since Beat Movement is optional, it need not apply in either case. But we suggest that it is less desirable for the clash to remain in (4.67a) than in (4.67b), because of what retaining the clash would mean for the "phonetic realization" of the utterance. It would mean, for (4.67a), that *looking* would somehow have to occupy the (ideal) time span of a fourth-level beat, while *-tana* in (4.67b) would have to occupy only the time span accorded a third-level beat. Presumably, the former pronunciation is more ungainly than the latter, and for that reason is avoided.[29] We suggest this answer only tentatively, of course, since so little is at present known about the phonetic realization of the grid.

It turns out nonetheless that an explanation of this sort can be extended rather naturally to account for certain cases mentioned by Bolinger 1981. Bolinger observes that although stress shift is possible in both *fast-trotting colt* and *fast-galloping giraffe*, it is more likely in the former than in the latter. These examples have exactly the same syntactic analysis (and hence exactly the same possibilities for SDA). All that differs is the number of weak syllables between the clashing prominences. The potential effects of SDA aside, the two examples have the following different grids:

(4.68)

a.
```
               x
     x₁      x₂
   x   x       x
   x   x       x
   x   x x     x
   fast-trotting colt
```

b.
```
                        x
     x₁               x₂
   x   x                x
   x   x    x           x
   x   x x  x          xx
   fast-galloping giraffe
```

Like *good-looking lifeguard*, *fast-trotting colt* contains a fourth-level clash in which the clashing beat syllables are separated by only one syllable. If we assume, as in the earlier case, that it is preferred that two syllables not be used to realize a fourth-level beat, then we can explain the preference for Beat Movement in (4.68a). In (4.68b), by contrast, there is simply more phonetic material in (after) the clashing fourth-level beat. Quite conceivably this is what makes it easier to maintain the clash in (4.68b) and avoid Beat Movement.

We turn next to a set of cases that seem to raise problems for Beat Movement. In these cases it appears that the rule's structural description is *not* met; that is, there does not appear to be a stress clash, but Beat Movement takes place nonetheless. In one sort of case, enough weak syllables intervene between the relevant beats to require the application of Beat Addition and hence the elimination of a clash, as in *phònological rĕséarch* (4.69).[30]

(4.69)

```
                  x
     x            x
 x   x            x
 x  x x  x x (x)  x x
phonological    research
```

In (4.69) the initial stressless *re-* will always constitute the kind of lapse with *-ical* that would give rise to Beat Addition and hence an elimination of the clash. Yet of course Beat Movement does apply in this case: *phònological rĕséarch*. In the other problematic case, the first beat in the second word is not a third-level beat, but only a second-level one, as in *telegraphic commùnicátion, ideal èditórial, psychological trànsformátion*, etc.:

(4.70)

```
a.                 x        b.             x
         x         x             x         x
     x   x       x   x         x x  x   x
    x x  x  x  x  x x x x      x x  x xx xx
    telegraphic communication    ideal editori al
```

Here there is no clash either, yet Beat Movement is possible: *tèlegraphic communicátion, ìdeal editórial, psỳchological transformátion*. If a clash is a necessary condition for Beat Movement, how can it apply here?

We suggest that (4.70a,b) are not in fact the appropriate pre–Beat Movement configurations for the stress-shifted pronunciations of these phrases. When the shift does take place, we claim, the first word bears a pitch accent (as does the second). Assuming that a syllable associated with a pitch accent has at least a fourth-level grid alignment, then the pre–Beat Movement grid alignments would be those given in (4.71a,b), for example, where subscripts indicate a clash, and Beat Movement could apply.

(4.71)

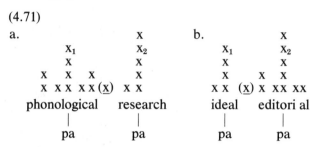

a.
```
                      x         b.                      x
      x₁            x₂                  x₁            x₂
      x             x                   x             x
   x   x   x        x                   x         x   x
   x  xx xx (x)   x x                 x x  (x)  x  xx xx
   phonological   research            ideal     editori al
       |            |                   |          |
       pa           pa                  pa         pa
```

It may seem that we are introducing a wild card here: pitch accent saves the day! But there is some indication that the presence of pitch accent produces greater rhythmic prominence (Halliday 1967b, and section 5.3.4).[31] Thus the issue here is the truth of the claim that when there is no pitch accent on phrases such as these, there is no stress shift. Consider in particular (4.69) without a pitch accent on *phonological*. With or without SDA, it would not have a clash (if our assumptions about Beat Addition are correct).[32] In the linguistic milieu, occasions are fairly common on which the adjective *phonological* is not a word requiring any sort of highlighting and hence is not prone to bearing a pitch accent. When it occurs without a pitch accent, the stress-shifted pronunciation *phònological reséarch* is felt to be unfluent and awkward. This is what a clash-motivated Beat Movement would predict, if pitch accents resulted in an extra rhythmic prominence. Our suggestion, then, is that the presence of pitch accents acts to make Beat Movement possible where it otherwise would not apply, and it does so in a way understandable in terms of the grid. We will develop this account in chapter 5, which contains a more precise description of both the conditions under which pitch accents appear and their contribution to intonational meaning.

Bolinger 1981, building on an earlier proposal (Bolinger 1965b), has a different view of the shift in prominence that we have discussed. He contends that the shift takes place when two pitch accents are too close together, and that what is sought in the prominence shift is a more optimal *pitch contour,* the "hat pattern," shaped like a mesa with H tones defining the outer edges. His analysis does not take into account rhythmic considerations of the sort outlined in this chapter. We submit that such an analysis cannot make sense out of the variability in the operation of the "Rhythm Rule"—whether that variability is due to syntactic timing, timing that involves familiarity, or another factor. Moreover, an account not based on essentially rhythmic considerations would not be able to explain why the most prominent element in a clash is stable. It is also difficult to see how such an account could extend to cases where more than two pitch accents occur in sequence and where the medial accent undergoes a shift. In such a case, the medial pitch accent is already contained within a hat pattern, so that its function in moving cannot be to produce one. That is, why should (4.72a) shift to (4.72b)?

(4.72)
a. thirtéen Tennessée míners   ⇒   b. thírteen Ténnessee míners

In this case an earlier pitch accent is already there. Moreover, there are many more "tunes" than the so-called hat pattern in English (see, for example, Pierrehumbert 1980), and stress shift applies in all of them. Pierrehumbert (personal communication) has made the point that the only conceivable prosodic common denominator in utterances with these various tunes would be their stress pattern, i.e., their rhythmic structure. These, then, are some of the reasons why we believe that prominence shift should be understood in rhythmic terms.

4.4 Levels of Prominence, Syntactic Structure, and the Cycle

We have assumed in the previous discussion, that there exist differences in degree of phrasal prominence that cannot be reduced to the presence of absence or pitch accent or to the distance between prominences in the horizontal dimension. We claim that these prominences are properly rhythmic in character and that their degree reflects the level of the highest beat with which a syllable is aligned in the metrical grid. We have observed that the relative prominence of the words in the sentence reflects their organization into phrases and compound words, the major prominence of a phrase or compound word being located roughly speaking toward the right or left extreme (respectively) of the constituent (unless the presence of a pitch accent within the constituent demands otherwise). We have proposed the grid-based Nuclear Stress Rule and Compound Rule as an account of this syntax-motivated pattern of prominences. The NSR is a right domain-end prominence rule, and the Compound Rule is a left domain-end prominence rule (cf. Prince 1981, 1983). The first applies within the domain of constituents of type Phrase and the second within constituents of type Word.

The fact that text-to-grid alignment rules like these have characteristic syntactic domains does not entail that the rules should follow any particular mode of application. It does not imply that they should apply in *cyclic* fashion, though the cycle does presuppose that the rules have syntactic domains, and it is certainly a natural hypothesis to entertain about their mode of application. The important competing hypotheses about the mode of application of the rules constructing the metrical grid would involve some sort of *simultaneous* application on the various domains on which the rules must be satisfied within the sentence. (An A-over-A account is excluded because phrasal prominence patterns reflect *embedded* structure; see section 3.6.)

Our cyclic hypothesis is that text-to-grid alignment rules and grid euphony rules are met simultaneously *within each successive cyclic domain,* and that they are subject to the Textual Prominence Preservation Condition within those successive domains. Thus we do not claim that these rules are all "surface true," for the effects of rules on lower cycles may be undone on higher cycles as described in preceding sections. All the evidence so far is consistent with this particular version of the cyclic hypothesis.

In chapter 3, we considered two alternatives to the cyclic hypothesis, both based on some implementation of the notion of simultaneity. According to one, TGA rules and GE rules are all met simultaneously on all domains on which they are satisfied. This version is untenable because it is simply not true that the effects of TGA rules on all domains are compatible with the effects of GE rules on all domains. Beat Movement may undo (move) a lower domain prominence required by the NSR, for example. According to an alternative theory of simultaneous application, all TGA rules are met simultaneously on all their appropriate domains and are then followed by the GE rules, which might be ordered among themselves or not. Significantly, this theory allows the possibility that all grid construction rules that do have syntactic domains of their own—the TGA rules—are not cyclic (and hence are not ordered in any fashion).

The latter version of a simultaneous theory seems to deal successfully with the complex derivations discussed in preceding sections. Consider, for example, the derivation of *rather lily white hands.* If the

NSR were simply a well-formedness condition on pre-shift and pre–
Beat Addition syllable-to-grid alignments that simply had to be met
simultaneously on all relevant domains, the result for *rather lily white
hands* would be the output given on cycle 3 in (4.56): *white* more
prominent than *lily, white* more prominent than *rather, hands* more
prominent than *white*. We repeat the representation here:

(4.56)

```
                    x
            x     x
x     x     x     x
x     x     x     x
x   x  xx   x     x
```
rather lily white hands

To simplify matters, let us consider that the problem is merely how to
get from this representation to either of the two representations (4.57)
or (4.60), repeated here.

(4.57)   (4.60)

```
                                                      x
                x            x_                       x
        x_      x            x               x        x
x       x   x   x            x       x       x        x
x       x   x   x            x       x       x        x
x   x  xx   x   x            x      xx       x        x
rather lily white hands      rather lily white hands
```

Let us suppose that Beat Movement and Beat Addition are unordered
with respect to each other. If Beat Movement preceded Beat Addition
in a derivation, the result would be (4.57). Beat Addition could not then
apply to that output (so that *rather* would be left less prominent). If
instead Beat Addition applied first (on *rather*) and then applied again,
something close to (4.60) would be derived (whether or not Beat Addition applied at the lower levels). Thus it is not entirely obvious that
there is a need for the cycle.

Recall, though, that we endorsed the cycle not because it is the only
theory capable of ensuring the rule interactions that allow the correct
patterns to be generated, but rather because it is the most constrained
theory of those that are descriptively adequate. Given the theory of GE
rules as it stands, with the rules of Beat Addition, Beat Movement, and
Beat Deletion, the problem is to provide the general theory with a
means of keeping these rules in check; and the theory of the cycle,
accompanied by the TPPC, is just such a theory. In effect it keeps Beat

Addition from overapplying and destroying the local prominences required by the TGA rules, as in the word-level examples given in chapters 2 and 3. And indeed some mechanism is needed to keep Beat
Addition in check on the phrase level as well. Were it not constrained,
it could derive the ungrammatical (4.72) from (4.56), for example, or
the ungrammatical (4.73b) from (4.73a).

(4.72)

```
X
X                   X
X           X   X
X   X       X   X
X   X       X   X
X   X   XX  X   X
```
rather lily white hands

(4.73)

```
a.                          b.  X
                X               X           X
    X   X       X               X   X       X
    X   X       X               X   X       X
    X   X       X               X   X       X
    three blind mice            three blind mice
```

To avoid these patterns, the simultaneous theory would also require
something like the TPPC. But the statement of the TPPC requires that
TGA rules and GE rules be satisfied simultaneously on the relevant
domain. For it to take effect in a noncyclic theory, TGA rules and GE
rules would have to be met simultaneously on all domains, and that, we
have shown, is impossible. The theory that would try to dispense with
the cycle thus reaches an impasse, and we must therefore relinquish
this alternative.

We owe to Janet Pierrehumbert (personal communication) a rather
different argument in favor of the cycle, one that Prince 1983 takes up
as well. Consider the stress pattern of the complex phrase *Alewife
Brook Parkway subway station:*

(4.74)

$$\overset{2}{\text{Alewife}} \; \overset{4}{\text{Brook}} \; \overset{3}{\text{Parkway}} \; \overset{1}{\text{subway}} \; \overset{4}{\text{station}}$$

Greatest prominence is on *subway*, which bears the main prominence
of the rightmost constituent in the NP. What is of interest in the location of the second greatest prominence, on *Alewife*. We submit that the

version of a simultaneous theory that we have considered cannot produce this prominence, whereas a cyclic application of TGA rules and GE rules applying in tandem can. The structure of the NP is as in (4.75a), and to simplify matters we will assume that each of the words bracketed there has the same level of word stress, noted in (4.75b). Now, if the NSR and the Compound Rule were to apply simultaneously on all relevant domains before the GE rules applied, the grid representation in (4.75c) would be derived. The clash created is circled. It could only be alleviated by an operation of Beat Movement, shifting the secondary prominence from *Parkway* to *Brook* as shown in (4.75d).

(4.75)
a. [[[[Alewife] [Brook]] [Parkway]] [[subway] [station]]]

```
b.    x         x      x        x        x
                                         x
                       (x       x)
            x          (x        x)

c.    x         x      x        x        x
                                         x
               x                x
               x         x      x

d.    x         x      x        x        x
```

This creates an ungrammatical stress pattern for this phrase:

(4.76)
*Alewife Brook Parkway subway station
 (4)   (2)   (3)   (1)   (4)

Consider next the result of applying both the TGA rules and the GE rules cyclically. On the basis of (4.75a,b), repeated as (4.77a,b), the following sequence of cyclic operations takes place.

(4.77)

a. [[[[Alewife] [Brook]] [Parkway]] [[subway] [station]]]

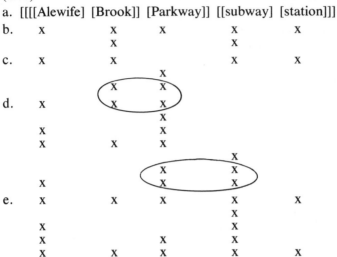

On the second cycle in (4.77d), the NSR is followed by Beat Movement, eliminating the circled clash. And on the third cycle, where the NSR gives greatest prominence to *subway*, Beat Movement again steps in to alleviate a clash. As shown in (4.77e), the errant beat lands again on *Alewife*, giving it secondary prominence in the phrase and thus the pattern desired.

Because of its success with complex cases like this, and for the reasons given above, the cycle appears to be necessary to an adequate account of the syntax-phonology mapping in sentence grammar. In chapters 6 and 7 we will show still more evidence for the cycle on the sentence.

Chapter 5
The Grammar of Intonation

5.1 The Issues

In this chapter we address two questions. The first—answered briefly in chapter 4 and in more detail here—concerns the relation between the "stress pattern" or rhythmic structure of an utterance and what we will call its *intonational structure*. The second—a large and much-debated question—concerns the relation between intonational structure and meaning. Though a full treatment of this question is beyond the scope of the book as a whole, in this chapter we will lay out our assumptions about the nature of intonational meaning and advance, in what can only be preliminary fashion, certain proposals concerning the relation between intonational structure, syntactic structure, and that property relevant to intonational meaning known as *focus*.

The first question concerns the relation between two aspects of phonological representations. One aspect, the "stress pattern," is to be understood as an alignment of the syllables of the sentence with a metrical grid. The other, the intonational structure, involves three things. First, it involves the *intonational phrasing* of the sentence, the division of the sentence into one or more *intonational phrases*. An intonational phrase is a unit of prosodic constituent structure with respect to which the characteristic intonational contours of a language are defined. Second, intonational structure involves the representation of the particular *intonational contour* of each intonational phrase. Following Pierrehumbert 1980, we will characterize the intonational contours of English as a sequence of pitch accents, flanked at the beginning by an (optional) boundary tone and at the end by a phrase accent and a final (obligatory) boundary tone, all of which are represented on an autosegmental tier separate from the tier(s) including segments and syllables (see section

5.3.1).[1] Third, the intonational structure of a sentence involves the assignment of pitch accents to the words of the sentence: every pitch accent of an intonational contour will be assigned to some usually word-sized constituent of the sentence, though not every word will have a pitch accent associated with it. The set of pitch-accent-to-word assignments of a sentence will be called its *pitch accent assignment.*

To the question "What is the relationship between intonation and stress?" we replied in chapter 4 that intonation "comes first," in a sense to be made precise, and that the intonational structure of a sentence, in conjunction with its surface syntactic structure, determines the rhythmic relations of its words and phrases. Specifically, we proposed that this be accomplished through the combined effects of the (grid-based) Nuclear Stress Rule (NSR), the Compound Rule, and the Pitch Accent Prominence Rule (PAR). Here we will elaborate on this proposal, which departs from other recent ones according to which phrase stress is defined independently of intonational structure (Liberman 1975, Liberman and Prince 1977, Bing 1979a, Ladd 1980, Pierrehumbert 1980).

Our theory that the assignment of intonational structure to a sentence is logically prior to the assignment of phrase stress entails that phrase stress plays no role in determining where and how the tonal units of the intonational contour (specifically, the pitch accents) are aligned with the syllables of a sentence. The opposite assumption, that phrase stress determines the alignment of the elements of the intonational contour with the "text," was made explicit by Liberman 1975 and has been explicit or implicit in all other generative works on the topic. In section 5.3 we will show the inadequacies of this "stress-first" account and the advantages of the "pitch-accent-first" account.

The second question concerns the relation between the intonational meaning of a sentence, on the one hand, and its intonational structure, on the other. We will use the term *intonational meaning* simply to designate any aspects of the meaning of a sentence that are defined wholly, or in part, with respect to its intonational structure. Studies of intonational meaning in English have led to partitioning it into two components; one might be called the *expressiveness component,* and the other the *informational structure* or *focus structure component* (Halliday 1967b, Crystal 1969, Bolinger 1965a, Ladd 1980). (It is not to be excluded that, in other languages, intonational meaning might include other, more conventional aspects of semantic representation, such as the scope of logical operators, variable binding, and so on.) The various components of intonational structure relate in different ways to these components of intonational meaning.

The expressiveness of an utterance concerns, among other things, the information it conveys about the speaker's attitude, mood, personality, etc. It may also involve such things as the so-called question intonation and other aspects of the illocutionary force of the sentence (see Liberman 1975, for example). Of the three aspects of a sentence's intonational structure, the one that contributes most obviously to its expressiveness is its (sequence of) intonational contours—that is, the *choice* of pitch accents, phrase accents, and boundary tones. The literature contains many discussions of the "expressive force" of intonational contours,[2] and we will examine some examples illustrating these relations in section 5.3.1. As for the other two aspects of intonational structure, it does not seem unlikely that pitch accent assignment (the choice of which words bear pitch accents) and intonational phrasing also contribute to the expressiveness of the utterance, though little has been said about this in the literature and we will not discuss it here. We may also note that whereas in English the burden of expressiveness is borne almost entirely by intonational structure, in other languages it is shared in varying degrees, or borne entirely, by particles of various sorts (as for example in Finnish (Carlson 1982) or Navajo (Schauber (1977)). All in all, we will not discuss considerations of expressiveness here, except insofar as they permit the establishing of the accent repertoire of the language (as illustrated in Pierrehumbert 1980, reviewed in section 5.3.1), for the expressiveness of a sentence, as determined by its intonational contour, does not appear to be systematically related to other grammatically relevant properties of the sentence.[3] In this way, expressiveness is radically different from the other component of intonational meaning in English, which involves the focus properties of the sentence.

Following Chomsky 1971 and Jackendoff 1972, we view the relation between intonational structure and focus-related intonational meaning as being mediated by a representation that we will call *focus structure*.[4] On this view, the characterization of that relation consists of two parts: a description of the relation between intonational structure and focus structure, on the one hand, and a description of the relation between focus structure and intonational meaning, on the other. One of the most important roles of a sentence's focus structure is in defining the sentence's presumed "informational contribution" to a discourse. Roughly speaking, what is focused in a sentence is understood to be "new" information in a discourse, what is not focused is understood to be "given." (This view will be refined in section 5.2.) Thus a grammar of discourse, which concerns itself with determining the appropriateness of a sentence within a particular discourse context, must clearly take focus into consideration. In English, the focus structure of a sentence is inextricably related to its intonational structure.[5] Our empirical claim is that in English it is the pitch accent assignment of a sentence that is directly related to its focus properties. Again roughly speaking, the presence of a pitch accent correlates with a focus (and thus with "new information"), while the absence of a pitch accent indicates the lack of focus (or "old information"). It may also be that the intonational phrasing of a sentence relates to its focus structure, though we will ignore that possibility until section 5.4 and in the meantime deal only with sentences consisting of one intonational phrase. As for the choice of intonational contour (the choice of particular elements from the tonal repertoire), it appears that, in English at least, this is irrelevant to focus structure. Finally, we explicitly deny that phrase stress bears any direct relation at all to focus structure (see section 5.3).

Various authors (for instance, Chomsky 1971, Jackendoff 1972, Bing 1979a,b, Williams 1980b, Halliday 1967b) assume that focus is a property of syntactic constituents. We will adopt that assumption here and will often use the term *a/the focus* to abbreviate *a/the focused constituent*. It is also necessary to assume that a sentence may have more than one focus, though this has been less generally recognized (see section 5.2). Jackendoff's proposal, building on Chomsky's, is that there is a property *Focus* that may be assigned to, and thereby "annotate," the constituents of the surface syntactic representation of the sentence. The set of assignments of the property of *Focus* to the constituents of a sentence is what we will call its *focus structure*. For Jackendoff, the role of focus structure in surface structure is a purely formal one. Focus structure marks the syntactic domain(s) within which the focus-related prosodic phenomena are defined, and it has a correspondingly special role in the semantic interpretation of the sentence and in determining its appropriateness in discourse. Here, we will follow Jackendoff in assuming that focus structure is represented in the surface structure of a sentence, by means of the *Focus*-label device.[6] We will assume as well that the same sort of representation of focus structure is present in logical form.

The arguments for including focus structure as part of the representation of logical form are due originally to Jackendoff 1972. Jackendoff showed that the scope of logical operators (such as negation) within a sentence may be delimited by the focus structure of the sentence, and that the meaning of such words as *only* and *even* is intrinsically bound up with focus.[7] For Jackendoff, this amounted to saying that focus structure contributes to defining the semantic representation of a sentence. Within the more recently developed revised extended standard theory framework (Chomsky 1981, for example), the conclusion would be that focus structure contributes to defining logical form (where scope and other such aspects of meaning are represented) and/or that focus structure is represented in logical form. Probably both conclusions are warranted.

It should be pointed out that focus structure on this theory is not in and of itself a representation of intonational meaning. Rather, it is a representation that itself requires interpretation. What it "means" for a constituent to be focused and, correspondingly, what it "means" for a constituent to be unfocused (or "presupposed") are questions that must be answered. And finding the correct answers is not a trivial matter. The various proposals include characterizing focus-related intonational meanings in terms of the given-new distinction (Halliday 1967a,b, Chafe 1976), in terms of relations defined between presupposition-focus pairs (Chomsky 1971, Jackendoff 1972, Williams 1980b), in terms of topic and comment (Kuno 1972), in terms of a notion of dominance (Erteschik-Shir and Lappin (to appear)), and more. Below we will briefly discuss these proposals concerning the focus structure–meaning relation, and we will make our own tentative contribution to the matter, building on Halliday 1967b and to some degree on Bolinger 1965b, 1972a.

As for the other half of the problem, which concerns the focus structure–intonational structure relation, we will argue that it should be construed in a way somewhat different from the one our predecessors have chosen. According to the theory we will propose (again, somewhat tentatively), an analysis of the relation between focus structure and intonational structure is based on two rules. The first, the Basic Focus Rule, says simply that a constituent to which a pitch accent is assigned is focused. For reasons to be explained, the effect of this rule is to say, roughly speaking, that a word is focused if it has a pitch accent. The second rule, the Phrasal Focus Rule, involves a recursive definition of focus. It says that a constituent may be focused if its *head* constituent (usually a Word) is focused and/or if a constituent contained within it that is an *argument* of its head is focused (which is to say, for example, that a VP may be focused if either a verb, or its argument(s), or both are focused). We mention these details here to bring out the fact that, according to the theory we will be defending, the focus structure–intonational structure relation is governed not only by the constituent structure relations of surface structure (as is conventionally assumed) but also by the predicate-argument structure of the lexical items of the sentence. And we point out, moreover, that neither focus rule pays heed to word order in surface structure. This theory thus makes rather different predictions about the focus structure of sentences from those made by the theories with which we are familiar.[8] These differences will be examined in section 5.2, where we will show that the focus rules allow new insight into the focus properties of English sentences. We will also show that, because they pay no heed to word order, the focus rules can be extended without modification to describing the prosody-focus relation in sentences of a language like German, whose word order may differ from that of English, but whose dominance relations and argument structure may be the same.

Clearly, our theory gives no place to the notions "normal intonation" or "normal stress," where these are taken to be either intonational patterns or phrase stress patterns that are computed automatically on the basis of syntactic structure alone. (In this our theory converges with those of Schmerling 1976 and Bolinger 1972b.) We consider it the task of the grammar to define the relation between focus structure and intonational structure, and we propose that the focus rules serve to define that relation, between focus and intonational structures that are freely and independently assigned to (surface) syntactic structure. On this theory, there is no intonational structure that is defined on focus-independent grounds to be "normal." While there does exist a "normal" range of possible intonational structures for any particular focus structure, as long as there is no focus structure independently defined as "normal" (according to some criteria yet to be determined), there will be no "normal intonation" for a sentence. Of course, given our pitch-accent-first theory, once an intonational structure is assigned to a sentence, the NSR, the Compound Rule, and the PAR will give rise to a stress pattern that is "normal" in the sense that it is automatically computed (on the basis of the syntactic structure along with that intonational structure). But this is not "normal stress" in the sense in which the term has previously been used—that is, to describe the distribution of the nuclear pitch accents in the sentence.

To sum up, we have sketched a theory that takes Chomsky's and Jackendoff's representation of focus structure to be the linchpin in the connection between prosody and focus-related meaning, and, like Chomsky's and Jackendoff's theory, views its descriptive task as divided into two distinct parts: the characterization of the prosody-focus relation, on the one hand, and the characterization of the interpretation of focus, on the other. These essential features of Chomsky's and Jackendoff's theory are pictorially represented in figure 5.1.

Our theory of the prosody-focus relation differs from that of Chomsky and subsequent workers in the generative tradition in two fundamental ways. First, it involves the claim that the intonational structure of a sentence rather than its phrase stress pattern is directly related to the focus properties of the sentence. On our theory, the relation between focus structure and phrase stress pattern is mediated by that intonational structure. This of course implies a theory of the intonation-stress relation that puts intonation first. It also implies a rather different theory of the prosody-focus relation from that of Chomsky and the others, which is formulated in the appropriate pitch-accent-based terms. The focus rules we have proposed are not, however, a mere translation into the present framework of Chomsky's and Jackendoff's conception of the stress-focus relation. Instead they involve the novel claim that it is the location of prosodic prominences (i.e., pitch accents) with respect to surface constituent structure *and* the place of focused elements within a predicate-argument structure that determine the full focus structure possibilities of a sentence. This is the second major difference between our theory and the one derived from the generative tradition. The organization of the grammar implied by the account sketched here is depicted in figure 5.2. (Note that we have not bothered to distinguish in the figure between surface structure (S_n) and the intonated surface structure (S_n'); cf. chapter 1. The distinction is immaterial to the present discussion.) The various sections of this chapter are devoted to fleshing out, and justifying, the different parts of this model.

In section 5.2 we present our theory of the prosody-focus relation, embodied in the set of focus rules. We make two central claims: first, that the location of a focus-relevant prosodic prominence within a focused constituent is *not* determined by principles like the NSR; second, that it is the argument structure of the phrase and the sentence that is

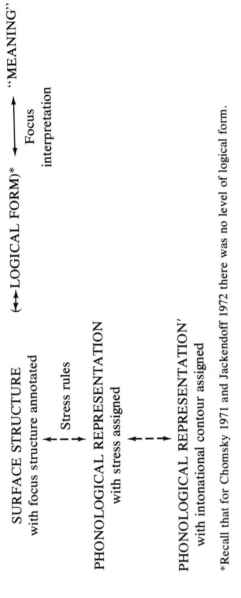

SURFACE STRUCTURE
with focus structure annotated

Stress rules

PHONOLOGICAL REPRESENTATION
with stress assigned

PHONOLOGICAL REPRESENTATION'
with intonational contour assigned

(↔LOGICAL FORM)*   "MEANING"

Focus
interpretation

*Recall that for Chomsky 1971 and Jackendoff 1972 there was no level of logical form.

Figure 5.1

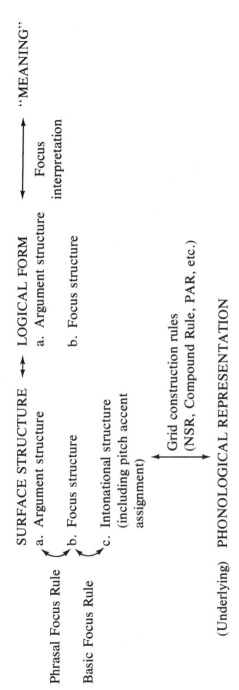

Figure 5.2

crucial in determining the focus properties of higher constituents on the basis of the prominences located within them. We also present a proposal for the interpretation of focus in the framework we have developed.

In section 5.3 we present evidence that it is the pitch accent assignment of a sentence, rather than the phrase stress relations, that is relevant to its focus structure, and we show that the pitch-accent-first theory accounts better for the intonation-stress relation than a stress-first account.

In section 5.3 we also provide evidence, based on the operation of the "Rhythm Rule," that a fully elaborated focus structure (i.e., annotation of focused constituents) must form part of surface structure, the representation in terms of which the rhythmic structure of the sentence is defined. We thus reject a possible alternative to our model, according to which only the focus properties of Words are annotated in surface structure and the focus structure of higher constituents is confined to logical form.

Finally, in section 5.4 we address the issue of intonational phrasing, raising questions and providing a few answers concerning, in particular, the relations holding among intonational phrasing, syntactic structure, and semantic relations.

5.2 The Prosody-Focus Relation

5.2.1 The Basic Analysis and Some Alternatives

This section examines the relation between prosody and focus structure in general, and in particular the claim that the argument structure of a sentence is relevant to determining its focus structure. Given the framework outlined in section 5.1, any difference in the intonational meaning of a sentence that relates to its "information structure" (Halliday 1967b) must be represented as a difference in focus structure. For the time being, we consider that a focused constituent contributes "new information" to the discourse, while a nonfocused constituent is understood to be "old information" or is "presupposed." (We defer a more refined characterization of focus-related intonational meaning until later in the section.) Since the appropriateness of a sentence with a particular intonational structure in a given context is (in part) a function of its intonational meaning and hence of its focus structure, we will appeal in our discussion to intuitions concerning discourse appropriateness in deciding the possible focus structures of a sentence and in ascertaining the relation between the focus structure(s) and intonational structure of a sentence.

The theory of the prosody-focus relation that is shared by Chomsky 1971, Jackendoff 1972, and Williams 1980b, for example, is that the location of prosodic prominence within a focused constituent is determined by the stress rules of the language. They claim that the greatest prominence within a focused phrase falls on the main-stressed syllable of the word that has been assigned prominence within the phrase by the NSR—more specifically, that greatest prominence will fall on the greatest prominence of the rightmost word of the phrase. We will call this the *NSR-Focus analysis*. Many authors have shown that it faces serious problems. Some attempts have been made to refine it (e.g., Bresnan 1971a, 1972); others have rejected it entirely, offering analyses based on rather different principles (e.g., Bolinger 1972a, Schmerling 1976, Ladd 1980). While drawing on the insights of the critics of the NSR-Focus analysis, we are not satisfied with their proposals and instead offer our own. We will emphasize the ability of our theory to account for the data that are problematic for the NSR-Focus analysis, and in so doing we will comment on some of the alternative analyses. Though there is not enough space here to fully examine these alternatives, it will become clear why we have chosen our approach over the others.

Our analysis involves three essential elements. The first element is the analysis of pitch accent assignment and association. We propose that pitch accents are *assigned to* (paired up with) constituents of type Word or smaller in syntactic structure, and that the pitch accent assigned to a constituent is *associated with* (realized upon) the rhythmically most prominent syllable of that constituent. The second and third elements are the focus rules:

(5.1)

a. *Basic Focus Rule*

A constituent to which a pitch accent is assigned is a focus.

b. *Phrasal Focus Rule*

A constituent may be a focus if (i) or (ii) (or both) is true:
(i) The constituent that is its *head* is a focus.
(ii) A constituent contained within it that is an *argument* of the head is a focus.

This analysis embodies three quite general factual claims, which are independent of the specific claim that focus structure depends on argument structure. The first claim is that pitch accents, and not rhythmic stress, are relevant in the prosody-focus relation. The second claim is that the principles for determining the location of focus-related prominences within words are different from those determining their location in phrases. Through pitch accent assignment and association, a pitch accent will (usually) find its way to the main-stressed syllable of a word (section 5.3.3), but the location of a pitch accent in a phrase is claimed not to be determined by the rhythmic makeup of the phrase at all. The third claim is that a focus may be embedded within another focus. This assumption is necessary to the very formulation of the Phrasal Focus Rule, which gives a recursive definition of focus. We will show that any theory must allow for embedded foci. The second claim is also central to our analysis: our focus rules are a particular articulation of that claim. As for the first, it is in fact not crucial to our demonstration. As long as the word-phrase distinction is maintained, which entity constitutes the focus-related prosodic prominence of a word is not of immediate importance. To make this clear, in this section we will use the neutral term *prominence* in speaking of the prosody-focus relation, waiting until section 5.3.2 to demonstrate that it is pitch accent, not stress, that is at issue. Thus we will temporarily revise the Basic Focus Rule as follows:

(5.2)
Basic Focus Rule (provisional)
A Word constituent that is prominent is a focus.

The capitalized words in the examples below are the "prominent" ones. As a rule of thumb, this means that a pitch obtrusion is associated with those words and probably some rhythmic salience as well.

   To begin with, consider sentence (5.3).

(5.3)
She SNEEZED.

Two intonational meanings, and hence two focus structures, may be associated with this sentence. In the first case, it seems appropriate to say that the VP is in focus, for the sentence is an appropriate answer to a question asking for information that the full VP in principle provides: "What did she do?" Our specific claim here is that the V is also in focus, along with the VP (though it is a bit difficult to sort out in this example what the additional meaning might be that focus on the verb might contribute). The second case involves a meaning that is commonly called *contrastive*. The verb *sneezed* here may be being used to contrast with another (intransitive) verb, as in the discourse "I don't think she SNIFFLED, she SNEEZED." In general, we will identify the intuition of contrast with a "narrow" focus in a sentence (and, correspondingly, with a greater amount of "presupposed" or "old" information in the sentence). In this we will follow Bolinger 1961 and Ladd 1980. Thus the two possible intonational meanings for (5.3) differ in that focus in the latter is "narrow" and encompasses only the verb, whereas in the former it is broader and also encompasses the VP.

Both intonational meanings are consistent with the prediction made by our grammar of focus. There is a prominence on *sneezed*. By the Basic Focus Rule, this is necessarily correlated with a focus on the verb. The Phrasal Focus Rule is in a sense optional; it says that there *may be* a focus on a higher constituent if such and such conditions obtain. It is consistent with the Phrasal Focus Rule that there *not* be a higher focus, and thus narrow focus on just the verb is allowed. It is also consistent with the Phrasal Focus Rule that there be a focus on VP, since the head verb of the VP is focused. (Note also that if the VP were an argument of the sentence, or if it were the argument of the tense-modal complex (named INFL in Chomsky 1981) and that were the head of the sentence, then VP focus would allow for S focus as well, given the Phrasal Focus Rule.) Our focus rules therefore predict the right array of focus structure here.

The NSR-Focus analysis also has no trouble with (5.3). Prominence on the (main stress of the) verb is consistent both with verb focus and with VP focus. It is, of course, not necessary to assume that when there is VP focus, there is also a focus on a lower element, but this, we will show, is not an advantage of the NSR-Focus analysis.

Consider next the sentence (5.4).

(5.4)
She watched "KOJAK".

Here again two different intonational meanings are possible. There may simply be a narrow (contrastive) focus on the object NP (she didn't watch "M*A*S*H," she watched "KOJAK"). And there may be VP focus as well. (5.4) is an appropriate response to the question "What did Mary do last night?" Our analysis is that the prominence on the noun *Kojak* means that the noun is focused, which in the case of proper names probably automatically guarantees that the NP is focused as well. Focus only on the NP gives the contrastive reading. The focus on the VP is made possible by the focus on the NP, which is an argument of the verb *watched*. As for the NSR-Focus analysis, it too predicts the right array of prosody-focus relations for the sentence. But as this example begins to show, it does so for the wrong reasons. If prominence falls on the NP within the focused VP here, it is because that NP is the rightmost constituent and receives main stress by the NSR. And the fact that the NP is necessarily interpreted as new information in (5.4) would have to be seen as an automatic consequence of VP focus, for the NSR-Focus analysis does not permit embedded foci.

With the next examples we will show that, because it lacks the notion of embedded foci, the NSR-Focus analysis cannot properly characterize the range of focus structures and intonational meanings that are available given a particular intonational structure for a sentence.[9] We will also show (as others have done) that the generalization concerning rightward prominence within focused constituents is incorrect and therefore that the notion that the rules of phrase stress determine the location of prominence within focused phrases must be rejected if we are to arrive at a correct characterization of the prosody-focus relation in phrases. And we will begin to amass evidence that it is the Phrasal Focus Rule, which appeals to the argument structure of sentences, that defines relations among foci (embedded in each other) and makes a straightforward treatment of the prosody-focus relation possible. We should point out that the first sets of facts to be discussed are consistent with a version of the Phrasal Focus Rule that does not appeal to argument structure; only later will we show cases that will decide between the argument-structure-based version in (5.1b) and the version in (5.5):

(5.5)
Alternative Phrasal Focus Rule
A constituent may be focused if it contains a focused constituent.[10]

A theory without embedded foci implicitly claims that the interpretation of NPs within a VP is somehow automatic (and cannot be immediately related to the NPs' own focus or lack of it). Without the notion of embedded foci, VP focus and the focus of NPs within a VP cannot be independently manipulated. But the evidence shows that they must be. Consider the two sentences below:

(5.6)
She sent a BOOK to MARY.

(5.7)
She sent a/the book to MARY.

Both have an intonational meaning in which the VP is focused. Either
may answer a question about what she (Jane) did next (or even the
question "What's happened?", in a discourse in which Jane is salient
and thereby "presupposed"). But the full focus structure of the two
sentences when they have VP focus is not identical. In (5.6), both NP
constituents of the VP represent new information. Given this, (5.6) is
an appropriate out-of-the-blue response to a question about Jane's activities. (5.7) is also a possible response to the same question, but for it
to be appropriate, it must be uttered in a discourse context in which
a/the book is "old information," for this is how the lack of prominence
on *book* is interpreted. Such a context is easily imaginable. Jane's job is
illustrating books, and her current book is the topic of conversation. A
question is raised about her recent activities. One of the speakers mentions that yesterday she (Jane) sent the book to Mary (a common
friend), and that she was looking forward to getting some comments
back on it. (5.7) would be an appropriate utterance of the sentence.
Thus a VP may be focused while one of its NP constituents may not be.
The pair of sentences (5.6) and (5.7) shows that the focusing (and interpretation) of a constituent within VP is indeed independent of the
focus of the VP. In order to give representation to this state of affairs,
we must allow for representations in which foci are embedded. We thus
claim that the focus structures for (5.6) and (5.7) when there is VP focus
are (5.8) and (5.9), respectively.

(5.8)

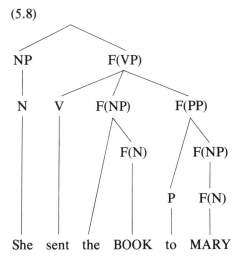

(5.9)

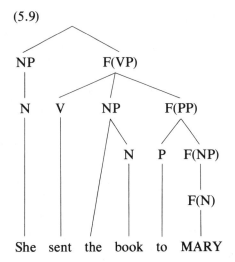

She sent the book to MARY

The focus rules declare these to be well-formed prosody-focus combinations. The Basic Focus Rule is satisfied, since every prominent word is a focus. And the Phrasal Focus Rule is satisfied, since for every higher-order constituent that is a focus, a head or an argument of the head within it is focused. These focus structures provide the basis for the appropriate intonational meanings.

But is the notion of VP focus really needed at all? If there is no VP focus in examples like (5.6) and (5.7), then there is no need to allow for embedded foci. We believe the notion of VP focus is required in order to represent the potential of such sentences to have (at least) two different intonational meanings. Sentence (5.6) may be appropriately uttered when it is presupposed (i.e., old information) that *she sent something to someone*. It may be one of a series of sentences itemizing what she sent to whom: . . . *and she sent a record to Paul and a pen to her brother,* etc. In such a case each individual NP is focused, but the VP is not. The other possible meaning is the one alluded to earlier, where no part of the VP is presupposed. We are claiming that in such a case the VP should be said to be focused as well. When we consider other examples, the need for the notion of VP focus, or of higher focus in general, will become even more evident.

The existence of embedded foci, and in particular of focus structures in which a focus may contain unfocused material, has important implications for a theory of the interpretation of focus. The presupposition of a sentence (its "old information") cannot be conceived as Jackendoff 1972 does, for example. For Jackendoff (p. 240), "the semantic material associated with surface structure nodes dominated by F is the Focus of the sentence. To derive the Presupposition, substitute appropriate semantic variables for the focused material." As we have shown, however, the presupposition is not merely a "sentence frame" from which the foci have been removed, leaving behind variables. Thus our outlook commits us to a new theory of focus and presupposition. Unfortunately, we are not in a position to offer such a theory here, and in what follows will only make partial attempts at solving the problem.

Judging from the cases considered so far, one important observation to be made about the interpretation of focus is that *lack* of focus is not uniformly interpreted. A nonfocused NP is necessarily interpreted as old information, but a nonfocused verb is not. In most of the preceding examples there is no prominence on the verb, and hence no F(V), yet the verb may be understood as new to the discourse. We believe the generalization to be that only the focus of constituents that are *arguments* is relevant to the aspect of intonational meaning where the discourse-relevant distinction between old and new information is represented, and we hypothesize that the (major) principle of focus interpretation at work in the grammar is (5.10):

(5.10)
Focus Interpretation Principle

F(argument) ⇔ new information

In what follows we will present other evidence suggesting that this is a correct hypothesis about the interpretation of focus. The point here is that a principle such as (5.10) leaves the interpretation of the focus of nonarguments such as the verb of the preceding examples totally vague. Lack of focus is consistent with such nonarguments' being new information. Of course prominence (and hence focus) are possible on "new" verbs as well: *She SENT the book to MARY* is an alternative to (5.7), appropriate in the same discourse context. Later evidence will confirm this approach to the interpretation of verbs and other nonarguments. There will be cases where there *is* focus on a verb and where this must *not* be interpreted as new information.

An alternative principle for the interpretation of focus is also consistent with many of the facts that will be discussed:

(5.11)
Alternative Focus Interpretation Principle

F(phrase) ⇔ new information

(5.11) draws a distinction between phrases and words, not arguments and nonarguments. Thus (5.10) and (5.11) clearly make different predictions. For the moment we will not examine these differences, instead assuming (5.10) as a working hypothesis. Later, in sections 5.2.3 and 5.2.4, we will evaluate the relative merits of the two principles.

Neither (5.10) nor (5.11) constitutes a full theory of focus interpretation. Neither says exactly what the focus of a verb, for example, might contribute to intonational meaning. Nor have we spoken precisely about what is meant by "old" and "new." (Halliday 1967b makes some very interesting observations on this matter.) But we are not in a position to attempt much more than this here, and we submit this partially worked-out analysis more as a suggestion for research than as an attempt at a definitive statement on the problems.

Let us return to the main thread, the analysis of the prosody-focus relation. Since our analysis makes no appeal to the position of a prominence in the linear sequence of constituents contained within a higher focused constituent, it can account for yet another set of cases that are problematic for the NSR-Focus analysis. Consider (5.12):

(5.12)
She sent her SKETCHES to the publisher.

This sentence, too, may have VP focus and thus constitute an informationally appropriate comment about Jane the illustrator's recent activities, provided that her publisher is somehow present in the discourse. It shows that there need not be a prosodic prominence in the rightmost position in the VP in order for VP focus to be present, and it shows, again, that a focused VP may contain an unfocused NP. On our account, this meaning of (5.12), wherein the VP is itself somehow "new" (even though one of its parts is "old"), corresponds to the focus structure in (5.13).

(5.13)

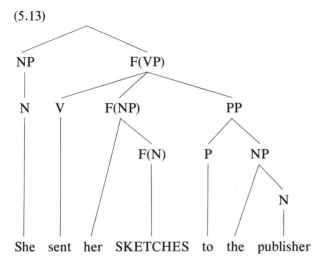

She   sent   her   SKETCHES   to   the   publisher

The focus rules declare (5.13) to be well formed since there is a chain of foci from the prosodically prominent word *sketches* up through the VP, wherein the crucial links are focused constituents that are either heads or arguments of the relevant phrases.

There is some disagreement whether sentences with a constituent structure, argument structure, and intonational structure like (5.12) may have a focused VP. Chomsky 1971, citing the example (5.14), claims they may not.

(5.14)
Did John give the BOOK to Bill?

He claims that a natural response to this question is "No, something ELSE" and *not* "No, he KEPT it." Since the focus structure of the response is taken to be the same as that of the question, the "narrowness" of the focus in the natural response is taken to indicate the narrowness of the focus in the question. We agree that narrow focus on *the BOOK* is the preferred intonational meaning here. But as long as there is a possible reading in which VP focus is also present, our account will hold up, for our theory permits both narrow focus on NP *and* broad VP focus when there is a prosodic prominence on *BOOK* in (5.14). Imagine that the questioner had asked John to do several errands on her behalf: return a certain book to Bill, photocopy some papers, etc. John, however, was notoriously forgetful and when the questioner ran into a roommate who (a) knew about the errands and (b) reported having seen John and Bill together, it seems to us that (5.14) would be an appropriate query and "No, he KEPT it" or "No, he FORGOT it" an appropriate response. Actually, the need to construct such an elaborate discourse to show VP focus in (5.14) has nothing to do with the focus rules, only with the fact that circumstances in which a noun phrase with the definite article *the* may be appropriately focused and represented as new information are harder to construct. Suppose the sentence had been (5.15).

(5.15)
Did John give a BOOK to Bill?

Such a sentence might be appropriate when only John, Bill, and, say, Bill's recent birthday are "old information" in the discourse. An appropriate response might be "No, this time he grew a pot of NARCISSUS for him." Other examples are plentiful in which an argument NP in second position in the focused VP is unfocused and the first argument focused:[11]

(5.16)
a. She offered all her RECIPES to Pete.

   (Discourse: a discussion of the unusual divorce settlement between Susan and Pete.)

b. They told us not to put our ELBOWS on the table.

   (Discourse: a discussion of family conflicts at the dinner table.)

c. La Guardia used to read the FUNNIES to the kids (on the RADIO).

   (Discourse: a discussion of why even New York's youngest generation liked the mayor.)

These examples and others discussed below show quite well that VP focus does not require a prosodic prominence on the right within the VP.

But the Phrasal Focus Rule does require that a focused head or argument be located somewhere within a higher focused constituent. This is the content of the proviso "that is contained within it" in formulation (5.1b) of the rule. That this proviso is indeed required is shown by the fact that the focusing of subject noun phrases, which are arguments of the verb, is not sufficient to allow VP focus. In (5.17a–c), where the sole prosodic prominence of the sentence is within the subject NP, there is only narrow focus on that NP; in other words, none of these is an appropriate response to the question "What's happening?"

(5.17)

a. JOHN writes poetry in the garden.

b. JOHN eloped.

c. JOHN was arrested.

It has been claimed that some sentences having a prosodic prominence only within the subject NP, like these, are perfectly appropriate when uttered out of the blue. Consider the examples in (5.18).[12]

(5.18)

a. The SUN is shining.

b. My UMBRELLA's been found.

c. My MOTHER's coming.
   etc.

Does their appropriateness when uttered out of the blue require us to consider the VP to be focused here, and therefore to allow for the possibility that a focused argument not contained within the constituent with its head may focus that constituent? We think not. It may simply be that it is possible in a felicitous discourse to utter sentences out of the blue where only the subject NP, and not the entire sentence, is being focused.[13] Thus we will leave our Phrasal Focus Rule intact for the moment.

The phenomena considered so far have also been analyzed by Schmerling 1976. Our account is like Schmerling's in that it gives no role to the Nuclear Stress Rule in determining the location of phrasal prominences within a particular utterance, and views the presence or absence of every prominence as related to the potential for the sentence to serve as an appropriate utterance within a given discourse context. There is a fundamental difference between this account and Schmerling's, however. Schmerling's system includes no representation of focus structure mediating between prosody and intonational meaning, and for this reason there are certain types of phenomena that it cannot describe.

Two principles form the crux of Schmerling's system. The first is (5.19) (1976:76):

(5.19)

Principle I

Those portions of a sentence receive reduced stress which contain material presupposed by the speaker to be true and to be known to the addressee(s).

In the absence of a level of focus structure, Schmerling's Principle I may seem to commit her theory to the claim that there is a one-to-one relation between prosody and intonational meaning. For example, with such a principle it is not possible to represent the difference in meaning that we have characterized as the difference between narrow (contrastive) and broad focus. Nor is it possible to speak of the scope of such focus-related words as *even* and *only,* and other matters discussed by Jackendoff that require the notion of focus structure. So while the intuition behind Principle I is sound, it does not constitute the basis for a theory of the prosody-meaning relation.

Schmerling offers a second principle as part of her theory (p.82):

(5.20)

Principle II

The verb receives lower stress than the subject and the direct object, if there is one; in other words, predicates receive lower stress than their arguments, irrespective of their linear position in surface structure.

Such a principle is taken to apply when a sentence is spoken out of the blue, when all of the sentence is "news" (p. 81). There is a lack of clarity here that stems, we believe, from the failure of Schmerling's theory to "modularize" the account of the relation between prosodic prominence and intonational meaning through the intermediary of focus structure. Schmerling attempts to sustain an analysis in which the presence or absence of prominences (her "stresses") is defined directly in terms of (a) the presumed old/new information content of the sentence in discourse (Principle I) and (b) its predicate-argument structure (Principle II). In particular, her analysis is committed, by Principle II, to a *lack* of prominence on verbs in "news" sentences, and this is wrong, as we have shown. In Schmerling's analysis, Principles I and II are rules for assigning "stress," but not *degree* of stress. (In her framework, like ours, it is whether a constituent has prominence (stress), or not, that is relevant to intonational meaning, and the degree of stress is determined by a late-level rule (see section 5.3.4).) We believe an intermediate level of focus structure helps to clarify the issues.

The point is that the presence or absence of focus on the verb is not relevant to the discourse-relevant information content of the sentence, as long as there is a focused argument within the VP when verb focus is absent. This means that a verb may be prominent, or not, when there is a prominent NP and the sentence is spoken out of the blue. That this should be the case follows from two principles: the Focus Interpretation Principle, which does not interpret the verb as old or new; and the Phrasal Focus Rule, which allows the argument NP to do the work of guaranteeing the possibility of VP focus, necessary in an out-of-the-blue context. The predicate-argument distinction that Schmerling recognizes to be relevant has a rather different function in our theory than in Schmerling's. On our theory, it has a place both in characterizing the prosody-focus relation and in the interpretation of focus. It will become increasingly clear that the problem must be broken down in this way.

Let us consider more fully the implications of part (ii) of the Phrasal Focus Rule, according to which focus on a constituent that is a head may allow for focus on the higher constituent of which it is head. This provision is needed in order to assign NP focus on the basis of N focus in *"KOJAK"* in (5.4), for example. (This is because of our assumption that only words (and not phrases) are attributed the property of focus on the basis of their prosodic prominence, an assumption we will justify in section 5.2.3.) The same provision will permit the focusing of VP and hence the focusing of yet higher constituents in (5.21a–d).

(5.21)
a. JOAN ELOPED.
b. JOHN was ARRESTED.
c. The SUN is SHINING.
d. My UMBRELLA has been FOUND.

It will also permit the focusing of a VP or NP in a situation where only the head word is focused and none of its arguments are. This is an important result.

Ladd 1980 has drawn attention to facts showing that a higher constituent may be focused when only its head and none of the head's arguments are focused, pointing out that these facts raise problems for any NSR-based account of focus assignment. Consider the discourse in (5.22) (Ladd's (19)):

(5.22)
A. Has John read *Slaughterhouse-Five?*
B. No, John doesn't réad [READ] books.

Ladd comments (p. 81):

The accent in (19) is in no sense "contrastive," as it is often said to be: the meaning of B's reply is not the explicit contrast 'John doesn't read books, he writes (reviews, collects, burns, etc.) them.' Rather the point of the accentual pattern is that *books* is deaccented; the focus is broad, but the accent falls on *read* by default.

We agree with Ladd's observation that the prominence on *read* in B's response does not involve a narrow "contrastive" focus and that instead there is a "broader" focus here. Neither NP is focused, with the result that, on our account, the focus structure of B's response must be as given in (5.23).

(5.23)

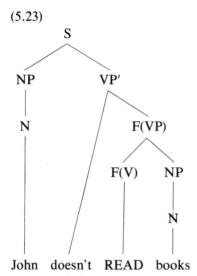

John   doesn't   READ   books

F(VP) is the minimal assignment of focus that would capture the intuition that focus is broad here. (F(VP′) and F(S) could also in principle be foci, given F(VP) and the Phrasal Focus Rule, though it is not clear to us whether these constituents are indeed focused in this particular discourse.) The point here is that the focus of VP must be attributed to the focus of the verb.

Discourse (5.22) thus presents a situation in which there is VP focus, where at the same time it is not necessary (in fact it is impossible) for an argument NP to be focused. The prominence of the verb allows for the VP focus (via the Basic Focus Rule and the Phrasal Focus Rule) and, given the Focus Interpretation Principle (5.10), such a focus structure commits the speaker only to the "newness" of the VP, not to the "newness" of the verb. This is a desirable result here, for *read* is certainly not "new." These principles of grammar therefore admit a possible pronunciation of the sentence that gives the intonational meaning appropriate to this discourse—the one in which only the verb is prominent. This is the only pronunciation of the sentence with the appropriate intonational meaning.

Ladd's analysis of cases like this is rather different. The analysis is embodied in his Focus Rule, (5.24).

(5.24)
Focus Rule (Ladd 1980)
Accent goes on the most accentable syllable of the focus constituent.

(In the discussion, we will substitute the neutral term *prominence* for Ladd's *accent*.) Given (5.24), the claim is that the prominence of the focused VP falls on the verb by *default*, only because the NP cannot be accented (is less accentable) in this discourse. But there is no factual basis for this general claim. When VP is focused, accent is possible in *two* places (at the least) when the NP is focused. For example, it is possible to say *John/he TEACHES CLASSICS* or *John/he teaches CLASSICS*.[14] Both cases may have VP focus. They differ in the presence or absence of focus on the verb, which—given the Focus Interpretation Principle—makes no contribution to the old/new informational content. The point is that prominence on a verb in a focused VP cannot in general be claimed to arise from the lack of focus on some other constituent in the VP. The reason that the verb *must* be prominent in the "default" cases is that the only way for VP focus to result when the arguments of the verb are not focused is for the verb itself to be focused, hence prominent.

Another pair of examples will help make the same point. Both questions in (5.25) have a focus on the NP *Lake Hill.*

(5.25)
a. Where is Lake HILL?
b. Where is LAKE HILL?

The noun phrase is in fact ambiguous, depending on whether the component nouns are interpreted as proper names (Mrs. Lake, Mr. Hill) or as designations of features of the landscape (lake, hill). And indeed, each prominence pattern illustrated in (5.25) has a preferred interpretation. *Lake HILL* designates the lake by the name of *HILL* (cf. *Lake ERIE, Lake HURON, Lake TAHOE*), while *LAKE HILL* designates a hill given the name *LAKE* (*BLAKE HILL, NOB HILL, FORT HILL*).

These examples show that one cannot predict on the basis of NP focus alone whether there will be one prominence (accent) or two within a constituent; the contrast shows that we must allow for at least two (and allow for each to receive an interpretation).[15]

There is another more serious problem with Ladd's Focus Rule: it is based on a conceptual distinction that is not valid, between "accentability" and "focus." Ladd does not define accentability. He suggests that it is a property that nouns inherently have to a greater degree than other categories of words, and he would attribute the prominence of *classics* in *teaches classics* to this inherently greater accentability. But, Ladd acknowledges, context may (somehow) render a noun less accentable. In such a case its sister verb, for example, is rendered "more accentable," and susceptible of receiving prominence (accent) when in a higher focused constituent. It would seem that focus and accentability are both the same notion, conceptually speaking. Both are relevant to intonational meaning and the appropriateness of a sentence in a particular discourse. What distinguishes between the two in Ladd's account is that focus is a property of a higher constituent and accentability is the property of a constituent contained within a focus. What is needed to unify them is simply the notion that foci may be embedded within each other.

The notion that foci may be embedded within each other provides the basis for a unified account of the focus structure of sentences and its relation to intonational meaning. Our focus rules and the accompanying Focus Interpretation Principle are just such an account. Would it be possible to reformulate Ladd's Focus Rule to provide such an account? We think not. Once the notion of accentability is eliminated, there is no way of avoiding a recursive definition of focus like the Phrasal Focus Rule. Thus, although we agree with Ladd's factual observations concerning broad focus in the so-called default accent cases, we reject his account of those cases. We also emphasize that the Basic Focus Rule and Phrasal Focus Rule account for the prosody-focus relation in these cases as they do in the earlier ones, without need for modification.

Before turning to other facts that our analysis accounts for, we would like to examine additional cases of "default accent" and thereby drive home two observations fundamental to our account of the prosody-focus relation: (i) that prominence need not be present at the rightmost extreme of a constituent in order for that constituent to be focused, and (i) that although a higher focus in some sense "derives" its focus from a focused constituent within it, it is not necessary for all constituents within a higher focus to be focused themselves.

Consider the following examples, drawn from Ladd 1980:81:

(5.26)
A bill was sent to Congress today by President Carter which would require peanut butter sandwiches to be served at all government functions. At a press conference today, a group of Senators led by Republican Barry Goldwater of Arizona DENOUNCED the measure. Goldwater said . . .

(5.27)
I can't imagine what it would be like to be a dentist—but I'm awfully glad there are guys who want to BE dentists.

(5.28)
A: Man, it's hot! Doesn't feel like it'll cool off till tomorrow at least.

B: Yeah, they SAID it would be hot all day.

In all these examples, the complement sister to the verb in VP is old information and so cannot be appropriately focused. However, the focusing of the verb is not understood to be contrastive. From this we conclude that there is VP focus here, allowed because of the focus on the verb. Examples such as these are actually no different in character from examples like (5.29) where the object of a verb is an unfocused pronoun.

(5.29)
I SAW her again today.

No narrow focus on *saw* is implied. Such a sentence could be uttered even to begin a discourse, if the referent is clear enough to the interlocutor. (It could be spoken upon entering the house, in reference to a particularly strange bag lady who inhabited the neighborhood, in which case *see* could not possibly be contrastive, since *see* is probably all one ever does with respect to this individual.)

Consider next some examples of "default accent" in prepositional phrases. Just as in VPs, when the NP object must be unfocused but the mother constituent focused, it is the head that carries prominence and hence focus, making the higher focus possible. We give the entire array of prominences for the first example, (5.30), though what interests us most here is the italicized prepositional phrase:

(5.30)

For THEM, it is *WITH metrical trees* that the pattern of prominences must be REPRESENTED.

The italicized PP is in a syntactically defined focus position: the constituent following *it is* must be a focus. Here the prominence that ultimately guarantees the possibility of PP focus is borne by the preposition. The context of such an utterance is clear: metrical trees (and patterns of prominence) are old information and so cannot be focused, which leaves the work of focusing the PP to the prepositional head. The Phrasal Focus Rule guarantees that the prominence of the preposition can do that work. Other examples of preposition prominence with broad focus are abundant:

(5.31)

The buttermilk's the best part OF it.

(*it* = a morning cereal concoction)

(5.32)

Some expressed concern that the President wouldn't be able to get a budget resolution THROUGH Congress.

(5.33)

I didn't even know it was BY Beethoven.[16]

(5.34)

IN such circumstances, people are likely to try something else.

None of these cases can be considered to have narrow focus on the preposition. The preposition is just the carrier, so to speak, of the prominence that allows for PP focus. It can do so by virtue of the fact that Focus Interpretation does not force the reading that the preposition constitutes new information.

As Ladd points out, the (so-called) default accent is not limited to this sort of VP and PP configuration. Indeed, whenever an unfocused argument occurs within a higher focused constituent, that higher constituent must contain another focused argument or a focused head. Compare example (5.30) to (5.35).

(5.35)

For THEM, it is in TERMS of metrical trees that . . .

Here, too, PP focus is guaranteed by a nonargument, though the example has a different shape. In this case, *terms,* the head of the NP object of *in,* is prominent; thus the NP object may itself be focused and thereby guarantee that the PP in syntactic focus position is focused. It is within that NP itself that we find a case of "default accent." *Terms* bears the prominence allowing for the higher NP focus because its argument NP, old information, cannot.

Such cases of "default accent" are extremely problematic for a number of the extant theories of the prosody-focus relation. Advocates of the various versions of the NSR-Focus analysis (e.g., Chomsky 1971, Jackendoff 1972, Bing 1979a, Williams 1980b) are committed to viewing the focus on verbs and prepositions in such cases as narrow, and hence contrastive. Such cases are also problematic for any account (such as Schmerling's) that does not incorporate focus structure, and in particular for any account that cannot separate the focus of the head from the focus of the higher constituent. The ability of our theory to deal successfully with the "default accent" cases is a strong indication that we are on the right track in giving the semantic relations *head* and *argument* a central role in characterizing the prosody-focus relation, rather than the linear order of constituents.

5.2.2 Prosody and Focus in German

Because our theory of the prosody-focus relation makes no appeal, either direct or indirect, to the *position* of prosodic prominence(s) in the linear order of constituents, it can be extended without modification to describing the prosody-focus relation in a language where the order of heads and their arguments differs from their order in English. Consider for example a German sentence with a verb in final position preceded in the VP by an argument NP, one in which the verb is *not* prominent and the major prominence of the sentence is on the preceding NP.

(5.36)
PETER hat ein BUCH betrachtet.
Peter   has a   book   looked at
'Peter has looked at a book.'

This sentence can be appropriately uttered out of the blue. Both NPs provide new information, and the VP may be interpreted as new information as well. The focus structure corresponding to the meaning that includes the "broad" focus of VP is, minimally, (5.37):

(5.37)

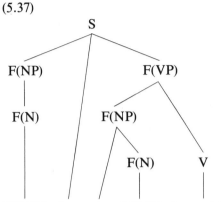

PETER   hat   ein   BUCH   betrachtet

(See Thiersch 1977 for justification of this phrase structure.) The focus rules pronounce this a well-formed prosody-focus structure relation. Moreover, the Focus Interpretation Principle interprets the focused subject and direct object NP arguments and the focused VP as new information and leaves the old/new status of the verb *betrachtet* vague.

Sentences like (5.37) present difficulties for the analysis of "normal phrase stress" in German within an SPE-like standard framework. The problem (addressed by Kiparsky 1966, for example) is to explain why there is no final prominence on the verb in an out-of-the-blue "normal stress" utterance like this, even though final prominence is (generally) the rule for other constituents, including the sentence. In (5.36), for example, *Buch* is more prominent than *Peter,* showing the effects of the NSR on the S. And sentences like (5.38a–c) (from Bierwisch 1968) exhibit rightward prominence of the NSR variety.[17]

(5.38)

a. [[Die Schuhe von Heinrich] sind kaputt]
$\quad$ the shoes   of   Heinrich   are   ruined
$\quad$ 'Heinrich's shoes are ruined.'

b. [[Bücher, die   zu teuer   sind], taugen   nichts]
$\quad$ books   which too expensive are   are worth nothing
$\quad$ 'Books which are too expensive are worth nothing.'

c. [Peter betrachtet ein Buch]
$\quad$ Peter looks at   a   book
$\quad$ 'Peter is looking at a book.'

Since the assumptions made by Kiparsky about German surface phrase structure are different from the assumptions we make here, following Thiersch 1977 and others, a detailed examination of Kiparsky's proposal and the difficulties it encounters would not be particularly fruitful. Suffice it to say that Kiparsky proposed that German had a rule like the English NSR that applied in some phrases but not in others. In these other constituents another phrase stress rule was said to apply, assigning leftmost prominence. Judging from the prominence pattern of (5.36) and (5.37), the VP would seem to be a phrase in which a rule assigning leftmost prominence applies. But even this special rule for VP is unable to cope with the facts, for if the VP contains two complements preceding the verb (and if both of them are new information), as in (5.39), then it is the rightmost that receives greatest prominence, not the leftmost, as the rule assigning leftmost prominence in VP would predict.

(5.39)
Sie hat ihrer   MUTTER das BUCH gegeben.
She has her (dat) mother   the book   given
'She has given her mother the book.'

(Capitalization fails to reflect *degrees* of prominence: *Buch* is more prominent than *Mutter* in this sentence. See note 17.)

It should be clear, of course, that German is no different from English with respect to focus. Lack of focus (and prominence) on the verb in any out-of-the-blue utterance (or any utterance where VP is focused) is perfectly permissible, and NPs (but not necessarily verbs) must be focused if they are to be interpreted as new. Another pair of examples involving a focused VP containing an unfocused NP will underline this similarity. Consider a discourse whose topic is the horrendous mess that typically occupies the living room. To give additional evidence of the lamentable state of affairs, one interlocutor, speaking of her brother, utters the sentence (5.40), which contains but one prominence.

(5.40)
Er hat sein BUCH im Wohnzimmer   verloren.
he has his book   in the living room lost
'He has lost his book in the living room.'

Actually, given the freedom in German word order, another sentence (5.41) with the same meaning is possible, where the order of the verb's complements has simply been reversed. As long as the prominence remains on the direct object *sein Buch,* the intonational meaning is the same.

(5.41)
Er hat im Wohnzimmer sein BUCH verloren.

The prominence on *Buch* does not give rise merely to NP focus in these sentences. Rather it seems appropriate to think of the entire VP as being focused. (5.40) is quite comparable to the English sentences cited above where the focus of a single NP within VP allows for VP focus, even when that NP's neighbor (sister) PP or NP in the VP is not focused. Sentences like this are of course problematic for any theory attempting to compute the location of a prominence within a higher focused phrase on the basis of purely linear or structural considerations.

Note finally that the "default" accent phenomenon that is found in English is found in German as well. (5.42) and (5.43) are quite appropriate as new utterances in a context in which books are old information:

(5.42)
PETER hat ein/das Buch BETRACHTET.

(5.43)
PETER BETRACHTET ein/das Buch.

(Bierwisch 1968 underscores the problematic character of these examples for a standard theory account of phrasal prominence.)

In sum, the theory according to which the position of greatest prominence within a focused constituent in German is determined by the rules of phrase stress has several undesirable consequences. It must posit two different rules for phrase stress (though this still leaves unexplained the prominence pattern of VP when it has two prominent complements). Even with that, it is not equipped to deal with sentences like (5.40) and (5.41), where the same focus structure may allow for two different loci of prosodic prominence. Nor is it equipped to deal with cases of "default accent" like (5.42) and (5.43). The focus rules and the Focus Interpretation Principle, however, account for these facts in a straightforward way. Bierwisch 1968 has noted the problematic character of these sentences for the NSR in German. But his conclusion that these facts show that the NSR must apply to levels of representation other than the surface syntactic level is unwarranted, as we have shown.[18]

There is one fact from German that our analysis does not account for. The sentence (5.44), wherein the verb is focused in addition to its complements, is considered to be distinctly odd, if not impossible, as an out-of-the-blue utterance where VP focus is in order.

(5.44)
PETER hat ein BUCH BETRACHTET.

Prominence on the verb here seems to indicate narrow focus on the verb. We do not know what to make of this fact, particularly because, when the verb is more semantically rich, it may be prominent and focused and still permit a broader VP focus interpretation, as in (5.45).

(5.45)
Er hatte diese MORALVORSTELLUNGEN INTERNALISIERT.
he had   these moral ideas   internalized
'He had INTERNALIZED these MORAL IDEAS.'

However, the verb *internalisiert* in no way requires a prominence. But note now that (5.46), where the same verb is *not* prominent, is reportedly the preferred pronunciation when the sentence is uttered out of the blue.

(5.46)
Er hatte die SELTSAMSTEN MORALVORSTELLUNGEN
he had   the strangest   moral ideas
internalisiert.
internalized
'He had internalized the strangest moral ideas.'

Perhaps focusing the verb here would "detract" from the focus on the NP. We have obviously not plumbed the depths of focus interpretation: principle (5.10) so far has no way of drawing the distinctions between cases like these in German or between comparable ones in English (of which Bolinger 1958a, 1972a cites many). Clearly an elaboration of the account is in order. Nonetheless, these facts, and our current inability to explain them, should not obscure the general point. The facts of German phrasal prominence we have examined show that the location of prominence within a focused constituent is not determined by phrase stress rules, that the focus of VP and its constituent NPs are independently variable, and that the focus rules account well for the prosody-focus structure relation in the language.

One remaining fact must be discussed before we leave the topic of German phrasal prominence. Sentence (5.47) (= (5.43)) is a case of "default accent" like those discussed in English.

(5.47)
Peter/PETER BETRACHTET das Buch.

The NP *das Buch* is unfocused, as old information, and the focus on the verb is not (necessarily) narrow. We may understand the VP to be focused. The important point is that the verb here is not *in* the VP. German is underlyingly verb-final, and the verb moved into second position is no longer a constituent of VP. (See Thiersch 1977 for arguments to this effect.) Note that the Phrasal Focus Rule does not in fact require that the focused *head* of a constituent be contained within it in order to be a focus itself. Yet (5.1b) could have been formulated to require that both head and argument be contained within the higher focus constituent if they are to "transmit" their focus to it. The facts of English would be consistent with either formulation, since the head verb does not leave the VP in English. But the facts of German seem to be compatible only with the original version; they seem to show that a head verb can focus the VP of which it is head even if it is not contained within it. There is an alternative solution, however. If the verb in second place were to have left a trace in VP, and if the surface structure focus of an antecedent translates into a focus of its trace, then the focus of the apparently verbless VP could be attributed to the focus of the trace of the head within it, and the requirement that a focused head be contained within a higher constituent if that higher one is to be focused could be maintained. We leave it to the reader to speculate about such matters, making no attempt to decide the issue here and turning instead to offer more observations of a similar kind.

5.2.3 Argument Structure and the Phrasal Focus Rule

So far we have not actually given decisive evidence in favor of the Phrasal Focus Rule, (5.1b), which clams that it is the focus of arguments and/or heads that is crucial to the focus of the higher dominating constituent. The facts examined so far have been consistent with the Alternative Phrasal Focus Rule, (5.5), according to which a higher constituent may be focused as long as it contains a focused constituent, of any sort.

We have also not given decisive evidence for our characterization of the Focus Interpretation Principle, (5.10), which relies on the distinction between arguments and nonarguments in interpreting the sentence for its old/new informational content. The facts considered would be consistent with the Alternative Focus Interpretation Principle, (5.11), which views the relevant difference merely in terms of the distinction between *phrases* and *words* that are not themselves phrases.

In order to show that the notions *argument* and *head* are indeed crucial, we must examine the focus and interpretation of words and phrases that are neither heads nor arguments in the predicate-argument structure of the sentence, and the focus and interpretation of the phrases that dominate them in surface structure. Syntactic constituents that are neither arguments nor heads of larger phrases will be called *adjuncts*. They include modifiers, quantifiers, and others. The Phrasal Focus Rule claims that the focus of an adjunct will *not* allow for the focus of the phrase that is its mother. And the Focus Interpretation Principle claims that the presence or absence of focus on an adjunct will not contribute to the old/new information content of the utterance.

Consider sentence (5.48):

(5.48)
JOHN bought a red TIE.

(5.48) could be uttered out of the blue, the VP and both NPs being taken to introduce "new information." Since the adjective *red* is not prominent here and hence not focused, the adjective phrase dominating *red* is not a focus. This sentence is not relevant to deciding which version of the Phrasal Focus Rule is correct. The lack of focus on the AP *red* has no effect on the potential of the higher NP *a red TIE* to be focused, since, given either version of the Phrasal Focus Rule, the focus of *TIE* would allow for the higher focus. Sentence (5.48) does permit us to ask about the status of the adjunct *red* in its informational structure, however. Does uttering (5.48) commit the speaker to the assumption that *red* is "old information"? Must *red* have already been mentioned in the discourse (or somehow be present in the discourse context) in order for (5.48) to be an appropriate utterance? We think not. If this intuition is well founded, then it follows that the original version of the Focus Interpretation Principle is the correct one. This is because *red* is not merely a word, but also a phrase, and as such would necessarily be interpreted as old information if it were the Alternative Focus Interpretation Principle that was at work.

Consider next sentence (5.49).

(5.49)
JOHN bought a RED shirt.

The question is whether the focus on the adjunct *red* permits focus on the entire NP, and hence on the VP. The answer here is no: focus is narrow, confined to the AP. (5.49) can be appropriately uttered when it is intended to be "contrastive" (as would be the case if it followed *Sue bought a blue shirt,* for example). But as an out-of-the-blue utterance, even in a discourse context where shirts are somehow salient, (5.49) does not seem to be appropriate. We conclude that focus on *red* ulti- mately does not allow for focus on VP. Given the Phrasal Focus Rule, the explanation for this is that the NP of VP is not focused, which is to say that focus on the adjunct *red* does not result in focus on the NP. This, too, is what the Phrasal Focus Rule predicts. The Alternative Phrasal Focus Rule, by contrast, would predict that focus of *red* would allow for focus on NP, and hence on VP. Here, then, is evidence fa- voring the characterization of the prosody-focus relation that invokes the relations involved in the argument structure of phrases.

Consider next a sentence in which the focus of the (adjunct) quan- tifier *three* varies:

(5.50)

$$
\text{There were} \begin{cases} \text{a.} & \text{three GUYS} \\ \text{b.} & \text{THREE GUYS} \\ \text{c.} & \text{THREE guys} \end{cases} \text{out there who were making a lot}
$$

of noise.

(5.50a,b) seem quite appropriate spoken out of the blue (where the referent of *there* is part of the discourse). In either pronunciation the NP may be understood to be new information. In such a case it is not necessary for *three,* which is not presupposed, to be focused. (This is predicted by the Focus Interpretation Principle.) But it *is* necessary for *guys* to be focused if the NP is new information: (5.50c) is not appropri- ate, unless *guys* is understood to be old information. The explanation for this, provided by the Phrasal Focus Rule, is that the adjunct *three* cannot "transmit" its own focus to the NP, so that, in order for the NP to be focused, its head *guys* must be focused. Note that the Phrasal Focus Rule does not require that the head of a "new" NP be focused. In this case the head must bear the focus because no other constituent within the NP can.

Compare in this regard sentence (5.51).

(5.51)

When THREE opponents of REAGAN gather together, everyone thinks there's a caucus taking place.

In the utterance as given there is no focus on the head noun *opponents,* yet it would be quite appropriately spoken where opponents had not been mentioned in the discourse. The NP can be interpreted as new because it may itself be focused. Here its focus comes not from its head, but from the NP argument of the head, *Reagan.*

As a final example of a prenominal adjunct within an NP whose focus does not allow for focus on the higher NP, consider the partitive quantifier *half* in (5.52).

(5.52)

$$\text{The lady gave me} \begin{cases} \text{a. half a PIE} \\ \text{b. HALF a PIE} \\ \text{c. HALF a pie} \end{cases}.$$

(5.52a,b) both have NP focus (hence, VP focus) and thus can be used in a situation in which the information corresponding to the entire VP is new. However, (5.52c) seems to give only narrow focus on *HALF* and would be appropriately used only if it were presupposed (old information) that "the lady gave me (some part of) a pie."

Before examining sentences involving adjuncts in other positions within phrases, we must deal with some apparent counterexamples to our claim that the focus of an adjunct does not give rise to the focus of its mother phrase. Bolinger 1972a cites a number of examples, among them (5.53) and (5.54), in which an adjunct is prominent and the head not, and where we would want to say that the entire NP is in focus:

(5.53)

My GERANIUM plant is almost dead.

(5.54)

There were CRAWLING things all around.

Both narrow focus on the modifier alone and broad focus on the entire NP are possible here. Bolinger attributes this pattern of prominence to the "relative semantic weight" and "predictability" of the words involved. (Indeed, Bolinger takes the notion "relative semantic weight" to explain most facts concerning the location of prominences in utterances—a position that Schmerling 1976 and Ladd 1980 show to be untenable.) In this instance we believe Bolinger's insight permits the explanation of what, on our theory, is an apparently anomalous focus structure. There is some reason to think that an additional focus rule is at work in defining the well-formedness of prosody–focus structure pairs in the language:

(5.55)
The Redundant Focus Rule

If a constituent is *redundant* in S_j, it may be a focus in S_j.

Redundant in S_j is defined as follows:

(5.56)
A constituent C_i is *redundant in S_j* if the meaning of the sentence S_j dominating C_i follows from the meaning of the sentence S_j' that is identical to S_j except that the contents of C_i are absent. (The lexical item(s) dominated by C_i (and their structural relations, if there is more than one lexical item) are the *contents* of C_i.)

Given this definition, the head nouns of both apparent counterexamples are redundant. (5.57) implies (5.53), and (5.58) implies (5.54).

(5.57)
My GERANIUM $_N[\phi]_N$ is almost dead.

(5.58)
There were CRAWLING $_N[\phi]_N$ all around.

Thus, given the new rule (5.55), the nonprominent heads may nonetheless count as foci, and the focus of the higher NP is ensured by the Phrasal Focus Rule. Of course, (5.55) can only be a primitive first approximation, for the "meaning" referred to will necessarily involve some knowledge of the world—in other words, it cannot be defined strictly in terms of the sentence.

This notion of redundancy and the Redundant Focus Rule based on it account for other examples cited by Bolinger:

(5.59)
a. He was arrested because he KILLED a man.
b. I'm going over to the DOCTOR'S place.
c. I'm doing it for JOHN'S sake.

In none of these cases must it be understood that *a man, place,* or *sake* is old information. In the latter two, the NP dominating the nonprominent head is apparently new (hence focused). The focus structures of these sentences, and their interpretation, require us to say that *a man, place,* and *sake* are focused, if our general theory is to be retained. Since these nonprominent would-be foci are redundant within their respective sentences,[19] we can claim that it is the Redundant Focus Rule that is at play here. Compare these to the quite similar examples offered by Bolinger:

(5.60)
a. He was arrested because he KILLED a POLICEMAN.
b. I'm going over to the DOCTOR'S BARN.
c. I'm doing it for JOHN'S WELFARE.

Here, the prominence pattern is as expected. The difference between these and the earlier examples is that the constituents *a policeman, barn,* and *welfare* are not redundant within the sentence, so that the focus of the NPs must be ensured by more conventional means—the presence of prominence on the head.

By adding the Redundant Focus Rule, then, we are able to bring a variety of new cases into the purview of our basic analysis (the Phrasal Focus Rule and the Focus Interpretation Principle), still preserving the generalizations that arguments and heads behave differently from adjuncts in the prosody-focus relation and that arguments are interpreted differently from nonarguments in the interpretation of focus structures. In our discussion of compounds (which draws on insights of Ladd 1981), we will again call on the Redundant Focus Rule to explain otherwise problematic prominence patterns.

We would now like to show that our grammar of focus, with its reliance on predicate-argument structure, accounts nicely for certain classic puzzles in the prosody-focus domain, puzzles that have proven quite vexing for previous accounts of this relation. The first involves the apparent contrast in "normal stress" between noun phrases containing relative clauses and noun phrases containing complements to the head noun, first mentioned by Newman 1946. Newman compares the examples in (5.61) and (5.62) (p. 178).[20]

(5.61)
a. I have INSTRUCTIONS to leave. ('I am to leave instructions')
b. I have INSTRUCTIONS to LEAVE. ('I have been instructed to leave')

(5.62)

a. With their PLANS to write, . . . ('their having plans to write')

b. With their PLANS to WRITE, . . . ('their having planned to write')

As his glosses indicate, the prominence pattern associated with the (a) sentences is taken to be appropriate when the *to*-phrase is a relative clause and the one associated with the (b) sentences to be appropriate when the *to*-phrase is a complement to the head noun. Bresnan 1971a, 1972 accepts the factual judgments and proposes an account for the "stress differences" in which the NSR is said to apply not at surface structure, where from the point of view of the NSR the phrases are identical, but at earlier stage(s) in the derivation (specifically, at the end of each transformational cycle). Subsequent investigation has shown that the original empirical generalizations were not entirely sound (see Berman and Szamosi 1972, Lakoff 1972b, Bolinger 1972a, Schmerling 1976, for example), and the new facts show that Bresnan's account, which we will review below, cannot be upheld. We suggest, however, that although the difference between the NP-relative clause and NP-complement cases are not as Newman and Bresnan have claimed, there is nonetheless one pronunciation that distinguishes the two.

Let us start by looking at prominence patterns where the syntactic differences are "neutralized." Consider first (5.63) (= (5.61a)).

(5.63)

I have INSTRUCTIONS to LEAVE.

The factual claim, which we share with the others cited above, is that such a sentence is ambiguous. We also claim that for both the relative clause and complement interpretation there are intonational meanings available in which focus may be just limited to the parts of the NP or may be as broad as possible, with focus on the higher NP and the VP. This is in fact what the focus rules predict, as the focus structure "tables" (5.64a) and (5.64b) show.

(5.64)

a.

$_{S_1}[I\ _{VP_1}[have\ _{NP_1}[_{NP_2}[INSTRUCTIONS]_{NP_2}\ _{S_2}[to\ _{VP_2}[LEAVE]_{VP_2}]_{S_2}]_{NP_1}]_{VP_1}]_{S_1}$

F(N)	F(V)
F(NP$_2$)	F(VP$_2$)
F(NP$_1$)	F(S$_2$)
F(VP$_1$)	
F(S$_1$)?	

b. $_{S_1}[I\ _{VP_1}[have\ _{NP_1}[INSTRUCTIONS\ _{S_2}[to\ _{VP_2}[LEAVE]_{VP_2}]_{S_2}]_{NP_1}]_{VP_1}]_{S_1}$

F(N)	F(V)
F(NP$_1$)	F(VP$_2$)
F(VP$_1$)	F(S$_2$)
F(S$_1$)?	F(NP$_1$)
	F(VP$_1$)
	F(S$_1$)?

The Basic Focus Rule gives the focus of N and V written above the line. Below the line, each successive focus is available (via the Phrasal Focus Rule) because of the focus of the constituent noted above it in the column, and each successive focus is in principle optional. In (5.64a), given that the head N of NP$_1$ is prominent, the entire NP$_1$ (and hence the highest VP$_1$) may be focused. The relative clause is also focused in (5.64a), though as the "focus chain" of *LEAVE* in (5.64a) shows, it does not contribute to focusing the higher NP (it is not an argument). In (5.64b), the fact that both the head N and the complement are focused means that there are in effect two routes to the focusing of NP$_1$ and VP$_1$, via the head or the argument. Thus the Phrasal Focus Rule predicts the possibility of "wide focus" in both cases. And this, the consensus says, is as it should be.

Consider next sentence (5.65) (= (5.61b)).

(5.65)
I have INSTRUCTIONS to leave.

Again, we claim that this pronunciation is possible either for the NP with the relative clause or for the NP with the complement. Moreover, we claim that it is appropriate to utter the sentence with either syntactic analysis when the higher NP and the highest VP are "new information." In other words, we are saying that the highest VP and its daughter NP may be new, while the unfocused VP that is the relative clause or complement is nonetheless old. ((5.65) with the relative clause interpretation could answer the question "What are you doing here?" addressed to the speaker as she enters an office; (5.65) with the complement interpretation could answer the question "Why are you going?" put as the speaker walks out. In either context *to leave* becomes old information.) Again, these possibilities are predicted by the focus rules:

(5.66)

a. $_{S_1}$[I $_{VP_1}$[have $_{NP_1}$[$_{NP_2}$[INSTRUCTIONS]$_{NP_2}$ $_{S_2}$[to $_{VP_2}$[leave]$_{VP_2}$]$_{S_2}$]$_{NP_1}$]$_{VP_1}$]$_{S_1}$

      F(N)

      F(NP$_2$)
      F(NP$_1$)
      F(VP$_1$)
      F(S$_1$)?

b. $_{S_1}$[I $_{VP_1}$[have $_{NP_1}$[INSTRUCTIONS $_{S_2}$[to $_{VP}$[leave]$_{VP}$]$_{S_2}$]$_{NP_1}$]$_{VP_1}$]$_{S_1}$

      F(N)

      F(NP$_1$)
      F(VP)
      F(S$_1$)?

Where the focus rules predict that the sentences diverge, and where it seems in fact they do, is in the utterance of (5.67).

(5.67)
I have instructions to LEAVE.

With the complement meaning, this sentence is appropriate where "broad" NP and VP focus are called for. Its focus structure is entirely comparable to that of the sentence *I was instructed to LEAVE*. With the relative clause meaning, however, we believe that only *narrow* focus, on *to leave*, is possible. The claim is that the prominence pattern in (5.67) for the relative clause analysis commits the speaker to the assumptions that (i) *instructions* is old information and (ii) the higher NP and VP are old information. If this indeed correctly represents the facts, and we believe it does, then the characterization of the Phrasal Focus Rule that invokes the predicate-argument structure of phrases must be correct. A relative clause is an adjunct, not an argument, so that focus on the relative clause *to leave* does not alone allow for focus on the higher NP, given the Phrasal Focus Rule. But the noun complement *to leave* is in fact an argument, and its focus may therefore be "transmitted" to higher phrases. Thus the Phrasal Focus Rule predicts the difference that we believe to exist between the prosody-focus possibilities of the two types of sentences. The relevant focus structure "table" is as follows:

(5.68)

a. $_{S_1}[I \ _{VP_1}[\text{have} \ _{NP_1}[_{NP_2}[\text{instructions}]_{NP_2} \ _{S_2}[\text{to} \ _{VP_2}[\text{LEAVE}]_{VP_2}]_{S_2}]_{NP_1}]_{VP_1}]_{S_1}$

$$\frac{F(V)}{\begin{array}{c} F(VP_2) \\ F(S_2) \end{array}}$$

b. $_{S_1}[I \ _{VP_1}[\text{have} \ _{NP_1}[\text{instructions} \ _{S_2}[\text{to} \ _{VP_2}[\text{LEAVE}]_{VP_2}]_{S_2}]_{NP_1}]_{VP_1}]_{S_1}$

$$\frac{F(V)}{\begin{array}{c} F(VP_2) \\ F(S_2) \\ F(NP_1) \\ F(VP_1) \\ F(S_1)? \end{array}}$$

To sum up, then, our description and analysis of the facts are rather different from Newman's and Bresnan's. Yet we accept that there is a difference in the prosody-focus patterns between the two types of cases, and we attribute it to the fact that the rules defining the relation between prominence and focus structure in surface structure appeal to the argument structure of the phrase.

Before examining one other set of cases that Bresnan discusses, which is relevant to the general theory of focus structure, we will review why Bresnan's theory of the supposed difference between Newman's sentences in (5.61) and (5.62) cannot be right, on phonological grounds. Bresnan's theory is that the SPE Nuclear Stress Rule (which assigns numerical values of the feature [n stress]) applies in the syntactic (transformational) cycle, and that within each cycle its application follows the application of all transformational rules on that cycle. Given this theory, along with a particular theory of the deep structure of relative clauses, the difference in the surface stress patterns of the pairs in (5.61) and (5.62) is computed automatically. Two sample derivations are given in (5.69):

(5.69)

a. $[$I $[$have $_{NP_1}[$instructions $_S[$ ____ to $_{VP_2}[$léave instructions$]_{VP_2}]_S]_{NP_1}]]$

VP₂ cycle

NSR   léave instructions

⋮

NP₁ cycle

Relative Clause   instructions   to   leave ϕ

Formation

NSR   (no change)

⋮

Surface pattern   I have instructions to leave

b. $[$I $[$have $_{NP_1}[$instructions $_{S_2}[$ ____ to $_{VP_2}[$léave$]_{VP_2}]_{S_2}]_{NP_1}]]$

⋮

NP₁ cycle

NSR   instructions   to   leave

⋮

Surface pattern   I have instructions to leave

The analysis relies crucially on some assumptions about the nature of the representation of stress that are questionable, to say the least, in view of our new understanding of stress. For example, the 1 stress that is the main word stress of the head of the relative clause is automatically vaulted to the status of main phrase stress by the deletion (in Relative Clause Formation) of the lower *instructions* that had borne the 1 stress that had caused the preceding verb to assume 2 stress. Neither a metrical tree nor a metrical grid theory of stress would have an analogue to this particular numerology, and an analysis of the sort Bresnan proposes would simply not be possible. In fact, even if the NSR "applied" in the syntactic cycle, and even if deletion occurred as part of Relative Clause Formation, the "main stress" that would be derived by either the tree or the grid theory would fall on *leave*. The derivation itself we leave as an exercise for the reader. The point is that, given a different understanding of the representation of stress, an analysis such as Bresnan's is in principle impossible.

We now turn to the other relevant set of cases that Bresnan discusses (1971a, 1972). She notes a contrast in the stress patterns of questions, which she says depends on whether or not the underlying object of the verb would have been susceptible to receiving main phrase stress or not:

(5.70)

a. John asked what Helen has $\overset{1}{\text{written}}$?

b. John asked what $\overset{1}{\text{books}}$ Helen has $\overset{2}{\text{written}}$?

(5.71)

a. Whose have I $\overset{1}{\text{taken}}$?

b. Whose $\overset{1}{\text{umbrella}}$ have I $\overset{2}{\text{taken}}$?

Bresnan's analysis of this contrast suffers from the same sort of empirical inadequacies as the earlier one. As others have demonstrated, main prominence may indeed fall on the (lower) verb even when its deep object (the surface *wh*-phrase) is a "full" NP (see Berman and Szamosi 1972, Lakoff 1972b, Bolinger 1972a, Schmerling 1976, for example). The phonological underpinnings of the analysis are equally problematic. But while Bresnan's particular analysis must go, the problem remains. It is still a fact that (5.70b) and (5.71b) are possible out-of-the-blue pronunciations, and it is the task of a theory of the prosody-focus relation to explain why this is so.

The crucial issue is whether there is VP focus in these questions. If there is VP focus in (5.70b) and (5.71b), even though the surface structure VP contains no prominence, then the focus of the VP would presumably have to be attributed to the focus of the NP argument of its head verb, even though that argument is not contained within it in surface structure. But we showed that an argument must be contained within a phrase if it is to "transmit" its focus. From this we would then have to conclude that the *trace* of the focused *wh*-argument is what allows for the VP focus. In other words, there would have to be a principle in the grammar stating that focus on an antecedent results in focus on the element bound by the antecedent. And even that would be too general, for focus on antecedents of argument traces left behind by NP movements such as Passive ultimately does not allow for VP focus (in *JOHN was arrested t* the focus is narrow, on *JOHN* alone). A lot rides, then, on whether or not the VP is focused in questions like (5.70b) and (5.71b). And the solution isn't obvious. Clearly, questions are "about" the questioned NP—which, if prominent, is certainly "new" in some sense. And clearly, new information may be introduced elsewhere in the sentence in the form of a focused NP that is not the *wh*-NP:

(5.72)
What BOOKS has HELEN written?

The verb may be focused as well:

(5.73)
What BOOKS did HELEN REVIEW?

But is there VP focus here?

What is needed are some operational tests for ascertaining the presence of VP focus that will apply when the utterance is a question. We have not invented such tests, and so must leave the question open here.

To conclude, we have shown in this section that there are good reasons for accepting the Phrasal Focus Rule and the Focus Interpretation Principle as the proper generalizations about the phenomena in question. We have been able to explain the different contributions of phrasal prominence to focus structure and ultimately to intonational meaning, by assuming that the argument structure of the sentence plays a crucial role in the analysis.

5.2.4 Focus and English Compounds

According to the analysis of English compounds given in SPE, the locus of greatest prominence in a compound is by rule on the left, and the cases of right-hand prominence are simply exceptions. There is some truth in this analysis, and indeed in chapter 4 we claimed that English has a Compound Rule that assigns rhythmic prominence to the greatest prominence of the left-hand constituent of a compound word. This proposal is in effect a translation into metrical grid terms of the SPE Compound Rule. But we also claimed that a different sort of prominence may be assigned to the words contained within compounds, one that is directly relevant to the focus properties of the sentence, and, as we will show, this latter sort of prominence is by no means generally assigned to the left-hand member. This additional sort of prominence, we claim, is the presence of a pitch accent, and the association of a pitch accent with a syllable guarantees (through the Pitch Accent Prominence Rule) that the syllable will be more rhythmically prominent than any non-pitch-accent-bearing syllable. The assignment of a focus-related pitch accent to the right-hand member of a compound will therefore give right-hand rhythmic prominence and thereby override the Compound Rule. (The assignment of pitch accent to the left-hand member will give greatest rhythmic prominence on the left. In such a case, the Pitch Accent Prominence Rule and the Compound Rule predict "main stress" in the same location.) On our account, then, the Compound Rule, like the NSR, comes into effect only where it is not overridden by the presence of focus-related pitch accents. In the discussion that follows we will continue to use the neutral term *prominence* to designate the suprasegmental property of words that is related to their place in a focus structure, though the relevant prominence is not merely "greatest (rhythmic) stress," but has a pitch component as well.

The proposed focus rules and Focus Interpretation Principle go a long way toward explaining the location of prominence in English compounds. Particularly interesting is the fact that the distinctions drawn among arguments, heads, and adjuncts are central to an explanation of focus in compounds. We will first consider as evidence the "isolation pronunciation" of compounds. As with any utterance, a compound uttered in isolation has a focus structure and an intonational structure, and, minimally, it will contain one (nuclear) prominence. The generalization is that, in an isolation pronunciation of the compound uttered in a "neutral" discourse context, (nuclear) prominence is located in the position within the compound that will guarantee "wide focus"—that is, focus on the compound as a whole, rather than just on the particular word bearing the prominence.

Compounds are generally right-headed in English (M. Allen 1978, Williams 1981a, Selkirk 1982), and they have a (recursive) bipartite structure. The left-hand element of a compound may bear a host of possible semantic relations to the head (M. Allen 1978, Downing 1977, Levi 1978, Selkirk 1982, Adams 1973). For our purposes, it is enough to distinguish between two general types of relationship: argument-head and adjunct-head. The focus rules and Focus Interpretation Principle predict that in the two different sorts of cases, prominence will be assigned differently. The demand for wide focus means that in the adjunct-head case prominence *must* fall on the head. There may also be a prominence on the adjunct, but prominence on the adjunct alone would give narrow focus on the adjunct. As for the first case, wide focus results if there is prominence on the argument alone. It would also result if there were prominence on the head as well, or on the head alone. But if the argument were not itself prominent, the Focus Interpretation Principle would assign it an "old information" status, so that such a pronunciation would not be appropriate in a neutral context. In sum, the following prominence possibilities are predicted for "neutral" isolation pronunciations of the two different sorts of compounds:

(5.75)

a.	ARGUMENT head	b.	Adjunct HEAD
	ARGUMENT HEAD		ADJUNCT HEAD
	*Argument HEAD		*ADJUNCT head

Before investigating the truth of these claims about the location of prominence in compounds, we should point out that many compounds, perhaps the majority of those invested with the status of lexical items, do not have a meaning that is a lawful product of semantic rules of combination. Examples are *greatcoat, greenhouse, high school, rainbow, funny bone, bluebird, redskin, kingfisher*. In such cases, of course, there is no argument-head or adjunct-head relation. We will say about these that the compound itself is the smallest syntactic-semantic unit relevant to focus structure and the appropriateness of the utterance in discourse. The prominence of such compounds is therefore irrelevant to our analysis of focus structure and focus interpretation. Nevertheless, we do consider the fact that prominence is on the left in such cases of "frozen" compound meaning to be significant. We believe that it demonstrates the correctness of the claim that there is indeed a Compound Rule in English, obscured though it may be in the other cases by focus-related prominence.[21] We will return to this point in section 5.3.3, restricting our discussion until then to compounds whose meaning is rather transparently a function of their component parts.

Consider the compound adjectives in (5.76).

(5.76)

a. waist HIGH   lily WHITE[22]
   world FAMOUS   crystal CLEAR
   Boston TRAINED   dirt CHEAP
   ash BLOND   stone DEAF

b. FROST bitten   WAGE earning
   DISEASE prone   GERM resistant
   BLOOD thirsty   COLOR blind
   BREATH taking   FIRE proof

These compounds all have the structure $_A[\text{N A}]_A$. Clearly the difference in the location of prominence here cannot be explained in purely structural terms. What differentiates between the (a) and (b) cases, aside from their prominence patterns, is the semantic relation holding between the head and its sister. In (5.76b), the head has an argument to its left: *bitten by frost, prone to disease, thirsty for blood, resistant to germs*, etc. In (5.76a), the head's sister has either the character of an adjunct modifier (e.g., *as white as a lily, as high as (the) waist, as cheap as dirt*) or a locative force (Adams 1973). The generalization that arguments take prominence here, whereas adjuncts do not, seems quite plausible. Consider next compound adjectives of the form $_A[\text{A A}]_A$ or $_A[\text{Adv A}]_A$. In the vast majority of cases the left-hand A or Adv is a modifier; thus, prominence in the compound falls on the head on the right, as in (5.77).

(5.77)

a. hard HITTING   worldly WISE
   long SUFFERING   red HOT
   wide AWAKE   ever LASTING
   well BEHAVED   blue GREEN

But note that when the deverbal adjective takes an adjective argument, the prominence pattern is reversed.

(5.78)

a.   NICE seeming
   ?RED-turning (leaves)

Finally, note that when the first element in an adjective compound is a preposition, it often has the force of an adjunct modifier, as in (5.79).

(5.79)

over RIPE	in BORN
under COOKED	out GOING

As these words show, left prominence is by no means the rule in adjective compounds. In fact, the opposite seems to be true (see Adams 1973, Kingdon 1958a for lists). The reason, we submit, is that most adjective compounds have adjuncts on the left. Such instances of left prominence as there are correlate with the presence of (left-hand) arguments.

Noun compounds are by far the most numerous in English. When the head N is deverbal and clearly requires a sister argument, prominence is always on the left:

(5.80)

WAGE freeze	CHICKEN thief
SCHOOL teacher	FOOTBALL coach
TIN mining	TRASH removal
SLUM clearance	HOUSE keeper
URANIUM enrichment	SOUL searching

(Note that prominence is also possible, and perhaps not so uncommon, on both the left argument constituent and the head (e.g., SLUM REHABILITATION), in particular when the head is especially "contentful.")[23] And there are a fair number of other cases of left prominence where the left-hand constituent might conceivably be construed as an argument:

(5.81)

APRON string	PERSONALITY cult
BEE sting	CARVING knife
DEATH penalty	LEATHER tool
BLOOD pressure	ORGAN pipe

Admittedly, we are straining the notion of argument here, and work needs to be done on characterizing the array of semantic relations involved in such cases, and just how such cases of left prominence differ from cases of right prominence. Among right prominence compounds are those in (5.82):

(5.82)

kitchen TOWEL	plate GLASS
peach BRANDY	town HALL
ginger ALE	kid GLOVE
bull TERRIER	cream CHEESE

It is not implausible to ascribe adjunct status to some of the left-hand members here—perhaps all. Of course we must also take care to establish that these are indeed instances of compounds and not phrasal collocations. Thus the contrasts in (5.83) could quite possibly simply be contrasts between compounds with arguments and phrases with adjuncts:

(5.83)

a. STEEL warehouse   'a warehouse for steel'
    vs.
    steel WAREHOUSE   'a warehouse made of steel'

b. LEATHER tool   'a tool for working leather'
    vs.
    leather TOOL   'a tool made of leather'

In any case, when the left-hand element clearly has adjunct status (as a modifier, for example), the head is prominent and the adjunct may not be.

We are not planning to undertake any more detailed analysis of noun or adjective compounds here. The examples we have given are intended to show, first, that semantic considerations, not merely structural ones, govern the placement of prominence in such compounds, and, second, that it is quite possible that our focus rules help to explain why particular compounds have the prominence they do.

Bolinger 1972a, 1981 has suggested that the notion of information content plays a role in determining prominence possibilities. His position is that relative semantic weight, predictability in context, and so on, account for the placement of prominences. Still, although these notions are useful to a certain extent, they are not sufficiently precise or articulated to account for important contrasts that we have noted here. It is necessary to appeal to rather specific aspects of the semantics of compounds in order to explain why *nice-seeming* should have left prominence and *easy-going* right prominence. We submit that a distinction in terms of argument structure (or lack of it) is fundamental to characterizing the prosody-focus relation for these cases.[24]

As Bolinger points out, the assignment of prominences in compounds is fairly variable, in particular when they are embedded in larger discourse contexts, and some of that variability can be understood as reflecting the amount of information conveyed by particular lexical items. Bolinger points to a difference between *pípe organ lesson* and *pipe organ tutórial* (our representation of the difference would be *PIPE organ lesson* vs. *PIPE organ TUTORIAL*) or *old schóol chum* (*old SCHOOL chum*) vs. *old school sídekick* (*old SCHOOL SIDEKICK*), for example. The assignment of prominence to the heads here is not a necessity, but may seem an appropriate highlighting given the circumstances. It does not add anything to the old/new information structure of the sentence (a fact predicted by the Focus Interpretation Principle). These cases are comparable to the ones cited earlier for German where the prominence of the verb depended on its semantic richness, and they are comparable to many other such cases discussed by Bolinger 1972a.

Severynse 1977 discusses another instance of this sort of variation, noting that the uniformly left-branching compound *labor union scandals investigation* may have greatest prominence either on *labor* or on *scandal*. We would represent the differences as in (5.84) and (5.85), where the focus tables indicate the focus structures of the examples. (We are assuming that *labor, labor union,* and *labor union scandals* are all arguments of their respective constituents.)

(5.84)

$_{N_4}[_{N_3}[_{N_2}[LABOR_1 \text{ union}]_{N_2} \text{ scandals}]_{N_3} \text{ committee}]_{N_4}$
$F(N_1)$

$F(N_2)$
$F(N_3)$
$F(N_4)$

(5.85)

$_{N_4}[_{N_3}[_{N_2}[LABOR_1 \text{ union}]_{N_2} \text{ SCANDALS}_5]_{N_3} \text{ committee}]_{N_4}$
$F(N_1)$ $F(N_5)$

$F(N_2)$	$F(N_3)$
$F(N_3)$	$F(N_4)$
$F(N_4)$	

The foci originating on *labor* and on the upper head *scandals* converge on the same wide focus structure, so that either pronunciation is appropriate with respect to the same range of discourses. Interestingly, the location of a pitch accent on the leftmost word in an example like (5.84) will allow for the broadest possible focus. The reason is that (5.84) contains a chain of arguments, and by the Phrasal Focus Rule the focus of an argument allows for the focus of its mother, which, if it is an argument, allows for the focus of *its* mother, and so on up. Other examples comparable to (5.84)–(5.85) are *1980 FOOTBALL season ticket application* and *SHOE string tip machine operator*. Like the earlier ones, these could have variants in which a later prominence appeared as well.

Finally, another extremely important fact about the prominence of compounds follows from our analysis. It is noted by Chomsky and Halle in SPE and discussed at length by Liberman and Prince 1977 that when the right-hand element of a compound is itself branching (composed of two constituents), the right-hand (upper) constituent is prominent. Liberman and Prince cite example (5.86), with greatest prominence on *language,* and compare it to (5.87), with greatest prominence on *law.*

(5.86)
[[LAW degree] [LANGUAGE requirement]]

(5.87)
[[[LAW degree] requirement] changes]

This fact is built right into Liberman and Prince's Compound Rule, which says, essentially, "Assign a greater prominence to the left-hand constituent of a compound, unless the right-hand constituent is branching."

These facts can be described in different terms. Observe that (5.87) has a single prominence in a "neutral" isolation pronunciation, and it falls on *law.* This is the unmarked prominence assignment for the entire compound, just as it is for each compound embedded in it: the pitch accent is contained within an argument of (each of) the head(s). (By the PAR, the syllable associated with that pitch accent will be the most rhythmically prominent of all.) The prominence assignment of (5.87) contrasts with that of (5.86). In (5.86) the right-hand daughter constituent *language requirement* contains a prominence (on *language,* the argument); the left-hand constituent may also contain one, on *law.* (If both contain a pitch accent, the NSR will guarantee the correct prominence on *language;* if only *language* has one, the PAR will make it more prominent. In either case, the rightward prominence is ensured.) The problem, as we see it, is to explain why the right-hand constituent should contain a prominence in the first place. Once it is there, the right-hand prominence of the whole is derived as described. The answer, we think, is quite straightforward. In a compound configuration like $[_A[CD]_A \ _B[EF]_B]$ it is impossible for A and B to stand in an argument-head relation to each other. (See Selkirk 1982:ch. 2, where it is shown that a word with an open argument position—e.g., *requirement*—must have that argument satisfied by a sister constituent (if it is to be satisfied at all)—e.g., *language.* Since branching constituents like *language requirement* do not, on that theory, have open argument positions, it follows that the sister to a branching constituent will never be an argument with respect to it.) The relation is instead a somewhat "looser" connection, of a vaguely attributive or adjunct sort, which requires that the unmarked prominence assignment give the pitch accent to the head, B, which is on the right. Within B, of course, the unmarked internal prominence assignment gives prominence to the argument, *language.*

Needless to say, this approach to explaining the facts differs radically from the essentially syntax-based approach of SPE or Liberman and Prince, according to which the rule assigning prominence relations to compounds is sensitive to the geometry of the syntactic tree (whether via boundaries, as in SPE, or directly, as in Liberman and Prince 1977). Our claim is that there is a correlation between right-hand branching and right-hand prominence in compounds because there is a relation between right-hand branching and the semantic characteristics of the compound, which are reflected in the unmarked right-hand prominence assignment, which is in turn reflected in right-hand rhythmic prominence. The appeal of the analysis is that this correlation follows from general principles, each motivated on quite independent grounds. There is no need in our grammar, then, for a rule specifying, in ad hoc fashion, that syntactic branching determines the possibilities of prominence.

5.2.5 Summary
This brings to a close our examination of the evidence in favor of construing the prosody-focus relation in terms of our focus rules, which crucially appeal to the predicate-argument structure of the sentence

rather than to the linear order of its elements. Our approach has been successful in solving certain "classic" problems concerning the prosody-focus relation: the problems of "default accent," the NSR in German, the so-called Bresnan sentences, and right prominence in compounds, along with the general problem that there is no "normal stress" for a sentence. To be sure, we haven't written the last word on the topic. But viewing the prosody-focus relation in our general terms, rather than in terms of the NSR-Focus approach, has much to recommend it and offers promising lines of research on problems still left unresolved.

5.3 The Primacy of Pitch Accents

The *location* of focus-relevant prominences within a focused compound or a phrase is governed by principles that ignore relations in rhythmic prominence. We have previously shown that the location of "normal phrase stress" and "normal compound stress" is irrelevant in characterizing the prosody-focus relation. In this section we will show that stress, or rhythmic prominence, is also not involved in the *representation* of prominence differences relevant to focus. Our claim is that the prominence referred to in the focus rules (specifically, the Basic Focus Rule) is a *pitch accent*.

Because the notion of pitch accent, and the specific sense in which we are using it here, may be unfamiliar to many readers, the first part of this section (5.3.1) describes the theory of intonational contours in which this notion has a place, specifically, the theory of Pierrehumbert 1980. We will then discuss the pitch-accent-first theory of the intonation-stress relation, which involves, among other things, certain assumptions about the nature of the Pitch Accent Prominence Rule and its relation to other text-to-grid alignment rules like the NSR and the Compound Rule (section 5.3.4).

We have already presented our pitch-accent-first theory of the prosody-focus relation. It involves two things: the rule of Pitch Accent Assignment, which says that pitch accents may be assigned to Words in surface structure, and the (original) Basic Focus Rule, which says that a constituent to which a pitch accent is assigned is a focus. (The other focus rules make no appeal to prosody. As far as the Phrasal Focus Rule is concerned, for example, the basic focus of words, upon which it depends, could just as well have been based on the presence of some particle or focus-related affix.) The focus-relevant prosodic "prominence" referred to in the preceding discussion is on our theory the presence of pitch accent on a word. We will have nothing more to say about the pitch accent–focus relation here. (We will, however, repeat the arguments for assuming that pitch accents are assigned only to words, in section 5.3.3.)

In elaborating here on the pitch-accent-first theory of the intonation-stress relation first presented in chapter 4, we will take the opportunity to show why a stress-first theory provides a less adequate account of that relation, even when modified in view of what has been said about the prosody-focus relation (section 5.3.2). We will show that, if stress (or rhythmic prominence) is taken to be the *representation* of focus-relevant prominence, the general theory of the prosody–intonational meaning relation must take on certain undesirable features. For this reason, we take pitch accents to be primary, and pivotal, in a theory of this relation. Moreover, we relegate rhythmic patterns to a quite secondary role, pursuing, as we have, the idea that rhythmic structure is produced (in cyclic fashion) on the basis of surface structure, that it does not form part of surface structure, and that it is therefore not part of the representation of an utterance that is relevant to intonational meaning.

The last topic that we treat in this section is the role of focus structure in restricting the displacement of pitch accents brought about by Beat Movement (the "Rhythm Rule"). We will show that focus structure does indeed need to be "marked" in surface structure, since that surface structure is what circumscribes the operation of such grid construction rules (section 5.3.5).

5.3.1 The Phonology and Phonetics of English Intonation

The major element of a theory of intonational structure for a language is the theory of its intonational contours. It is doubtless in the specifics of their intonational contours that languages differ most, and this is consequently where the greatest descriptive burden lies. A theory of intonational contours itself has two subparts, which are interdependent. First, it must be able to characterize, in phonological terms, the intonational contours of a language. Usually this has consisted in describing contours in terms of a linear sequence of atomic tonal units. Second, it must be able to characterize the phonetic interpretation of the contours, i.e., to characterize the relation between the intonational contour, phonologically defined, and the attested pitch contour (the fundamental frequency or F_0 contour). We adopt here the view of

Pierrehumbert 1980, whose work amply and persuasively demonstrates that the description of intonation must be sorted out in this way. And, with Pierrehumbert, we therefore take issue with approaches to intonation that have attended only to one aspect or the other. Pierrehumbert has shown, as have others, that it is necessary to provide a phonological characterization of the intonational contour and, moreover, that the phonological analysis cannot be made independently of the analysis of its phonetic interpretation—that different assumptions about phonetic interpretation have different consequences for the range of hypotheses that can be entertained concerning the phonological representation. This of course is normal in linguistic research, where the analysis of underlying linguistic representations is made in concert with the analysis of their interpretation by linguistic rules. Pierrehumbert's theory of intonation is then simply an instance of the familiar sort of linguistic theory that is found in a variety of domains. What is of particular interest in the case of Pierrehumbert's theory is that, while the underlying representation of intonational contours is cast in terms of discrete linguistic entities, the output of the rules (of phonetic interpretation) that apply to it is cast in strictly "phonetic" terms, as a continuously varying fundamental frequency (F_0) contour, rather than in terms of a (surface) representation having the same formal properties as the underlying one.[25]

In the present chapter, we will simply assume Pierrehumbert's theory of intonation and will not present the arguments for it and against competing theories. Our exposition of her theory will be limited to those elements most relevant to our present concern, which is the characterization of the relation between intonational structure and rhythmic structure, on the one hand, and intonational structure and intonational meaning, on the other. For a full defense and exposition of this theory, we refer the reader to Pierrehumbert 1980.

Pierrehumbert's theory of the phonology of intonational contours is based on three fundamental and essentially independent assumptions. The first is that the phonological representation of the contour is autosegmental. This amounts simply to claiming (a) that the intonational contour is phonologically represented on a separate (autosegmental) *tier,* independently of the segmental and/or syllable properties of the utterance, and (b) that it consists of a sequence of discrete tonal entities (Goldsmith 1976a,b). Such an assumption has been implicit or explicit in many works on intonation (of which Ladd 1980 gives a useful review). We should point out that Pierrehumbert explicitly denies that any more than a single linear representation is necessary for characterizing the tonal contours of sentences; she thus takes issue with proposals according to which the tonal properties of sentences are represented hierarchically or in any more "global" way.[26] One could say that the theory, in this sense, is *strictly autosegmental*. Needless to say, this is an extremely restrictive, and therefore highly interesting, hypothesis.

The second basic assumption is that the tonal elements (= *tones*) making up an intonational contour consist of a specification of tonal *levels,* of which there are moreover only two, *High* and *Low*. In this respect, the theory once again contrasts with others in its restrictiveness. Some authors have suggested that more than two levels are needed to characterize intonational contours (e.g., Liberman 1975); others have suggested that both level tones and contour tones (falls and rises) are at play (e.g., Ladd 1980). Still others have proposed viewing intonational contours only in terms of contour tones, suggesting also that there are only two of these, *Fall* and *Rise* (e.g., Clark 1978, Bing 1979a). While the latter sort of proposal is comparable in the simplicity of its tonal repertoire to the High-Low theory, Pierrehumbert shows that it encounters numerous empirical problems, among them a (principled) difficulty in the assignment of phonetic interpretation to contour tones (Pierrehumbert 1980). Again, it is an extremely interesting result of Pierrehumbert's work that the basic atoms of tonal representation (the *tones*) can be restricted to the set {High, Low}.

The third and from our point of view the most directly relevant aspect of Pierrehumbert's theory is the idea that three distinct types of tonal entity make up the intonational contour of every intonational phrase in English, and that these entities have different compositions in terms of tones, different distributions within the intonational phrase, different manners of associating with the syllables of the sentence, and possibly different sorts of contributions to make to its expressiveness. The theory is that the intonational contour of English consists of (a potentially infinite sequence of) *pitch accents,* a *phrase accent* (appearing after the rightmost pitch accent), and *boundary tones* (appearing at the right and left extremes of the intonational phrase). (See note 1.) Call this the theory of the "syntax" of the intonational contour. A pitch accent is associated (normally) with the "primary-stressed" syllable of a word; the phrase accent is realized not on any particular syllable, but within a certain time period after the final (nuclear) pitch accent; and the initial and final boundary tones are associated with the initial and final syllables, respectively, of the intonational phrase. According to Pierrehumbert's analysis, a pitch accent of English may consist of either one or two tones. One of those tones is tropic to the syllable that has the greatest rhythmic prominence within the word. Following in the autosegmental tradition, an asterisk (or "star") is used to mark a stress-tropic tone. Thus the general form of pitch accents in English is either T*, T*+T, or T+T*, where T = H or L. (For reasons explained in Pierrehumbert 1980, only H*, L*, L*+H, L+H*, H+L*, H*+L, and H*+H can actually be said to form part of the pitch accent repertoire of English.) The phrase accent is a single tone, either H or L. The boundary tone is also a single tone, H or L, which will be written T% to distinguish it notationally from tonal entities of other types.

According to Pierrehumbert, the minimal intonational contour of an intonational phrase consists of a pitch accent, a phrase accent, and a final boundary tone. Sentences (5.88a) and (5.89a) exhibit just such minimal contours.[27]

(5.88)

    H*   L   H%

    |

a. Legumes are a good source of vitamins.

(5.89)

    L*   H   H%

    |

a. Are legumes a good source of vitamins?

In these examples, the first tone is the (sole) pitch accent, the second is the phrase accent, and the third is the final boundary tone.

According to Pierrehumbert, the phonetic realizations of these underlying intonational contours as F_0 contours are as shown in figures 5.3 and 5.4. In these figures, the alignment of the typed text with the contour is only a rough one. There are local perturbations in the contour, due to segmental effects. A circled segment such as ② gives a point of reference, indicating what part of the contour corresponds to what part of the sequence of segments. The tones are written in to indicate the points of the F_0 contour they correspond to.

Of course, just how such underlying contours are realized depends on where in the sentence the assignment (and association) of pitch accent to text is made. These same contours could be realized in an utterance consisting of a single syllable, in which case there would be considerable F_0 fluctuation within the confines of that syllable. The steepness of the slope of an F_0 rise or fall and the length of the realization of a particular gesture (rise, fall, or level) will clearly depend on the tune-text relation. Sentences (5.88b,c) and (5.89b,c) with their F_0 contours in figures 5.5–5.8, respectively, contain instances of the same minimal contour as in (5.88a) and (5.89a).

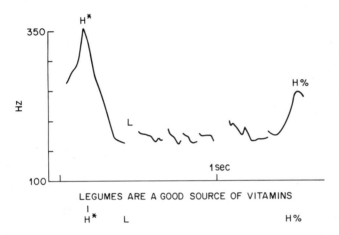

Figure 5.3

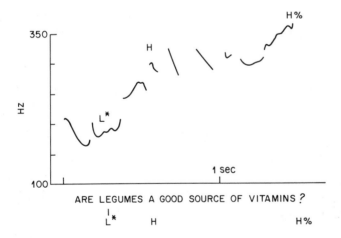

Figure 5.4

Figures 5.3 through 5.17 are copyrighted in Pierrehumbert (1980) and are reproduced with her permission. Drafted versions were provided courtesy of AT&T Bell Laboratories.

(5.88)

$$H* \qquad L \qquad\qquad H\%$$

|

b. Legumes are a good source of vitamins.

$$H*LH\%$$

|

c. Legumes are a good source of vitamins.

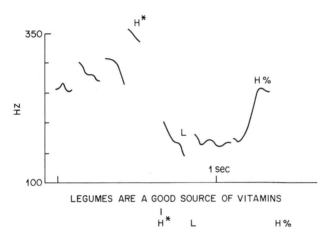

Figure 5.5

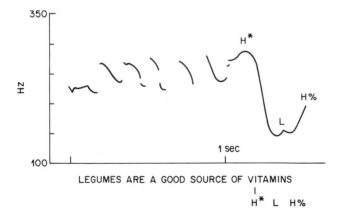

Figure 5.6

The Grammar of Intonation   258

(5.89)

$$L^* \qquad H \qquad H\%$$
$$|$$

b. Are legumes a good source of vitamins?

$$L^*HH\%$$
$$|$$

c. Are legumes a good source of vitamins?

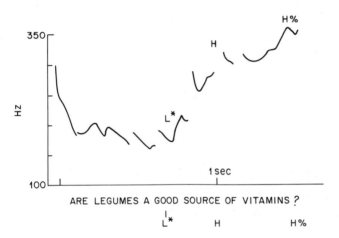

Figure 5.7

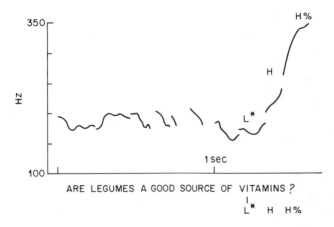

Figure 5.8

All that differs here, phonologically speaking, is the locus of pitch accent association. (This is related to a difference in focus structure for the sentence.)

In the next examples the intonational contour is not minimal, but contains more than one pitch accent (and sometimes an initial boundary tone as well). The phrases of (5.90) contain underlying intonational contours of this sort, realized as shown in figures 5.9–5.13.

(5.90)

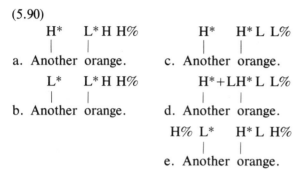

(These different combinations of tone are related, of course, to different possibilities of expressiveness.)[28]

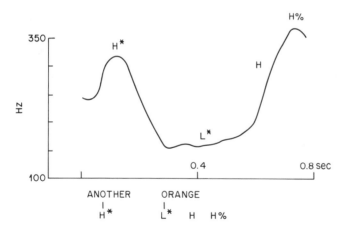

Figure 5.9

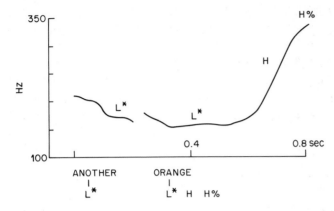

Figure 5.10

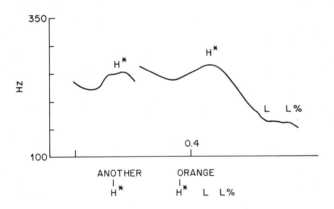

Figure 5.11

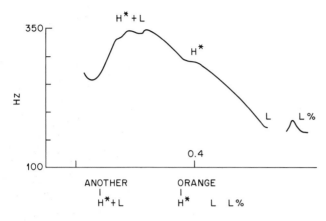

Figure 5.12

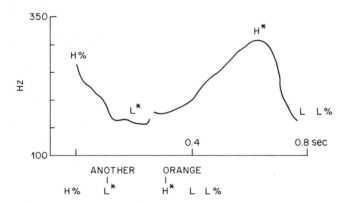

Figure 5.13

Sentences (5.91) and (5.92) are yet longer examples exhibiting varying combinations of pitch accents; they have the F₀ contours shown in
figures 5.14–5.17.

(5.91)

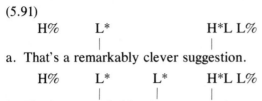

a. That's a remarkably clever suggestion.

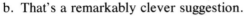

b. That's a remarkably clever suggestion.

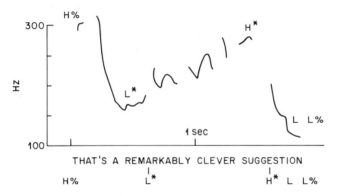

Figure 5.14

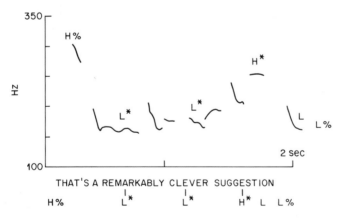

Figure 5.15

(5.92)

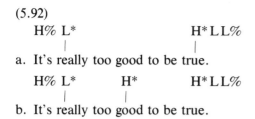

a. It's really too good to be true.

b. It's really too good to be true.

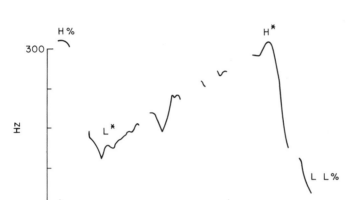

Figure 5.16

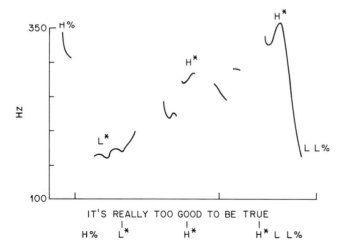

Figure 5.17

(The examples in (5.91) and (5.92) involve differences both in expressiveness and in focus structure, since what is varied is not only the choice of contour but also the pitch accent assignment.)

We will say nothing here about the particulars of the phonetic interpretation of these contours, i.e., about the relation between the underlying intonational contour and its surface phonetic realization as an F_0 contour. For aspects of the phonetic interpretation that will have to remain mysterious here, we recommend Pierrehumbert 1980. An understanding of the details of this interpretation is not crucial to our concerns here, however. It will be enough to recognize that the presence of a pitch accent (usually) coincides with some audible (or visible) pitch obtrusion, either upward or downward, in the pitch contour.

Note that this theory of the intonational contour claims that there is no difference between nuclear and prenuclear tonal entities. The nuclear pitch accent of an intonational phrase is simply the last in the series of pitch accents that, along with the phrase accent and boundary tones, make up the intonational contour of the phrase. This theory thereby differs from several others which assign a different status to the nuclear and prenuclear portions of the intonational contour (again, see Ladd's 1980 review). Moreover, what is said to be nuclear in this theory is a more confined stretch of the contour than in some theories, which have viewed the tonal material belonging to the final pitch accent and the phrase accent, and sometimes even the final boundary tone, as constituting a single tonal entity. By factoring out the phrase accent, as in Bruce 1977, and the boundary tone, as in Liberman 1975, Pierrehumbert's theory offers a representation of the intonational contour in which the nucleus emerges as a tonal entity entirely like the tonal entities that precede it; and this, Pierrehumbert argues, is as it should be. It is important to any theory of the relation between intonational structure and intonational meaning, of course, that there should be a (potentially infinite) sequence of tonal entities of the same type (the pitch accents) associated with words in a sentence. This theory of the intonational contour, coupled with the observation that there may be more than one intonationally cued focus within a sentence (more precisely, a sentence consisting of just one intonational phrase), leads to the hypothesis that was offered above, namely, that focus is related to pitch accent assignment. Roughly speaking, according to this hypothesis the more words there are bearing pitch accents in the sentence, the more foci there will be.

We will not consider the differences in meaning that may be conveyed by the tonal content of the various pitch accents. As mentioned in section 5.1, this appears to be entirely a matter of expressiveness and as such is not of direct interest here. We should point out, though, that English is far richer than some languages in its repertoire of pitch accents: Stockholm Swedish has only H*L (Bruce 1977), and it is not implausible to assume that French has only H* (Delattre 1966). This means that the intonational contours of an utterance have the potential for making a much greater contribution to expressiveness in English than they do in these other languages. We will also not consider the meaning conveyed by the various boundary tones. This matter is discussed to some degree in Liberman 1975, as well as in Pierrehumbert 1980. Nor will we consider the meaning, if any, of the High and Low phrase accents.

Pierrehumbert's hypothesis is that, within the confines of the above-described "syntax" of the intonational contour, the choice of particular tonal elements is free.[29] That is, any pitch accent may appear in combination with any other pitch accent, or any phrase accent, or final boundary tone, and so on.[30] This free combination for the expressiveness component implies that, if principles of "expressive interpretation" exist, they must be compositional in nature. Note that this theory of free combination does not exclude the existence of intonational idioms, which are contours with a fixed composition in terms of tonal entities and a "frozen," conventional interpretation. The "contradiction contour" discussed by Liberman and Sag 1974 and Ladd 1980 is doubtless one such idiom. But according to Pierrehumbert's hypothesis, such conventionalized contours, referred to by some as *intonational words,* are the exception, not the rule.

In the following sections (except the last), we will make the simplifying assumption that only one intonational phrase corresponds to each sentence discussed. This will permit us to ignore, for the time being, the presence of anything but pitch accents within the span of the sentence. It will also permit us to ignore, temporarily, questions relating to phrasing and focus.

5.3.2 The Representation of Focus-related Prominence

In discussing the prosody-focus relation in section 5.2, we did not specify the nature of the "prominence" that is relevant to focus structure. Phonetically speaking, it has both a tonal and a rhythmic component. But what of the representation of that prominence in surface structure, where the prosody-focus relation is defined? Does it include both the tonal and the rhythmic attributes of the prominence; or is one of them somehow "prior," and if so, which one? Our theory, as we have said, is that the assignment of a pitch accent to a word is what constitutes the prosodic prominence relevant to focus structure, and we take that pitch accent assignment to (partially) determine the rhythmic prominence patterns on the phrase (via the Pitch Accent Prominence Rule).

Any theory of the prosodic prominence relevant to focus structure must be able to represent and distinguish all the prominence patterns in (5.93), for example, for each pattern has a distinct focus structure. The abstract patterns of (5.93) are exemplified in (5.94).

(5.93)

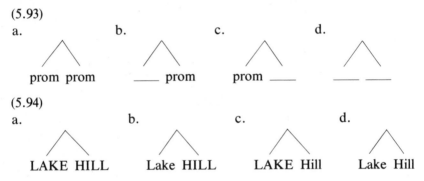

(5.94)

a.   b.   c.   d.

LAKE HILL   Lake HILL   LAKE Hill   Lake Hill

The pitch-accent-first theory represents those distinctions directly as the presence (or absence) of a pitch accent assignment to the word. We represent these assignments as follows, using *pa* to stand for any of the English pitch accents, as described in section 5.3.1.

(5.95)

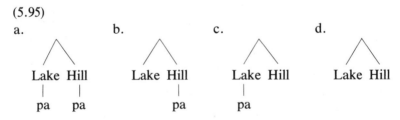

(The capitalization used informally to represent the prominence distinctions in section 5.2 is replaced here by the representation of a pitch accent assignment.) Putting it more explicitly, our theory is that pitch accents form part of the intonated (syntactic) surface structure representation, and that the focus rules constitute a definition of the well-formedness of such a structure with respect to the prosody-focus relation. Moreover, the theory says that the intonated surface structure is mapped into a rhythmic structure—the metrical grid—by text-to-grid alignment rules that pay heed both to constituent structure (the NSR and the Compound Rule) and to the presence of pitch accents (the Pitch Accent Prominence Rule) and by rules of grid euphony.

The central empirical claim made by this theory—a correct one, we believe—is that for every (word with a) pitch accent in the utterance there is at least one focused constituent, and that for every focused constituent there is at least one pitch accent.[31]

What would a possible stress-first theory look like? According to such a theory, the presence of the tonal material of the intonational contour is predictable—on the basis of rhythmic prominence(s) of the utterance—and it is the utterance's rhythmic properties that are relevant to (in direct relation with) its focus structure. How might a stress-first theory represent differences in focus-relevant "prominence" patterns, such as those exemplified in (5.94)? Whatever the distinctive stress-based representation of the differences in "prominence" is, it must be adequate to distinguish this sort of prominence from any other rhythmic prominence in the sentence that is *not* related to focus, for a focus-relevant rhythmic prominence must constitute an unambiguous instruction to "add a pitch accent" to it—if the empirical claim made above is indeed true.

Just what could that representation of focus-related prominence be? Clearly, a strictly *relational* representation of stress is inadequate. Neither an *s/w* tree of the sort in (5.96) nor the metrical grid configuration in (5.97) (where the grid positions must be taken to be on the third level or above) can represent the appropriate distinctions in (5.94).

(5.96)

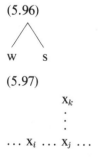

w   s

(5.97)

$$x_k$$
$$\vdots$$
$$\ldots x_i \ldots x_j \ldots$$

The rhythmic prominence of a syllable relative to some other syllable is not a guarantee that it will receive pitch accent, and being less rhythmically prominent must not be a guarantee that it will *not* receive a pitch accent. All combinations are possible, as (5.95) shows.

Bing 1979a has sought to overcome this problem for a purely relational metrical tree theory of stress. Her claim is that for every focus
there is an intonational phrase, and that it is the "strongest *s*" (the
designated terminal element, DTE) of the metrical tree within each intonational phrase that determines the placement of the tonal element.
Williams 1980b presupposes (more or less) this account. (5.98a) and
(5.98b) would thus represent the distinction between *Lake HILL* and
LAKE HILL, or *John LEFT* and *JOHN LEFT.*

(5.98)

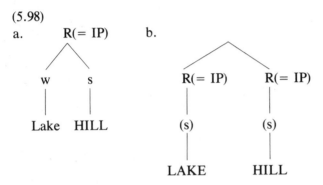

Rephrasing a bit, the claim would be that within each intonational
phrase (IP) a pitch accent is assigned to the DTE of the metrical tree
contained in the IP. (When an IP contains just one syllable, that syllable is the DTE.) But this claim about the representation is simply false.
First, as Pierrehumbert's investigations have shown, it is not the case
that for every pitch accent there is an intonational phrase. Second, the
claim that there are two intonational phrases in a representation like
(5.98b) is not supported by the actual facts of pronunciation. The various phonetic correlates of intonational phrasing, such as timing and
details of the realization of the pitch contour, are not necessarily present whenever there are two pitch accents in sequence, and in this case
not at all (see section 5.4).

A final version of a stress-first theory might be attempted within a
metrical grid framework, which permits the representation of degrees
of prominence in nonrelational terms. It might be suggested, for example, that focus-related prominence corresponds to the presence of a
grid position on a particular metrical level—say, the fifth. In intonated
surface structure, the story might go, the main stress of a focused word
is aligned with a fifth-level grid position. Since there are no English
words whose main stress would be higher than fourth-level as a result
of the word stress rules, fifth-level prominence would guarantee the

right distinction. But note that the automatic pitch accent assignment that this stress-first theory presupposes would have to take place crucially *before* the operation of grid construction rules like the NSR, since they might create fifth-level prominences (and higher). But then, the rhythmic prominence of the pitch-accent-bearing syllables would still have to be protected. On this theory the NSR would have to be prevented from creating prominences on non-pitch-accent-bearing syllables that were greater than those on pitch-accent-bearing syllables. In other words, this theory would also have to have a Pitch Accent Prominence Rule. The grid-based "fifth-level-prominence-first" theory thus begins to resemble the pitch-accent-first theory.

One reason for choosing the pitch-accent-first theory is that it is simpler. There is but one thing to be said about surface structure: "A pitch accent may be assigned to a word." From this pitch accent assignment, everything else follows. As for the "fifth-level-beat-first" theory, it requires stating that "A fifth-level beat may be assigned to a word." And it also requires stating that a pitch accent is assigned to a fifth-level beat. The pitch-accent-first theory makes one step unnecessary.

Another reason for choosing the pitch-accent-first theory is that it allows for a representation *in intonated surface structure* of *which* pitch accent, among the many available, is assigned. The choice of pitch accent is (apparently) not relevant to focus structure and the old/new informational content of an utterance, but it is relevant to expressiveness. A pitch-accent-first theory would therefore allow all aspects of intonational structure that are relevant to intonational meaning to form part of one and the same level of representation—the surface structure. This would seem to be a desirable result.

5.3.3 Pitch Accent Assignment and Pitch Accent Association

In this section we take up the *assignment* of pitch accents to constituents of English sentences and their consequent *association* with individual syllables within their assigned constituents. By *Pitch Accent Assignment* (PA Assignment) we mean the pairing of a pitch accent with a particular constituent of syntactic structure. It is this pairing of pitch accent and constituent that is appealed to in the Basic Focus Rule ("A constituent to which a pitch accent is assigned is focused"). We make the important assumption that pitch accents are assigned only to word-level constituents. We also assume that pitch accent assignment is "free"—that is, that the appearance of a pitch accent in (surface) syntactic structure is regulated by no other principle than (a) that it be paired only with a constituent of word size or smaller and (b) that the constituent with which it is paired must be a focus. (The Basic Focus Rule may be viewed as a well-formedness condition on (surface) syntactic structure.) Once a pitch accent assignment is made, the (auto-segmental) association of that pitch accent with a particular syllable within the focused constituent is automatic. The pitch accent is associated with the most rhythmically prominent syllable within the constituent to which it is assigned, where rhythmic prominence is defined in terms of the alignment of syllables with the metrical grid.

With the assumption that pitch accents are assigned to words, the association of pitch accents with the main-stressed syllable of the word is accounted for by the same sort of principle operative in other languages, where pitch accents are a property of words. (This sort of association is standard in pitch accent languages such as Lithuanian (Halle and Kiparsky 1981), Serbo-Croatian (Ivič and Lehiste 1973), Swedish (Bruce 1977), and so on.) However, the additional assumption that pitch accents could be assigned to phrases and associated with the primary-stressed syllable of the phrase by a comparable association mechanism simply makes the wrong predictions. As we have shown, normal phrase stress in no way determines which word of a phrase will bear a pitch accent, but normal word stress does determine which syllable of a word will bear the pitch accent assigned to that word. Thus our proposal that Pitch Accent Assignment is not made with phrases, but only with constituents of word size (or lower), is consistent with the fact that the location of pitch accents in words and phrases is determined by entirely distinct sorts of principles.

Not just any word is susceptible of being assigned a pitch accent relevant to focus. The word must be in some sense semantically transparent, or meaningful on its own. This is shown by the fact that in compounds with "frozen," noncompositional meanings the pitch accent is always found on the left, e.g., *high school, high chair, yellow jacket, funnybone, blackboard, kingfisher*. Assuming that a pitch accent is assigned only to the higher compound word constituent and not to any of the component parts, which do not have individual meanings in the context of these compounds, then Pitch Accent Association will align the pitch accent with the greatest prominence of the (compound) word in regular fashion. In a compound, that prominence is on the left. (Indeed, the behavior of such words may be viewed as supporting the claim that there is a Compound Rule in English that assigns left prominence.)

A higher compound word will not be assigned a pitch accent if the compound is "regular," in that the meaning of the whole is more obviously a function of the meaning of its parts. In such cases, the location of a pitch accent within a focused compound is determined by the Phrasal Focus Rule and depends on the argument structure of the compound, as shown in section 5.2.5. Thus the assignment of pitch accent relevant to focus must be restricted to what are in some sense the "minimal" transparently meaning-bearing constituents of the sentence. The vast majority of these are noncompound words.

An obvious question is whether or not pitch accents are assigned to constituents smaller than words that are transparently meaningful in themselves. The answer quite probably is yes. The transparently negative prefixes *in-*, *un-*, and *non-*, for example, quite regularly bear pitch accents. Such a prefix will of course always have narrow focus in these instances, since it is not the head of its word constituent (see M. Allen 1978, Williams 1981a, Selkirk 1982).

We should distinguish between the intonational meaning associated with a prominence on affixes like these and the meaning associated with prominence on affixes not meaningful in themselves, such as might occur in the contrast between *TRANSfer* and *REfer*, for example. In such cases something of a metalinguistic statement seems to be involved: possibly a comment is being made *about* the morphemes themselves. The "intonational meaning" in such instances is analogous to that found when syllables rather than morphemes are being contrasted: *I said coFFIN, not coFFEE*. It is also analogous to the pitch accenting ·of one of the parts of a frozen compound: *I said kingFISHER, not kingPIN*.

Perhaps the generalization is that pitch accents can be assigned to anything of level word or below, but that a pitch-accent-bearing element is only interpreted along the lines of a normal focused constituent when it has an identifiable separate meaning. When the pitch-accent-bearing element cannot be interpreted in this way, the presence of pitch accent is interpreted instead in metalinguistic terms. We will take this as our working hypothesis.

Let us consider now the formulation of Pitch Accent Association. If a pitch accent is assigned to a particular word in English, as in (5.99a), it will be associated with the main prominence of the word, as for example in (5.99b).

(5.99)

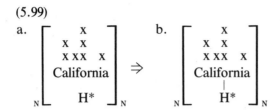

(We are assuming, obviously, that Pitch Accent Association will take place only after the prominence patterns have been established within the domain of the constituent to which it is assigned. We could think of the association itself as being cyclic and therefore applying only on the relevant domain.)

If a pitch accent is assigned to a particular morpheme of a category type smaller than Word, such as a prefix, it will be associated with the most prominent syllable of the prefix, as in (5.100).

(5.100)

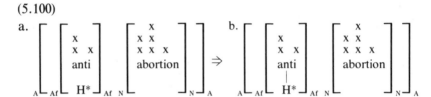

(This sort of assignment might be made when *antiabortion* is being contrasted with *proabortion,* for example.) Finally, a pitch accent may even be assigned (and associated) to a particular syllable, and a weak one at that, as in *coFFEE* vs. *coFFIN.*

These examples show that there is no absolute minimum level of prominence required for pitch accent association—only greatest prominence within a specified domain. That domain is delimited by the bracketing of the constituent to which the pitch accent is assigned. Pitch Accent Association could be formulated as follows:

(5.101)
Pitch Accent Association (PA Association)

$$
\alpha \begin{bmatrix} x_j \\ \vdots \\ x_i \\ \ldots\ \sigma\ \ldots \\ T^* \end{bmatrix} \alpha \Rightarrow \alpha \begin{bmatrix} x_j \\ \vdots \\ x_i \\ \ldots\ \sigma\ \ldots \\ | \\ T^* \end{bmatrix} \alpha
$$

Condition: x_j is the most prominent beat of the metrical grid in α.

(Another way of stating the condition would be to require that x_j be both initial and final in α, a condition that can be met only by a most prominent beat.)

The distinction between PA Assignment and PA Association is a useful one. First, it allows the association of the pitch accents forming part of English intonational contours to be considered an instance of a quite general rule of association, (5.101), which is responsible for associating pitch accents with (prominent) syllables in languages where pitch accents may not be freely assigned but instead may be part of the lexical entries of words. Second, and more important for the analysis of English, it accounts for the *re*association of a pitch accent in a constituent that has undergone Beat Movement and whose locus of greatest prominence has consequently changed. If pitch accent association were only part of an initial pitch accent assignment, then it would not be available as a separate principle having the power to associate pitch accents already assigned.

Consider (5.102a–c):

(5.102)

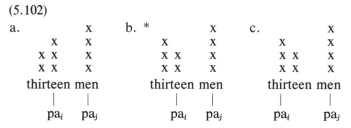

When Beat Movement applies in this NP, the (locally greatest) prominence with which the pitch accent on *thirteen* had been associated is moved to an earlier syllable, as in (5.102b). This creates a representation that PA Association judges to be ill formed, wherein the pitch accent is not associated with the greatest prominence. The association (5.102b) is not attested. What is attested is (5.102c), where the pitch accent has "followed" the prominence. This pitch accent movement can be accounted for by assuming (a) that an ill-formed association is automatically eliminated, creating a "floating" pitch accent and (b) that PA Association automatically reapplies, docking the floating pitch accent on the newly prominent syllable. This is the main reason, then, for distinguishing PA Assignment from PA Association. (We will discuss the movement of pitch accents by the "Rhythm Rule" further in section 5.3.5.)

It is possible for more than one pitch accent to be assigned/associated with a word. Pierrehumbert 1980 gives the examples below (we have supplied the grids):

(5.103)

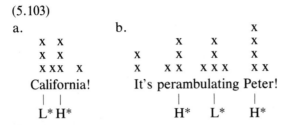

The additional pitch accents do not seem to modify the focus-related properties of the utterances. (This could simply mean that the Basic Focus Rule does not care how many pitch accents are assigned to a constituent.) It does seem that the presence of a second pitch accent does introduce a difference in the expressiveness of an utterance, though it is hard to say just what the difference is. Whether additional pitch accents like these have the same status in the grammar, and in particular whether they are assigned in (surface) syntactic structure and associated by PA Association or by some revision of it, we will leave open. What we will have to say does not require us to ascertain the status of these secondary pitch accents.

5.3.4 The Intonation-Stress Relation

The proposed pitch-accent-first theory of the intonation–phrase stress relation has two main components: the Pitch Accent Prominence Rule (PAR) and the Nuclear Stress Rule (NSR). The PAR guarantees that the rhythmic prominence of any syllable bearing a pitch accent will be greater than one that does not. For example, it is responsible for the differences in rhythmic prominence displayed in *Lake HILL* and *LAKE Hill* that correlate with differences in the presence of a pitch accent. Following the PAR, the grids constructed for these are (5.104b) and (5.105b), respectively.

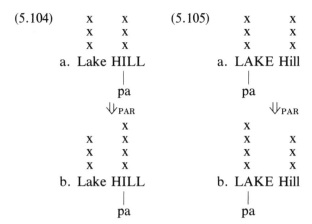

(5.104)   X   X   (5.105)   X   X
                 X   X   X   X
                 X   X   X   X
           a. Lake HILL   a. LAKE Hill
                 | |
                 pa   pa
                 ⇓PAR   ⇓PAR
                       X   X
                 X   X   X   X
                 X   X   X   X
                 X   X   X   X
           b. Lake HILL   b. LAKE Hill
                 | |
                 pa   pa

The NSR guarantees the greater rhythmic prominence of the right-hand constituent in a cyclic domain when all syllables bear a pitch accent, as in LAKE HILL. We will argue in this section that each pitch-accent-bearing syllable has at least a fourth-level beat in the metrical grid (introduced by the PAR), so that the derivation of LAKE HILL would be as follows:

(5.106)

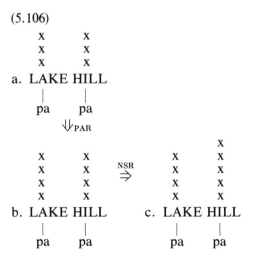

           X   X
           X   X
           X   X
      a. LAKE HILL
           | |
          pa   pa
           ⇓PAR
                                        X
           X   X   X   X
           X   X   NSR   X   X
           X   X   ⇒   X   X
           X   X   X   X
      b. LAKE HILL   c. LAKE HILL
           | | | |
          pa   pa   pa   pa

The NSR is also claimed to apply in the absence of any pitch accents at all, giving the derivation in (5.107).

(5.107)

```
                             X
X      X    NSR    X      X
X      X     ⇒     X      X
X      X           X      X
Lake Hill          Lake Hill
```

Thus it is the NSR that is responsible for the generalization made by Newman 1946 that the last "heavy stress" (pitch-accent-bearing) syllable is the most prominent.

There is one phenomenon our theory does not explain: namely, the relative prominence within compounds when both component constituents bear a pitch accent. As Bolinger 1981 points out, compounds like *CHINESE EXPERT* or *SLUM REHABILITATION* have rightmost prominence. This is not predicted if our Compound Rule applies, like our NSR, when "all else is equal." If it were to apply, the left-hand member of the pair bearing pitch accents should be prominent. We cannot explain this divergence in the behavior of these two text-to-grid alignment rules, and for the moment we will simply stipulate that the Compound Rule may not apply if the syllable belonging to the beat that it would promote bears a pitch accent.

Having already described in chapter 4 our general theory of the intonation-stress relation and the interaction of the PAR and the NSR, we will not elaborate it further here. However, we do need to formulate the PAR more explicitly. There is good reason to think that the PAR always introduces at least a third-level beat and probably even a fourth-level one. Indeed, we will argue that the rule should be formulated as follows:

(5.108)
Pitch Accent Prominence Rule

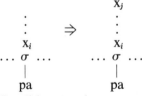

Conditions: x_j is on a metrical grid level n, where

      (i) n is (minimally) greater than the level of any other beat *not* aligned with a pitch accent;

      (ii) $n \geq 4$.

The rule applies to a syllable associated with a pitch accent. Recall that there is no minimum prominence required for PA Association. It is the PAR, we claim, that is responsible for the fact that all pitch-accent-bearing syllables have a certain minimum rhythmic prominence.

Let us first consider why it is that the PAR must introduce at least a third-level prominence. Note first that no syllable bearing a pitch accent is susceptible of *destressing*. A second-level prominence does not prevent destressing, but a third-level prominence does, as we showed in section 3.3. By assuming at least a third-level prominence on normally weak syllables in words, we can explain the lack of destressing.

(5.109)

coffin	vs.	coFFIN
refer	vs.	REfer
intolerable	vs.	INtolerable

We should emphasize that the lack of destressing and consequent vowel reduction here cannot be attributed to the mere presence of a pitch accent. While it is indeed true that the presence of a pitch accent (and, more generally, any tonal material) might cause a lengthening, that lengthening must be considered to be rather "late-level," or phonetic, for the presence of a certain amount of tonal material on a syllable does not prevent this "phonological" destressing and vowel reduction. This is shown by the fact that when a phrase accent and a boundary tone are both realized on a stressless syllable in final position in an intonational phrase, as in (5.110), the vowel (though lengthened) has its reduced quality.

(5.110)

H* LH%
|
President?

Note also that assuming a third-level beat would account for the failure of function words to undergo destressing, vowel reduction, and other rules that give them their "weak forms" when they happen to bear a pitch accent, even though they may be in an environment where destressing would otherwise have been possible (cf. chapter 7).

(5.111)

a. Joe HAD planned to LEAVE.

   (vs. Joe'd [d] planned to LEAVE.)

b. I'm traveling TO Boston, not FROM there.

   (vs. I'm traveling to [tə] Boston.)

Another reason for assuming a third-level beat with pitch accents is that it would explain the *displacement* of "main word stress" in *perambulating* when both the first and the second stressed syllables bear a pitch accent. In *peRAMbuLAting,* a formerly second-level stress on *-at-* is now even greater than the original main word stress, a fact that could be guaranteed by the NSR if *-at-* were at least third-level. (Recall that the NSR "sees" only third-level beats.)

Finally, there is a consideration indicating that it may be at least a fourth-level beat that the PAR introduces. In discussing the likelihood of the application of the "Rhythm Rule" in section 4.3.2, we suggested that the prominence shift is more likely when the first word carries a pitch accent on the clashing syllable. The claim is, for example, that Beat Movement is more likely to apply in *FUNDAMENTAL THEOREM* than in *fundamental theorem/THEOREM.* Assuming a fourth-level prominence with pitch accents, the explanation is that there is a greater clash (at two levels) in the former case than in the latter, as shown in (5.112a) and (5.112b).

(5.112)

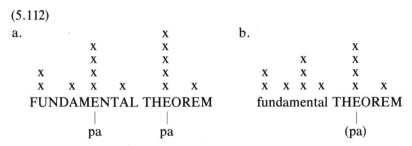

More specifically, the claim is that (5.112a) would be less tolerated as a clash because of the extremely unwieldy stress-timing pronunciation it would require, given that only two syllables are there to realize the fourth-level beat.

5.3.5 Focus Structure and the "Rhythm Rule"

We have shown that the "Rhythm Rule" may bring about the displacement of a pitch accent in a word, through Beat Movement and the consequent disassociation and reassociation of the pitch accent. (Recall the derivation of *THIRteen MEN* from *thirTEEN MEN* in section 5.3.3.) It is also the case that the "Rhythm Rule" may bring about the displacement of a pitch accent from one word to another within a phrase. (5.113a) may be changed into (5.113b):

(5.113)
a. lily WHITE HANDS   b. LILY white HANDS

In this section we will examine the implications of such a phenomenon for our theory of the prosody-focus relation.

First note that (5.113a) and (5.113b) share an intonational meaning, corresponding to broad focus on the entire compound *lily white*. This is predicted in our theory because the compound *lily white* is in a context in which it could have undergone Beat Movement and consequent pitch accent displacement. In surface structure the pitch accent of *LILY* in (5.113b) could have been on *white,* in a position where broad focus would have been possible. Thus, there is a surface structure source for (5.113b) identical to that of (5.113a); as a result, they may share an intonational meaning and hence a focus structure. Note in contrast that when *lily white* is not in a Beat Movement environment (at the end of a sentence, for example), a pitch accent on *lily (Her hands were LILY white)* will not allow for a broad focus interpretation. It cannot mean the same thing as it does in *Her hands were lily WHITE.* These facts are consistent with our general approach to the stress-intonation-focus relation. The level of representation at which the prosody-focus relation is established is not the level of the surface rhythmic pattern (created in part by grid euphony rules); rather, it is a more abstract representation—the intonated surface structure. It is the position of the pitch accents in intonated surface structure that is crucial to focus, not the position they may be moved to because of grid construction rules of the syntax-phonology mapping.

Lest it be thought that the phenomenon of pitch accent displacement with preservation of broad focus is not perfectly general, we provide a list in (5.114) of examples where the prominence of a prenominal phrase consisting of an adjunct followed by a head falls on the adjunct and the entire prenominal phrase may nonetheless have broad focus. (These locutions are ambiguous, of course; the adjunct focus could be interpreted as narrow focus on the adjunct.)

(5.114)

PRETTY good TEACHER   VERY nice PAPER
THIRTY-nine STEPS   HOME made JAM
POST-Kafkaesque NOVEL   a REMARKABLY clever
TOO many PEOPLE   SUGGESTION
a REALLY good COACH   a HARD hitting DELIVERY

Yet the displacement of pitch accents through Beat Movement is not as free as it might seem. If there is *narrow* focus on the head of a prenominal phrase, the pitch accent *cannot* be moved. The pronunciation *LILY white HANDS,* like that of the phrases in (5.114), cannot be interpreted to mean that the head (here, *white*) and the head alone in the phrase is focused. That is, the surface structure prominence pattern (5.113a), which is ambiguous, may be converted into (5.113b) with only one of its focus structures, the broad one. Narrow focus impedes prominence shift. Moreover, as Liberman and Prince 1977 observe, although examples (5.115a,b) have an identical phonological structure, they differ in whether or not they can undergo the "Rhythm Rule."

(5.115)

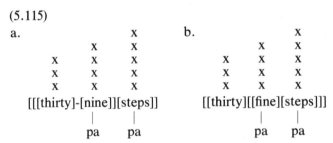

THIRTY-nine STEPS and *thirty-NINE STEPS* do share an intonational meaning. They are just like the pairs in (5.113). But *THIRTY fine STEPS* does not share an intonational meaning with *thirty FINE STEPS*. Here the pitch accent on *thirty* indicates only narrow focus.

The generalization seems to be that a pitch accent cannot be moved outside the focused constituent to which it imparts focus. The focus structures of (5.115a) and (5.115b) are (5.116a) and (5.116b), respectively.

(5.116)

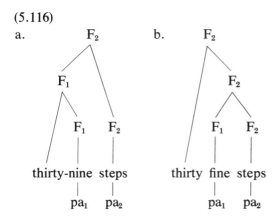

(The focus constituent marked F_n "gets" its focus from the pitch accent marked pa_n via the focus rules.) Clearly, moving the pitch accent from *fine* in (5.116b) would move it out of a constituent that it serves to focus, whereas moving the pitch accent from *nine* would do nothing of the kind, since *thirty-nine* as a whole is a focus for which the pitch accent of *nine* is ultimately responsible. Compare now the two focus structures possible for the surface structure prominence pattern of *lily WHITE HANDS:*

(5.117)

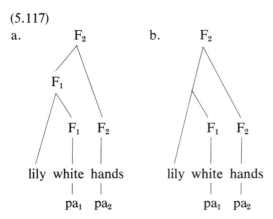

In the narrow focus case (5.117b), if the pitch accent on *white* were moved, it would move outside the only constituent with which it has a focus relation. In (5.117a), on the other hand, the moved pitch accent would still be dominated by one of the foci for which it is (ultimately) responsible.

Apparently, then, there is a constraint on the rhythm-motivated displacement of pitch accents, a constraint involving not phonological representation but rather the syntactic structure and focus structure upon which that representation is built. In order to formulate it precisely, we must be able to identify the focus or chain of foci that "belong to" (trace their focus to) a particular pitch accent. We will do this by subscripting (coindexing) the pitch accent and "its" foci, as in the preceding examples. The constraint will be formulated as follows:

(5.118)
Focus Domination of Pitch Accent

A pitch accent pa_n must always be dominated by some focus F_n.

Consider now the derivation of *LILY white HANDS* from the more basic surface syntactic representation with the prominence pattern *lily WHITE HANDS*. Entering the highest cycle in the syntax-phonology mapping, it has the following representation:

(5.119)

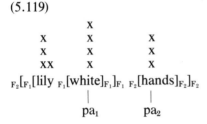

The NSR and subsequent Beat Movement will produce (5.120a) and (5.120b), respectively.

(5.120)

We assume that the latter is ill formed, because it violates both the PAR and PA Association. The violation could conceivably be undone by reapplying the PAR (and recreating the clash). This does not occur. Apparently, what happens instead is that the pitch accent is made to "float," as in (5.121a), thereby eliminating the violation. It then reassociates to the greatest prominence not already associated within the cyclic domain—the prominence on *lily*—giving the surface structure (5.121b).

(5.121)

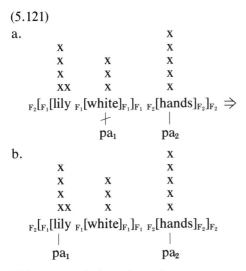

This reassociation gives rise to a representation that is grammatical, according to Focus Domination of Pitch Accent, so that all ends well. The same would not be true for a structure involving narrow focus on *white*. The derivation would proceed in the same way, but this time Focus Domination would rule out the result. Of course, since Beat Movement is not obligatory, the pitch accent need never have been dislodged in the first place. Only the pronunciation in which Beat Movement does not take place is consistent with narrow focus.

To sum up, we have shown evidence for a constraint on the syntax-phonology mapping that refers to focus structure and in particular to the focus structure of higher-order constituents. If the constraint is to be expressed "locally," within the confines of the syntax-phonology mapping, then it follows that focus structure must be annotated in surface syntactic structure. This of course is Jackendoff's position, which we have been assuming here. It is interesting that evidence for such an important aspect of syntactic-semantic representation should be provided by the phonological interpretation of that structure, accomplished in the syntax-phonology mapping.

5.4 Intonational Phrasing

In preceding sections we have ignored intonational phrasing, in order to simplify the exposition of our theory of intonational structure and the theory of the relation of that intonational structure to rhythmic structure (the metrical grid alignment) on the one hand and focus structure on the other. Our examples have consisted of just one intonational phrase (IP). It is in fact a quite normal state of affairs for a (matrix) sentence to correspond to a single IP. Yet to complete the picture of the role of intonational structure in the grammar we must examine sentences consisting of more than one IP. The mere existence of such sentences immediately raises several important questions:

> What, if any, is the relation between intonational phrasing and syntactic structure?
> Does the intonational phrase have any distinctive semantic properties?
> Does the intonational phrasing of a sentence carry with it any particular contributions to the meaning of the sentence?
> What, if any, is the relation between the intonational phrasing and the focus structure of the sentence?
> What is the effect of intonational phrasing on the metrical grid alignment of the sentence?
> Are there any cooccurrence restrictions on the tonal contours of successive intonational phrases?

It being impossible to treat all these questions here, we have chosen to comment (albeit in preliminary fashion) on the ones closest to the central preoccupations of this book. These concern the relation between intonational phrasing and syntactic structure, on the one hand, and intonational phrasing and rhythmic structure, on the other.

5.4.1 Intonational Phrasing and the Organization of the Grammar

In analyzing intonation and focus structure, we showed that two principles of well-formedness—the Basic Focus Rule and the Phrasal Focus Rule—lead to an insightful characterization of the relation between the focus structure of a sentence and the distribution of pitch accents within it. This approach permits us to assume that both pitch accents and focus structure are freely and independently assigned to surface structures (with the restriction that a pitch accent be assigned only to constituents of type Word or smaller). The focus rules define which of these freely generated combinations are well formed. (Of course, other approaches are possible: pitch accent assignments could be made on the basis of a prior assignment of focus structure, or focus structure could be assigned on the basis of a prior assignment of pitch accents. In either case, the focus structure of the sentence would still be governed by the same sort of conditions on focus structure–pitch accent combinations.) The point is that syntactic structure per se in no way determines the location, number, or tonal characteristics of the pitch accents assigned to the sentence. (See Halliday 1967a,b, who makes the same general point.) The situation is no different with intonational phrasing: on different utterances, the same sentence may be differently partitioned into intonational phrases. In other words, the syntactic structure of a sentence cannot be said to *determine* its intonational phrasing. (This point is made in Halliday 1967a,b and Selkirk 1978c.) Thus the relation between syntactic structure and all aspects of intonational structure can be depicted as a one-to-many mapping.

In assuming that (i) there is a phonological representation of intonational structure whereby the sentence may consist of one or more IPs, and where for each IP there is a contour consisting of phonologically distinct tonal elements (pitch accents, boundary tones, and phrase accents) associated in different ways with syllables of the utterance, and that (ii) the phonetic realization of a sentence's F_0 contour is defined in terms of its intonational structure, syllable content, and metrical grid alignment, we are taking issue with writers like Cooper and Sorensen 1981, who would have it that a sentence's F_0 contour is computed automatically, in virtue of its syntactic structure, without appeal to any of the aspects of phonological representation we have referred to as intonational structure. The latter sort of theory, according to which the F_0 contour is syntactically determined, is seriously misguided. (See Pierrehumbert and Liberman 1982 for an important critique of this position.) A central fact that any treatment of sentence intonation must account for is that a given sentence, with a given syntactic structure, may have many linguistically distinct (contrasting) realizations. This fact alone necessitates a theory of F_0 contours appealing to some linguistic representation other than the syntactic—namely, a representation of intonational phrasing, intonational contours, and the association of tonal elements with syllables of the sentence, or what we have been calling "intonational structure."

We view the relation between syntactic structure and intonational phrasing in the same general way as the relation between surface structure, focus structure, and pitch accent assignment. We will consider the surface structure of a sentence as being freely partitioned into intonational phrases, that phrasing then being subject to certain well-formedness conditions. It is known that there are indeed limits on intonational phrasing—that there may be some that are simply ungrammatical. Our major task in this section is to define the well-formedness conditions on intonational phrasing. The hypothesis we have to offer is that the well-formedness conditions are of two general types, neither of them syntactic in character. The first, which is quite trivial, we will call the *Syntactic-Prosodic Correspondence Rule for Intonational Phrase:*

(5.122)
Syntactic-Prosodic Correspondence Rule for Intonational Phrase

A matrix sentence must be exhaustively parsed into a sequence of (one or more) intonational phrases.

The second, the *Sense Unit Condition,* is more substantive and will require some elaboration. It places essentially semantic conditions on intonational phrasing.

(5.123)
The Sense Unit Condition on Intonational Phrasing

The immediate constituents of an intonational phrase must together form a sense unit.

(In section 5.4.3 we will define both *immediate constituent of IP* and *sense unit.*) Our position, then—again following Halliday 1967a,b—is that there are no strictly syntactic conditions on intonational phrasing. Any apparently syntactic conditions on where "breaks" in intonational phrasing may occur are, we claim, ultimately to be attributed to the requirement that the elements of an intonational phrase must make a certain kind of semantic sense.

As for the relation between intonational phrasing and the metrical grid alignment of the sentence, we will simply assume, without going into details, that the IP is an honorary phrase of the syntax—that the grid construction rules apply in cyclic fashion both to the immediate constituents of an IP and on the IP itself (producing the appropriate "nuclear" prominence on the last pitch accent within the IP). It is quite probable that the IP is the highest phrasal constituent to which rules like the NSR apply, or in other words that the domain of grid construction does not include more than one IP. We are claiming, then, that a sentence's intonational phrasing determines certain aspects of its rhythmic structure. Along with the claim made earlier that the pitch accent assignment (and association) of a sentence determines certain aspects of its "stress pattern," this amounts to the more general claim that a level of linguistic representation combining intonational structure and syntactic structure determines the rhythmic structure of a sentence. We call this level of representation the *intonated surface structure* (see chapter 1).

We hypothesize, moreover, that it is the intonated surface structure, annotated for focus structure, that is ultimately submitted to semantic interpretation. (This means that the intonated surface structure is put directly into relation with logical form.) One reason for taking this view is that the particular choice of tonal elements in the intonational contour (pitch accents, phrase accents, and boundary tones) may contribute, in some languages, to various aspects of semantic interpretation that require grammatical description. (Of course, we have not shown this so far; what we have shown is that, in English, only the *presence of* a pitch accent, not its tonal composition, is ultimately relevant to semantic interpretation. This generalization is expressed in the Basic Focus Rule.) Another reason for thinking that it is the intonated surface structure that is put in relation to logical form and semantic representation is that the semantic relations that must be invoked in characterizing the well-formedness constraint on intonational phrasing may not all be expressible in syntactic structure, but instead require appeal to some level of semantic representation other than surface structure.

5.4.2 Some Phonetic Indices of Intonational Phrasing

Pierrehumbert's 1980 theory of intonational contours in English is a theory of the contour of an intonational phrase. When an English sentence consists of a single IP, there are only two boundary tones (at the left and right extremes of the sentence), one phrase accent (after the last pitch accent), and (in principle) any number of pitch accents. The intonational contour of a single-IP sentence and a multiple-IP sentence will differ, therefore, in that the latter will contain phrase accents and boundary tones in medial position, before and after other pitch accents. Thus the presence of a medial boundary tone is a reliable indication that the sentence consists of more than one IP, and since its effects on the F_0 contours are quite salient, we will center our attention on it, rather than on the phrase accent. Recall that boundary tones are either H or L, and that they are realized on the syllable immediately adjacent to the left or right limit of the IP.

The so-called continuation rise, often found medially in a sentence, involves a boundary tone (Pierrehumbert 1980); thus the appearance of a continuation rise sentence-medially signals the presence of more than one IP in the sentence and, more precisely, a "break" between IPs located immediately after the syllable on which the rise occurs. Sentence (5.124), with a continuation rise on the stressless syllable -cal, can only have the IP analysis (5.125), where there is a high boundary tone on -cal.

(5.124)

H

After the musical, they went for a late snack to Ella's.

(5.125)

H

IP(. . . . . -cal)IP IP(. . . .)IP

There is no other way that a rise like this could be introduced, given the rhythmic context of the sentence. (The H is too distant from any main-stressed syllables to be part of the realization of a pitch accent.) Consider next sentence (5.126).

(5.126)
HLH

After lunch, we think we'll go for a drive.

The monosyllable *lunch* has a fall-rise contour. Given our assumptions about the phonological representations of pitch contours and their phonetic realization (based on Pierrehumbert 1980), such a fall-rise can be localized on a single syllable only when a (stressed) syllable bearing a pitch accent is at the end of an IP. In such circumstances, the pitch accent, the phrase accent (which necessarily follows the last pitch accent in an IP), and the boundary tone must all be realized on the same syllable. (Normally, when the last pitch accent is farther from the end, no such changes in the slope of F_0 are possible.) Thus the presence of a medial continuation rise, and especially one following a fall on the same syllable, is very good evidence of the presence of a break between two IPs in the sentence.

There is another clear indication of the presence of the end of an IP: a sharp and deep fall in F_0, to the baseline of the speaker's range. According to Pierrehumbert 1980, such a fall occurs when a low boundary tone is present, i.e., only at the end of an IP. This sort of fall contrasts with a much less dramatic one that takes place inside an IP in proceeding from one pitch accent to another. (It is produced not because of the presence of an L between two Hs, but because of what Pierrehumbert calls *rules of interpolation*.) The contrast between the deep fall occasioned by an IP-final L boundary tone and the fall introduced by "interpolation" is visible in figure 5.18, showing the F_0 contour of the sentence *An earlier warning would allow remedy*. The NP *an earlier warning* constitutes a single IP containing two H* pitch accents, one on *earlier* and one on *warning*. The VP *would allow remedy* is an IP, with a single H* on *remedy*. Observe that the dip in F_0 between the pitch accents on *early* and *warning,* contained within a same intonational phrase, is significantly less marked than the dip between the pitch accents on *warning* and *remedy*. This latter dip is of the sort only to be found at the end of an IP.

The timing of a sentence may provide supporting evidence for its division into intonational phrases. There is typically a lengthening or pause at the end of an IP. Some of the lengthening may be an effect of the tonal contour at the end of IPs: certain types of tonal configuration simply take longer to realize (Lyberg 1979). But a pause could not be explained in the same way. Moreover, if the degree of lengthening present at the end of an IP cannot be explained by other influences, then both it and the pausing must be explained as an effect like syntactic timing. We suggest they result from the addition of silent demibeats

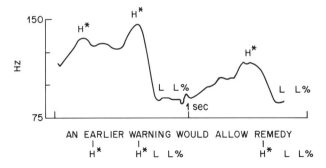

Figure 5.18

by the rule of Silent Demibeat Addition (chapter 6). If there is indeed a regular timing effect associated with the end of IP (and independent of the pitch contour), then, this is another way in which IP is treated as an honorary phrase by the syntax-sensitive rules of grid construction.

5.4.3 Semantic Conditions on Intonational Phrasing

In taking the position that intonational phrasing is syntactically free but semantically constrained, we align ourselves with Halliday 1967a,b, for example, and against Downing 1970, 1973, Bing 1979a,b, and Selkirk 1978c, for example, who claim that there are at least some surface configurations, defined in syntactic terms, that in effect require particular intonational phrasings. We will argue for a particular conception of the semantic constraints on intonational phrasing, the Sense Unit Condition (5.123), according to which the immediate constituents of an IP must together form a sense unit. We will show that this condition alone accounts for the range of variable or optional phrasings available to a sentence, the ungrammaticality of others, and the instances of apparently obligatory phrasing as well.

The definition of *immediate constituent of an intonational phrase* is straightforward:

(5.127)

Definition: An *immediate constituent of an intonational phrase* IP_i is a syntactic constituent contained entirely within ("dominated" exclusively by) IP_i and not dominated by any other syntactic constituent contained entirely within IP_i.

To illustrate, in sentence (5.128a), with its intonational phrasing (5.128b), the NP constituent *Mary* and the V constituent *prefer* are immediate constituents of the first IP, and the NP constituent *corduroy* is the (only) immediate constituent of the second.

(5.128)

a.

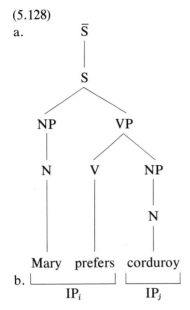

Mary   prefers   corduroy

b.

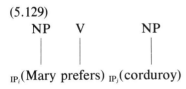

IP_i IP_j

We will find it convenient to write IPs with their immediate constituents as follows:

(5.129)

    NP   V   NP
     | | |
$_{IP_i}$(Mary prefers) $_{IP_j}$(corduroy)

To give substance to condition (5.123), we need to define what it means for constituents to form a "sense unit." It goes without saying that a single constituent on its own forms a sense unit. As for larger groups of constituents, our basic hypothesis is embodied in (5.130):

(5.130)
Two constituents C_i, C_j form a sense unit if (a) or (b) is true of the semantic interpretation of the sentence:
a. C_i modifies C_j (a head)
b. C_i is an argument of C_j (a head).

If more than two constituents form a sense unit, it will be because the appropriate relations of the type just defined exist among them. Clearly the IPs in (5.129) satisfy the Sense Unit Condition, with *sense unit* so defined. In IP_i an argument-head relation obtains between the subject NP and the verb, so they constitute a sense unit. In what follows, we will see that the well-formed intonational phrasings all consist of IPs that are well-formed according to the Sense Unit Condition, and that the ill-formed intonational phrasings consist of IPs that do not.

Let us first consider instances of intonational phrasing that are obviously ungrammatical. Pierrehumbert 1980 points out that sentence (5.131) may not be realized with an intonational phrasing wherein the PP complement *in ten* belonging to the subject NP is included in the same IP with the VP, but separated from the rest of the subject NP, as in (5.132).

(5.131)

$_S[_{NP}$[Three mathematicians in ten]$_{NP}$ $_{VP}$[derive a lemma]$_{VP}]_S$

(5.132)

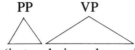

*$_{IP_i}$(Three mathematicians) $_{IP_j}$(in ten derive a lemma)

Our explanation for the ungrammaticality of (5.133) is that the two immediate constituents of IP$_j$ do not form a sense unit, given the meaning of sentence (5.131). Another simple illustration of the effect of the Sense Unit Condition is provided by the sentence *Jane gave the book to Mary,* for which we assume the sentence structure (5.133). (Even if the VP structure were more complex, with V and NP forming a constituent, our argument would be unchanged.)

(5.133)

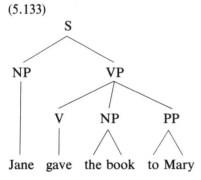

There are of course a variety of well-formed intonational phrasings for this sentence, ranging from (5.134a) to (5.134d) and from (5.134g) to (5.134h). What is notable is the ungrammaticality of (5.134e) and (5.134f).

(5.134)

a. (Jane gave the book to Mary)
b. (Jane) (gave the book to Mary)
c. (Jane gave the book) (to Mary)
d. (Jane gave) (the book) (to Mary)
e. *(Jane) (gave) (the book to Mary)
f. *(Jane gave) (the book to Mary)
g. (Jane) (gave the book) (to Mary)
h. (Jane) (gave) (the book) (to Mary)

(To check these intuitions about phrasing, we suggest pronouncing the last syllable of each phrase with a "continuation rise.") The two ungrammatical phrasings are the ones with the IP (*the book to Mary*), an IP that does not satisfy the Sense Unit Condition. The NP *the book* and PP *to Mary* that are the immediate constituents of that IP bear neither an argument-head nor a modifier-head relation to each other. Thus compare (5.134e,f) to (5.134g), for example. In (5.134g) the immediate constituents of the medial IP are the V *gave* and the NP *the book*. Though they do not form a syntactic constituent together, they do form a sense unit, so that (5.134g) represents a well-formed phrasing. Compare also (5.134c), where the first IP is not a syntactic constituent, but is well formed because each of its immediate constituent NPs bears an argument relation to the other immediate constituent, the V. Thus (5.133) shows quite well that a single syntactic structure can have a host of intonational phrasings and that some of them contain IPs that are not isomorphic to any syntactic constituent. The ungrammatical IP is distinguished not by the fact that it does not correspond to a syntactic constituent, but rather by the fact that its own immediate constituents do not form a sense unit.

Consider next the much-discussed example of a sentence whose "phonological" phrasing is at odds with its syntactic phrasing, (*This is the cat) (that chased the rat) (that ate the cheese*). This example is sometimes regarded as evidence that a "readjustment" of syntactic structure is required, in order to create the right sort of input to the phonological component (SPE, chapter 2, Langendoen 1975). This sort of example is also discussed by Schmerling 1980, who advocates a Montague-grammar-based approach to the problem of syntax-phonology nonisomorphism in phrasing. In our view, however, this example simply illustrates that the intonational phrasing assigned to a sentence is not necessarily isomorphic to its syntactic phrasing. The syntactic structure of the sentence is entirely right-branching, as shown in (5.135a). It is analyzed into successive IPs, whose immediate constituents are noted in (5.135c).

(5.135)

a. s[NP[VP[NP[s[VP[NP[
b.   This   is   the cat   that   chased   the rat
c.   (NP   V   NP)   (Comp   V   NP)

   s[VP[NP[   ]]]]]]]]]]
      that   ate   the cheese
      (S   )

Each of these IPs is well formed according to the Sense Unit Condition. Consequently, we do have a theory of why this sentence should be able to have this particular phrasing.

This example raises an interesting question. We are saying that the first two IPs are well formed because the immediate constituent NPs bear an argument relation to the verb. (We ignore the status of complementizers here.) Yet in neither case is *the cat* or *the rat* the "complete" argument of the preceding verb. Indeed, their modifying relative clauses are contained fully, or partially, within the next IP. This apparent problem for the Sense Unit Condition dissolves, however, if (for the purposes of this condition at least) we view the argument-head relation as obtaining between the *head* of an argument phrase and the immediate constituent head. Thus, since *rat* is the head of the entire NP (including relative clause) that is the argument of *is*, we will consider it (and any other constituent of which it is the head) to qualify as the argument of *is*, and therefore to form a sense unit with it in the IP.

This same extension of argumenthood to the head of an argument phrase permits us to invoke the Sense Unit Condition to characterize as well formed the following intonational phrasings for *Jane tried to begin to learn Spanish:*

(5.136)

   Jane tried to begin to learn Spanish.
a. (NP) (VP   )
b. (NP   V) (VP   )
c. (NP   V   V   )(VP   )
d. (NP   V   V   V   )(NP)
e. (S   )

At issue are the phrasings (5.136c,d), where we want to say that the final V is an argument of the preceding V (and for (5.136d) that this V is in turn an argument of the first). In a strict sense it is the S (or VP) that dominates the final V that is the argument of the preceding V. But by extending argumenthood to the word that is the head of the argument constituent (or the head of its head), we can say that the final V and the preceding V form a sense unit together. (Note that if an S is argument to *try,* for example, we are forced to consider VP to be the head of S in order that *begin* qualify as head of the head of the argument constituent here.)

With regard to obligatory phrasing, the well-formedness condition on IPs—the Sense Unit Condition—does not directly state what *must* constitute an IP. But it does implicitly have something to say about the matter, for it prohibits constituents that do *not* bear a sense unit relation from occupying the same IP and as a result forces such constituents into separate IPs. Thus, it would seem to follow (correctly) from the Sense Unit Condition that vocatives, certain types of parentheticals, tag questions, and other sorts of nonargument, nonmodifier expressions should be fated to constitute IPs on their own. (Bing 1979a,b has a useful discussion of this class of phrases and their intonational properties. However, we dispute her claim that it is the syntax of these phrases that is responsible for their realization as IPs.) It also follows from the Sense Unit Condition that a preposed phrase is not obligatorily an IP on its own—if it bears a modifier or argument relation to another constituent with which it could be grouped in an IP. This is a correct result, as the next sentence illustrates.

(5.137)

$$\text{H* \qquad H*}$$

$_{IP}$(When Geordie and I went to Scott's, it was pouring rain)$_{IP}$

((5.137) was uttered as Irene and I were on our way to Scott's through the pouring rain.) Focus is narrow, on the conjoined subject of the preposed clause (a modifier of the following sentence), and the entire sentence would appear to constitute one IP. Such examples are not rare. We are not denying, however, that it is often—even quite often—the case that preposed material is set off as a separate IP. This, we suggest, has nothing to do with well-formedness conditions on intonational phrasing; instead, it is probably to be explained in terms of the discourse function or "meaning" of preposing and the "meaning" or discourse function of intonational phrasing, about which we unfortunately have nothing to say at present.

There is a last sort of apparently obligatory phrasing that we cannot yet explain. Nonrestrictive modifiers such as nonrestrictive relative clauses are always separate IPs, not included in the same IP with the constituent they modify. The Sense Unit Condition as formulated obviously provides no explanation for this. We suspect that the intonational separation required by nonrestrictive modifiers does follow from their meaning in the sentence, however. In many respects, such phrases function as separate assertions, or expressions, and it may be that in this capacity they must be in different IPs. Perhaps for one constituent to form a sense unit with another, the two must form part of the same assertion. We are in no position to elaborate here on what we mean by "assertion" or "expression," however, so we must leave the problem unresolved.

We believe we have shown that characterizing the well-formedness condition on intonational phrasing in rather simple and straightforward semantic terms has much to recommend it. The Sense Unit Condition, based on the essential notions "argument-head" and "modifier-head," declares ill formed those phrasings that are indeed ungrammatical, allows for the great amount of attested variability in grammatical phrasing, and succeeds in accounting for a certain amount of obligatory phrasing as well. We have not undertaken to compare this semantic approach to phrasing with syntax-based approaches such as Downing's 1970, 1973 and Bing's 1979a,b, believing the burden of proof is now on the advocates of the syntax-based approach to show that the facts reviewed here reduce to some essentially syntactic generalization.

Chapter 6
Syntactic Timing:
Juncture in the Grid

In the preceding chapters, we have been primarily concerned with the representation of patterns of prominence. We have argued for representing prominence patterns at both the word and the phrase level in terms of a rhythmic structure, specifically the metrical grid proposed by Liberman 1975. We have also been concerned with the relation between these prominence patterns and the structure (syntactic and/or morphological) of words and phrases. As in the standard theory, we have viewed the role of syntactic structure with respect to prominence patterns as one of demarcating the domains (continuous spans of the utterance) within which relations of relative prominence are defined. In this chapter we will focus on certain other grammatically relevant contributions to the timing of an utterance and on the role of syntactic structure in delimiting that contribution.

Considerable evidence has accumulated that there is an important relation between surface syntactic constituent structure, on the one hand, and timing phenomena such as pausing and lengthening, on the other.[1] Pauses, in varying degrees of length, may form part of the fluently uttered realization of a sentence; moreover, the likelihood of the appearance of a pause within an utterance, as well as its magnitude, is related to the syntactic structure of the utterance.[2] Thus, for example, between the last element of a verb phrase and a following adsentential phrase, like a vocative, there may appear a pause of some size, as in (6.1).[3]

(6.1)
Here is the famous duke, James.
$\cdots$ $_{VP}[\cdots$ $_{NP}[\cdots\cdots\cdots]_{NP}]_{VP}$ $_{NP}[\cdots]_{NP}$

But a pause of this magnitude will not appear between two elements of a single noun phrase, such as the one in (6.2):

(6.2)

Here is the famous Duke James.

... $_{NP}[$....... $_N[$...$]_N$ $_N[$...$]_N]_{NP}$

(Indeed, it could be said that no pause at all appears in this context, other than the minimum required by the cessation of voicing associated with the voiceless stop k.) The contrast between (6.1) and (6.2), and between other such pairs reported in the literature, suggests strongly that syntactic structure determines in some fashion the possibilities of pausing in the utterance. Similarly, it appears that differences in the syntactic structure of utterances correlate with differences in the length of their syllables (see notes 1 and 2). There is a lengthening that is localized on the syllable that stands in absolute final position in a constituent[4] (except at the end of a sentence, where a general slowdown effect seems to result in the lengthening of a number of syllables at the end (Klatt 1976)). Moreover, the degree of this final lengthening seems to depend on the magnitude of the "constituent break" that the syllable precedes. In section 6.2 we will examine some of the data on which these assertions about pausing and lengthening are based, while investigating just what aspects of syntactic structure appear to be relevant to these timing phenomena.

We will be considering two fundamental questions. First, are syntactic timing effects to be represented as part of the *same* rhythmic structure as the prominence patterns of the utterance, or not? Second, how is the relation between syntactic structure and this representation of "syntactic timing" properly characterized in a grammar? Obviously, the second question is not independent of the first. If syntactic timing is ultimately to be represented in terms of the metrical grid, as we will argue it must be, then the relation between syntactic structure and pausing/lengthening must be understood to be indirect, mediated by the relation of both to the metrical grid of the utterance. But if syntactic timing were otherwise represented, then other conceptions of the relation of syntactic structure to timing in phonetic interpretation would of course be possible.

We hypothesize, with Liberman 1975, that both pausing and final lengthening come about as a result of the presence of silent positions in the metrical grid of an utterance (i.e., positions in the grid that are not (underlyingly) aligned with syllables). A hypothesis not unlike this is put forward by Catford 1966, Abercrombie 1968, and others. Abercrombie's term to describe such a hiatus in the rhythmic progression of syllables is *silent stress*; the term *rest* used by Catford aptly expresses the idea that these pauses and lengthening have an integral place in an overall rhythmic structure quite analogous to a musical score, i.e., that they are not merely "performance" effects.

We hypothesize moreover that these silent positions are introduced by a set of rules that are sensitive to the syntactic structure of the utterance. Formally speaking, we will construe these rules as operations that contribute to constructing the metrical grid of a sentence: silent positions will be "added" to the metrical grid of a constituent, presumably after the patterns of prominence have been defined, under syntactically specified conditions. We call these the principles of *Silent Demibeat Addition* (SDA), discussed in preliminary fashion in section 4.3.2. Our claim, then, is that the full rhythmic structure of an utterance, its metrical grid, is constituted by the (underlyingly) silent positions of syntactic timing, as well as by the positions that represent prominence patterns, and thus that principles of prominence and principles of syntactic beat addition together define the metrical grid (or grids) for an utterance.

The theory of syntactic timing outlined here differs in significant respects from other theories that have been entertained. There is an important line of research on speech production, including work by Klatt, Cooper and his colleagues, and others (see note 1), according to which surface syntactic structure has a direct role in the production of speech. These researchers claim that there are rules (or "processes") for lengthening syllables and rules for placing pauses that appeal directly to syntactic structure. The rules themselves are presumed to be rather "low-level"—indeed, part of the phonetic implementation of the linguistic representation of the sentence. The theory presupposed in these works therefore gives syntactic structure a pervasive role in the phonology, right "down to" the rules governing the quantitative details of duration. We will show, however, that the data that are taken to motivate this theory underdetermine the conclusions drawn and are in fact consistent with the theory we have outlined.

The other important, and related, difference between our theory of syntactic timing and most others is the role given to rhythmic structure in characterizing grammatically relevant pausing and final lengthening. Cooper and Paccia-Cooper 1980, for example, explicitly deny that there is any connection between syntactic timing and matters relating to rhythm (though they present no arguments or data for this denial). Others have more or less ignored the issue. By contrast, Lehiste 1973b,

1980 and Lea 1974 do indeed point to a connection among syntactic timing, rhythmic structure, and syntactic structure. Neither offers a theory of the representation of rhythmic structure or of the representation of syntactic timing in terms of that structure, however. Nor do they make any explicit proposals concerning the relation between syntactic structure and rhythmic structure. The challenge, of course, is to develop such a theory, and to thereby gain deeper insight into the web of relations and correlations that are attested. Elaborating on a simple basic idea first proposed by Liberman 1975—that syntactic timing is to be understood in terms of silent positions in the metrical grid of an utterance—we hope to begin to answer that challenge.

6.1 Syntactic Timing as Silent Grid Positions

Some representation of syntactic timing effects such as final lengthening and pausing is necessary as part of the set of instructions governing the speech production mechanism. The claim we are making here is that an abstract *phonological* representation of these timing effects is required, and that this abstract representation is converted into a phonetic representation—a very low-level one—that provides explicit quantitative information about the duration of segments and pauses. That more abstract representation, we suggest, is the alignment of syllables with a metrical grid, which may contain silent positions, unaligned with syllables. The grid alignment of a syllable (this includes its "vertical" alignment, i.e., the representation of prominence, and its "horizontal" alignment, crucially involved in final lengthening) will combine with other factors such as the segmental composition of the syllable, rate of speech, and so on, to give a quantitative characterization of the durations of the segments contained within that syllable.[5] As for pauses, our theory holds that they are grid positions not aligned with any syllable (i.e., any phonated material); the duration of a pause will depend on the number and type of silent positions, rate of speech, and so on.

Counterposed to this theory would be one involving no nonquantitative, phonological representation of these syntactic timing effects, where final lengthening and pausing would be represented only as part of the quantitative specification of duration that is expressed in very low-level phonetic representation, having been introduced by rules that compute duration on the basis of the syntactic structure of the utterance, among other things. This is the view of Klatt 1976 and Cooper and Paccia-Cooper 1980, for example. In this section we take issue with this view and argue that timing effects must be represented in terms of the metrical grid.

What sort of evidence would one look for in trying to determine the appropriate representation of final lengthening and pausing? Clearly, one might logically look first at the rules of the phonology and of the syntax-phonology mapping. If syntactic timing is appropriately represented in terms of the grid, then it might be expected that rules of grammar that are sensitive to the syllable-to-grid alignment of an utterance (which include rules of the phonological component as well as rules of grid construction) would be affected by the presence of the silent beats and demibeats that we claim to be the source of pausing and final lengthening. And indeed there is evidence that the silent positions of syntactic timing do have an influence on phonological phenomena.

6.1.1 Syntactic Timing and the "Rhythm Rule"

The grid euphony rule of Beat Movement (the "Rhythm Rule") is defined as an operation on the metrical grid. The rule applies when two beats are adjacent on the same metrical level, i.e., when they constitute a *clash*. As shown in section 4.3.2, the theory according to which the contribution of syntactic timing is represented as silent positions in the grid explains the *lack* of Beat Movement in cases where, on the basis of the prominence patterns of the syllable sequences alone, it would be expected that there would be a clash and thus a propensity for Beat Movement to occur. The contrasting pair *Marcel Proust/Marcel proved,* discussed in section 4.3.2, is a case in point. It must be explained why Beat Movement is common in the first example and rarely occurs (if at all) in the second. The idea that in the latter case there is a not insignificant number of demibeats (and hence, through Beat Addition, beats) between the subject NP and the verb immediately explains the lack of Beat Movement. The requisite clash is simply not there. Thus, because the "Rhythm Rule" (Beat Addition) must be cast in grid terms, it provides important evidence for representing the varying degrees of "disjuncture" between words in the sentence in grid terms as well. (In section 6.2, we examine other examples of contexts where the "Rhythm Rule" does and does not apply, further substantiating the approach defined in chapter 4.)

6.1.2 Syntactic Timing and External Sandhi

A somewhat more subtle argument can be made for a grid representation of timing on the basis of evidence from the operation of rules of segmental phonology that apply to segments belonging to adjacent words in the sentence (rules of external sandhi). It is fairly common to find that rules of consonant assimilation, vowel contraction, and the like apply "between words." It is also fairly common to find that whether or not such rules of external sandhi do apply depends in some fashion on how "closely" the words are "connected"—where "closeness of connection" is defined, ultimately, in terms of surface syntactic phrase structure. Some researchers have taken the position that the "connectedness" or "adjacency" relevant to sandhi processes is to be characterized directly in terms of surface phrase structure (e.g., Pyle 1972, Rotenberg 1978, Napoli and Nespor 1979, Cooper and Paccia-Cooper 1980). An alternative approach, of which SPE is representative, claims instead that the surface structure translates into a phonological representation, which in turn governs rules of phrasal segmental phonology. In SPE, *boundaries* of various types are inserted into the string of phonological segments, by boundary conventions making appeal to surface phrase structure, and it is the number and type of boundaries separating segments that influences the operation of external sandhi rules. (This theory is developed in Selkirk 1972.) McCawley 1968, Basbøll 1978, and Selkirk 1980a,b have argued that boundaries qua segmental entities do not provide the sort of phonological representation that sandhi rules require. These authors give a central role to the notion of domain, and in fact in Selkirk 1980a,b we proposed that phonological representation includes a set of prosodic constituents, hierarchically organized, which in effect demarcate the appropriate domains for sandhi rules of phrasal phonology. Here we will argue for another phonological representation of connectedness, or *juncture,* which also presupposes that syntactic structure is mapped into a phonological representation that mediates between syntax and rules of the phonology.

We hypothesize that the metrical grid represents the "degrees of connectedness" of words in sequence that are appropriate for governing the applicability of external sandhi rules. On this theory, juncture—more precisely, *disjuncture*—is a matter of the number of *silent grid positions* lying between the syllables at the limits of words. The hypothesis that the juncture relevant to sandhi rules is a matter of syntactic timing permits an explanation for the fact that sandhi rules are more likely to apply in just those syntactic environments where pauses are less likely. We will show that it also permits an explanation for the fact that the range of syntactic environments in which sandhi rules apply increases as the speed of utterance increases.

The basic idea behind this proposal is that it is *adjacency in time* that governs the application of external sandhi rules, and that the grid gives an appropriate (abstract) representation of these timing relations. Let us first entertain the hypothesis that sandhi rules require (some degree of) *adjacency defined with respect to the grid*. Imagine that some rule—a rule of nasal assimilation, for example—required that the syllable containing the (final) nasal to be assimilated be separated by no silent beats from the syllable containing the consonant to which it assimilates. With such a restriction, the rule would be confined to applying only inside words. Or imagine that the rule allowed at most one silent demibeat to intervene. Then the rule would apply both inside words and between certain words in the sentence (but not in all syntactic contexts), depending on how many silent positions had been inserted. Such a theory would also need to explain why in faster speech sandhi is more likely in a greater range of environments. To assume that a rule is sensitive to the number of grid positions that might separate the segments involved would require that in different styles (speeds) of utterance there be different representations of the grid (the rhythmic structure) for the sentence. The claim would be, then, that fast speech involves not only speeding up the utterance, but also eliminating the silent grid positions (i.e., changing its phonological representation). Now it is certainly not out of the question that changes in basic rhythmic structure might accompany changes in tempo, but there is something to be said for a theory that does not require that there be differences in the phonological representation for every tempo. (Note that all other theories of the domain of sandhi rules have the same problem: requiring either a different set of representations for different speeds or some provision specifying ad hoc that the domains of rules might change according to speed.)

The metrical grid approach to disjuncture permits a theory that does not require changing the representation when tempo changes. Suppose that the requirements on *adjacency in time* specified by sandhi rules were not a matter of adjacency *on the grid,* but *adjacency in real time*. This idea, along with the assumption that a representation of silent beats in the grid is the representation of syntactically governed disjuncture, allows us to explain the different sandhi possibilities in different syntactic contexts at different rates of speech.

The grid is like a musical score, and that score may be implemented at faster or slower tempos. Given a particular tempo, we may assume that a particular (ideal) time value (i.e., a particular duration) is assigned to the beats and demibeats of the metrical grid. The faster the tempo, the shorter the real-time duration of a grid position. Now suppose that a nasal assimilation rule in language L applies only when the nasal and the following consonant are separated in time by fewer than n milliseconds. And suppose that at a given tempo T a demibeat is given the value of $\frac{n}{2}$ msec. At that tempo the rule would apply in syntactic contexts where the grid alignments (including silent positions) were those of (6.3a) and (6.3b), but not (6.3c) and (6.3d).

(6.3)

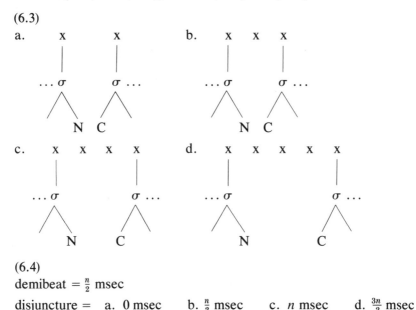

(6.4)

demibeat $= \frac{n}{2}$ msec

disjuncture $=$ a. 0 msec   b. $\frac{n}{2}$ msec   c. n msec   d. $\frac{3n}{2}$ msec

This is because, in the latter cases, the real-time duration of the underlying silent positions would add up to n msec or more, as indicated in (6.4). But now suppose that the tempo is speeded up to T', in which the real-time value of a demibeat is only $\frac{n}{3}$ msec. The same rule with the same time adjacency requirements (no time disjunction of length n or larger may separate N and C) will apply to the same syllable-to-grid alignment and give different results. (6.5) shows what the real-time value of the disjuncture in (6.3) in tempo T' would be.

(6.5)

demibeat $= \frac{n}{3}$ msec

disjuncture $=$ a. 0 msec   b. $\frac{n}{3}$ msec   c. $\frac{2n}{3}$ msec   d. n msec

At such a tempo, the rule will also apply in a syntactic context with two silent grid positions, as in (6.3c).

With three very natural assumptions, then, we can straightforwardly explain the behavior of sandhi rules in the sentence—not only the discriminations they make between syntactic contexts, but also their greater likelihood of applying in a larger range of contexts (i.e., across greater constituent breaks) once the tempo increases. The first assumption is the one we are arguing for in general here—that syntactically determined phonological disjuncture is a matter of silent grid positions. The second assumption—that for any tempo a real-time (ideal) value is assigned to individual grid positions—is not specific to the case at hand either. It is required by the very idea that the grid is an abstract rhythmic structure akin to a musical score, something that requires an orderly interpretation (or performance). The third assumption is that there will be associated with any particular sandhi rule a specification of the real-time adjacency it requires. Any theory of sandhi rules, whether based on syntax, boundaries, or prosodic categories, must say what adjacency requirements (domain requirements) a sandhi rule imposes. Thus the third assumption merely specifies the nature of that adjacency requirement in our theory.

The appeal and the promise of this theory reside in the possibility it offers of rather subtly characterizing both the domains of sandhi rules and what happens under different tempos. It seems that it may well correspond to the facts of sandhi more closely than other analyses. (We will give evidence for this in section 6.2.) Though we are not in a position to defend this analysis in detail here, if such an analysis of sandhi can be shown to hold water, then it provides important evidence for the notion that there are silent positions in the metrical grid, the numbers of which in any syntactic context are determined by a mapping of syntactic representation into phonological representation, via rules of silent demibeat addition that collaborate in constructing the grid.

6.1.3 The Pausing/Lengthening Relation

There is another, somewhat different sort of argument for a metrical grid representation of syntactic timing. This argument is based on a particular empirical claim, namely, that pausing and final lengthening

are part of the same phenomenon, not independent "processes" of the
grammar (see Pike 1945, Catford 1966, and Martin 1970a,b, for example). The significance of this fact, assuming its validity, is that a representation of syntactic timing in terms of the metrical grid affords a
real possibility of explaining in a principled way why it should be a
fact—why final lengthening goes hand in hand with pausing—while
theories such as those of Klatt 1976 and Cooper and Paccia-Cooper
1980 are forced, in the absence of further ad hoc stipulations, to view
this connection as a matter of mere coincidence.

Suppose, for the sake of argument, that in some sentence in which
the sequence of words *traveling tomorrow* occurs, the rules of Silent
Demibeat Addition (SDA) introduce two silent demibeats between the
two words. The word stress patterns of the words, shown in (6.6), are
assumed to be defined prior to SDA.

(6.6)

```
x           x
x           x
x x x   x   x   x
traveling tomorrow
```

Ignoring the potential contribution of phrasal prominence, the words in
phrasal combination would have the syllable-to-grid alignment (6.7),
where syntactic silent grid positions are underlined.

(6.7)

```
x               x
x       x       x
x x x   x x x   x   x
traveling   tomorrow
```

(The underlined basic beat on the second metrical level we assume to
be present by virtue of the absolutely general rule of Beat Addition
(section 4.3.2).) If the syllable-to-grid alignment remains as it is, (6.7)
will serve as input to the phonetic rules that interpret the utterance,
assigning quantitative values for duration and so on. A straightforward
interpretation of the syllable-to-grid alignment (6.7) would be that the
first three syllables are sounded in time with the grid, followed by a
pause the length of a basic beat, followed by syllables four through six

sounded in time with the grid. We suggest the following principle of (universal) grammar that would give this interpretation as its result:

(6.8)
A grid position not aligned with a syllable is realized in time by an absence of phonation, namely, a pause.

We do not consider this principle to be an ad hoc stipulation. Given the theory of phonological representation as the alignment of the syllables of an utterance with a metrical grid, there is really no other interpretation that a representation such as (6.7) could have. The grid marks out points in time; it is spoken only insofar as it has syllables aligned with it. Nonaligned silent grid positions, like the rests of music, are pauses in the sounded realization of a rhythmic scheme. It would seem a necessary feature of the theory, then, that principle (6.8) should govern the interpretation of phonological representation.

How then to explain the appearance of final lengthening, which, we claim, may either supplant pausing or coexist with it? All that needs to be explained is why the grid alignment (6.7) may be modified to give (6.9a) or (6.9b).

(6.9)
a. x   x
    x   (x)   x
    x x x x̲ x x   x   x
    traveling   tomorrow

b. x   x
    x   (x)   x
    x x x x̲ x̲   x   x   x
    traveli n g tomorrow

Actually, a more precise expression of these alignments would be (6.10a) and (6.10b), which are "real" representations, not merely an expository convenience.

(6.10)

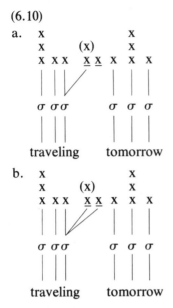

(On this theory, it is the syllables of the utterance themselves, and not the segments of the syllables, that are directly related to (aligned with) the grid.) In (6.10a) the grid alignment of the final syllable *-ling* is modified, to include an alignment with the first syntactic silent position; in (6.10b) *-ling* is aligned with both (underlying) silent demibeats. In both cases the syllable also retains its original alignment. In the latter case, there would be no pause, and *-ling* would be considerably lengthened; in the former, there would still be a pause, though shorter than the one in (6.7), and *-ling* would be lengthened, though less than in (6.10b). On our theory, if there is to be a phonological representation of final lengthening, then it must be as shown in (6.10a) or (6.10b).

Assuming, then, that (6.10a) and (6.10b) are representations of final lengthening, and that one or the other derives from the more basic (6.7), it is crucial that the theory provide a principled answer to two basic questions. (i) Why does the basic syllable-to-grid alignment undergo this modification in the first place, so that an already aligned syllable is aligned with silent positions as well? (That is, why aren't the putative silent positions always simply realized as pauses, with no lengthening anywhere?) (ii) Given that additional alignments are possible, why do they take the form (6.10a) or (6.10b), but not for example, (6.11a) or (6.11b), which would seem to be possible (among others) on the basis of (6.7)? (That is, why is it that syntactically relevant lengthening phenomena are always limited to syllables in constituent-final position?)

(6.11)

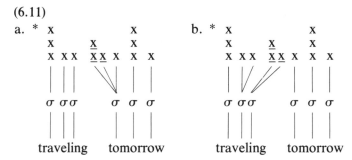

(In the impossible (6.11a), the syllable *following* the silent positions has been elongated, aligned at the surface with the additional positions preceding it. In the impossible (6.11b), both the penult and the final syllable of the word preceding the silent positions have been realigned and lengthened.)

We believe that our theory can provide insightful answers to these questions, answers that are motivated on quite independent grounds. In order for this to happen, though, some rather general principles of grammar governing the representation of other sorts of phonological phenomena must be allowed a role in governing the alignment of syllables with the metrical grid. We have in mind certain principles of autosegmental phonology, which has been successfully applied to the analysis of tonal phenomena and is being extended to other areas of the phonology as well (see chapter 1). The fundamental idea in autosegmental phonology is that a phonological representation consists simultaneously of distinct "tiers," each containing a linearly ordered sequence of linguistic units. It is proposed, for example, that tones are represented independently of segments or syllables and specifically that they occupy their own tier, "in parallel" with the syllable tier. A major component of this theory of phonological representation is the set of principles governing the "associations" or relations between the entities on the various tiers (see Clements and Ford 1979, for example). Now suppose that by appropriately generalizing these principles of autosegmental association, they can be made to govern the alignment of syllables with the metrical grid. There is no doubt that, formally speaking, such a generalization is possible, since the sequence of syllables of an utterance is a tier and its metrical grid (or perhaps the demibeats of the first metrical level) can be thought of as a tier. If, indeed, such a generalization of principles permitted the correct characterization of the phenomena of these two domains, then it would be wrong not to adopt this generalization and view these phenomena as superficially somewhat different manifestations of the same basic sort of phonological organization.

We are not prepared here to undertake a wholesale examination of autosegmental theory and the possibility of generalizing it to the syllable-to-grid alignment. We merely point out that if several of the most fundamental principles of association in autosegmental phonology are extended, they provide the answers to the questions posed above. We are seeking to explain the derivations that give (6.10a) or (6.10b) as a surface realization of (6.7). In other words, thinking of these representations and the derivations in (rather schematic) autosegmental terms, we are seeking to explain the derivation of either (6.12b) or (6.12c) from (6.12a). (E_n stands simply for "(linguistic) entity or unit.")

(6.12)

a. $E_1\ E_2\ E_3\ E_4\ E_5\ E_6\ E_7\ E_8$ $\Rightarrow$ b. $E_1\ E_2\ E_3\ E_4\ E_5\ E_6\ E_7\ E_8$

$\qquad \sigma\ \ \sigma\ \ \sigma \qquad \sigma\ \ \sigma\ \ \sigma \qquad\qquad \sigma\ \ \sigma\ \ \sigma \qquad \sigma\ \ \sigma\ \ \sigma$

c. $E_1\ E_2\ E_3\ E_4\ E_5\ E_6\ E_7\ E_8$

$\qquad\qquad\qquad\qquad\qquad\qquad\qquad \sigma\ \ \sigma\ \ \sigma \qquad \sigma\ \ \sigma\ \ \sigma$

It turns out that in tonal systems (where E_n = "high" or "low"), if underlying nonassociated tones such as E_4 and E_5 in (6.12a) are phonetically realized at all, they are realized through the associations represented in (6.12b) or (6.12c). That is, a syllable preceding nonassociated tones extends its association to them: all syllables retain their original associations, and additional associations are established in right-to-left fashion (Haraguchi 1977, Clements and Ford 1979). Obviously the principles of phonology that guarantee this sort of left-to-right association between syllables and tones in tonal systems could and indeed should be invoked to guarantee the same sort of alignment between syllables and grid positions. This, then, is the theory's answer to the second of the two questions posed earlier.

It may happen that under specific conditions in a particular language no additional association of a syllable with nonassociated entities on another tier is possible. In a tonal system, it could be that the representation (6.12a) could not be realized as either (6.12b) or (6.12c). This would be the situation if, for example, the language permitted no contour tones (combinations of H and L) on any syllable, and if in (6.12a) the tone E_3 were not the same as E_4 or E_5. But the point is that there is in general an "impulse" to associate every entity on one tier with at least one entity on another tier. The literature on autosegmental phonology contains various formulations of this "impulse" (see Goldsmith 1976a,b, Haraguchi 1977, Clements and Ford 1979). However it is to be expressed in formal terms, we suggest that it will also explain why the additional (final lengthening) alignments of a syllable with silent positions in the metrical grid occur in the first place, thus answering our first question.

A final point remains to be made, which is specific to the syllable-to-grid alignment. We think it quite likely that syllables may have a maximum extendability or "stretchability." These limitations on stretchability might be roughly analogous to the proviso in some tonal languages that additional associations not create contour tones (though they might not be so language-particular). It may be that (i) no syllable can be aligned with more than a certain maximum number of demibeat positions, at a given rate of speech, and moreover that (ii) syllables of different types differ with respect to how many grid positions they can occupy. (A syllable ending in a sonorant would probably have a greater ability to "fill the gap" than a syllable ending in a voiceless stop, for example.) The idea is that, in spite of the "impulse" to fill silent positions in the grid, there will be pauses, just when the number of silent positions in the grid exceeds the threshold of stretchability of the syllable preceding the silent positions. At present, we have no evidence bearing on this proposal; we offer it merely as a speculation in our attempt to understand why pauses would appear at all as reflexes of silent grid positions, given the "impulse" to association between tiers. Even without a full explanation at this point, however, we feel that there are enough similarities between autosegmental "spreading" and the realignments we are arguing for here to permit us to seriously entertain the hypothesis that a single, unified theory encompasses both sorts of phenomena.

To sum up, then, in advocating the analysis of syntactic timing as nonaligned (silent) positions in the metrical grid, we have argued that pauses are a plausible phonetic interpretation of silent grid positions in our theory, in fact the only one (principle (6.8)). That it is precisely pauses that are a major manifestation of syntax-related timing would seem to force the conclusion that there are silent positions. We have also argued that this representation of syntactic timing permits a principled explanation for the attested syntax-related syllable lengthening. It explains not only why lengthening should exist, but also why that lengthening should be localized as it is on constituent-final syllables. So far, then, our theory makes just the right predictions.

Also encouraging is the evidence from the experimental literature that final lengthening and pausing are perceptually equivalent. It appears that listeners perceive instances of final lengthening as pauses (Martin 1970a,b, Lehiste 1979b). On our theory of syntactic timing, these results are perfectly understandable, if we assume that listeners translate what they hear into its more abstract phonological representation. At a deeper level of representation, according to our theory, these superficial manifestations of syntactic timing are equivalent.

Our theory would seem to make yet another sort of prediction about the facts, namely, that there should be a trading relation or negative correlation in the amount of final lengthening and pausing to be found in any particular syntactic context. Let us assume that, for any particular syntactic "break" (where "break" means the point lying between two words in sequence), there is a fixed, nonvariable number n of silent demibeat positions in the grid. These are introduced by the rules of syntactic silent demibeat addition, according to the nature of the constituent structure relations at that break. (This is doubtless too strong an assumption, in part because there is probably some optionality in syntactic beat addition (see section 6.2). Still, we will adopt it for the sake of argument.) Given this assumption, and given our theory of pausing and final lengthening, it should turn out that the duration of pausing and the duration of final lengthening always add up to the same amount of overall duration, when syntactic context and speech rate are held constant. We expect to find variability in lengthening in any position, if indeed there is variability in the "stretchability" of particular syllables. The important point is that our theory appears to predict that the duration of pausing following the lengthened syllable will vary accordingly, in inverse proportion to the duration of syllable lengthening. Unfortunately, the literature on duration in speech production offers no data bearing on this issue. But our theory makes rather specific predictions about what those data should be.[6]

Two facts apparently confirming this general approach are (i) that some syntactic contexts will exhibit final lengthening, but no pause, and (ii) that the opposite situation does not arise. The contexts in which only lengthening appears are those where the constituent break is smaller. These facts are understandable if we assume that the number of silent positions correlates with the size of the constituent break: the smaller the break, the smaller the number of silent demibeats. When the silent demibeats are few enough that no syllable would exceed its threshold of stretchability in aligning with them, as might well be the case at smaller constituent breaks, we predict that an (autosegmental) realignment to all those positions will always take place. This means that there will only be lengthening and no pausing in those positions. This is the limiting case of the negative correlation between lengthening and pausing that our theory predicts. It predicts that such a situation should arise only at smaller constituent breaks, as is in fact the case.[7]

Let us now compare the apparent successes of our theory of syntactic timing to the apparent limitations of theories such as those of Klatt 1975, 1976 or Cooper and Paccia-Cooper 1980, wherein final lengthening and pausing are viewed as totally independent processes whose effects are not to be represented phonologically. First, the latter sort of theory does not explain why pausing and final lengthening should both be present in speech production: why does one accompany the other? Second, it does not explain why lengthening should be localized as it is, on constituent-final syllables. A nonphonological account of lengthening would be consistent with a lengthening spread over a number of syllables, for example.[8] Third, it cannot immediately explain the perceptual equivalence of pauses and final lengthening. Fourth, it cannot explain a negative correlation between pausing and lengthening (if such a correlation in fact exists) and in particular cannot explain what is known to be the case—that there is final lengthening but no pausing at smaller constituent breaks. We conclude, then, that the case is extremely strong for interpreting both pausing and final lengthening as realizations of underlying silent nonaligned positions in the rhythmic structure of the sentence, represented here as a metrical grid.

6.2 The Syntax of Rhythmic Disjuncture

6.2.1 The Rule of Silent Demibeat Addition

If silent positions in the metrical grid are the appropriate representation of syntactic (dis)juncture, the grammar must include a set of rules that define, for any particular sentence (with a particular surface phrase structure), the possibilities of (dis)juncture between the words and phrasal constituents making up the sentence. Because rhythmic disjuncture reflects (in ways yet to be made precise) the surface constituent structure of the sentence, the rules for disjuncture must be construed as operations that "look at" surface structure and add silent grid positions as a function of it. In chapter 4 we made a tentative proposal concerning the grammar of disjuncture, one that we showed to be generally successful in explaining the differing likelihood of application of the "Rhythm Rule" in different syntactic environments. We proposed that a rule (or rules) called *Silent Demibeat Addition* applies in three syntactic contexts: at the end of a word, at the end of a branching constituent, and at the end of a constituent that is daughter of S. These rules were understood to apply cyclically, in the grid construction that constitutes part of the mapping from syntactic to phonological representations, and their cumulative effects were viewed as a representation of different degrees of disjuncture in the sentence. In this section we will refine this proposal so that it is more consistent with various sorts of evidence about different degrees of disjuncture that are found in different types of syntactic context. We must emphasize, though, that even this proposal will undoubtedly need to be refined, when further evidence becomes available. Indeed, the topic of phrasal (dis)juncture is a vast one, and relatively little detailed evidence is available that would permit anything like a definitive statement about it. We offer our tentative proposal here because we believe that, even in its perhaps primitive state, it permits a better understanding of the known facts than other extant proposals concerning the representation of juncture and its characterization by rule.

We will take the following formulation of Silent Demibeat Addition as our working hypothesis:

(6.13)
Silent Demibeat Addition

Add a silent demibeat at the end (right extreme) of the metrical grid aligned with
a. a word,
b. a word that is the head of a nonadjunct constituent,
c. a phrase,
d. a daughter phrase of S.

Two provisions require some comment. First, clause (b), which differentiates between words depending on the place they and their mother phrases have in the argument structure of the sentence. This clause would discriminate, for example, between sequences of modifier plus head (e.g., A–N) and head plus complement (e.g., N–A, V–N, etc.). This is a desirable result, as we will show. Note that clause (b) comes into play only in syntactic phrases and not in compound words: *nice-seeming* and *hard-hitting* are not distinguished by their internal junctural relations. Second, clause (c) is subject to a particular restriction. This clause places a silent demibeat at the end of a phrasal constituent, and one of its effects is to ensure that deeply embedded multiply right-branching phrasal configurations will be followed by the appropriate amount of pausing or lengthening. Note, though, that the rule itself does not appeal to branchingness. However, we will stipulate that if a word *is a* phrase, that configuration will not receive two demibeats, only one. This means, for example, that a prenominal AP consisting of just an adjective will not be made juncturally distant from what follows merely by its phrasal status.

The application of Silent Demibeat Addition is governed by a number of quite general principles. First, we assume that it is cyclic, an assumption consistent with our general approach to the syntax-phonology mapping and in particular with our theory of the construction of the metrical grid by rules of text-to-grid alignment and grid euphony. We will assume the cyclicity of SDA in our discussion and also more specifically that it applies *after* the rules generating prominence patterns on a cyclic domain, as the last rule on the cycle. The rationale behind this is that silent positions do not affect prominence patterns of constituents within the cyclic domain they terminate. (For example, basic patterns of Beat Addition at the second level are not affected by the presence of silent grid positions.) Their effect is on the relations *between* the constituents that flank them, an effect that is felt only on the next higher cyclic domain. This, then, is one reason for viewing Silent Demibeat Addition in cyclic terms. In chapter 7 we will give an additional sort of evidence that SDA applies in cyclic fashion, involving its interaction with phrasal Monosyllabic Destressing. Most of the facts that we will consider in the present chapter do not bear on the cyclicity of SDA, though, and we will ignore the issue in our discussion.

Another general principle governing the application of SDA is one that we will first present fully in section 7.2.1: the *Principle of Categorial Invisibility of Function Words* (PCI). Its effect is to make the categories belonging to the class of function words (e.g., determiners, auxiliary verbs, personal pronouns, conjunctions, prepositions, etc.) "invisible" with respect to rules of the grammar that crucially appeal to the categorial status of constituents mentioned in their structural descriptions. Given this principle, the clauses of Silent Demibeat Addition that mention "word" will apply only to major category words. Thus no silent demibeat will be inserted after a preposition, for example, even though it may be the head of a phrase. This gives the right result, since it is known that the junctural properties of function words differ significantly from those of "real" major category words. The effect of the PCI, then, will be to confine clauses (a) and (b) of SDA to applying only to words of the categories N, V, A, Adv.

It turns out to be necessary to restrict clause (a) of SDA to applying on the higher cyclic domain that includes the word under consideration. At this point it is not clear what general principle of grammar this might follow from. It might seem that clause (a) of SDA should be able to apply within the cyclic domain of a (major category) word. But this will give the wrong result, given that, as a rule of grid construction, SDA will precede destressing within any cyclic domain. If SDA applied within the word before Monosyllabic Destressing, then that rule would (incorrectly) be forever blocked from destressing word-final syllables. In order for Monosyllabic Destressing to apply freely to word-final syllables, we must require that SDA not insert its word-final silent demibeats until the next cycle—that is, until it is applying on the phrasal or some higher word domain. What seems to be happening is that words are ignored by Silent Demibeat Addition until they have an identifiable place in a higher-order syntactic structure.

Let us consider the effects of SDA in the sentence *Mary finished her Russian novel*. The metrical grid alignment (6.15) shows the output of applying the rule to the surface structure (6.14). The silent demibeats added are underlined.

(6.14)
$_S[_{NP}[_N[Mary]_N]_{NP}$ $_{VP}[_V[finished]_V$ $_{NP}[[her]$ $_{AP}[_A[Russian]_A]_{AP}$ $_N[novel]_N]_{NP}]_{VP}]_S$

(6.15)
```
X          X                   X          X
X          X            X    X          X
X XXXX XX        XX   X      X   X   X   X   X XXXXX
Mary   ↑    finished ↑   her Russian ↑ novel     ↑

    (a,b,d)        (a,b)              (a)      (a,b,c,d)
```

For reasons of visual clarity, only the prominences introduced by the rules of word stress are represented in (6.15). The effects of the NSR and the PAR are ignored here, as are the effects of Beat Addition (which would apply to the long lapses created by SDA). By virtue of its status as a major category word, an argument (of verb phrase), and a daughter of S, *Mary* is followed by three silent positions introduced by clauses (a), (b), and (d), respectively, of SDA. The verb *finished* is set off by two positions, through the effects of clauses (a) and (b), whereas *Russian,* being the head of an adjunct phrase, is followed only by the one position that its major category status merits it. The possessive pronoun *her* is followed by no silent positions, a fact in part explained by its function word status. (The special status of NPs that are pronouns will be discussed at greater length in chapter 7.) And after *novel* there is a host of silent positions, inserted not only by virtue of the fact that *novel* itself is a major category word that is the head of an argument phrase, but also by virtue of the fact that *novel* is at the end of two phrasal constituents (the NP and the VP), and at the end of a daughter of S as well.

In following sections we will bring various types of evidence to bear on the particular choices that we have made in formulating SDA. We will rather briefly survey the facts involving the application of the "Rhythm Rule" in English, facts about pausing and final lengthening in English, and facts from other languages involving rules of external sandhi. Our intent is to show the wealth of the types of evidence that bear quite directly on specific hypotheses concerning the translation of information about syntactic structure into a representation of disjuncture in the rhythmic structure of the sentence. The study of phrasal Monosyllabic Destressing undertaken in chapter 7 will further confirm our approach to SDA. Of particular interest is the fact that empty categories (like traces) present in surface structure are *not* "seen" by SDA and given interpretation in terms of silent demibeats. (In this, we depart from an earlier claim (Selkirk 1972) that there should be a junctural representation of traces and other empty categories.)

One of the important features of SDA is its asymmetric application. A silent position is added at the end (the right extreme) of the metrical grid aligned with a constituent C by virtue of certain designated properties of C (whether it is a word; what kind of word it is; whether it is a phrase; whether it is a daughter of S). Thus, at a constituent "break," it is the character of the constituent on the left that determines the disjuncture between itself and what follows. Information about the constituent on the right is irrelevant according to SDA as formulated in (6.15). An asymmetry in the effect of syntax on phrasal phonology has been noted by a number of researchers working on the phonology and phonetics of the sentence (see Napoli and Nespor 1979 on Italian sandhi, Clements 1977 on Ewe tone sandhi, Cooper and Paccia-Cooper 1980 on pausing and lengthening in English).[9] We will show that other phenomena, including the English "Rhythm Rule," constitute further evidence that this asymmetry exists. What we cannot do at present is explain *why* it exists. The explanation may reside, as Cooper and Paccia-Cooper 1980 and their colleagues believe, in a theory of sentence processing. For the moment, we will not pursue any such functional explanation.

There are of course factors other than syntactic ones that create disjuncture in time between words of a sentence; thus it is only when these other factors are kept constant that we will be able to clearly discern the syntactic contribution to rhythmic disjuncture. As we mentioned in section 5.4, intonational phrasing may affect the timing of a sentence. We also argued in section 5.3 that the presence of a pitch accent correlates with a fourth-level rhythmic prominence, and in section 4.3.2 that prominence in a clash context may result in a certain amount of lengthening.[10] We mention these facts not to say that these features of phonological representation are correlated with additional silent grid positions (though we would not exclude the possibility that they are), but only to caution that there are timing effects related to other aspects of phonological representation that might in fact obscure the syntactic contribution. Compare, for example, the possible pronunciations of *This is the CBS Evening News*. On one pronunciation, fluently uttered without any particular emphasis, the entire sentence consists of a single intonational phrase and, accordingly, has but one intonational contour. On another occasion, the same sentence, spoken with an announcer's flourish, is divided into two intonational phrases: (This is) (the CBS Evening News).[11] On this pronunciation, *is* is not only stressed, but also followed by a pause and lengthened considerably (though the nuclear accent of the phrase is nonetheless located on *this*). This pausing and the lengthening of *is*, not attested in the earlier version, are presumably to be attributed to the presence of *is* at the end of the intonational phrase.[12] They cannot be attributed to the syntactic structure of the utterance, since in the two cases the surface structure is the same. Any study of the contribution of syntactic structure to pausing and final lengthening must therefore control for this independent variable, the intonational phrasing. Unless this is done, it is impossible to distinguish the contribution of syntactic constituent structure to syntactic timing from the contribution of phonological constituent structure.[13] The same can be said for the presence of pitch accents in the sentence.

6.2.2 The Phonology and Phonetics of Rhythmic Disjuncture

6.2.2.1 The English "Rhythm Rule"   In first discussing the "Rhythm Rule" in English (section 4.3), we noted that the failure of Beat Movement to apply in certain syntactic contexts, despite the apparent existence of a clash in the stress patterns of the items in sequence, could be explained by assuming that in those contexts a sufficient number of silent demibeats (and, through Beat Addition, silent beats) were present to in effect eliminate the clash. Given this account, we expect to find that where Silent Demibeat Addition has applied a sufficient number of times (and where Beat Addition has followed on its heels), there will be no Beat Movement.

This account correctly predicts that Beat Movement will be common with modifier-noun sequences. (Most of the examples in preceding chapters have been of this type: *àchromatic léns, thìrteen mén, àbstract árt, fùndamental théorem, Dùndee mármalade,* etc.) The reason for the readiness of Beat Movement to apply is that no more than *one* silent demibeat will be inserted in such a context, so that a clash will often occur. Because it is a major category item, a prenominal adjective will have one silent position introduced after it, for example. But because the AP of which that adjective is head is an *adjunct,* clause (b) of SDA will not introduce another position. Because AP contains only A, clause (c) is inapplicable; and (d) is inapplicable as well. So *abstract art* is derived as follows:

(6.16)

```
              x                         x
      x       x               x         x
x     x       x     ⇒    x     x         x
x     x     x x          x     x     x x
abstract   art           abstract   art
```

Note that if the A were a compound or the AP were branching, an additional silent demibeat would be inserted, by clause (c), but this would not necessarily mean that Beat Movement would be less likely to apply, since the NSR would vault the prominence of the head A up one level, creating a clash at a higher level, as shown in (6.17). This is avoided, if possible (section 4.3.2).

(6.17)

```
                    x
        x           x
x       x           x
x       x   (x)     x
x       x    x x    x
really good      play
```

The theory also predicts that other [Adjunct Head] configurations will have a similar paucity of silent grid positions between words and that Beat Movement will therefore be more likely to apply. This seems to be the case. In Adverb-Adjective sequences Beat Movement also applies quite regularly: *àbsolutely cértain, psỳchologically réal, ànaphorically bóund,* etc.

It is by no means the case, however, that the "Rhythm Rule" is limited to prehead positions. Consider the following examples, where a head N or V is followed by its complement within NP or VP and undergoes the rhythmic inversion:

(6.18)
a. the thìrteenth of Máy (cf. thirtéenth)
    the tòwn hall of Ámherst (cf. the Amherst town háll)
    a ràtification of the tréaty (cf. ratificátion)
    the òverripeness of the péars (cf. overrípeness)
    a rèconciliation of párties (cf. reconciliátion)

b. to òverthrow the góvernment (cf. overthrów)
    if you còntradict your móther . . . (cf. contradíct)
    They're going to ìncrease spénding (cf. incréase)
    He'll never còmprehend phýsics (cf. comprehénd)
    a rule that ìnterchanges constítuents (cf. interchánge)

Our claim is that, all else being equal, Beat Movement will be less likely in a V N sequence than in an A N sequence, for example, because there is an additional silent position after the verb, in view of its status as the head of a nonadjunct phrase (the VP). Consider *increase spending:* if there is no pitch accent on *increase,* then the grid alignment of the phrase is as in (6.19).

(6.19)

```
                x
      x         x
  x   x   (x)   x
  x   x   x x   x   x
  increase      spending
```

Should Beat Addition apply, the clash at the third level would be eliminated and Beat Movement averted, but should Beat Addition not
apply, Beat Movement would bring about the reversal.

The differential treatment accorded to adjuncts and nonadjuncts by
SDA is illustrated quite well by another sort of example. Consider the
pair *(the)* *ÙB líbrary* and *UB̀'s líbrary*. In the former, the noun *UB* (the
old nickname for the University of Buffalo) has some sort of adjunct
status (compare *stone wall, brick chimney, town common,* etc.); in the
latter, *UB's* is a possessive NP, an argument (of sorts). SDA assigns
them different numbers of silent positions, as in (6.20) and thereby predicts, correctly, that Beat Movement is more likely to apply in one case
than the other:

(6.20)

```
a.           x            b.             x
        x    x                 x         x
       x x   x x              x x        x x
       x x x x x x           x x   x x   x x x
     (the) UB  library       UB's        library
```

Beat Movement is virtually obligatory in the first case, and possible,
though less necessary, in the second. Observe next that the mere addition of one weak syllable and hence one demibeat makes the inversion
within the possessive even less probable: the normal pronunciation of
UMass's library, with the *pre* –Beat Movement pattern (6.21), is *without* inversion.[14] (This would seem to imply either that Beat Addition
must apply here, or that the *Montana* Filter (section 3.2.4) has come
into play.)

(6.21)

```
                x
      x         x
  x   x   x     x x
  x   x   x x x x x x
  U Mass's      library
```

The "Rhythm Rule" also provides evidence of the essentially asymmetric character of SDA. Consider the sentence (6.22). Here, Beat Movement in the preposition *underneath* is virtually obligatory (compare *undernéath*).

(6.22)
I put those five $_{PP}[_P[\text{ùnderneath}]_P\ _{NP}[[\text{her}]\ [\text{bóok}]]_{NP}]_{PP}$

This is to be expected, given SDA as formulated, for *underneath* is only a preposition and thus would receive no silent demibeats. If the constituent following *underneath* is made more complex, by increasing numbers of embeddings of possessive NPs, the behavior of *underneath* is unchanged. Beat Movement carries on as usual.

(6.23)
a. I put those five $_{PP}[\text{ùnderneath}\ _{NP}[_{NP}[[\text{her}]\ \text{sìster's}]_{NP}\ \text{bóok}]_{NP}]_{PP}$

b. I put those five $_{PP}[\text{ùnderneath}\ _{NP}[_{NP}[_{NP}[[\text{her}]\ \text{sìster's}]_{NP}\ \text{frìend's}]_{NP}$
$\text{bóok}]_{NP}]_{PP}$

This would seem to imply that the degree of embedding of the right-hand constituent at a constituent break is irrelevant to SDA and therefore that whether or not there is a clash bringing on Beat Movement depends only on the constituent's ending with *underneath*. Finally, in (6.24), where *underneath* is still on the left of the constituent break but now embedded within a subject NP, there is no Beat Movement in *underneath*.

(6.24)
I bet $_S[_{NP}[\text{those five}\ _{\bar{N}}[_{PP}[_P[\text{undernèath}]_P]_{PP}]_{\bar{N}}]_{NP}\ _{VP}[\text{are cóoked}]_{VP}]_S$

Various clauses of SDA will apply (and reapply) in such a configuration, inserting a sizeable number of silent positions after the subject NP and thereby quite effectively eliminating any possibility for a clash and hence any possibility for Beat Movement to apply.

6.2.2.2 Pausing and Final Lengthening in English Though data from pausing and final lengthening would in principle constitute major evidence in evaluating any proposal concerning the rules of SDA and their syntactic environments, the data that are available can for the most part be taken only as suggestive and do not bear directly on a proposal whose predictions are as explicit and as differentiated as ours. With the exception of work by Cooper and his colleagues (see note 1), little research on final lengthening and pausing had adequately controlled for details of syntactic analysis and even their work permits only limited conclusions to be drawn, as we will show. We will nonetheless draw on this literature, showing how our proposal could account for some of the facts that have been cited.

It has long been recognized that the division of a sentence into words is reflected in the sentence's rhythmic properties, even when stress (or prominence) pattern is kept constant. D. Jones 1964:239–240 remarks that

the rhythm of the sentence is determined not only by the number and nature of the speech sounds in the word-group and the positions of the stresses in the words of more than one syllable, but also by the grammatical relations between words. If an unstressed syllable occurs between two stressed syllables it tends to be shorter if it is grammatically more closely connected with the following stressed syllable than if its closer relationship is with the preceding stressed syllable.

He gives ♪. ♪ ♩ as the time relation among the syllables of *Buy the book* or *quite forgot* and ♫ ♩ as the time relation for *either book* or *Take it out*. A further example of this well-known sort of contrast is discussed by Abercrombie 1967: *Greater London* vs. *Grey to London*. In British Received Pronunciation, the two preceding examples are identical in terms of segments and stress. But *Grey* is longer with respect to *to* than *Grea-* is to *-ter*.[15] This contrast does not speak directly to any particular one of the clauses of SDA, but it does lend support to the hypothesis (embodied in SDA) that major category words would be followed by one silent demibeat at the least (and function words by fewer or none). Our account would align the two examples as follows:

(6.25)

```
a.          x           b.                      x
      x     x                 x                 x
      x     x                 x                 x
      x  x  x  x  x            x  x  x  x        x
     Greater  London         Grey    to London
```

These representations provide the basis for explaining the timing contrast (though they by no means tell the whole story). In (6.25a), the final syllable *-ter* will stretch out and align with the following demibeat, and in that way it will contrast with *to,* which is confined to just one demibeat. The greater length of *Grey* with respect to *to* may simply be a matter of the number of demibeats that it should be aligned with phonetically—three of them, if (6.25b) is the correct representation. The length of the first syllable of *Greater* would seem to suggest that main stress itself contributes to length, accounting for what is said to be the equivalence of the two syllables in this case. The details of some of this interpretation remain to be worked out and more fully justified, but the central point should be clear. Our theory of rhythmic disjuncture predicts timing differences of just the sort observed: a stressless syllable preceding a constituent break should be longer than a stressless syllable following one.

This sort of evidence points to the existence of at least one silent grid position between words in sequence (more precisely, to the existence of at least one position after a major category word). Data from experimental studies on speech production confirm this. It is consistently reported that word-final syllables are longer, on the average, than word-medial or word-initial syllables (Oller 1973, Klatt 1975, Umeda 1975, Nakatani, O'Connor, and Aston 1981). This effect is predicted by assuming, as we have, the presence of silent position(s) between words and an account of final lengthening as left-to-right autosegmental spreading. Notice, however, that such data, while confirming the left-to-right spreading and the presence of silent positions, do not give evidence concerning any details of SDA, e.g., the asymmetry of SDA and its sensitivity to only certain sorts of syntactic information.

There is, however, some evidence of the need for clause (b), which places an additional silent demibeat after the head word of a nonadjunct phrase. Catford 1966 notices, for example, that the sentences *That was a man-eating fish* and *That was a man eating fish* are distinguished by the presence of a "rest" between *man* and *eating* in the latter case.[16] Catford marks the rest with the symbol $_\wedge$, representing the rhythmic differences between the two sentences as follows:

(6.26)
a. | That was a | man-eating | fish
b. | That was a | man $_\wedge$ eating | fish

We interpret this rest as a silent beat. The relevant parts of the structures of these two sentences are shown in (6.27a,b):

(6.27)
a. This is $_{NP}$[a $_{AP}$[$_A$[$_N$[man]$_N$ $_A$[eating]$_A$]$_A$]$_{AP}$ [fish]]$_{NP}$
b. This is $_{NP}$[$_{NP}$[a [man]]$_{NP}$ $_S$[eating fish]$_S$]$_{NP}$

We would argue that the silent beat in (6.27b) arises from the combined (and cumulative) effects of (at least) two syntax-dependent principles of timing: word-end silent demibeat addition (clause (a) of SDA), and clause (b) of SDA. These two rules account for the presence of two silent demibeats after *man* in (6.27b), and those two silent demibeats translate, by grid euphony, into one silent beat. We illustrate the resulting grid alignment below, noting only the beat and demibeat levels of the grid:

(6.28)

```
      x     x     x
      x    x x   x   x
NP[...man]NP      S[eating...]S
```

Because the second of the two rules of SDA will not be applicable when *man* is the first element of a compound, the grid alignment for the compound *man eating* is merely (6.29):

(6.29)

```
      x        x
      x    x   x   x
N[...man]N    A[eating...]A
```

The grid clearly permits a simple and straightforward representation of these subtleties of non-stress-related timing.

It is known, moreover, that the branching character of a constituent on the left at a constituent break will translate into a pause or lengthening effect. Pairs such as those in (6.30) and (6.31) have identical prominence patterns, as shown, but they may nonetheless be rhythmically distinguished (Liberman 1975).

(6.30)
a.
```
                        x
          x             x           x
          x             x           x
      x   x x x     x x x     x     x
NP[AP[American]AP N[N[history]N N[teacher]N]N]NP
```

b.
```
                        x
            x           x           x
            x           x           x
        x   x x x     x x x     x     x
NP[N[N[A[American]A N[history]N]N N[teacher]N]N]NP
```

(6.31)

a.
```
                      x
        x             x        x
        x             x        x
        x   x         x        x
```
$_{NP}[_{AP}[crystal]_{AP}\ _N[_N[beach]_N\ _N[boat]_N]_N]_{NP}$

b.
```
                      x
        x             x        x
        x             x        x
        x   x         x        x
```
$_{NP}[_N[_N[Crystal]_N\ _N[Beach]_N]_N\ _N[boat]_N]_N]_{NP}$

We submit that what disambiguates the two is a disjuncture in the (b) examples, located after the left-hand branching (compound) constituent (introduced by an iteration of clause (a) of SDA) and realized as a lengthening of the final syllable of the compound.[17]

In general, the first three clauses of SDA, whether in combination or through an iteration based on embedded words or phrases, provide the explanation for the general observation that *longer* constituents are followed by greater pauses, for length usually translates into a greater constituent complexity or depth of embedding. Since constituents tend to be right-branching in English, the length of a constituent on the left usually does correspond to a greater depth of embedding.[18] It is worth noting that Cooper and Paccia-Cooper 1980, who show that depth of embedding correlates with length of pause, have found that it is the depth of embedding of the left-hand constituent at a constituent break that is important.

As for clause (d) of SDA, which assigns a silent demibeat at the end of constituents daughter to S, it receives a certain support from timing evidence. Parentheticals, preposed adverbials, postposed phrases, vocatives, and the like, are set off from the rest of the sentence by a disjuncture in time (Klatt 1976, Bing 1979a,b). Furthermore, a subject NP may be followed by a more substantial pause than, say, a possessive NP (Klatt 1975). These sorts of data are to be expected, if daughters of S are given a special status by rules adding silent positions to the grid alignment of the sentence.

There is obviously much more to be said about these issues, and much more research to be done. With this cursory review we hope merely to have shown that there appears to be some basis in fact for the distinctions between syntactic contexts drawn by our proposal for Silent Demibeat Addition.

6.2.2.3 External Sandhi   The rules of Silent Demibeat Addition as formulated in (6.13) together generate different amounts of rhythmic disjuncture in different sorts of syntactic contexts. If, with (6.13), we are approximating a correct description of rhythmic disjuncture and if phonological rules applying between words (external sandhi rules) are indeed sensitive to the adjacency in time of the sound segments involved, then we should find that, for any given rate of speech, it is more likely for the sandhi rules to operate in contexts where fewer silent grid positions are added than in contexts where SDA would predict more. In what follows we will briefly review some facts of external sandhi from a small number of languages, showing that the theory's predictions appear to be borne out.

The various clauses of SDA define what is in effect a "hierarchy" of rhythmic disjuncture for the various sorts of "constituent breaks" encountered in a sentence. (6.32) is a partial list of "constituent break types" and the place they occupy on the hierarchy of disjuncture (a larger Roman numeral corresponds to a larger amount of disjuncture). The letters appearing after the descriptions of the syntactic contexts name the clauses of SDA responsible for adding a silent demibeat in those environments.

(6.32)
(i)   Function word and first word of its sister on the right[19]
       Examples: the cat, in old houses

(ii)   Single word adjunct phrase and first word of right sister (a)
       Examples: old houses, first attempt to leave

(iii) a. Once-branching adjunct phrase and first word of right sister
         (a,c)
         Examples: extremely old houses, many more people
      b. Head word of nonadjunct phrase and first word of right sister
         (a,b)
         Examples: saw Nelly, top of the mountain
      c. Nonbranching nonadjunct phrase and first word of right sister
         (a,b)
         Example: gave books to Mary

(6.32)

(iv) a. Once-branching nonadjunct phrase and first word of right
sister (a,b,c)
Examples: gave many books to Mary, elect a stupid
person president

b. Nonbranching daughter of S and first word of right sister
(a,b,d)
Example: Mary left town

(v) a. Twice-branching nonadjunct phrase and first word of right
sister (a,b,c,d)
Example: gave many books on architecture to Mary

b. Once-branching daughter of sentence and first word of right
sister (a,b,c,d)
Example: Mary's mother left town

If external sandhi rules are sensitive to adjacency in real time, it is
predicted that, at a given rate of speech, they will apply in syntactic
contexts falling in a continuous subsequence of this hierarchy, starting
with (i). The cutoff point will depend on the rate of speech, and it may
also depend on the rule itself (rules may possibly vary in their adjacency requirements). The prediction is that a sandhi rule will apply in
contexts in increasingly higher positions in the disjuncture hierarchy in
increasingly faster rates of speech.

Mandarin tone sandhi, as described by Cheng 1968, bears out this
prediction. In Mandarin, a word with tone 3 preceding another word
with tone 3 is changed into a word with tone 2. (Tone 3 is a low falling-
rising tone; tone 2 is a high rising tone.) The rule requires a certain
degree of "connectedness" between the words with the tones involved,
and the constituent breaks across which tone sandhi applies grow ever
larger as speech rate increases. Cheng offers the example shown in
(6.33), consisting entirely of words with underlying tone 3, to illustrate
these properties of the rule:[20]

(6.33)

3 3   3   3   3
[[lau li] [mai [siau pi]]]
'Old Li buys a small writing brush.'

a.   2 3   3   2   3
b.   2 3   2   2   3
c.   2 2   2   2   3

In a more deliberate rate of speech, tone sandhi takes place only in the A N sequence (6.33a). At a somewhat faster rate, the verb also loses its tone 3 in view of the following context (6.33b). And at a yet faster rate, the head of the subject NP also loses its tone 3 (6.33c). Again, this is just the sort of data that our theory of rhythmic disjuncture and time-sensitive sandhi rules predicts should exist.

The well-known phenomenon of *raddoppiamento sintattico* (RS) in Italian[21] also lends itself to analysis in terms of our theory. RS is usually described as gemination of a word-initial consonant arising in certain sentential contexts under certain phonological conditions. The phonological condition that seems generally to hold is that the preceding word must end in a main-stressed vowel.[22] Compare, for example, *più caldo* [pjù kkáldo] 'more hot' and *meno caldo* [mèno káldo] 'less hot'. This *raddoppiamento* is in fact an instance of a quite general phenomenon of interword resyllabification; it is subject to a variety of phonological restrictions that we will not consider here (Vogel 1977, Chierchia 1982a,b,c). The question we wish to address (in rather cursory fashion) is that of specifying the syntactic environments in which this resyllabification applies. (A grid-based analysis of RS sharing some features with ours is developed in Chierchia 1982b.)

If the resyllabification of which RS is an instance is governed by rhythmic disjuncture (represented in terms of the metrical grid), then we expect (a) that it happens more readily in contexts lower in the disjuncture hierarchy than in contexts higher in the hierarchy and (b) that it happens in contexts higher in the hierarchy in faster speech. Unfortunately we have no data on the influence of speech rate on RS, but data are available on the syntactic contexts in which RS is more or less likely to apply. Napoli and Nespor 1979 make quite a detailed examination of the syntactic contexts in which RS applies. Nespor and Vogel 1982 point out that the earlier analysis needs elaboration and refinement in order to account for the fact that RS is more likely to apply in some syntactic contexts than in others. They observe that RS is more likely between a modifier and a following head (e.g., *tre cani* 'three dogs', *più caldo* 'more hot') than between a head word and a following complement (e.g., *fa caldo* 'it's hot out', *la città vecchia* 'the old city'). This is what our account predicts, since the latter environment is higher in the disjuncture hierarchy than the former. Chierchia 1982b observes moreover that RS is more likely between, for example, the two words *caucciù* 'rubber' and *giallo/gialla* 'yellow' in the context of the phrase in (6.34), where *giallo* modifies *caucciù*, than in (6.35), where *gialla* modifies the entire complex *sfero di caucciù* 'sphere of rubber'.

(6.34)
[una [sfera [di [[caucciù] [giallo]]]]]
'a sphere of yellow rubber'

(6.35)
[una [[sfera] [di [caucciù]]] [gialla]]
'a yellow sphere of rubber'

The lesser likelihood of RS in (6.35) may be attributed to the greater amount of embedding of the left-hand constituent, which translates on our theory into a greater number of silent demibeats. Chierchia gives other contrasts of a similar sort, RS being more likely in the (a) cases than in the (b) cases:

(6.36)
a. Ho picchiato [il [re con lo scettro]]
   'I hit the king with a scepter (the king had a scepter).'
b. Ho picchiato [il re] [con lo scettro]
   'I hit the king with a scepter (I did it with a scepter).'

(6.37)
a. Mio fratello mangiò le fragole e [finì [tutto il resto]]
   'My brother ate the strawberries and finished all the rest.'
b. Mio fratello mangiò le fragole e [[Fifì] [tutto il resto]]
   'My brother ate the strawberries and Fifi all the rest.'

It is also noted that RS is virtually impossible when the constituent on the left is very long and heavy, as in (6.38) and (6.39). (The italicized words border the potential RS environment.)

(6.38)
[La religione que tutti pensano Mario stia praticando con *fedeltà*]
[*perde* fedeli]
'The religion which everybody thinks Mario is practicing faithfully is losing followers.'

(6.39)
Ho visto [il ragazzo che Maria ama con *onestà*] [*per* fortuna]
'I saw the boy that Maria loves honestly, luckily.'

Given the grid-based analysis of disjuncture embodied in SDA, it is
expected that these facts should be as they are.

Napoli and Nespor's 1979 account of the RS facts in effect denies
that phonological representation has a role to play in determining the
possibilities of RS in the sentence. They suggest that a syntactic condition (the *Left Branch Condition*) governs the applicability of RS (in
other words, that RS is directly sensitive to syntactic structure):

(6.40)
The Left Branch Condition
"RS can apply between a word *a* and a following word *b*, where *a*
is immediately dominated by the preterminal category symbol A, and
b is dominated (not necessarily immediately) by the category
symbol B, only if A is a left branch of the first node that dominates
both A and B." (1979:824)

They specify that "A [is a] left branch of a given node C if no branching
nodes intervene between A and C, and if there are no daughters of C to
the left of A" (p. 824).

The claim, then, is that RS applies only in the following configuration:[23]

(6.41)

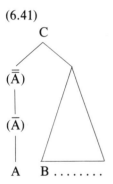

But, as Nespor and Vogel point out, the likelihood of application of RS
in syntactic configurations of type (6.41) is not the same—it depends on
what sort of word or phrase *A* is. And, as Chierchia points out, the Left
Branch Condition rules out RS in contexts where it does indeed apply.[24] This is the case with (6.35), (6.36b), and (6.37b). It is also the
case with the sentences of (6.42), where the italicized words are the RS
environment.

(6.42)

a. Io ho [[amato] [*più*] [*Carlo*]]
   'I (have) loved Carlo more.'

b. Loro hamo [[eletto] [*Artù*] [*papa*]]
   'They elected Artu pope.'

c. Ho [[messo] [*Artù*] [*per* strada]]
   'I put Artu on the road.'

Conceivably, a more adequate syntax-based account could be offered, in order to come to terms with the facts. But there are a number of reasons for considering that RS applies in terms of a phonological representation that mediates between syntactic structure and phonological processes such as resyllabification in general. First, of course, the grid-based account, motivated on quite independent grounds, appears to be consistent with the facts. Second, viewing RS as being governed ultimately by the grid helps to explain why it is that RS and the Italian "Rhythm Rule" (Nespor and Vogel 1979) go hand in hand. Chierchia 1982b has shown that in dialects where both RS and a stress shift rule operate to eliminate clashes, either both rules apply or neither does, in a given syntactic context. Whether or not the "Rhythm Rule" applies is a function of "closeness" defined with respect to the grid. That RS should apply in just the contexts that the "Rhythm Rule" indicates have less rhythmic disjuncture would follow if RS itself were sensitive to that disjuncture. Finally, there is another reason why phonological representation needs to mediate between syntactic structure and RS. It is observed in the traditional literature on RS (e.g., Camilli 1911) that RS does not arise when there is a considerable pitch movement (*dislivello di tono*) on the last syllable of the first word. We might take this to mean either that the first word bears a pitch accent, or that the first word is at the end of an intontional phrase. In either case, the rhythmic structure or timing, of the sentence would be affected, with greater disjuncture introduced between the two words in sequence. And this impedes RS. It seems clear that no syntax-based account can make sense of such a fact.

Both Nespor and Vogel 1982 and Chierchia 1982b suggest that the intonational phrase serves as a domain for RS, implying that the lack of RS between two words is an indication that they belong to separate intonational phrases. This is probably too strong a claim, for it would imply, among other things, that any lack of RS in contexts where the other phonological conditions were satisfied, and in contexts where at a different speed there might be RS, would have to be explained in terms of a different intonational phrasing for the sentence. It is not at all obvious that the data from pitch contours would support this position. Our position is that RS is governed by considerations of *adjacency in time* and is thus affected by the nature of the rhythmic disjunctures in the grid and their interpretation in any particular performance. If intonational structure appears to affect RS, we submit that it is because intonational structure affects the nature of the grid itself, or the realization of the grid in time.

Another well-known case of apparently syntactically governed external sandhi, French *liaison,* behaves in a way that is reminiscent of Italian RS, but unlike it in certain details. Liaison involves the pronunciation of a word-final consonant in the context of a following word with an initial vowel, e.g., *les enfants* [lezãfã] 'the children' vs. *les filles* [le fij] 'the girls'. It is only in certain syntactic contexts that a final consonant will be maintained when a vowel follows. In others, it will delete regardless of what follows: *les enfants/accouraient* [lezãfã akurɛ], not **les enfants accouraient* [lezãfãzakurɛ] 'the children ran up'. In Selkirk 1972, 1974 we attempted to describe the range of contexts in which liaison does and does not appear. Since then we have come to a fuller understanding of the facts, and a new description reflecting that understanding would require substantial revisions. We are not prepared to undertake that task here, but simply wish to point out that, to the extent to which liaison is a viable phonologically based phenomenon in French, its behavior is consistent with what would be predicted if it were governed by rhythmic disjuncture and the rules for Silent Demibeat Addition proposed in (6.13). Liaison is known to be obligatory in the following contexts, for example:

(6.43)
a. Clitic pronoun plus verb
   Examples: nous‿aimons, nous vous‿aimons
b. NP determiner plus right sister
   Examples: les‿autres filles, les‿animaux
c. Numeral plus right sister
   Examples: trois‿enfants, trois‿autres filles
d. Adjective plus noun
   Examples: ancien‿ami, petit‿enfant
e. (Certain) prepositions and right sister
   Example: dans‿une minute

These are of course just the contexts where SDA creates the least amount of rhythmic disjuncture—zero or one silent grid position. In certain other contexts, liaison is said to be optional. These include contexts where the head word of a phrase is followed by a complement: *des politiciens américains, (il) mangeait une pomme,* etc. (see Selkirk 1974). The curious thing in the latter environments is that liaison only takes place when the final consonant involved belongs to an inflectional morpheme: **un politicien américain.* This fact, and the fact that liaison in these contexts appears only in more formal self-conscious styles of speech and not at all necessarily in conditions of faster speech (if anything, the contrary), leads us to speculate that in such contexts liaison is no longer an essentially phonological phenomenon, but one being maintained by some rules that may be quite "grammaticized" or "syntacticized" and no longer reflect the processes of "core phonology." This said, the fact that it is in just those syntactic contexts where SDA would predict the presence of the next smallest amount of rhythmic disjuncture that this syntacticized liaison takes place cannot be accidental. In some way, then, even these facts about liaison lend support to the general approach being taken here.[25]

Studies of external sandhi that attend to the particulars of the syntactic contexts in which the rules apply or do not apply are fairly rare. (Among those familiar to us are, for example, Kaisse 1977, 1978 on Modern Greek, Rotenberg 1978 on Modern Irish, Clements 1977 on Ewe, Kisseberth and Abasheikh 1974 on Chi Mwi:ni, Egido and Cooper 1980 and Cooper, Egido, and Paccia 1978 on English.) Since we have not undertaken to review them from the theoretical perspective being laid out here, our proposal must be taken as quite programmatic. Nonetheless, the nature of the predictions should be quite clear.

Chapter 7

Function Words: Destressing and Cliticization

A description of the metrical grid alignment of words and phrases in English, and of the role of syntactic structure in determining that alignment, would not be complete without some discussion of the class of words traditionally described as having "strong" and "weak" forms (Sweet 1891, 1908, D. Jones 1931, Gimson 1970). These are for the most part monosyllables belonging to the syntactic class of "function words": auxiliary verbs, modals, prepositions, determiners, conjunctions, personal pronouns, etc. In their strong forms, these monosyllables are "stressed" (in a degree yet to be specified—though we have argued in sections 3.2.3 and 4.1.1 that they do not have a third-level alignment)—and their vowels are the full vowels characteristic of stressed syllables. In their weak forms, these monosyllables are stressless, their vowels undergo the reduction typical in English of stressless syllables (in certain cases, they may even delete), and the surrounding consonants may also be modified or deleted because of the stressless status of the syllable.[1] The function words in the phrases of (7.1), for example, normally appear in their weak forms, as noted in column (a), though they may also be pronounced with their strong forms, listed in column (b).[2]

(7.1)

	a.	b.
a fence	[ə]	([ej])
can pile (up)	[kən, kn̩, kəm, km̩]	[kæn]
for Timothy	[fr̩]	[fɔr]
in confidence	[ɪn, n̩, ɪŋ, ŋ̩]	[ɪn]
need *him*	[ɪm, m̩]	[hɪm]

The strong, stressed forms of function words are their citation forms, and the form in which they must appear in certain syntactic configurations; the weak forms normally appear in the complement set of syntactic configurations. It is generally observed that, in order for a function word to take its weak form, it must be sufficiently "close," syntactically speaking, to what follows (or, in a few cases, to what precedes).

It is also characteristic of function words that they may exhibit an extremely close phonological connection, or juncture, with an adjacent word—usually to the word that follows, but sometimes to one that precedes. This closeness in juncture is illustrated by the great likelihood that phonological rules of sandhi will operate between a function word and an adjacent word, in the appropriate syntactic circumstances, and also by the concomitant absence of rhythmic disjuncture between the two. The examples of (7.2a) are representative. The strong tendency for a nasal ending the function word to assimilate in place of articulation with the consonant beginning the following word is evidence of very close juncture. And, rhythmically speaking, there is no apparent hiatus between the words, as comparison with the corresponding words in (7.2b), in this respect identical, shows rather well.[3]

(7.2)

a. a fence	b. offence
can pile (up)	compile
for Timothy	fertility
in confidence	incompetence
need him	Needham

In the framework we are developing here, both stress and juncture are a matter of the metrical grid alignment of an utterance. We may surmise, therefore, that if function words differ from nonfunction words in properties relating to stress and juncture, then function words do not have the same basic metrical grid alignment as nonfunction words. Indeed, our hypothesis is that the grammar draws a distinction between function words and nonfunction words in the syntax-phonology mapping, where the syllable-to-grid alignment of words and phrases is defined and where the silent demibeat addition of syntactic timing is determined. The hypothesis is that the specialness of function words resides essentially in their not being treated like "real" words by the grid construction principles of this mapping, and more specifically, (a) in their not being attributed the following silent demibeat that their word status would otherwise merit them (section 6.2.1) and (b) in their not being attributed a third-level "main word stress" (sections 3.2.4 and 4.1.1). We claim that these and other ways in which function words are not treated like "real" words in the grammar are to be attributed to a single principle, the *Principle of the Categorial Invisibility of Function Words* (PCI), which says (essentially) that rules making crucial appeal to the syntactic category of the constituent to which they apply are blind to the presence of function word constituents. As a consequence of the PCI, function words will lack the particular features of the metrical grid alignment of "real" words, and from these peculiarities of metrical grid alignment all (or virtually all) else follows automatically.

The central role in our analysis of the phonology of function words is played by Monosyllabic Destressing (3.56), a rule that eliminates the basic beat (second-level) alignment of a single syllable, under certain conditions. Recall from section 3.3.3 that for a syllable to be susceptible to this destressing rule, it must have the appropriate internal rime composition—a CV syllable (V is a lax vowel) is the most likely to destress, a CVVC or CVCC syllable is the least likely to do so, and so on. A number of general conditions govern destressing. Two play a role in constraining Monosyllabic Destressing within "real" words: the Higher Prominence Preservation Condition (HPPC) and the Alternation Maintenance Condition (AMC). In what follows we will show that the HPPC and a further condition, the Grid Culmination Condition, govern the operation of Monosyllabic Destressing on the phrase.

Clearly, a monosyllabic function word is in principle susceptible to Monosyllabic Destressing as we know it, given our assumptions about the basic phonological representation of function words: it does not (necessarily) have a third-level stress, and it is not (necessarily) followed by a weak demibeat. Some of the sequences in (7.2a) have the basic phonological representations shown in (7.3), given the foregoing assumptions (and ignoring silent demibeats after the head N).

(7.3)

```
  x              x          x
x x           x   x       x   x
x x           x   x       x   x    x x
a fence       can pile    in confidence
```

From these representations, the rule can produce the destressed versions in (7.4).

(7.4)

```
 x              x          x
 x              x          x
 x  x           x  x       x  x  x x
a fence      can pile    in confidence
```

Our task will be to offer a theory of the configurations in which Monosyllabic Destressing is *blocked*. One purpose of this chapter, then, is to demonstrate that Monosyllabic Destressing and its governing conditions, in conjunction with the general theory of grid construction and the theory of the basic phonological representation of function words embodied in the PCI, together constitute a very good theory of the distribution of the strong and weak forms of function words within the sentence.

This analysis shares certain general features of the analysis of function word phonology proposed in Selkirk 1972. However, the latter analysis is couched within a standard SPE framework; it assumes the SPE theory of phonological representation and with it both the conception of stress as an *n*-ary feature assigned to vowels and the conception of juncture as boundary segments having their place in the linear string of sound segments. In both analyses, the syntax-phonology mapping is of central importance. In that mapping, general features of surface syntactic representation are translated into (degrees of) juncture in the phonological representation, and a distinction is made between the junctural properties of function words and those of "real" words. Both analyses assume the stressed form of the function word to be basic, and that the major descriptive task of the grammar is to characterize the destressing of function words in the appropriate environments. The reduction of vowels and the deletion of vowels and certain consonants are understood to be consequences of the stresslessness of a syllable, and the phonology of "contraction" is seen as a special case of the phonology of stressless syllables. Thus the central phenomenon in both analyses is destressing. In both analyses the destressing rule is defined on phonological representation and is crucially governed by the junctural properties of the utterance. The apparent sensitivity of the destressing rule to various syntactic characteristics of the utterance is explained as a sensitivity on the part of the rule not to aspects of surface syntactic structure but rather to the degrees of juncture that are the encoding of surface structure in phonological representation.[4] There are nonetheless important differences in the two approaches, not the least of which is that the main agent of function word destressing in the present analysis is a rule that is independently motivated in the grammar, Monosyllabic Destressing. The destressing rule of Selkirk 1972, the Monosyllable Rule, was an ad hoc invention, particular to monosyllabic function words. Moreover, the present analysis handles not only the facts treated in Selkirk 1972, but also new facts that the theory of Selkirk 1972 could not have analyzed, in particular those relating to the role of pitch accent assignment and other rhythmic factors in preventing destressing. Of course the present analysis has the further advantage of being consistent with a general theory of stress and juncture that can explain a greater variety of stress- and juncture-related phenomena than the standard SPE theory could.

Viewing Monosyllabic Destressing as the agent of the "alternation" between the strong and weak forms of function words in the sentence requires that the syllable(s) of function words be underlyingly stressed (aligned with a position on the second (basic beat) level of the metrical grid) and then, through application of the rule, reduced to stresslessness. An alternative to our basic analysis would be one in which function words were not normally stressed (aligned with the basic beat level); here, their strong stressed forms would arise from applying a rule *adding* a basic beat alignment under certain limited conditions. In the first part of section 7.1.1 we show that for quite general reasons, an alternative of the latter sort is not viable. The general framework that has been developed here requires in effect that the alternation between strong and weak forms be understood in terms of a stressed syllable losing its basic beat alignment, and not the reverse.

In section 7.1.2 we argue that the rule destressing function words must apply on a phrasal domain, and that it must precede the application of Beat Movement on that domain. This ordering follows from considering both phrasal destressing and Beat Movement to be cyclic, and it supports our general claim that the syntax-phonology mapping proceeds in cyclic fashion. The further demonstration that the rule of phrasal destressing is the same as Monosyllabic Destressing, which applies in words, leads to the conclusion that Monosyllabic Destressing is not "postcyclic" but cyclic, though restricted to a syntactic domain of word or higher.

In section 7.1.3 we justify in detail our claim that Monosyllabic Destressing, applying on a phrasal domain, is responsible for the strong-weak alternations in function words. In sections 7.1.4 and 7.1.5 we examine the influence of various principles of grid construction on the operation of Monosyllabic Destressing, showing that the effect of these principles on the metrical grid representation to which the destressing rule applies accounts for the rather subtle range of phenomena involved in the strong-weak alternations, including the blocking of the rule that leads to the systematic appearance of strong ("uncontracted") forms in certain syntactic contexts. We show evidence in section 7.1.5 that the presence of empty categories such as traces in surface structure is not reflected in the phonological representation (contra Selkirk 1972) and so does not affect the destressing of function words. The blocking of Monosyllabic Destressing in contexts preceding empty categories will be seen to follow from other principles of the grammar.

The weak forms of (7.1) could be referred to as *clitics,* if the term is used simply to designate a word that is stressless and immediately adjacent, juncturally or rhythmically speaking, to what follows or what precedes. The function words of (7.1) are *proclitic* (except for the last), in that the word to which each of these clitics is bound follows it. Note, however, that the proclitic status of these words in no way requires assigning them a syntactic analysis according to which they are "attached" (Chomsky-adjoined) to the word that follows, as in (7.5), for example.

(7.5)

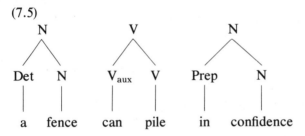

The more conventionally assumed syntactic analyses in (7.6) will be quite adequate as a basis for assigning the proper phonological interpretation of these sequences, given the theory outlined.

(7.6)

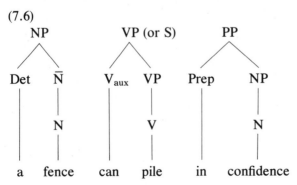

Because Silent Demibeat Addition, which is responsible for establishing the (rhythmic) juncture between words in sequence, adds silent demibeats only to the *right* of constituents (section 6.2.2) and because it adds none after a function word, no silent demibeat will intervene between the two words in the configurations in (7.6). (The basic phonological representations corresponding to (7.6) are given in (7.3).) Thus, even without "attaching" the function word further, the junctural properties of these clitics are ensured. It is of course because of this close juncture and lack of a following silent demibeat (and also, of course, because of a lack of third-level word stress) that Monosyllabic Destressing can apply. The conclusion, clearly, is that there is no motivation for a syntactic rule of procliticization (contra Bresnan 1971b and Zwicky 1977:9).[5] What the grammar does with the structures in (7.6) it would have to do with the structures of (7.5) as well. An additional rule ensuring greater closeness, syntactic or otherwise, is therefore superfluous.

The same is not true with certain *enclitics* in English, however. As in Selkirk 1972, we will see the need to posit several rules that all have the effect of *encliticizing* a function word—bringing it closer to what precedes than would otherwise have been expected on the basis of the surface syntactic analysis of the sequence. In certain cases, this encliticization has the appearance of a rule that is properly syntactic (or even "lexical"); two well-known instances are *To* Contraction (creating *wanna* from *want to*, for example) and *Not* Contraction (creating *don't* from *do not*, for example).[6] But in other cases the encliticization can be argued to be a readjustment in the rhythmic structure of the utterance, a rule of the syntax-phonology mapping that does not presuppose a syntactic encliticization. This, we will argue, is the case with the well-known Aux Contraction of *Nora's been here,* for example.[7] One goal of section 7.2 will be to contribute to refining the notion of cliticization in the theory and to demonstrate that a distinction must be drawn between syntactic cliticization, on the one hand, and rhythmic cliticization on the other.

7.1 The Basic Analysis

7.1.1 The Basic Grid Alignment of Function Words

We assume that, when the phrase cycle is entered, all (or virtually all) function words are "stressed" (basic-beat-aligned), but not "word stressed" (third-level-beat-aligned), regardless of their position in the sentence. We then propose that they may lose that stress (basic beat alignment) in certain phrasal configurations. One reason for this assumption is that there is an independently motivated rule, Monosyllabic Destressing, which eliminates that basic beat alignment in the appropriate contexts, thereby accounting for the proper distribution of the strong and weak forms of function words. An even more important reason is that this assumption seems to be the only one consistent with a quite general principle governing the mapping of function words into phonological representation, the above mentioned Principle of the Categorial Invisibility of Function Words. Finally, making the opposite assumption—that function words are basically unstressed (and thus that their stressed forms are derived by rule in certain specified circumstances)—requires considerable ad hoc complication in the grammar. We will support the last two arguments in this section, leaving the demonstration that Monosyllabic Destressing is the agent of phrasal destressing for section 7.1.3.

Our claim is that Monosyllabic Destressing, or some rule of destressing, is responsible for deriving the weak forms of function words, and that the presence of strong forms in a sentence can be attributed to a failure of the rule to apply. We suggest that when destressing fails to apply, the function word simply emerges on the surface with its original basic beat alignment (and perhaps also with alignments at a higher level, introduced by other principles of grid construction). Two features of the metrical grid alignment of function words require attention. One is the systematic presence of a basic beat alignment, which, when destressing fails to apply, accounts for the appearance of function words in their strong form. The other is the systematic absence of third-level "word stress" (except as introduced by the Pitch Accent Prominence Rule (PAR) or grid euphony). This is what accounts for the ability of Monosyllabic Destressing, or any other destressing rule, to reduce function words to stresslessness in the first place.

The assumption that function words bear no third-level stress is of course necessary, if Monosyllabic Destressing is indeed the agent of destressing, for the rule is blocked when the syllable has a grid alignment in this degree. There is also another reason to suppose this assumption is correct. Recall that the Nuclear Stress Rule will not accord phrasal prominence to a non-pitch-accent-bearing function word (section 4.1.2). Thus, for example, in (7.7),

(7.7)

[I [showed Paris to them] weeks ago]

|

pa

where *showed, Paris,* and its sister *them* all lack a pitch accent, rhythmic prominence falls on *Paris,* contrary to what the NSR would predict if *Paris* and *them* were equally prominent to begin with. We conclude that the NSR seeks out a prominence on at least the third level of the metrical grid and that *them* is ignored precisely because it does not have such an alignment.

How, then, is the grammar to avoid assigning a third-level prominence to function words? Recall that in English the Main Stress Rule that assigns third-level stress (or higher) operates within the domain of the category type Root. If we were to stipulate that function words are analyzed not in terms of Root but only in terms of Word, then a lack of third-level stress would be guaranteed. But this solution is undesirable, because it is too language-particular. The lack of rhythmic prominence in function words seems to be quite a general phenomenon, found in many languages, and it is doubtful that all of them have not only a Root-Word distinction in their word syntax but also a syntax-phonology mapping in which only Root serves as the domain of main word stress assignment. We will suppose, therefore, that the structure of function words is not unlike that of "real" words (that is, they are analyzed as both Roots and Words) and that the absence of main word stress is to be explained some other way.

What we suggest is that the syntactic category labels for function words are simply "invisible" to principles of the syntax-phonology mapping. This means that if a function word has the labeled bracketing (7.8a) or (7.8b), it will be treated as though it had the labeled bracketing (7.8c). (*FW* stands for the syntactic category feature complex(es) of function words.)

(7.8)

a. $_{fw}\text{root}[\ldots\ldots\ldots]_{fw}\text{root}$ b. $_{fw}\text{word}[\ldots\ldots\ldots]_{fw}\text{word}$ c. $[\ldots\ldots\ldots]$

This is the *Principle of the Categorial Invisibility of Function Words* (PCI). Given this general principle, any rule that crucially mentions the category name or type associated with the labeled bracketing in its structural description will simply not apply to function words. This categorial invisibility will guarantee the inapplicability of the stress rule of English assigning third-level prominence, for the rule specifies the category type (= Root) of the constituent to which it applies. This is the desired effect. This principle will also guarantee that Silent Demibeat Addition, which inserts a silent demibeat after a category of type Word, will not apply to function words. Thus it is not necessary to specify that SDA does not apply to function words (see section 6.2.1). Moreover, as we will show, the PCI guarantees that function words *will be* aligned with the second, basic beat, level of the metrical grid.[8]

Given our general framework, the presence of a basic beat alignment in any monosyllabic word, whether a "real" word or a function word, must be the result of the text-to-grid alignment rules of English applying at the second metrical level—either the Heavy Syllable Basic Beat Rule (HBR) or the Initial Basic Beat Rule (IBR). (In the case of the basic beat alignment of polysyllables, the grid euphony rule of Beat Addition might also play a role.) If the basic beat alignment of monosyllabic function words were in every instance attributable to the HBR, then the systematic presence of the alignment could *not* be taken as evidence that function words are treated as "real" words at this level, since the HBR applies only in terms of syllable type and makes no appeal to syntactic domain. However, if the IBR were to play a role in the basic beat alignment of function words, this would be an instance of function words being treated as "real" words and would violate the PCI, for the IBR makes appeal to the Word or Root status of the constituents to which it applies. (It does not apply to affixes, for example.) We believe, however, that the IBR need not be invoked here. The presence of basic beat alignment in function word monosyllables may be viewed as resulting from the HBR alone.

The following types of monosyllabic function words occur:

(7.9)

C_0V:	the, a
C_0VC:	in, up, at, on, has, is, was, that, it, them, him, her, us, from, for, are, does, can, could, will, etc.
C_0VV:	you, he, she, they, to, do, by
C_0VCC:	must[9]
C_0VVC:	our, might, your, these, whose

In the case of the last three types, a basic beat alignment by the HBR is unavoidable. A CVV or CVVC syllable is necessarily stressed, because of the tenseness of the vowel; CVCC is stressed, as a closed syllable, since at most its last consonant could be extrametrical, given the assumptions made in chapter 3. But in the case of CVC types like *in, at,* and so on, consonant extrametricality would seemingly be able to render the syllable honorarily open, so that CVC would join CV in not having its stressing guaranteed by the HBR. Yet function word monosyllables of the form CVC *are* systematically basic-beat-aligned, for they appear in strong form in contexts where (as we will show) Monosyllabic Destressing cannot apply. It might be thought that this systematic stressing of CVC is to be attributed to the IBR. But there is an alternative analysis—namely, that consonant extrametricality is excluded in function words. This being the case, the HBR will always stress monosyllabic CVCs.

Recall that extrametricality is established only with respect to particular syntactic domains (section 3.2.2) and that it is a relation between a particular consonant or syllable and a particular syntactic constituent. However, the PCI has the result that no relation can be established between a function word category and any other entity, be it a rule or a particular segment or syllable. It follows, then, that extrametricality is impossible in function words; and from this it follows that CVC function word monosyllables are always basic-beat-aligned. Thus the systematic appearance of a basic beat alignment in function words may be seen as a consequence of the PCI, rather than as a counterexample to it, as it would be if the IBR had to be invoked.

There is a last detail to consider here: CV function word monosyllables will never be stressed on this analysis. The HBR is unable to stress CV, and we are claiming that the IBR is inapplicable because of the PCI. However, the only two words with this syllabic type are *the* and *a,* and we will show that it is completely unproblematic to consider them always stressless.

To sum up, then, the PCI governing the syntax-phonology mapping of function words accounts for the fact that they bear second-level (basic beat) stress, the fact that they do not bear third-level word stress, and other properties as well. Thus, postulating the underlying basic beat alignment of function words that an analysis of the strong-weak alternations in terms of Monosyllabic Destressing requires is by no means an ad hoc feature of the analysis, but a consequence of a quite general principle of the grammar.

Let us consider now the alternative assumption about the original metrical grid alignment of function words with strong and weak forms—the assumption that they are basically stressless. Given this assumption, the strong forms are derived through stressing in phrasal contexts, and destressing plays no role. (A variant of such an analysis, couched in the standard SPE framework, is pursued by Suiko 1977, 1978a). However, we will show that this approach has a number of undesirable consequences and that we must therefore maintain our original assumption.

Presumably something like the PCI is necessary with this alternative approach, since third-level word stress is assumed not to be present and the (alleged) absence of second-level stress implies the inapplicability of the IBR. The lack of rhythmic disjuncture after function words also follows from the PCI.

The first problem lies in accounting for the presumed *lack* of basic beat alignment in function words having weak forms, namely mono-syllables of the form CV, CVC, and CVV. On this account *all* CVCs must be basically stressless. The only way to ensure this would be to require that all final consonants in function words *must* be extrametri-cal (and therefore incapable of being stressed by the HBR). Since this requirement follows from nothing we know to be true of extrametrical-ity or of function words, it is simply an ad hoc stipulation, one that is in fact inconsistent with the PCI. As for CVV function words, on this account they must all be analyzed as underlying CV, since as CVV they would be stressed by the HBR. Treating the CVV words as CV is not entirely outrageous, though, and so it is not itself a serious drawback of the approach.[1]

The second problem lies in deriving strong forms (i.e., the basic beat alignment) of CV, CVC, and CVV in phrasal configurations. There are in fact no independently motivated rules of the grammar that could introduce these basic beat alignments in the appropriate contexts. Beat Addition is the only conceivable candidate, but it is only optional on the phrase (sections 3.2.4, 4.3.1, 7.1.4) and so is in principle incapable of explaining the *obligatory* presence of strong forms in certain con-texts. Thus any derivation of a strong form of CV, CVC, or CVV could only be the result of some rule devised for the purpose. The necessity of such ad hoc inventions is doubtless a sign that the assumptions un-derlying the analysis is wrong, thus warranting a return to the original approach.

Excursus 1: The status of personal pronouns with respect to the PCI requires some clarification. These pronouns—*I, me, my, he, him, his, she, her, her, you, your,* etc.—behave just like function words in that they commonly take on a weak form. Yet these pronouns have a syn-tactic status different from that of other function words: they are phrases (NPs), and as such would be predicted to share some junctural attributes of phrases, despite the fact that they themselves, as words, would be treated like other function words, following the PCI. No matter what framework is chosen, something special must be said about NPs consisting only of a personal pronoun (cf. Selkirk 1972:section 3.2.4). We will assume that, by universal stipulation, such an NP is an honorary member of the class of function words and that it is treated as such in the syntax-phonology mapping in accordance with the PCI.

Excursus 2: The prepositions appearing in compound words behave in terms of the grid quite like nouns, verbs, and adjectives in compounds: *ínfìghting* (cf. *cóck fìghting*), *òutdó* (cf. *skỳ blúe*). The PCI must apparently be made to ignore function words inside structures generated by the word syntax component. In so doing, it would allow prepositions in compounds to be treated like any other word. Perhaps this differential treatment of prepositions in words and in phrases points to a principled difference between word grammar and sentence grammar, but for the moment we will leave this possibility unexplored.

7.1.2 Destressing and the Cycle

It can be shown that destressing takes place on a lower phrasal syntactic domain, preceding Beat Movement on a higher phrasal syntactic domain. This ordering, which can be explained in terms of the cycle, supports our hypothesis that the grid construction component of the mapping between syntactic and phonological representation is governed by the principle of the cycle (see especially chapter 4). The further demonstration that the phrasal destressing rule is the rule of Monosyllabic Destressing, which applies within words, leads us to conclude that Monosyllabic Destressing is a cyclic rule, but one that is restricted to a syntactic domain of word or higher.

The argument that the destressing of function words precedes Beat Movement on phrases is as follows. Function words lacking weak forms (i.e., function words that do not undergo destressing) are perfectly capable of receiving a third-level beat via Beat Movement, whereas function words that have weak forms (ones that undergo destressing) are not. For example, the unreducible *too* or *any*, appearing with only a basic beat alignment in *tòo múch* or *àny móre*, may acquire the greater prominence shifted from *much* and *more* by Beat Movement in the configurations *tóo mùch mèat* and *ány mòre mílk*. But the function words *as* and *some*, which appear in their destressed weak forms in *ăs múch* and *sŏme móre*, remain destressed in the complex configurations *ăs múch mèat* and *sŏme móre mílk*, where the clash between the quantifiers *much* and *more* and the following noun remains unresolved. The differing applicability of Beat Movement in these cases may be explained if destressing precedes Beat Movement.

We suggest that this ordering follows from considering both rules to be phrase-cyclic. If this is the case, the following derivations result:

(7.10) a. $_2[_1[[too] [much]]_1 [meat]]_2$ b. $_2[_1[[as] [much]]_1 [meat]]_2$

	too	much	meat		as	much	meat
		x	x			x	x
	x	x	x		x	x	x
	x	x	x		x	x	x
Word Cycle	too	much	meat		as	much	meat
Phrase Cycle 1							
NSR	vacuous				vacuous		
					x		
Destressing	inapplicable[10]				as		
Phrase Cycle 2			x				x
		x	x			x	x
	x	x	x			x	x
	x	x	x		x	x	x
NSR	too	much	meat		as	much	meat
			x				
	x		x				
	x	x	x				
BM	too	much	meat		blocked		

We consider that Beat Movement is blocked, correctly, on the higher cycle *as much meat* because the lack of basic beat alignment on *as* makes a shift impossible. (Recall from section 4.3.1 the principle of Basic Beat Integrity rules out Beat Movement in such cases.) The crucial assumption here, of course, is that the destressing of *as* and *some* applies on the *phrase*. If these function words "entered the phrasal domain" in their stressless form, then we would have no reason to invoke the cycle to explain the inapplicability of Beat Movement in these cases. But in fact, this crucial assumption is not at all independent. It is in effect the direct consequence of another element of the theory: the PCI.

The PCI rules out the possibility that weak forms like *as* and *some* are simply stressless to begin with. This original stresslessness would in principle be possible if the final consonants of such words were extrametrical, and the HBR therefore inapplicable. But we argued against this position in the preceding section. A conceivable alternative would be for destressing to apply to these function words on the word domain, before the phrasal cyclic domains are reached. But the PCI excludes this possibility as well. For destressing to apply to function words qua words it must "know" that they are words. But, given the PCI, information about the wordhood of function words is unavailable, invisible. Thus, the syllables of function words will be susceptible to destressing only when they form part of some larger non–function word domain, i.e., a phrase. The destressing of function words is therefore phrasal, and, given its relation to Beat Movement, it must be cyclic.

As pointed out in chapter 3, the destressing rules applying in words must in general follow the establishment of the basic stress pattern in words,[11] that is, destressing rules do not operate along with the cyclic rules constructing the metrical grid alignment of the word. (The latter rules include rules of text-to-grid alignment and grid euphony rules like Beat Addition and Beat Movement.) There are two possible interpretations of this fact (cf. chapter 3). One is that destressing in words is "postcyclic." According to this interpretation, destressing in words would belong to a class of noncyclic rules that would apply "after" the "word-cyclic" rules. The other interpretation is that destressing in words is itself cyclic, but that it is limited to applying on syntactic domains of the level Word (or higher). Given that in English the cyclic rules establishing the basic syllable-to-grid alignment in words have categories of type Root as their domain, it is enough to limit destressing to a supra-Root domain to ensure that it will follow the cyclic stress rules within words.[12]

Kiparsky 1979 has shown that destressing in words must precede the application of the Rhythm Rule (our Beat Movement) on the phrase. His point is that the impossibility of stress shift in *expect rain* (*expèct ráin*, not *èxpect ráin*) is to be explained as the impossibility of stress shift onto a stressless syllable (section 4.3.1), and therefore that the rule responsible for the stresslessness of the initial syllable in *expect* must precede the rule shifting the stress. This ordering of destressing in words before the phrasal application of Beat Movement is of course perfectly consistent with considering destressing to be cyclic, on the Word domain or above, and with considering Beat Movement to be cyclic as well. As for the interpretation according to which destressing in words is "postcyclic," it requires some elaboration in view of the necessity of ordering destressing prior to cyclic rules applying on the phrasal domain. A more apt characterization of destressing in words would be as a rule that is "postcyclic with respect to the word," taking

that to mean that it belongs to a class of rules that are not cyclic themselves, but would apply between the application of word-cyclic rules
and the application of phrase-cyclic rules. (An advocate of this characterization of destressing might want to allow in principle for the
existence of two sets of "postcyclic" rules: those following the "word
cycle" and those following the "sentence cycle.")

The facts concerning the distribution of the strong and weak forms of
function words in the sentence appear to remove the seeming indeter-
minacy in the status of destressing in words, ruling out the interpretation of this destressing as a "postcyclic" rule. If the agent of destressing
on the phrasal domain is the same rule as the (relevant) agent of destressing within words, Monosyllabic Destressing, we cannot plausibly
maintain that the latter destressing rule is at the same time "postcyclic
with respect to words" and cyclic on the phrase; we must conclude,
then, that Monosyllabic Destressing is a cyclic rule, limited to syntactic
domains of level Word or higher.[13] In the following section we defend
the assumption that Monosyllabic Destressing is the rule of phrasal
destressing.

First, however, let us consider the implications of the cyclicity of
destressing on our theory of the organization of the grammar. In previous chapters we have argued that the grid construction carried out by
text-to-grid alignment and grid euphony rules must be cyclic. Here we
have presented another argument for the cyclicity of grid euphony, as
well as an argument for the cyclicity of destressing. These results imply
that destressing must be viewed as forming part of the syntax-phonology mapping; it is not a (postcyclic) phonological rule applying to
the output of cyclic grid construction.

What we have not yet established is the respective ordering of grid
construction and destressing *within* a cyclic domain. We presume that
some general principle establishes this ordering, the likeliest hypothesis
being that all grid construction rules precede all destressing rules. This
ordering is consonant with the general observation, made in chapter 3,
that destressing serves only to "deepen" troughs in the rhythmic pattern created through the combined effects of the text-to-grid alignment
and grid euphony rules, and that it serves moreover to create a grid that
is yet more optimal than the one defined by those rules. This general
principle also has the effect of ordering Silent Demibeat Addition, another sort of grid construction principle, before destressing in a single
syntactic domain. In what follows, we will show that this is a highly
desirable result. Our hypothesis about the strong-weak alternations in

function words maintains in part that destressing is blocked under certain junctural conditions and specifically that the silent grid positions introduced by SDA within a phrasal domain will block the destressing of a function word in final position in that domain. One (desirable) effect of the general ordering hypothesis, then, is to ensure that those silent grid positions are inserted before destressing may apply and are therefore in position to block it.[14]

In sum, we propose that, within each cyclic domain of the syntax-phonology mapping, the various rules and principles are ordered as follows:

(7.11)
The Syntax-Phonology Cycle

Text-to-grid alignment rules
Grid euphony
Silent Demibeat Addition
Destressing

7.1.3 Monosyllabic Destressing

In claiming that Monosyllabic Destressing is the agent of phrasal destressing, we are claiming that, given our general theory about the nature of the metrical grid alignment of a sentence (and its manner of construction) and the particular theory of function words in the grid alignment that is embodied in the PCI, Monosyllabic Destressing (along with the conditions governing its application) correctly predicts (i) *which* function words may be destressed (i.e., the membership of the class of function words having weak forms) and (ii) *where* in the sentence destressing may occur. In this section we give evidence for prediction (i). In subsequent sections we give evidence for prediction (ii), examining the effect of various grid construction principles on the metrical grid alignment of function words and on the consequent applicability or inapplicability of Monosyllabic Destressing, and showing that these principles and Monosyllabic Destressing (with its governing conditions) do constitute a satisfactory (though only partial) theory of the distribution of weak and strong function words in the sentence.

The most important generalization about the class of function words having weak (destressed) forms is that they are all monosyllables. Bi- or polysyllabic function words have only a strong form. (See tables 7.1 and 7.2, where the function words of English are listed according to number and type of syllables.) Monosyllabic Destressing predicts this

Table 7.1
Monosyllabic Function Words

	C₀V	C₀VR	C₀VR̄	C₀VCC	C₀VV	C₀VVC
Prepositions		+for	+at	+since	by	down
		+from	+of		+to	out
		+in	+with		through	round
		on	+as			like
		+till	up			
			but			
Auxiliaries		+am	+is	aren't*	+do	
		+are	+was		+be	
		+were	+here			
		+been	+has			
			+had			
			+does			
			+did			
Modals		+will	+would	+must	may	might
		+shall	+should	can't		
		+can	+could			

Pronouns	+him	+it	+its	(+)I	+your
	+her	+us		(+)you	our
	+their	+what(rel)		(+)she	their
	one	+his		(+)he	whom(rel)
	+when(rel)			(+)we	whose(rel)
				(+)they	
				(+)me	
				(+)my	
				(+)why(rel)	
				(+)who(rel)	
Determiners	+a	+an**	+as	so	these
	+the	+some	that	no	those
		all	this	too	each
			such		both
Conjunctions,		+than	+and		
Complementizers		+that	+but		
		+for	+as		
		+or	+that		
		+nor	+if		

*Some speakers pronounce *aren't* as two syllables.

**An is of course only a sandhi form, found before vowels. For an interesting discussion, see Rotenberg 1978.

Table 7.2
Polysyllabic Function Words

	σ́ σ	σ σ́		
Prepositions	over	before	among	towards
	under	behind	along	until
	after	beneath	against	except
	during	beyond	across	
		below	above	
		between	about	
			around	
Auxiliaries	having			
	being			
	haven't			
	hadn't			
	isn't			
	etc.			
Modals	going			
	couldn't			
Determiners	any*			
	every			
	either			
	neither			
Conjunctions	neither	because		
	either			

Any may sometimes destress, giving [n̩i]. In this it is like *gonna*, one pronunciation of which is [ŋənə].

fact, thereby providing a first major source of support for our analysis of destressing.

Monosyllabic function words are clearly susceptible to Monosyllabic Destressing, given our theory of grid construction. If no pitch accent is assigned to a function word in surface structure, then principles of grid construction will assign it the grid alignment of (7.12) within the function word domain.

(7.12)

$$\begin{bmatrix} x \\ x \\ \sigma \end{bmatrix}$$

This is just the sort of entity that Monosyllabic Destressing may destress, so that (unless on the next higher cyclic domain either a third-level grid position is added (through Beat Addition or Beat Movement) or a weak demibeat position is made to follow) it is in principle capable of applying. Of course it does not apply with equal facility to syllables of all types: the farther a syllable type is down the hierarchy $C_0V - C_0VR - C_0VC - C_0VCC - C_0VV - C_0VVC$, the less likely it is to apply. And indeed the facts about which items among the monosyllabic function words do and do not have weak forms reflect this hierarchy, as we will show.

The inability of bisyllabic and other polysyllabic function words to destress is particularly well illustrated by bisyllables whose ever-stressed first syllable is a morpheme that as a monosyllable is perfectly able to destress. Compare (7.13a) and (7.13b).

(7.13)

a. *have* [hǽv, hɔ̌v, ɔ̌v, v]   b. *having* [hǽviŋ]
   has [hǽz, hæ̌z, ɔ̌z, z]   *hasn't* [hǽzn̩t]
   had [hǽd, hɔ̌d, ɔ̌d, d]   *hadn't* [hǽdn̩t]
   be [bí, bǐ, bǐ]   *being* [bíiŋ]
   is [íz, ǐz, z]   *isn't* [ízn̩t]

Other initial-stressed bisyllables whose stressed syllable is of the type that the rule might readily destress are *under, after, any, every,* etc. These words are all of the form (7.14):

(7.14)

$$\begin{bmatrix} x & \\ x & x \\ \sigma & \sigma \end{bmatrix}$$

What prevents phrasal Monosyllabic Destressing from applying in these cases, it would seem, is the constant presence of the following weak syllable. As pointed out in chapter 3, this rule must in general be prevented from applying in all instances where the "target" syllable is followed by a destressed syllable; the Alternation Maintenance Condition (AMC) was proposed to block the rule in such circumstances. This blocking effect could be invoked in the present case and therefore could account for the lack of weak forms for such bisyllables. Yet we will show that the lack of destressing here should be attributed to a different general condition on destressing.

There is another class of bisyllables that also do not destress, but whose failure to destress cannot be attributed to the AMC. These are the bisyllables that end in an ever-stressed syllable and have the configuration shown in (7.15).

(7.15)

$$\begin{bmatrix} & x \\ x & x \\ \sigma & \sigma \end{bmatrix}$$

The last syllable of many bisyllables with this stress pattern is of a type that cannot be readily destressed (if at all) by Monosyllabic Destressing: *about, behind, except, beneath.* But there do exist cases where that last syllable is eminently destressable in principle, but in fact never undergoes the rule: for example, *before* (cf. *for*), *among, along, above.* How can we account for this stability if the AMC is inapplicable here? Or is this just a matter of exceptionality? We think that these are not "exceptions" and that the question may have an interesting answer, involving a different general condition on destressing that seems to explain many of the limitations on phrasal destressing.

It turns out that the destressing of monosyllabic function words on the phrase does *not* respect the AMC: the presence of a following weak syllable does not block the phrasal destressing of a previous syllable, as shown by (7.16a–d).

(7.16)

a. They saw some astounding things. [smə]
b. The Suns have defeated the Braves. [əvdə]
c. Renee could have left by now. [kədəv]
d. Please get in the car. [n̥nə]

If destressing is cyclic, as we have claimed, then at the point at which
Monosyllabic Destressing would be applying to *some, have,* and *could,*
the immediately following syllable would already be stressless. (Recall
that *the* and *a* will be stressless to begin with.) The ability of the rule to
apply in these circumstances shows that it is not being blocked by the
AMC. Yet the AMC does play a role *within* ("real") words, in blocking
the destressing of basic beats followed by weak demibeat-aligned syllables. Apparently, the AMC needs to be confined to the appropriate
domain, and that domain would appear to be the smallest Word, which
coincides with a Root. Recall that Monosyllabic Destressing must be
said to cycle on consitutents of category type Word or higher (if indeed
destressing on both word and phrase is accomplished by the same rule).
By restricting the AMC to the Root domain, in effect, we leave
Monosyllabic Destressing free to create sequences of stressless syllables on the phrase (or in complex words). (And, by assuming that this
rule obeys the strict cycle, we can ensure that, on the phrasal domain,
it will not eliminate word-internal alternating basic beats.) This approach gives the right results for monosyllables on the phrasal domain,
but notice that it eliminates the AMC as a candidate for explaining the
lack of destressing in initial-stressed bisyllabic function words, for the
PCI will prevent the AMC, now confined to a syntactic domain, from
coming into play.

It can be argued that the lack of destressing in the initial- and final-
stressed bisyllabic function words should be explained as resulting from
another general condition on destressing, the *Grid Culmination Condition,* for which we will give more evidence in what follows. We will say
that a beat *culminates* the metrical level in d_i if it is alone on its metrical
level in d_i. The Grid Culmination Condition says the following:

(7.17)
The Grid Culmination Condition (GCC)

A basic beat that is culminating may not be deleted.

The GCC may be viewed as a condition that maintains relations of
second-level rhythmic prominence established on earlier cycles. It in-

volves only a limited amount of "globality," however. Because phrasal destressing obeys the strict cycle, the GCC is a condition that need look only at two subjacent domains, α and β, as illustrated in (7.18):

(7.18)

$$\alpha\left[\begin{matrix} \cdots\cdots \\ \cdots\cdots \\ \cdots\cdots \end{matrix} \beta\left[\begin{matrix} \cdots x \cdots \\ \cdots x \cdots \\ \cdots \sigma \cdots \end{matrix}\right]_\beta \begin{matrix} \cdots\cdots \\ \cdots\cdots \\ \cdots\cdots \end{matrix}\right]_\alpha$$

It governs the application of a rule to a basic beat on domain α as a function of the status of that basic beat defined with respect to β (or α). What is in question is whether or not the basic beat culminates in β (or in α).

The GCC cannot be generalized to metrical levels higher than the second. Were it to be quite general, the operation of Beat Deletion in examples like *sports contest,* where the rule applies to eliminate main word stress, would be wrongly excluded. The statement of the GCC in (7.17) makes it specific to the basic beat level.

From the GCC it follows of course that the basic beat in *before, above,* etc., appearing in configuration (7.15) may not be eliminated. It may also take responsibility for preventing the deletion in the initial-stressed bisyllables with configuration (7.14). Given the evidence presented thus far, the GCC might seem to be little more than the condition "Don't destress a bisyllable." Indeed, were its effects limited to impeding the destressing of bisyllabic function words, we would question whether Monosyllabic Destressing was involved here, rather than some other phrasal destressing rule that directly mentioned the number of syllables in the function words susceptible to destressing (like our 1972 Monosyllable Rule, for example). But we will show that the GCC can also be given responsibility for blocking the destressing of monosyllabic function words in certain phrasal configurations and thus does more than merely block the destressing of bisyllabic function words.

Summing up so far, we have suggested that the failure of polysyllabic function words to have weak forms is the result of restrictions placed on destressing by the Grid Culmination Condition. Since the condition will always apply in the case of polysyllables, destressing will never take place. In the case of monosyllables, however, the condition will not necessarily apply (though it may); thus monosyllabic function words may in principle be destressed and appear in weak forms.

Not all monosyllabic function words do in fact have weak forms, and it seems that Monosyllabic Destressing, with its sensitivity to syllable type, predicts reasonably well which of these monosyllables may destress. In the lists of function words given in tables 7.1 and 7.2, the symbols + and (+) indicate the words that have weak forms. Those marked + have forms with reduced vowels or syllabic sonorants; these are clearly destressed forms, since vowel reduction and the appearance of syllabic sonorants are possible only in stressless syllables. The words marked (+) have unreduced tense vowels, yet because (rhythmically speaking) they behave more like stressless syllables, we have included them in the weak form class. In this connection, note that the tensing of words in English is a partly positional phenomenon: no lax nonlow vowels appear in final position in words in English. Moreover, not all final tense vowels receive stress (see chapter 3). It is therefore not inconsistent to consider that (some) function words may at the same time be stressless and have a (final) tense vowel.[15]

Let us examine figure 7.1 in some detail. Note first that there are only two words, *a* and *the,* in the C_0V class. Recall that we are assuming these to be basically stressless, since the HBR is inapplicable to C_0V, and the PCI prevents the IBR from applying.[16] Among the closed syllables containing lax vowels, virtually all the $C_0V\bar{R}$ syllables ($\bar{R}$ = nonsonorant) have weak forms as well. (Those that do not are *up, but* (preposition), *not, what, such, this, that* (demonstrative).) Of the three nonnegative words in the C_0VCC class, all have weak forms, and one might speculate that this is explained in some way by the fact that the final cluster is composed of coronal consonants, which in English syllable rime structure have rather special properties (McCarthy 1977, Selkirk 1978b, Halle and Vergnaud 1980). Among the C_0VV syllables, the proportion having weak forms is lower than in the earlier classes; among the C_0VVC syllables, there are none. The general picture, then, is consistent with viewing Monosyllabic Destressing to be the agent of destressing here: the likelihood of its applying depends on the syllable's place in the same hierarchy of types that plays a role in word-internal destressing. Moreover, the rule is influenced not just by syllable type, but also by frequency. The generalization seems to be that greater frequency allows the rule to apply farther along the hierarchy. Thus *do* may destress, but *through,* with the identical vowel, may not; and the preposition *to* contrasts with the (underlyingly) homophonous *too.* The lesser frequency of *through* and *too,* along with their C_0VV syllable type, is probably what blocks Monosyllabic Destressing here. Frequency may also explain the failure of the impersonal pronoun *one* to destress, in the American dialect at least. But it does not explain all the vagaries of the rule; some words that lack weak forms, like *on* or *up,* will simply have to be listed as exceptions to it.

To conclude, then, Monosyllabic Destressing and the accompanying Grid Culmination Condition provide a good theory of which function words are *susceptible* to destressing (i.e., to appear in weak form). We will next show that they also constitute a good theory of where in the sentence these items may in fact take their weak forms, and where, conversely, they must remain strong.

7.1.4 The Blocking of Monosyllabic Destressing by Higher Prominences

In order for a destressing rule to apply to a syllable, the syllable must not be aligned with a third-level beat (or higher). This is a result of the Higher Prominence Preservation Condition. A function word receives at most a second-level alignment, qua word. Within the phrase, it receives no prominence from the Nuclear Stress Rule, which seeks out only a third-level beat or higher (chapter 4). There are, however, two other potential sources of higher-level rhythmic prominence on the phrase: the Pitch Accent Prominence Rule (PAR) and rules of grid euphony. Both of these grid construction rules may add higher beats to function words that "come into" the sentence with only a second-level metrical grid alignment. In so doing, they in effect block the phrasal destressing of those words.

Let us first examine the role of pitch accent assignment in maintaining a function word in its strong form. Recall that pitch accents are assigned to constituents in surface structure, where their distribution with respect to the annotated focus structure of the sentence is submitted to the well-formedness conditions we have called the *focus rules*. Within the constituent to which a pitch accent is assigned, it is associated with the most rhythmically prominent syllable. In the case of function words, this would mean that the pitch accent is associated with a basic-beat-aligned syllable. The PAR is a text-to-grid alignment rule that must be satisfied everywhere (on every cyclic domain); it says that a syllable bearing a pitch accent must be more prominent (in terms of the grid) than any syllable not bearing a pitch accent. It can be thought of as adding the requisite beats. Moreover, we suggested in chapter 5 that the PAR should always ensure at least a third-level alignment for a pitch-accent-bearing syllable, regardless of surrounding context. Given the PAR, then, a function word syllable bearing a pitch accent will have *at least* a third-level grid alignment on any phrasal domain, whether or not it contains another stressed syllable. Thus the presence of a pitch accent on a function word guarantees that it will be impervious to destressing.[17]

(We should point out here that in Selkirk 1972 there was no understanding of the role of pitch accents (or of intonation in general) in determining levels of stress, nor was there any understanding of the relation of those pitch/rhythm prominences to the focus properties of the sentence. Therefore, certain facts concerning the stress of function words cited in Selkirk 1972 need to be reexamined and reinterpreted. Some, but by no means all, of that reexamination is carried out below.)

Let us look at some examples of pitch-accented function words. The examples of (7.19) are naturally interpreted as instances of "contrastive" or narrow focus on the function word itself; in the presence of that focusing pitch accent, the monosyllables necessarily appear in their strong form.

(7.19)
a. Joan COULD try (but she WON'T).
b. HER father made one for her.
c. She's AS forgetful as you are (but probably not MORE).
d. Because we HAD tried, they agreed to it.
e. They were given SOME bread (though not MUCH).
f. I want to bring HER up, too.

Of course, not all instances of pitch-accented function words involve instances of narrow focus on the function word.[18] Cases of "default accent" abound, where the function word focuses a higher constituent:

(7.20)
a. These can BE contrastive only by virtue of the "normal" reading. (R. Stockwell)
b. There's nothing we CAN do.
   (Response to: We should DO something.)
c. Well, I don't think there's anything TO do.
   (Response to: Something must definitely be done.)
d. How many times have you BEEN there?
e. Yes, and I'm now IN these situations of more or less collaboration.
f. In any case, I don't think there's anything TO transparency and opacity.

Other examples of this sort occurred in section 5.2.1.

The presence of pitch accents on these function words in sentences with surface structures like those above is in no way obligatory. In general, surface structure does not determine the placement of pitch accents. Rather, it is the annotation of a surface structure by focus structure that is related to pitch accent assignment, and any one surface structure may have more than one focus structure. In sentences with the same surface structures as (7.19a–f), but with different focus structures, as in (7.21a–f), the function word may lack a pitch accent and thus be entirely capable of destressing:

(7.21)
a. Joan cŏuld [kəd] TRY (but she WON'T).
b. Hĕr [hr̩] FATHER made one for her.
c. She's ăs [əz] forgetful as YOU are, but probably not more.
d. Because we hăd [əd,d] TRIED, they agreed to it.
e. They were given sŏme [sm̩] BREAD (though not MUCH).
f. I want to bring hĕr [r̩] UP, too.

The point, then, is that blocking by the PAR may arise in syntactic environments where, without a pitch accent, the function word could very well reduce.

Let us turn next to the effects of rules of grid euphony (in particular, Beat Addition) on the destressing of function words. In a sequence of monosyllabic function words where each is in principle capable of being destressed (it lacks a pitch accent and is in a syntactic context where weak forms may appear), there is often a tendency to a rhythmic alternation of weak and strong forms. Sweet 1875–76 was to our knowledge the first to observe this fact (see also Jespersen 1909:156, 1962:652, cited by Giegerich 1978). Sweet remarked that though the "logical" pronunciation of sentence (7.22) would be (7.22a), where *can* and *you* are destressed, the sentence is in fact normally realized as (7.22b), with a stress on *can*.

(7.22)
Can you tell me the way to the station?

a. kən yu *tel* . . . (italics = "stressed")
b. *kæn* yu *tel* . . .

This, Sweet remarks, shows that the principle of (rhythmic) alternation is at play. An elaboration of Sweet's example drives the point home. When three monosyllabic function words appear in sequence, as in

(7.22), it is highly unnatural for all of them to be destressed, and the stressing maintained appears to be just the stressing that results in eurhythmic alternation:

(7.23)

a. $\left\{\begin{array}{l}\text{?Yŏu cŏuld bĕ} \\ \text{Yòu cŏuld bĕ} \\ \text{Yŏu còuld bĕ}\end{array}\right\}$ sléeping.

b. Jáne $\left\{\begin{array}{l}\text{?wăs fŏr thĕ} \\ \text{wăs fòr thĕ}\end{array}\right\}$ Dódgers.

c. They sáng $\left\{\begin{array}{l}\text{?ĭt ĭn ă} \\ \text{ĭt ĭn ă}\end{array}\right\}$ fúnny wáy.

The presence of these alternation patterns of weak forms is, we think, the result of the application of the grid euphony rule Beat Addition.

Beat Addition might in fact apply before Monosyllabic Destressing on a particular cyclic domain and so block its application. There is one possible derivation of this sort of Sweet's (7.22b), which is shown in (7.24). At the outset of the cyclic domain of S, the metrical grid alignment is (7.24a) (ignoring silent demibeats in VP).

(7.24)

$_{\bar{S}}[_S[[\text{Can}]\,[\text{you}]\,_{VP}[\text{tell me the way to the station}]_{VP}]_S]_{\bar{S}}$

```
                                              (x)
                          (x)                  x
                           x          x        x
          x    x           x          x        x
          x    x           x    x  x  x  x  x  x x
a.        Can  you         tell me the way to the station
                          (x)
          x                x
          x    x           x
          x    x           x
b.        Can  you         tell ...
                          (x)
          x                x
          x                x
          x    x           x
c.        Can  you         tell ...
```

Beat Addition, seeing the lapse constituted by *can you*, could (optionally) apply, giving (7.24b). Next, Monosyllabic Destressing would destress only the *you*, giving (7.24c).

Another conceivable derivation of Sweet's (7.22b) would also involve applying Beat Addition, but *after* the application of Monosyllabic Destressing. Suppose that Beat Addition had *not* applied to (7.24a). Then Monosyllabic Destressing would apply to that representation, destressing both *can* and *you* as in (7.24c').

(7.24)

```
        x
        x
  x   x   x
```
c'. Can you tell ...

This is not necessarily the end of the story (though it could be, since the sentence may be realized as such, with both function words unstressed). On the next cycle, the $\bar{S}$ cycle, Beat Addition may (optionally) apply again and introduce a basic beat over *can,* as in (7.24d).

(7.24)

```
      (x)
        x
  x     x
  x   x   x
```
d. Can you tell ...

The reason that Beat Addition gets a second chance and is able to reapply here, without violating the principle of the strict cycle, is that it is a rule *without a syntactic domain,* as are all rules of grid euphony (section 3.2.4). We suggest that this lack of domain allows it to apply wherever it pleases on the grid contained "within" the constituent currently being cycled on.

Monosyllabic Destressing does have a syntactic domain, however, and must therefore obey the strict cycle. This will remove the possibility that it might undo the later effect of Beat Addition on $\bar{S}$. Furthermore, the assumption that the phonological rules of reduction that accompany destressing are "postcyclic" (the unmarked case in our theory) will ensure that the monosyllable *can* will not have been reduced on the S cycle before being stressed again on the $\bar{S}$ cycle. In the latter derivation, then, a later application of Beat Addition partially undoes the effects of an earlier application of Monosyllabic Destressing. Below we introduce some more cases where the two rules must be ordered in this way.

Consider the derivation of *Jane was for the Dodgers.* (7.25a) is the output of the two NP cycles. Beat Addition cannot apply over *for*

(there is no lapse on the second metrical level), and Monosyllabic Destressing will apply, destressing *for* and giving (7.25b) on the PP cycle.

(7.25)

$_\text{S̄}[_\text{S}[_\text{NP}[\text{Jane}]_\text{NP} \; _\text{VP}[\text{was} \; _\text{PP}[\text{for} \; _\text{NP}[\text{the Dodgers}]_\text{NP}]_\text{PP}]_\text{VP}]_\text{S}]_\text{S̄}$

```
                                    x
           x                        x
           x         x    x         x
           x         x    x      x  x  x
a.         Jane      was  for    the Dodgers

                                    x
                                    x
                                    x
                     x           x  x  x
b.         . . .     . . .  for    the Dodgers

                                    x
                                    x
                                    x
                     x    x      x  x  x
c.         . . .     was  for    the Dodgers

                                    x
           x                        x
           x         x    x         x
           x         x    x      x  x  x
d.         Jane      was  for    the Dodgers
```

For could be *re*stressed in either of two ways. Beat Addition could
(optionally) apply on the VP cycle, or it could wait and apply on a
higher cycle. Let us suppose that Beat Addition does not apply on the
VP cycle. Monosyllabic Destressing will apply on the VP cycle, destressing *was,* as in (7.25c). Next, on the S cycle, Beat Addition may
apply to eliminate the long lapse . . . *was for the* . . . , thus deriving
(7.25d).[19]

This will conclude our examination of the "rhythmic alternation" in
weak forms. With these examples, we have barely begun the investigation of a pervasive and rather complex phenomenon, where the facts
are subtle and probably depend to a certain extent on factors like tempo
that fall outside the Beat Addition analysis we have offered here. It
should be clear from our examples, though, that it is entirely plausible
to view these alternations as being produced by Beat Addition, one of
the guardians of the Principle of Rhythmic Alternation in our conception of things.

Neither the PAR nor Beat Addition regularly blocks the destressing of function words in particular sorts of syntactic contexts. This is because neither Pitch Accent Assignment and Association (and the consequent application of the PAR) nor Beat Addition relies in any direct way on syntactic structure. However, there is a principle of grid construction—Silent Demibeat Addition (SDA)—that directly appeals to many aspects of the surface syntactic constituent structure of the sentence, and the silent demibeats it introduces do regularly block the destressing of monosyllabic function words in a certain type of syntactic context.

7.1.5 The Blocking of Monosyllabic Destressing by Silent Demibeats

There is an important generalization that any analysis of function words must explain: namely, that a monosyllabic function word that *is a phrase* itself or *is at the (right) end of a phrase* never destresses (i.e., will always appear in strong form). (This generalization holds except in a small number of cases, to be discussed in section 7.2, where encliticization has taken place and a weak form appears in final position.) Given the theory of grid construction and destressing proposed thus far, along with one additional assumption, it is predicted that this should be so. Consider first the case of a monosyllabic function word that *is a* phrase. The syllable appears in the syntactic configuration (7.26).

(7.26)

$$_{phrase}[_{fw}[\sigma]_{fw}]_{phrase}$$

(7.27)

$$
\begin{array}{c}
\text{x} \\
\text{x} \\
a. \quad _{fw}[\sigma]_{fw}
\end{array}
$$

$$
\begin{array}{c}
\text{x} \\
\text{x x} \\
b. \quad _{phrase}[_{fw}[\sigma \quad]_{fw}]_{phrase}
\end{array}
$$

Grid construction proceeds as follows. Demibeat Alignment and the HBR assign the alignment in (7.27a) on the domain of the function word itself. Monosyllabic Destressing does not apply on that cycle since it requires a domain of Word or higher and the PCI makes the function word "invisible" qua word. (The PCI also rules out any application of the Main Stress Rule and SDA from the function word domain.) So the monosyllabic function word is stressed (basic-beat-aligned) as it enters the next cycle. On the phrase cycle, SDA guarantees the addition of *at least* one silent demibeat at the right edge of the metrical grid delimited by the phrasal node (section 6.2.1). Thus SDA will produce the grid alignment in (7.27b). Monosyllabic Destressing, which follows SDA (since SDA is a principle of grid construction; section 7.1.2), will not now be able to apply, because the basic beat is now in culminating position and so must remain, given the Grid Culmination Condition.

We assume that application of SDA on the phrase in (7.26) creates a configuration like (7.27b), where the inserted silent demibeat is contained within (?dominated by) both the phrase and the function word immediately dominated by the phrase. The alternative would be to assume that the structure (7.27b') is the output of SDA in such a case.

(7.27)

$$\text{b'.} \quad _{\text{phrase}}[_{\text{fw}}[\overset{\text{x}}{\sigma}]_{\text{fw}} \overset{\text{x}}{}]_{\text{phrase}}$$

The effect of the assumption we have made is that the basic beat in the function word is in culminating position in both the phrase and the word. The culmination of the basic beat with respect to either constituent is enough to cause the GCC to block Monosyllabic Destressing on the higher (phrasal) domain. (Recall that in bisyllables a basic beat in culminating position within the function word is always blocked from destressing, whether or not it is also in culminating position on the phrase.) For cases where the function word *is a* phrase, then, it is immaterial whether we assume the output of SDA to be (7.27b) or (7.27b'), since under either assumption the basic beat is in culminating position on the phrase and Monosyllabic Destressing on the phrase is blocked by the GCC. But we will show that Monosyllabic Destressing is also blocked when the function word is final in a phrase, but not exhaustively dominated by it, and where that phrase may contain other basic beats. In such a case the basic beat of the function word would not be culminant on the phrase. Thus it must be that SDA produces a configuration wherein the basic beat of a phrase-final function word is made to occupy culminating position within the function word itself, as in (7.28a), not (7.28b).

(7.28)

$$\text{a.} \quad _{\alpha}[\ldots{}_{\text{fw}}[\overset{\overset{\text{x}}{\text{x x}}}{\sigma}]_{\text{fw}}]_{\alpha} \qquad \text{b.} \quad _{\alpha}[\ldots{}_{\text{fw}}[\overset{\overset{\text{x}}{\text{x x}}}{\sigma}]_{\text{fw}}]_{\alpha}$$

We assume then that the result of SDA on a higher constituent α is a representation in which the added silent demibeat is contained within any lower constituent at the right extreme of α, as in (7.28a). This seems a natural enough assumption. The point is, then, that a phrase-final function word and a function word that *is a* phrase are blocked from destressing for the same reason—the introduction of a culmination-producing silent demibeat on the higher phrasal domain. These cases, along with the undestressable polysyllabic function words, show the pervasive effect of the Grid Culmination Condition.

We thus claim, in general, that whenever the destressing of a monosyllabic function word is systematically blocked in a particular type of syntactic configuration, that configuration is one where the function word is phrase-final. (This simply amounts to claiming that our proposed assumptions about grid construction and destressing do account fully for the distribution of strong and weak forms in the sentence (except, of course, for the encliticization cases to be treated in section 7.2).) This claim seems to be borne out in fact. Consider verb particles, for example. The preposition that is a verb particle appears in its strong form, as in (7.29).

(7.29)

a. They boxed ìn the crowd.	b. They boxed the crowd ín.
Pat flew ìn the plane.	Pat flew the plane ín.
Would you let ìn a cat?	Would you let a cat ìn?

(Only *in* is used here, since *in* is the only preposition employed as a particle that has a weak variant (see table 7.1).) The (a) sentences of (7.29) contrast with those of (7.30), where *in* is the prepositional head of a prepositional phrase with an NP object. Here *in* may take on its weak form.

(7.30)

They boxed ĭn the crowd (and not inside the ring).
Pat flew ĭn the plane (rather than in the helicopter).
Would you sit ĭn the car?

There is a convincing piece of "segmental" phonetic evidence for the appearance of the weak form of *in* in (7.30), but not in (7.29). This evidence involves the behavior of final *t* before *in*. A final *t* may be phonetically realized as a flap or as a glottal stop, depending on what follows it in the sentence (Kahn 1976, Selkirk 1978b). It will be a flap if followed by a vowel, and a glottal stop if followed by a consonant. Now one variant of the weak form of *in* is a syllabic *n*, [n̩]. So it should be possible to pronounce the *t* of *sit in the car* as a glottal stop, and this is indeed the case: [sɪʔ n̩ nə kar]. In the verb particle cases of (7.29), on the other hand, the glottal stop pronunciation of *t* should be impossible, since the following *in* is stressed and could never reduce to [n̩]. This is also the case: *let in the cat* may be pronounced with a flap, [lɛDɪn̩nəkæt], but not with a glottal stop, *[lɛʔɪn̩nəkæt].

Following Emonds (1971), we assume that in the position after an NP object, as in (7.29b), the verb particle has the status of an intransitive preposition, i.e., it is a preposition that *is a* PP. (And as such, it will not destress.) The particle in immediately postverbal position may also be a PP, though we will not exclude the possibility that it has a different syntactic analysis in this position. It seems not unlikely that the verb and the particle together form a constituent—more precisely, a compound verb (Selkirk 1982). Of course, if the particle preposition is an immediate constituent of a compound, it will receive normal third-level word stress, just like the prepositions of *inbred, infighting,* and so on (section 7.1.1), and the destressing of the particle will be blocked. In either case, then, there is a relevant structural contrast between the cases in (7.29a) and the cases in (7.30) that accounts for destressing in the latter but not in the former.

(7.31)

$$
\begin{array}{ccc}
 & & \text{x} \\
\text{x} & & \text{x} \\
\text{x x} & & \text{x} \\
\end{array}
$$

$_V[\ldots]_V \ _{PP}[_P[_\sigma \quad]_P]_{PP} \ _{NP}[\ldots]_{NP}$ or $_V[_V[\ldots]_V \ _P[\sigma]_P]_V \ _{NP}[\ldots]_{NP}$

(7.32)

$$
\begin{array}{c}
\text{x} \\
\text{x} \\
\end{array}
$$

$_V[\ldots]_V \ _{PP}[_P[\sigma]_P \ _{NP}[\ldots]_{NP}]_{PP}$

As for the (7.29b) cases, they would have the structural analysis (7.33).

(7.33)

$$
\begin{array}{c}
\text{x} \\
\text{x x} \\
\end{array}
$$

$_V[\ldots]_V \ _{NP}[\ldots]_{NP} \ _{PP}[_P[_\sigma \quad]_P]_{PP}$

In its status either as a phrase or as the constituent of a compound, then, the verb particle is systematically blocked from destressing.

The phrase-final position of monosyllabic function words also accounts for their failure to destress in several other syntactic configurations. Among these configurations, exemplified below, are prepositional phrases with "stranded" prepositions, verb phrases containing only a modal or auxiliary verb (the rest of the VP having been deleted), noun phrases with only a determiner (and an empty head), and noun phrases with only a possessive pronoun (and an empty head).

(7.34)

a. What were you thinking $_{PP}$[of ____]$_{PP}$ last night? *[ɔ̌v]

b. That's the point we got $_{PP}$[to ____]$_{PP}$. *[tə]

(7.35)

a. She's not much taller than I $_{VP}$[am ____]$_{VP}$. *[(ɔ̌)m][20]

b. I'd like $_{VP}$[to ____]$_{VP}$, but I'm not sure
I $_{VP}$[should ____]$_{VP}$. *[tə];*[səd]

(7.36)

a. $_{NP}$[Some ____]$_{NP}$ complained. *[sm̩]

b. I saw $_{NP}$[some ____]$_{NP}$ crying.[21]

(7.37)

a. $_{NP}$[His ____]$_{NP}$ disappeared. *[ɪz]

b. I saw $_{NP}$[his ____]$_{NP}$ burn.

As the starred forms to the right indicate, the weak forms of the function words cannot be used in these contexts. We submit that the silent demibeat whose presence blocks Monosyllabic Destressing here is the one introduced by SDA at the right end of the higher phrase in which the function word itself is final.

There is a conceivable alternative explanation for the blocking of Monosyllabic Destressing in these cases. According to this explanation, an empty category follows the function word within the phrase (be it an empty (dummy) head N, an empty (dummy) VP, a *wh*-trace, or whatever). Despite its lack of a terminal string, this empty category is "seen" by SDA, which inserts (at least) one silent demibeat at the end of it; in turn, this silent demibeat blocks destressing. We took a position not unlike this in Selkirk 1972, where we proposed that the junctural representation of the sentence (and representation in terms of word boundaries) reflected the presence of all lexical and phrasal categories in surface structure, whether empty or not, and that the destressing of function words was blocked by the junctural entities associated with empty categories, including traces. (This analysis built on a proposal first made by Baker and Brame 1972.) We now believe that this claim is false, and that the presence of empty categories in surface structure has no systematic junctural reflection in phonological representation. The empirical claim that we now endorse is that the only syntactic context where function words are systematically blocked from destressing by junctural material (i.e., by SDA) is phrase-final position.

To investigate the validity of the revised claim, we must examine the behavior of function words in contexts where they are not phrase-final but do precede empty categories. None of the examples examined so far has this property; they are of the form (7.38a) or (7.38b).

(7.38)

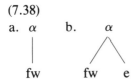

What we are looking for are cases like (7.39a) or (7.39b), where β is not empty and the function word is therefore not final.

(7.39)

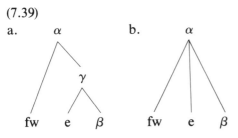

If Monosyllabic Destressing is systematically blocked in contexts like (7.39a,b), then we can draw two very interesting conclusions. First, we can conclude that it is indeed correct to posit an empty category where we have (otherwise the phonetic facts would go unexplained); second, we must conclude that SDA "sees" that empty category. A third conclusion must also be drawn: that the Grid Culmination Condition is the wrong explanation for the blocking of Monosyllabic Destressing. If SDA introduced a silent demibeat at the (right) end of the empty category, it would not cause the basic beat of the function word to be in culminating position, and so the function word would nonetheless destress. Clearly, much hinges on whether or not destressing is blocked in the environment of (7.39). Suppose, on the other hand, that destressing were not systematically blocked in that environment. This fact would be consistent with a variety of conceptions of surface structure and its phonological interpretation. It might mean simply that there are no empty categories in the positions investigated. (We would not draw this conclusion, however, since the syntactic evidence amply demonstrates that they are indeed there.) It might mean that empty categories are there but are not interpreted phonologically (i.e., are not "seen" by SDA). Or it might mean that they are there and are interpreted in terms of silent demibeats by SDA, but that the GCC does indeed govern Monosyllabic Destressing, so that that rule is simply not affected by the additional position(s). We believe that Monosyllabic Destressing in English is *not* blocked in the environment of (7.39), and in what follows we will attempt to show why this is a correct empirical generalization. For the time being we will accept the state of theoretical limbo this fact leaves us in, but at the end of the section we will review some reasons for concluding that, although empty categories are present in surface structure, they are *not* interpreted by SDA.

In investigating the status of empty categories in phonological representation, we will proceed through the taxonomy of empty categories, looking in turn at PRO, NP-trace, *wh*-trace, and empty heads (including the structures with gapping and VP Deletion). It turns out to be impossible to ascertain whether Monosyllabic Destressing is blocked by PRO or NP-trace. This is because, for reasons having to do with the particulars of English phrase structure, no nonphrasal function word in English precedes a PRO or an argument position from which an NP might have moved, either in surface structure or in deep structure. That is, there is no instance in English of the surface configuration (7.39), where *e* is PRO or trace of NP. There are, however, a variety of cases in which a *wh*-trace or an empty head may be the *e* of (7.39), and it is these cases we propose to examine.

Wh-trace appears in the general context (7.39a) when the function word belongs to either of two classes: complementizers, as in (7.40), or the forms of the copula *be,* as in (7.41).

(7.40)

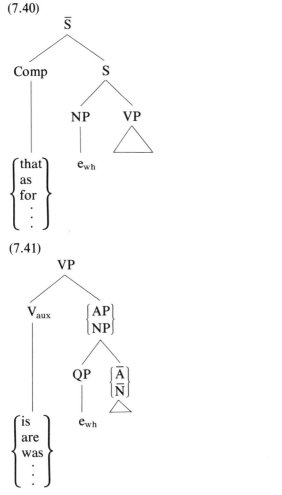

(7.41)

(7.42a–c) and (7.43a–c) provide examples of (7.40) and (7.41), respectively. (For (7.40), cf. also *That's as good as was expected.*)

(7.42)
a. the woman that _____ came by
b. the girl who _____ left
c. the same ones as _____ were treated last year

(7.43)
a. This table's longer than it is _____ wide.
b. Jane is as English as Irene is _____ German.
c. It was more fun than it was _____ trouble.

It has also been claimed (Selkirk 1972) that the copula appears in the context (7.44), illustrated by (7.45a–e).

(7.44)

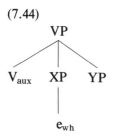

(7.45)
a. Do you know where the party is ____ tonight?
b. Some day he'd like to be what you are ____ now.
c. I wonder how tall he is ____ in his bare feet.
d. They told Mary how eager John is ____ to go.
e. I'm perplexed by what it is ____ you're saying.

For reasons having to do with the nature of English phrase structure and the nature of transformation(s), there are no other surface configurations in English that are conceivably of the general types (7.39a,b) and that involve *wh*-trace.

It turns out that examples like those of (7.42), (7.43), and (7.45) provide very weak evidence, if any at all, for the claim that *wh*-trace affects the phonological realization of the function words in its immediate environment. As has been noted (for example in Gazdar 1981, Suiko 1977), but was not in Selkirk 1972, destressing is never blocked in the case of the complementizers in (7.42). The reduced forms of *that* [ðət], *as* [əz], *who*[22] [ʊ], *than* [ðn̩], etc., can always be used before a following *wh*-trace of the subject NP. Perhaps this fact could be made to follow by ascribing some special status to *wh*-trace in subject position[23] or some special status to complementizers, but we are inclined to see this as representative of a general failure of empty categories to be subject to SDA.

The common appearance of a strong form of *be* in comparative constructions like (7.43a–c), noted first by Bresnan 1971b, led us to conclude in Selkirk 1972 that the quantifier phrase (QP) posited as part of the deep structure of the compared AP or NP left a trace that could block destressing.[24] A contrast is therefore predicted between comparative clauses with a missing QP and sentences where the copula simply precedes a predicate with no missing QP. Such a contrast does seem to occur; compare, for example, (7.46a) and (7.46b), due to J. Bresnan.

(7.46)

a. It's more trouble than $\left\{\begin{array}{l} \text{it is} \\ \text{*it's} \end{array}\right\}$ ____ fun.

b. It's more trouble than it's worth ____.

Yet it has come to our attention that judgments vary on these matters. Neidle and Schein (n.d.) report that not all speakers recognize a contrast here and that some find the destressed form perfectly acceptable in the comparative.[25] For a theory according to which SDA "sees" wh-traces, this "dialectal variation" is problematic, for it is not to be expected that a core concept concerning the (in)visibility of wh-traces to phonological interpretation will vary across dialects. Moreover, as R. Kayne (personal communication) has pointed out to us, the strong form of be may have to appear in comparative constructions even when it does not precede the putative location of wh-trace, as in (7.47).

(7.47)

Jane $\left\{\begin{array}{l} \text{is} \\ \text{'s} \end{array}\right\}$ a more brilliant doctor than Mary $\left\{\begin{array}{l} \text{is} \\ \text{*'s} \end{array}\right\}$ a promising lawyer.

(The wh-trace of QP is assumed to be part of the AP and therefore to follow a, not is.) This fact requires us to look for an alternative, non-trace-based explanation for the appearance of strong forms in comparative constructions. One, according to which the blocking is attributed to focus-related prosodic properties of the sentence, will be explored below. We hope that it will ultimately lead to an explanation of "dialectal variation" as well.

The one set of cases in which there is quite general agreement about the appearance of a strong form before a wh-trace is the set illustrated in (7.45). In these examples, the trace has been left by Wh Movement in either a question or a relative clause. But, although we agree that there is a systematic lack of destressing here, we disagree with the conclusion that the wh-trace is responsible for it. It is not implausible that (7.45a–e) might have the surface structure of (7.48) rather than (7.44).

(7.48)

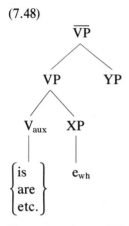

Since constituent YP is in no instance an argument of the copula, (7.48) is a structure perfectly compatible with what is known about the location of semantic types of complements with respect to heads. But if (7.48) is the structure for the relevant parts of (7.45a–e), then we have lost the strongest case for saying that *wh*-trace blocks Monosyllabic Destressing, for in this structure the copula not only precedes a *wh*-trace but also falls *at the end of a phrase*.

On balance, then, the evidence that *wh*-trace blocks the appearance of the weak forms of function words is shaky indeed. In the case of the complementizer, *wh*-trace never blocks destressing. In the case of the copula in comparatives, destressing is not always blocked; moreover, something else must be responsible in any event for blocking that cannot be attributed to traces. And in the last case it is quite likely the phrase-final position of the copula, and not its position before trace, that is the crucial factor.

We must say more about the prosodic factors we are alleging to be responsible for the absence of destressing in the comparative constructions mentioned above, though what we will say is quite preliminary and speculative in nature. We have already shown that the presence of a pitch accent impedes the destressing of monosyllabic function words, and it seems to us that in the case of comparatives it is the pitch accent association of the copula that accounts for some cases of the blocking of Monosyllabic Destressing. For example, in one pronunciation of *The table is longer than it is wide,* which is perhaps the preferred one, the second *is* bears a pitch prominence, along with the obviously focal compared constituents *longer* and *wide,* and the focal *table.* In this case the *is* remains rhythmically prominent as well:

(7.49)

H   H   H   H

The table is longer than it is wide.

Of course other focus structures are possible for this sentence that do not involve a pitch accent on the second *is,* and the fact that *is* still fails to destress for some speakers will have to be explained in some other way. But before exploring these other pronunciations, let us look more closely at (7.49), which seems to say something interesting about the prosodic properties of comparative sentences. The pitch accent and hence focus on *is* appears to add nothing to the intonational meaning of the sentence and could be eliminated with no change. We suggest that this is because it is redundant. The focused *is* cannot reasonably be interpreted as contrastive, for there is nothing but another form of *be* for it to contrast with in the preceding sentence part. And the broader focus allowed by *is,* in its capacity as head of VP, is already ensured by the focusing of *wide,* which is an argument of *is* within VP. Why does *is* have a pitch accent at all? We suggest that it is there for reasons of style. Comparative constructions involve structural parallelism, and it may be that speakers prefer to utter them with a prosodic parallelism as well. Indeed, as we will show, certain instances of comparative constructions *must* be parallel in terms of focus and hence in terms of prosody. Now in (7.49), there are only three nonredundant foci, two in the first part and one in the second. We suggest that the focus on *is* may be there simply to introduce parallelism on the intonational (pitch accent) level. We might expect speakers to vary with respect to such style-related matters, and this, then, would be one possible source of the interspeaker variation reported in the destressing of *is* and other forms of *be* in comparatives.

But we still need to explain why the copula may fail to destress when it does not bear a pitch accent. Sentence (7.50) is a case in point.

(7.50)

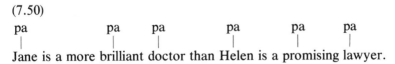

pa   pa   pa   pa   pa   pa
| | | | | |
Jane is a more brilliant doctor than Helen is a promising lawyer.

We have marked the location of the pitch accents in the most natural pronunciation of such a sentence. The two parts of the sentence are entirely parallel from the point of view of both focus structure and pitch accent assignment. *Is* lacks a pitch accent. Yet we believe that the absence of destressing on the copula here is still explained, ultimately, by the parallelism in focus exhibited in such constructions. We may think of sentence (7.50) as consisting of two parallel pairs of foci, illustrated in (7.51).

(7.51)
[Jane] is [a more brilliant doctor] than [Helen] is [a promising lawyer]
  F_1 F_2 F_1' F_2'

F_1 is paired with F_1' and F_2 is paired with F_2'. In such parallel constructions, it is not uncommon for the second member of the second pair to be preceded by a slight rhythmic hiatus or disjuncture. This can be seen as well in parallel constructions where F_2' is not preceded by the copula:

(7.52)
[Helen] ate [an apple pie] while [Jane] ate [a chocolate cake]
  F_1 F_2 F_2' F_2'

The judgments are subtle, but we believe that the phenomenon is a real one, and that it permits an account of the appearance of undestressed *is*. Let us call the rhythmic disjuncture produced before F_2' *paired focus framing*. We will represent that disjuncture as a silent demibeat in the metrical grid, to be introduced by the following rule:

(7.53)
Paired Focus Framing

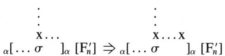

This rule says that a silent demibeat is added to the grid alignment of a constituent α that precedes a constituent F_n' that is the second member of a focus pair. As formulated, the rule produces a configuration where, if α were a monosyllabic function word, it could not destress, for the basic beat of the syllable would be in culminating position in α. Of course there are other conceivable ways of formulating the rule. One attractive alternative would simply be to add a demibeat before F_n', without appealing to the preceding constituent. But that alternative has the disadvantage that it would not create a metrical grid alignment in which a preceding copula would be prevented from destressing by Monosyllabic Destressing through the effect of the Grid Culmination Condition. We will therefore keep the formulation (7.53).

Notice moreover that the rule does not require the presence of more than one focus pair in the two sentences. Thus it applies in the following sentence, (correctly) blocking the application of Monosyllabic Destressing to *is:*

(7.54)
She's [a better doctor] than she $_\alpha$[is]$_\alpha$ [a linguist]
F$_1'$$F_2'$

The rule as formulated is still too crude: it would insert a silent demibeat before *Helen* in (7.51), thereby wrongly preventing the destressing of *than.* Clearly some further conditions need to be imposed. We will not pursue the matter here, however, hoping merely that this outline of an analysis renders plausible our claim that the failure of destressing in these constructions stems from focus-related timing rather than from *wh*-trace and its reflection in the grid.

Now it may be that some speakers do not have a rule like (7.53) in their grammars; they may simply never produce a rhythmic disjuncture in this environment. The existence of such a group of speakers would not be at all surprising, since here too the effect seems to be a "stylistic" one. Paired Focus Framing may be thought of as producing a timing configuration that sets off and supports the parallelism in the focus structure; its role is an auxiliary one. Rule (7.53) is a "grammaticization" of the phenomenon, and those who are not sensitive to or users of this sort of "expressive" timing may have no such rule at all. Without such a rule, of course, the copula would be expected to destress.

To sum up this speculative foray into the area of the prosodic realization of parallelism, we have suggested that the maintenance of unstressed *is, are,* etc., in comparative constructions has nothing to do with the presence of a *wh*-trace of QP in these constructions, but is related instead to the fact that comparative constructions characteristically exhibit parallelism of focus and prosody as well as structural parallelism. We have suggested that speakers may employ various devices to underscore this parallelism in prosodic fashion and that these devices, whether the addition of a (redundant) pitch accent or the addition of a silent demibeat, are what impede Monosyllabic Destressing.

It remains to discuss one last class of empty categories, which have been taken (in Selkirk 1972, for example) to show that empty categories in surface structure (sites of "deletion"[26] or extraction) find their reflex in the junctural representation of phonology. These are the empty or "dummy" heads that might be thought to remain in syntactic representation after the operation of a deletion rule like Gapping. (7.55) illustrates the general sort of configuration in question.

(7.55)

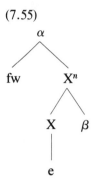

This sort of derived structure might with good reason be thought appropriate for the part of the sentences in (7.56) that includes the "deletion site."

(7.56)
a. John is proud of his daughter, and he [is ＿＿＿ of his son], too.
b. Mary can dance the tango better than I [can ＿＿＿ the rumba].
c. I have some pictures of Helen for you and [some ＿＿＿ of Edith] for John.

The function words that precede the gaps in (7.56) and other comparable sentences must appear in their strong form. Notice now that it is characteristic of gapped constructions like these that they display a parallel syntactic structure and a paired focus structure. The "deleted" head is nonfocal, because repeated, and always precedes a focused constituent, the second of a focus pair. What this "deletion" leaves behind in (7.56), then, is a function word preceding the second member of a focus pair. We are therefore inclined to invoke the concept of paired focus framing, and rule (7.53), to explain why it is that the function words do not destress in (7.56). Here too, then, as with comparatives, the fact that these syntactic structures have a typical focus structure ultimately explains the appearance of the strong forms of function words before the alleged sites of empty categories in surface structure.

We have argued that the empty categories of surface structure, whether dummy heads or *wh*-traces, have no role in determining the phonological representation of the function words that c-command them, as in the configuration (7.39). As mentioned earlier, this fact does not necessarily lead to the conclusion that SDA ignores empty categories, for it could be that empty categories receive one or more silent demibeats through SDA but that the position of the silent demibeat(s), outside the function word, makes it (them) unable to block the application of Monosyllabic Destressing via the GCC. However, there is evidence suggesting that, at least in the case of traces and PRO, empty categories are not interpreted by SDA. Cooper and his colleagues (see especially Cooper and Paccia-Cooper 1980) have studied the durational properties of surface structures, explicitly investigating whether the presence of *wh*-trace, NP trace, or PRO affects the timing of the production of the surrounding words. Their results suggest that traces and PRO make *no* contribution to the timing of the sentence. From this result, we conclude that SDA—which we argued in chapter 6 to be the source of the syntax-related timing differences studied by Cooper et al.—does not apply to these empty categories. Cooper and Paccia-Cooper do report a systematic durational effect of gapping, however: the syllable preceding the "deletion site" is lengthened. This is of course what Paired Focus Framing predicts. The conclusion then seems to be that empty categories are not reflected in the junctural representation of phonology, and thus that they do not "block" the application of Monosyllabic Destressing. While the destressing of function words *is* blocked by the junctural properties of certain syntactic configurations, this happens either because the function word precedes a paired focus or because it comes at the end of a phrase.

One more syntactic configuration in which Monosyllabic Destressing is blocked requires discussion—namely, the position before parentheticals:

(7.57)

a. Denise is a woman who, if she had the chance, would do great things.

b. Among the play's strongest numbers are, as might be expected, the dance or dance-associated pieces.

c. Josie was looking forward to—or should I say was nervously apprehensive about—her school play.

Notice that these examples have a natural pronunciation in which the function word does not bear a pitch accent.[27] Therefore the explanation for the lack of destressing here must be a junctural one. The stressed function word of these examples also does not precede a paired focus. Therefore the silent demibeats blocking destressing here must arise from the application of SDA in phrase-final position. The central question is, then, In what phrase is the function word final? It seems unlikely that the answer is to be found in the syntactic analysis of parentheticals—from which it would not follow that a phrase necessarily precedes a parenthetical expression.[28] But we know that a parenthetical is an intonational phrase (IP) itself and that it is preceded and followed by IPs (section 5.4). Given this, any pre-parenthetical function word is itself final in an IP. It seems entirely plausible that this IP-final status of the function words in (7.57) is responsible for their lack of destressing. In order for this account to work all that is required is that SDA be made sensitive to the IP constituency of the sentence, as well as to its syntactic constituency.

Given our theory of the organization of the grammar, the intonational phrasing of the sentence is established prior to grid construction, so the analysis of a sentence into IPs is certainly there for SDA to "see." We will consider that SDA does see IPs, just as it sees any other (syntactic) phrases, and that it adds one (or more) silent demibeat(s) at the right extreme of each. This appeal by a grid construction rule to the intonational phrasing of the sentence has a precedent. We showed in chapter 5 that the Nuclear Stress Rule must take the IP as a domain (the highest, in fact) on which it applies. A consistent picture thus emerges. Grid construction rules (of all sorts) respect IP constituency just as they do syntactic constituency. It is for this reason, we submit, that function words before parentheticals appear only in their strong stressed form.

There are some apparent counterexamples to the analysis presented so far, which suggest that function words remain in their strong form when located at the end of a phrase. These range from the infinitival *to* of *wanna* (I don't wanna ____) to the auxiliary *have* of *I could've* and object pronouns like *them* in *I saw'm*. Our position, stated also in Selkirk 1972, is that these pre-final stressless function words are not counterexamples to our basic analysis, but instead provide evidence for rules of encliticization that in fact alter the surface syntactic representation to which the rules of the syntax-phonology mapping apply. We will show in the following sections that, assuming an encliticized syntactic structure, the above phonological shapes are exactly the ones predicted, given our theory of grid construction and destressing.

7.2 Varieties of Encliticization in English

7.2.1 The Taxonomy

The above titles reflect our opinion that enclitics in English are a heterogeneous lot, and that the best one can offer as a general statement about enclitics in English is a taxonomy of the various sorts attested. We will argue for parceling them into two major classes: those produced by rules of *syntactic restructuring* and those produced by rules of *rhythmic restructuring*. Within these classes we will also point out various subclasses. The main purpose of this section is to show that this taxonomy has some basis in fact, and to argue for the place of a few well-known encliticization rules of English within it.

In ascribing encliticization rules to one or the other major class, we will use a set of criteria that distinguish them clearly. It is a property of *all* rules of encliticization that we have encountered that they mention the particular morpheme or class of morphemes that is made enclitic. Where the rules differ is in (a) what further sorts of contextual information they mention in their structural descriptions and (b) where in the grammar they apply. Properties (a) and (b) are not strictly independent, of course, since an appeal to a certain type of information about the representation may entail a particular place for that rule in the overall derivation, given our theory of the organization of the grammar.

We will say that an encliticization rule is a rule of syntactic restructuring (belonging to the syntactic component and preceding all operations of the syntax-phonology mapping) if it has one or more of the following properties:

(i)   The rule is constrained by general principles of the syntax.
(ii) The rule precedes other operations of the syntax.
(iii) The rule is confined to particular phrase structure configurations.
(iv) The rule mentions the categorial or morphological identity of the host to which the enclitic is attached.

It should be fairly obvious why we have included (i), (ii), and (iii) as properties giving membership in the class of syntactic encliticization rules, but the relevance of (iv) requires some explanation, which we give below.

As for rules of rhythmic encliticization, which we consider to be rules of the syntax-phonology mapping, we will say that a rule belongs to this class if it has either of the following properties:

(v) The rule is constrained by aspects of rhythmic (dis)juncture in the sentence.

(vi) The rule is constrained by aspects of the metrical grid alignment of syllables (i.e., their rhythmic prominence) as established on the phrasal domain.

It seems moreover to be a general fact about rules of encliticization displaying properties (v) and/or (vi) that they identify only the morpheme or set of morphemes that are made enclitic, but not the host or other aspects of the sentential syntax. Perhaps this combination of extreme "locality" and the properties (v) and (vi) is purely coincidental, but we suspect that it is not, and that it reflects something deep about the sorts of information made generally available to different sorts of principles of grammar. (We develop this point in chapter 8.)

Putting this hunch in the form of a (tentative) hypothesis, we suggest that if an encliticization rule mentions any more syntactic information than is required to specify the nature of the (set of) morphemes to be encliticized, it merits the status of a syntactic restructuring rule. It is predicted, then, that any rule involving such additional syntactic information will precede all rules of the syntax-phonology mapping, and thus that any rule with such syntactic conditions will *not* make appeal to any information about the metrical grid alignment of the utterance. Our examination of enclitic rules will bear out this hypothesis.

Among the syntactic restructuring rules, we will distinguish between on the one hand *To* "Contraction" and *Not* "Contraction" (giving, e.g., *wanna* and *shouldn't*) and on the other hand the rules encliticizing *have* and personal pronouns (giving, e.g., *I could've* and *I saw'm*). The former two may even be "lexical," in the sense that the encliticized forms may be lexical items themselves, but the latter two are decidedly "late-level" and apply only at the last minute, readjusting the surface structure in preparation for the syntax-phonology mapping.

Among the rules of rhythmic restructuring we include what has commonly been called *Aux Contraction;* it accounts for the (optional) attachment of a stressless *is* to what precedes, as in *Nora's having a birthday soon*. We also include here rules encliticizing such stressless elements as *to* (in its many forms), the article *a(n),* and the preposition *of*. All these rules of rhythmic restructuring have the effect of bringing a stressless syllable closer to a preceding rhythmic prominence; they might be viewed as instances of a general tendency to Tonic Attraction, wherein a (strong) beat draws to it the weak companion components of rhythmic structure that follows.

Recognizing the existence of rhythmic-structure-sensitive rules of encliticization and of a rhythmic rationale for the fact that encliticization occurs in the first place may permit us to better understand the entire phenomenon of encliticization. Suppose it were the case that the "core phenomenon" were Tonic Attraction. The various rules of encliticization itemized here might then be seen as progressive stages of the "grammaticization" of this essentially rhythmic effect. Consider the rules of syntactic restructuring. Certainly it is easy to view the cliticization of pronouns to preceding verbs as having a rhythmic origin. The object pronoun would relatively rarely be focused (and pitch-accented); thus it would typically find itself following a more rhythmically prominent (usually pitch-accented) verb. And by Tonic Attraction, the pronoun would be drawn to the verb. The fact that *have* attaches to a preceding modal could be similarly explained. In sentences with a modal–*have* sequence it is very likely that the modal will receive a pitch accent and very unlikely that *have* will. In earlier times, then, *have* too may have been drawn by Tonic Attraction to the rhythmically more prominent modal. Similar histories could be proposed for *Not* Contraction and *To* Contraction. Viewing the phenomenon of encliticization in this way suggests strongly that the taxonomy we have given is not of great theoretical interest, however. These rules grammaticizing the core tendency expressed in Tonic Attraction are simply rules of the syntactic or phonosyntactic periphery, with little, if anything, to say about universal grammar.

Nonetheless, there are a few interesting points to be made about enclitics. First, it is only the encliticization rules that are peripheral or ad hoc. As we will show, once a function word is encliticized, its phonological properties are entirely predictable, given our general theory of grid construction and destressing. Second, although the taxonomy is rather loose, it is nonetheless consistent with a clear-cut distinction between rules of the syntactic component, on the one hand, and rules of the component interpreting syntactic structure as phonological structure, on the other. In other words, there is apparently a discontinuity in this allegedly progressive grammaticization of encliticization—a point where a rule makes a qualitative leap from the "phonosyntactic" to the syntactic.

The analysis to be developed here differs in certain ways from the analysis proposed in Selkirk 1972. There we argued for a class of syntactic encliticization rules—including all those mentioned here—basing our discussion largely on arguments of Bresnan 1971b; but we did not recognize the class of rhythmic restructuring rules and, among them, Aux Contraction. Moreover, although the syntactic structures claimed to be derived by syntactic encliticization in Selkirk 1972 were the same ones we adopt here, the phonological interpretation of those structures was quite different. There we proposed an ad hoc rule of Clitic Destressing that now turns out to be unnecessary. We will show that the phonological interpretation of encliticized structures proceeds according to the general principles laid out here, deriving the correct results. Thus our present analysis of English encliticization represents a definite improvement over the analysis of Selkirk 1972. Part of this improvement, it should be said, is to be attributed to the greater understanding of the nature of stress and juncture that has been achieved over time and is reflected in this study.

7.2.2 Syntactic Restructuring

7.2.2.1 *Not* Contraction It has long been recognized that there is a rule of English grammar that attaches the negative form *not* to a preceding auxiliary verb or modal, and that, because this rule precedes the syntactic rule of Subject-Aux Inversion (SAI), it forms part of the syntactic component. *Not* Contraction is commonly taken to be responsible for producing the complex forms written with *-n't* (*didn't, don't, isn't, aren't, can't, couldn't,* etc.) from an input structure where *not* follows its host-to-be, in a position generated by the phrase structure rules (Chomsky 1957, Klima 1964, Katz and Postal 1964, Ross 1967). The fact that in sentences where SAI has applied the negative may appear before the subject NP only if it is contracted (i.e., enclitic to the inverted auxiliary or modal) has been taken as evidence that *Not* Contraction precedes SAI. Compare the ungrammatical sentences of (7.58b) to the grammatical sentences of (7.58a).

(7.58)

a. $\begin{Bmatrix} \text{Didn't} \\ \text{Couldn't} \\ \text{Hasn't} \end{Bmatrix}$ she leave/left?

b. *$\begin{Bmatrix} \text{Did not} \\ \text{Could not} \\ \text{Has not} \end{Bmatrix}$ she leave/left?

This ordering of *Not* Contraction before SAI seems to us a conclusive argument that the former is a rule of syntactic restructuring.

This conclusion is consistent with another property of *Not* Contraction: it makes crucial appeal to the categorial identity of the host morpheme. Notice that although the sentences in (7.59a) are perfectly well formed with an uncontracted *not,* they are ungrammatical if the *not* is attached to the preceding word, as shown in (7.59b).

(7.59)

a. They have more than often not left before midnight.
    She was asked to not wear her shoes inside.
    We didn't not see them, we simply didn't pay any attention to them.

b. *They have more than oftenn't left before midnight.
    *She was asked ton't wear her shoes inside.
    *We didn'tn't see them, we simply didn't pay any attention to them.

The generalization is that *n't* encliticizes only to modals and auxiliaries.

It may well be that the rule producing the contracted *n't* forms is now not a syntactic transformation, but instead a rule of English morphology. (See Zwicky and Pullum 1982 for arguments in favor of this position.) Or perhaps there is no rule at all in synchronic grammar, and the *n't*-contracted forms are simply listed in the lexicon. Two facts supporting the latter alternative are (a) the phonological shapes of some of the contracted and uncontracted forms are not alternations produced by regularly applying rules of the grammar (*do* [du]/*don't* [dont], *will* [wɪl]/*won't* [wont]) and (b) there exists at least one contracted form, *ain't,* which must certainly be regarded as a lexicalized or suppletive variant. (Note that if there were a syntactic transformation (or morphological rule) encliticizing *not,* some device also making appeal to the particular identity of the host morpheme (a rule of surface suppletion?) would still be needed in addition in order to produce the correct surface phonological shapes.) Whether *n't* encliticization is a rule at all would therefore seem to depend on whether a ruleless lexical listing of the forms can appropriately capture the facts about the distribution of *n't* and *not* in English sentences. If it can, then the lexical treatment would seem the more desirable.

7.2.2.2 *To* Contraction   Since it was first proposed in Bresnan 1971b, a rule of *To* Contraction (or *To* Encliticization) has been given a central role in deriving the forms sometimes written *wanna* (*want to*), *hafta* (*have to*), *gonna* (*going to*). This rule has generated considerable interest, since constraints on its operation would appear to provide evidence for important aspects of current syntactic theory. The original contrast that gave rise to the debate was pointed out by Larry Horn:

(7.60)
a. Teddy is the man I want to succeed.
b. Teddy is the man I wanna succeed.

(7.60a) is ambiguous between one reading where *want* is followed by a controlled PRO (the "Equi" case) and another where it is followed by a *wh*-extraction site, but (7.60b) is unambiguously interpreted as having a PRO subject after *want*. Our own original suggestion (Selkirk 1972) was that *wh*-trace (in the form of word boundaries) might be responsible for blocking the contraction, though we offered no explanation for why an empty category like PRO would not block the rule. In some sense, the proposal implied there mixed the vocabulary of phonology and syntax in allowing a rule of syntactic encliticization to be blocked by traces in the form of word boundaries. Subsequent investigation, however, has shown that the rule is not at all phonological.

Research on *to* contraction over the last ten years, effectively summarized in Postal and Pullum 1982, has provided several kinds of evidence for considering *To* Contraction as a rule of syntactic restructuring (if still leaving somewhat undetermined exactly what syntactic conditions govern the application of the rule). First, only *wh*-traces left in the deep structure position of the *wh*-moved phrase block contraction. (Neither the *wh*-trace left by the successive cyclic movements of the *wh*-phrase through Comp, nor the subject NP trace left by Raising, nor PRO impedes the rule.) Clearly, only in the syntax is it possible for this distinction to be drawn (unless these empty categories are mapped into different phonological representations, and there is no evidence for that). And, indeed, the relevant distinction has been drawn in a variety of ways by syntactic theorists (see Jaeggli 1980, Van Riemsdijk and Williams 1980, Postal and Pullum 1978, 1982, for example). Second, Postal and Pullum 1982 have noted (i) that the *to* that contracts with a preceding verb must "belong to" the infinitive complement of that host verb, and not to some other infinitival clause, and (ii) that the *to* cannot contract out of a coordinated infinitival structure, even though complement to the host. Third, the rule necessarily mentions the identity of the host morpheme: *I'm going to/*gonna the movies, She meant to/ *menna leave earlier*, etc.[29]

Rather than taking space here to argue for or against any particular position on the nature of *to* encliticization as a syntactic process and what it reveals about the nature of the grammar, we refer the reader to the extensive literature on the topic. We will say in passing, though, that we would not be at all surprised if the *to*-contracted verb forms ultimately turned out to be lexical items themselves (subcategorized for complements without *to*), rather than entities produced by a rule of the syntax.

We have chosen not to elaborate on the phonology of the enclitics *-n't* and *-to* here, partly because it is in some respects irregular. What is *not* irregular about these forms, however, is that they are stressless, regardless of what follows, and that they are juncturally very close to their host verbs (as shown by their effect on the phonology of the host). In what follows we will show that our theory of grid construction entails that syntactically encliticized function words are separated by no silent demibeat from the preceding word, and that they have a metrical grid alignment permitting them to destress (even though final) at the point where Monosyllabic Destressing applies. To illustrate these aspects of the phonological interpretation of syntactically encliticized function words, we will examine two further sorts of syntactic encliticization, involving *have* and pronouns, (both discussed in Selkirk 1972). In each case we will also show why there must indeed be an encliticization, why the relevant rule is one of syntactic restructuring, and why we place syntactic restructuring rules at the very end of the syntactic derivation.

7.2.2.3 *Have* Encliticization   The auxiliary verb *have* has the idiosyncratic property that it may destress even when in phrase-final position, as in (7.61):

(7.61)
I would have, you must have, they must not have, she couldn't have

Have may be pronounced [əv] in all these cases. In addition, this anomalous phrase-final destressing may take place only when a modal or *not* precedes, as shown by the ungrammaticality of the elliptical sentences in (7.62).

(7.62)
a. *We [əv].   vs.   We [hæv].
b. *John and Mary [əv].   vs.   John and Mary [hæv].
c. *I could never [əv].   vs.   I could never [hæv].
d. *They must all [əv].   vs.   They must all [hæv].

Finally, when *have* destresses in this pre-final position, it is impossible for the preceding modal to destress, though the modal is normally susceptible of destressing in that position before *have*. Compare the possible realizations of *I could have* to *I could have gone* (assuming that there is no pitch accent on either *could* or *have*).

(7.63)

    I could have gone.
a. ... cŏuld hăve ...   [kə̆də̆v]
b. ... còuld hăve ...   [kʊ̀də̆v]
c. ... cŏuld hàve ...   [kə̆dhæ̀v]

(7.64)

    I could have.
a. *... cŏuld hăve ...   *[kədəv]
b.   ... còuld hăve ...   [kʊdəv]
c.   ... cŏuld hàve ...   [kədhæv]

To explain these facts, we suggest that *have* may syntactically encliticize to *could,* optionally, and in any context, pre-final or medial. Our main argument for this syntactic analysis whereby *have* attaches to the modal is that all the facts concerning the stress of *have* and the preceding modal follow from it automatically. Another consideration, of course, is that a syntactic restructuring rule for *have* permits us to capture the dependence of *have*'s destressing on the preceding morpheme in that part of the grammar where the necessary information about the string is already available—that is, in the syntactic component. Note next that if it is indeed a syntactic rule, *Have* Encliticization nonetheless follows syntactic rules like SAI, as shown by the ungrammaticality of *Could [əv] you left earlier?* opposed to *Could you [əv] left earlier?* We see no reason not to think that *Have* Encliticization applies at the very end of the syntactic derivation.

    The syntactic structure of a modal – *have* sequence prior to encliticization is, schematically speaking, (7.65a); the postencliticization structure is (7.65b).

(7.65)

a.   b.

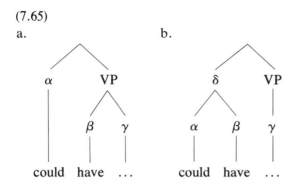

We avoid pinning names on the categories dominating *could* and *have*. What is important to the discussion is simply that α and β are function word categories and that δ qualifies as a Word-level category, but whether it is a function word or a "real" word is immaterial. Given these assumptions about syntactic structure, the syntax-phonology mapping will proceed as it should. On the α and β domains the syllables of *could* and *have* will be aligned with basic beats, but no silent demibeats; thus they "enter" the δ cycle with the following structure:

(7.66)

```
    x       x
    x       x
δ[α[could]α β[have]β]δ
```

On the δ cycle no silent demibeats will be added at the end. If δ is a "real" word, this is because SDA applies only on the next domain up from the word (section 6.2.1 and below). If δ is a function word, the lack of SDA can also be attributed to the PCI. The lack of SDA is crucial here. Because no silent demibeat is added to *have* within δ, the basic beat of *have* is not in culminating position within β; thus *have* may be subject to Monosyllabic Destressing. If δ is a function word, Monosyllabic Destressing will not be applicable until the next higher cycle, but if δ is a "real" word, the rule may apply to it. It doesn't matter which.

The important fact to be explained is that either *could* or *have* may destress here, but not both. If Monosyllabic Destressing were to apply first to *have*, it would create configuration (7.67) and could not then apply again to *could*, for the basic beat of *could* is in culminating position in δ in (7.67).

(7.67)

```
    x
x       x
```
₈[[could] [have]]₈

(7.68)

```
        x
x       x
```
₈[[could] [have]]₈

If, on the other hand, Monosyllabic Destressing destressed *could* first, deriving (7.68), the beat of *have* would be in culminating position and thus protected from another application of the rule. Apparently all we must specify is that Monosyllabic Destressing may not apply simultaneously to two configurations but only to one at a time. Given that stipulation, the derived structure (7.64b), and the limitations on the applicability of SDA, either (7.67) or (7.68) will be derived (giving [kʊdəv] and [kədhæv], respectively). But (7.69) and its corresponding pronuncition *[kədəv] will not be:

(7.69)

```
x       x
```
₈[[could] [have]]₈

It is not without interest that in these rather unexpected circumstances the Grid Culmination Condition should once again have the central role in blocking Monosyllabic Destressing.

7.2.2.4 Pronoun Enclitics   Much of the phonological behavior of English personal pronouns can be explained simply by assuming that they occupy the normal noun phrase positions in surface structure and that noun phrases consisting of, and immediately dominating, a personal pronoun are treated like function words, as far as the PCI is concerned. (The latter is one special assumption that does have to be made about personal pronouns; cf. section 7.1.1.) In their function word status, personal pronouns will fail to be assigned third-level stress by the rules of word stress and a following silent demibeat by SDA. If they are not phrase-final, then they should destress. And this is of course what happens: in *You talked about that yesterday, you* may appear in its weak form *yŏu*. Even if a subject pronoun does not destress, because of its syllable type, it is still juncturally rhythmically adjacent to what follows: in *I leaned over Carnap* the diphthongal *I* is to *leaned* what *Ei-* is to -leen in Eileen drove her car back. Possessive pronouns in headed NPs also behave as predicted: Your [jr̩] book's over there.

In final position in a phrase, however, we do not find just what would be expected on the basis of the pronoun's status as function word and its presumed location in surface phrase structure. Although in certain syntactic environments only the expected stressed form appears finally, in others the pronoun may appear in its stressless weak form:

(7.70)
a. She put ₙₚ[ₙₚ[his]ₙₚ]ₙₚ on the table
b. He ᵥₚ[showed his mother ₙₚ[them]ₙₚ]ᵥₚ
c. (I'll take a third of that piece,) if you'll ᵥₚ[saw me off ₙₚ[it]ₙₚ]ᵥₚ

(7.71)
a. She ᵥₚ[found ₙₚ[him]ₙₚ]ᵥₚ   him = [m̩]
b. They'll give it ₚₚ[to ₙₚ[you]ₙₚ]ₚₚ   you = [jə]
c. How ₛ[are ₙₚ [you]ₙₚ]ₛ   you = [jə]

In (7.70a–c) the weak form of the pronoun in the phrase-final position is ungrammatical: *She put his [ɪz] on the table (vs. She put his [ɪz] book on the table), *He showed his mother them [ðm̩]. This is the expected situation. What is unexpected is that weak forms should appear in (7.71). This phenomenon is not random, however: when the pronoun is weak phrase-finally, there is always an immediately preceding verb or preposition. This fact led us in Selkirk 1972 to posit rules encliticizing pronouns to a preceding verb or preposition. In the rest of this section we will elaborate on the syntactic conditions under which this putative rule of syntactic restructuring takes place. We will also show that there is no basis for assuming that these encliticization rules interact with other syntactic processes (transformations); the evidence seems to be that they are strictly surface readjustment rules. And we will show that the hypothesized derived syntactic structures automatically give rise to the correct phonological representations for the pronouns and their hosts.

The factual claim made about (7.70a–c), especially (7.70b,c), may require some comment. It has often been assumed that personal pronouns cannot appear as the second member of double object (Dative Movement) constructions, as in (7.70b), or after a verb particle, as in (7.70c). (See, for example, Ross 1967, Emonds 1971, Wasow 1975.) The correct generalization, we submit, is that the weak, stressless forms of pronouns cannot appear in this position. Sentences (7.70a–c) seem perfectly acceptable—when the pronouns are realized in their strong forms. Indeed, the acceptability of personal pronouns in these phrasal configurations is made all the more obvious when the pronoun happens to bear a pitch accent and be focused, as (7.72a–d) show quite well:[30]

(7.72)

a. Maybe they can wake up DEDE and then Dede can wake up US.

b. I wanna bring up HER, too.

c. (If you say you keep those ones for yourself,) and then go ahead and give the guy THEM, then . . .

d. They put HER on Pat's team, and gave Ann US.

The existence of the well-formed sentences (7.70a–c) and (7.72a–d) makes it quite clear that no condition on the pronominal character of the object NP should be built into any transformational rules for ordering the constituents of the VP, if such rules even exist.[31] In fact, however, recent work in syntactic theory (Bresnan 1982, Stowell 1981) has shown that the word order of subcategorized elements in VP is not governed by transformation, and (7.70a–c) and (7.72a–d)—along with their counterparts with the pronominal noun phrases in an earlier position in VP—would be generated as is.[32] Pronominal noun phrases in any of the positions in VP are susceptible of focusing, and with a pitch accent will not destress. Without a pitch accent, they are predicted to behave like normal function words with respect to Monosyllabic Destressing in any VP position.[33] This prediction is borne out except in immediately postverbal or postprepositional position, and this is where we suggest these pronominal noun phrases are encliticized, in a last-minute surface structure operation.

Hankamer 1973 has presented an argument for viewing Pronoun Encliticization as a rule that precedes certain syntactic operations, in particular Gapping. He observes that in (7.73) the two elliptical sentences are understood as having had the sequence *informed me* "gapped."

(7.73)

Paul Schachter has informed me that the basic order in Tagalog and related languages is VSO, Ives Goddard that the unmarked order in Algonkian is OVS, and Guy Carden that the basic order in Aleut is OSV.

With this observation we concur. Hankamer contrasts (7.73), with its pronoun object, to (7.74), where *Haj Ross* takes the place of *me*.

(7.74)
Paul Schachter has informed Haj Ross that the basic order in Tagalog and related languages is VSO, Ives Goddard that the unmarked order in Algonkian is OVS, and Guy Carden that the basic order in Aleut is OSV.

He claims that in (7.74) the gap can only be interpreted as *Paul Schachter has informed*. The contrast between (7.73) and (7.74), he suggests, may be the result of encliticizing the pronoun object to the verb in the former case, before Gapping applies. This would allow Gapping to treat *informed me* as a verb, whence the different possibilities of deletion and interpretation would ultimately follow. This argument does not go through, however, for the contrast is not accurately drawn. Presumably Hankamer was examining a pronunciation of (7.74) in which *Haj Ross* and the other proper names were under focus, which we rewrite here as (7.75).

(7.75)
PAUL SCHACHTER has informed HAJ ROSS that the basic order in TAGALOG and related languages (LANGUAGES) is VSO, IVES GODDARD that the unmarked order in ALGONKIAN is OVS, and GUY CARDEN that the basic order in ALEUT is OSV.

The interpretation of (7.75) is as Hankamer suggests. But suppose now that *Haj Ross* is "old information" and is unfocused in this mini-discourse, as written in (7.76).

(7.76)
PAUL SCHACHTER has informed Haj Ross that the basic order in TAGALOG and related languages is VSO, IVES GODDARD that the unmarked order in ALGONKIAN is OVS, and GUY CARDEN that the basic order in ALEUT is OSV.

The only interpretation now is that the "gap" corresponds to *informed Haj Ross*.[34] But surely we do not want to say that *Haj Ross* is enclitic to the verb. And if we don't adopt this solution for unfocused *Haj Ross*, then we have no reason to adopt it for the unfocused *me* of (7.73). Thus gapping provides no evidence that Pronoun Encliticization is a rule that precedes some other operation of the syntactic component.[35]

We do want to think of Pronoun Encliticization as a syntactic rule, however, for it obeys certain syntactic conditions. First, it mentions the character of the host: the pronoun attaches only to a verb or a preposition. Second, it seems that the host must c-command the pronoun. The evidence for this is that a pronoun does not attach to a preceding verb particle, as shown in (7.70c) and the following sentences:

(7.77)
When you roll over thém (roll them over), try not to mess up thém (mess them up).

(The pronunciations in parentheses are preferred.) The prepositional "particle" is a PP and thus does not c-command the following pronominal NP.[36] Finally, as we will show, the phonological properties follow automatically, assuming an encliticized structure.[37]

We formulate the rule as follows:

(7.78)
Pronoun Encliticization (optional)

$$[_{+\text{verb}}^{\quad X^0}] \; [N_{pro}] \Rightarrow 1 \; \# \; 2, \; \phi$$
$$\quad 1 \qquad\quad 2$$

Condition: 1 c-commands 2

This rule (Chomsky-)adjoins a personal pronoun (N_{pro}) to a preceding c-commanding word with the syntactic feature [+verb] (i.e., the class of verbs (including auxiliary verbs) and prepositions).

The phonological properties of the (putative) encliticized pronouns that must be explained are (a) their stresslessness and (b) the lack of (rhythmic) disjuncture between pronoun and host. (For an argument that, rhythmically speaking, a stressless pronoun object of the verb is enclitic to it, see Abercrombie 1964. For further phonological evidence supporting this characterization, see Selkirk 1972.) These properties are straightforwardly derived, given our theory of the syntax-phonology mapping and destressing. Consider the simple sentence *She saw them*. The result of syntactic encliticization would be the syntactic representation (7.79). The appropriate metrical grid alignment is (7.80).

(7.79)

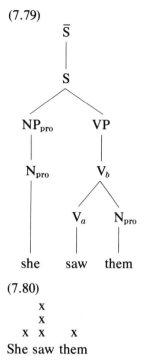

(7.80)

```
    x
    x
x   x    x
```
She saw them

(7.80) is derived from (7.81) in the following fashion:

(7.81)

$\bar{s}[_S[_{NP_{pro}}[_{N_{pro}}[She]_{N_{pro}}]_{NP_{pro}} \; _{VP}[_{V_b}[_{V_a}[saw]_{V_a} \; _{N_{pro}}[them]_{N_{pro}}]_{V_b}]_{VP}]_S]_{\bar{s}}$

Cycle on N_{pro}, V_a

```
                                  x
                          x   x   x
                          x   x   x
"word stress rules"       She saw them
SDA                       ──  ──  ──
```

Cycle on V_b
"stress rules"   ── ──
SDA   ── ──

```
                                  x
MD                            ──  them
```

Cycle on VP
"stress rules"   ── ──

```
                          x
                          x
                          x   x   xx
SDA                       [saw them   ]
MD                        ──  ──
```

Cycle on S
"stress rules"   ── ── ──

```
                              x
                          x   x
                          x   x   x   xxxx
SDA                       [She saw them        ]
                              x
                              x
                          x   x   x   xxxx
MD                        [She saw them     ]
```

On the lowest cycle, the pronouns are treated like all function words: they receive a basic beat alignment but no third-level main word stress, and they are assigned no silent demibeat. As for the verb, a "real" word, it is assigned normal "word stress," but no following silent demibeat. (Recall that SDA does not apply to words until a higher cyclic domain.) On the next higher cycle, on the V node created by the encliticization, no changes are made by either the "stress rules" or SDA. The only "stress rule" applicable here would be the Compound Rule, which has a Word domain, but it will not raise the degree of prominence above third-level if the relevant prominence is already most prominent.

SDA will not apply at the end of the derived constituent V_b, again because a ("real") word receives the silent demibeat it merits only on the next higher cycle. It is the lack of SDA at the end of V_b on this cycle that permits Monosyllabic Destressing to apply on this domain to demote the enclitic *them* to stresslessness. In this way, then, an enclitic function word is being treated just like a final syllable in a nonsyntactically derived word. As for SDA's failure to add a silent demibeat to V_a on the V_b cycle, we presume that V_b is not the proper sort of higher domain for its application. (The same point can be made about words containing neutral affixes, which are suffixed to categories of type Word. The internal word is not assigned a silent demibeat. Indeed, we predict that enclitic elements should show the same phonological properties as neutral suffixes in English.) On the VP cycle, silent demibeats will be added both to V_b in its capacity as a word and to the VP itself. But the silent demibeats are "too late" in coming to block the destressing of *them,* which took place on the previous cycle. Finally, on the S cycle, more silent demibeats are added at the end. The subject pronoun NP_{pro}, an honorary function word, is unaffected by SDA and thus will destress by Monosyllabic Destressing. The point, then, is that the mapping of the surface structure (7.79) into its appropriate metrical grid alignment (7.80) proceeds just as predicted, given the assumptions made about grid construction and destressing for independent reasons.

The syntactic structures derived by encliticization of a pronoun to a preposition or an auxiliary verb are interpreted somewhat differently, essentially because of the function word character of the host. In fact, these structures have the same interpretation as *could have.* Either the pronoun enclitic or the function word host is destressed, but not both:

(7.82)

a. Mary will give the documents $\begin{Bmatrix} \text{tò yŏu} & \text{[tùwjə]} \\ \text{tŏ yòu} & \text{[tə̆jùw]} \\ \text{*tŏ yŏu} & \text{*[tə̆jə̆]} \end{Bmatrix}$ soon.

b. The others are looking $\begin{Bmatrix} \text{àt thĕm} & \text{[æ̀tm̥]} \\ \text{ăt thèm} & \text{[ə̆tðèm]} \\ \text{*ăt thĕm} & \text{*[ə̆tm̥]} \end{Bmatrix}$.

c. I'll be thinking $\begin{Bmatrix} \text{òf yŏu} & \text{[ʌ̀vjə]} \\ \text{ŏf yòu} & \text{[ə̆vjùw]} \\ \text{*ŏf yŏu} & \text{*[ə̆vjə̆]} \end{Bmatrix}$.

(7.83)

a. How tall $\left\{ \begin{array}{ll} \text{àre yŏu} & [\text{àrjə}] \\ \text{ăre yòu} & [\text{řjùw}] \\ \text{*ăre yŏu} & \text{*[řjə]} \end{array} \right\}$?

b. What sign $\left\{ \begin{array}{ll} \text{àre yŏu} & [\text{àrjə}] \\ \text{ăre yòu} & [\text{řjùw}] \\ \text{*ăre yŏu} & \text{*[řjə]} \end{array} \right\}$?

(Note that we are discussing only pronunciations where neither the pronoun nor the host bears a pitch accent, i.e., where main prominence in the sentence precedes the encliticized structures. Only when pitch accent is out of the picture do we have a clear view of the role of Monosyllabic Destressing and SDA in interpreting these structures.)[38]

There do seem to be cases where both a preposition and a following pronoun object may destress, as in *What did they gíve tŏ yŏu* [təjə]? This pronunciation is most natural in fast speech, and may be the result of the application of something like the Abracadabra Rule (section 3.3.2). Notice that fast speech involves other reductions of what would have been stressed syllables at more measured rates: for example, *I'm gonna* [gʌ́nə] *leave* becomes *I'm* [gə̆nə] *leave* (and sometimes even [áŋə̆nə] *leave,* [ámə̆nə] *leave, or* [áŋnə̆] *leave*). But it may also be that the preposition itself encliticizes to the preceding verb, with the pronoun then following on its heels, in which case they would be treated just like a sequence of neutral affixes and could both be stressless at the outset. We have not investigated the matter enough to know what the right approach is. In any event, a simple extension of the grammar already provided would account for the cases of double destressing that do exist.

7.2.3 Rhythmic Restructuring: The Case of Aux Contraction

Auxiliary verbs and modals behave in many respects just like other function words. They normally destress, unless they bear a pitch accent or a rhythmically added beat, or appear at the end of a phrase or before a parenthetical, or have a stressless syllable enclitic to them (such as *-n't, -ing,* or a personal pronoun). But there is one property peculiar to auxiliaries and modals: in their weak forms they may lose their syllabicity entirely (through vowel deletion or the "desyllabification" of syllabic sonorants) and be realized on the surface only with a nonsyllabic consonantal residue.[39] This is reflected in the conventional spellings of *'s* (for *is, has*), *'d* (for *had, would*), *'m* (for *am*), *'ve* (for *have*), *'re* (for *are*), and *'ll* (for *will*). We will refer to these forms as *contractions* and to the rule or rules involved in deriving their phonological shape as *Auxiliary Deletion* (Aux Deletion). However the details of Aux Deletion are to be described,[40] it is clearly a rule (or set of rules) that carries somewhat further the well-attested tendency in the language to reduce stressless syllables, accomplishing what can be thought of as a "coalescence" with an immediately preceding syllable.

We now agree with Lakoff 1970, Zwicky 1970, Kaisse 1981b, and others that the phenomenon of Aux Deletion requires the auxiliary to be juncturally adjacent to what precedes[41] and that there must therefore be a rule of grammar bringing at least some of the auxiliaries closer to what precedes. But we submit that an insightful characterization of this rule, which we will call *Auxiliary Contraction* (Aux Contraction), requires that it be cast in rhythmic structure terms—that it is a rule of rhythmic restructuring, not a rule of the syntactic component.

As we have shown, function words that are syntactically enclitic have the characteristics required for Aux Deletion: they are stressless, and they are juncturally close to what precedes. Thus it is plausible that the same general sort of rule of syntactic restructuring that created the enclitic configurations in the earlier cases also creates the configuration in which Aux Deletion takes place. According to a syntactic analysis of Aux Contraction, a structure like (7.84) is submitted to the syntax-phonology mapping:

(7.84)

$\ldots {}_N[{}_N[\text{Jane}]_N \, {}_{V_{aux}}[\text{is}]_{V_{aux}}]_N \ldots$

But there is one important difference between the auxiliary contraction cases and the earlier cases of encliticization: auxiliary contraction is ungrammatical in positions we have characterized as phrase-final or pre-focus (though some might call them pre–empty category positions), as well as before parentheticals, as illustrated in (7.85) and (7.86).

(7.85)

a. Mary's as tall as you $\begin{Bmatrix} \text{are} \\ *\text{'re} \end{Bmatrix}$ —— wide.

b. Tell me where the party $\begin{Bmatrix} \text{is} \\ *\text{'s} \end{Bmatrix}$ —— tonight.

c. The water's bad, and the air $\begin{Bmatrix} \text{is} \\ *\text{'s} \end{Bmatrix}$ ——, too.

(7.86)

a. The play's strongest number $\begin{Bmatrix} \text{is} \\ *\text{'s} \end{Bmatrix}$, as might be expected, a dance piece.

b. The best show $\begin{Bmatrix} \text{has} \\ *\text{'s} \end{Bmatrix}$, it seems, won a prize.

(Such facts have been noted by Bresnan 1971b, King 1970, and others.) However, the enclitics *n't, to* (as in *wanna*), *have* (as in *could've*), and *him, her,* etc. (attached to verbs and prepositions) have no such distributional restrictions:

(7.87)

a. You shouldn't ____.
Do you wanna ____?
I could've ____.
They found 'm.

b. You shouldn't, it seems, be too upset by this.
I could've, if I'd wanted, been more attentive.
They found 'm, according to Jane, in the closet under the stairs.

The more limited distribution of auxiliary contractions may imply nothing more than that a syntactic rule encliticizing the auxiliary to what precedes must be more complicated than the encliticization rules described earlier. And, indeed, a richer structural description for a putatively syntactic Aux Contraction rule, placing conditions on what must or must not follow the auxiliary on its right, would permit this peculiarity to be encoded in the grammar. (Kaisse 1981b offers such a formulation.) But to approach the problem in this way is to ignore what seems to be a highly significant generalization, given what is known about function words in general: that Aux Contraction fails just where an auxiliary would have to remain in its strong stressed form, had it *not* been made syntactically enclitic to what precedes. If we were to assume that the auxiliary were not syntactically encliticized, we would have an immediate principled explanation for why auxiliary contraction does not occur in these environments: stress impedes Aux Deletion. Or, in positive fashion: auxiliary contraction is possible in just those syntactic configurations where, given standard assumptions about surface phrase structure, the syntax-phonology mapping would assign an auxiliary a stressless status. It looks, then, as though a syntactic rule of encliticization has little to recommend it.

Let us take it as a given that there are two necessary conditions for Aux Deletion: (i) that the auxiliary is stressless and (ii) that it is juncturally adjacent (in grid terms) to the preceding syllable. There is probably no disagreement on this matter. Now, given this characterization of Aux Deletion, the assumption that auxiliaries are *not* syntactically encliticized to what precedes, and our theory of grid construction and destressing, the correct distribution of most auxiliary contractions is predicted without further ado. All the auxiliary contractions appear in configurations where it is predicted that they will be stressless *and* where a non-phrase-final function word precedes. A preceding non-phrase-final function word would be followed by no silent demibeat(s) and hence would be juncturally adjacent to the following auxiliary. We predict, then, that contraction will take place in the following contexts:

(7.88)
a. She's a gas.
b. You've done it again.
c. I'm up to my ears in it.
d. We'll give it a try.
e. They're about to go.
f. Who've you been seeing?
g. Who'll be there?
h. Where've you been?
i. How'm I supposed to do that?
j. The one that's over there.
   etc.

The surface phrase structures of such sentences, some of which are given in the (a) examples below, would give rise to the metrical grid alignments in the (b) examples, where Aux Deletion can apply.

(7.89)
a. $_{\bar{s}}[_s[_{NP_{pro}}[you]_{NP_{pro}} \text{ }_{VP}[_{V_{aux}}[have]_{V_{aux}} \text{ }_{VP}[_V[done]_V \ldots]_{VP}]_{VP}]_s]_{\bar{s}}$

```
b.            x
              x
      x   x   x
      you have done
```

(7.90)

a. $_{\bar{s}}[_{Comp}[_{NP_{pro}}[who]_{NP_{pro}}]_{Comp}\ _{s}[_{NP}[e]_{NP}\ _{VP}[_{V_{aux}}[will]_{V_{aux}}$
$_{VP}[_{V_{aux}}[be]_{V_{aux}}\ \cdots]_{VP}]_{VP}]_{s}]_{\bar{s}}$
(*who, be* have pitch accents)

b.
```
x       x
x       x
x   x   x
who will be
```

(7.91)

a. $[\cdots\ _{\bar{s}}[_{Comp}[that]_{Comp}\ _{s}[_{NP}[e]_{NP}\ _{VP}[_{V_{aux}}[is]_{V_{aux}}\ _{PP}[_{P}[over]_{P}]_{PP}]_{VP}]_{s}]_{\bar{s}}$

b.
```
    x
    x
x x x x
that is over
```

On the other hand, had any of the preceding noun phrases here been constituted of anything but a single personal pronoun, or had any other sort of phrase preceded, there would be no junctural adjacency, for the obvious reasons; thus it would be predicted that Aux Deletion would be inapplicable and that no auxiliary contractions would appear. This prediction is borne out for *'ll, 've, 're, 'm*, as shown by (7.92a–d), but not for *'s* and *'d*, which are possible even when full phrases precede, as in (7.93a–d). (This sort of contrast is pointed out in Zwicky 1970.)

(7.92)

a. *The foci've been altered.
b. *Mary'll [l] try that.
c. *You and they're in this together.
d. *How low'm I going to go?

(7.93)

a. The foci'd been altered.
b. Mary's leaving soon.
c. My mother'd do it better.
d. Which typewriter's been fixed?

The fact that *'s* and *'d* are available in environments such as (7.93) is the one fact about the distribution of auxiliary contractions in the sentence for which we do not already have an explanation. What we propose to account for these cases is a rule of rhythmic restructuring, which in effect alters the metrical grid alignment that has been assigned to these auxiliaries by the "core" rules of the grammar. It says this:

(7.94)

Rhythmic Aux Contraction

$$
\begin{array}{cc}
\vdots & \\
\ldots\ldots \; X \;\ldots\ldots\; X \;\ldots\ldots \\
\ldots\ldots \; \sigma_i \qquad \sigma_j \ldots\ldots \\
\end{array}
$$

1 2 3 4 5 $\Rightarrow$ 1,2,4,3,5

σ_j = *has, is, had, would*

This rule is part of the syntax-phonology mapping. It alters only the metrical grid alignment of the sentence, affecting syntactic relations not at all, and will produce (7.95b) from (7.95a), for example.

(7.95)

```
a.           x        b.                 x
      x      x              x            x
      x      x              x            x
      x x xx x  x  xxx       x x   x  xx  x  xxx
     Rosie   has left       Rosie has    left
```

Once this rule has operated, Aux Deletion will be able to apply.[42]

Note that the rule has one crucial rhythmic condition: the auxiliary that is "contracted" must be stressless. This condition is consistent with the central generalization: that only auxiliaries that would be realized as stressless in their surface context may appear in contracted form. As written, the rule has no further rhythmic conditions, but it is not to be excluded that there may be some condition on factor 3, placing limits on the rhythmic distance between the auxiliary and what precedes. There do seem to be constraints on Aux Contraction involving the left-hand context. Kaisse 1981b has argued in fact that the auxiliary moves to the left and encliticizes (on her analysis, syntactically) only when the constituent on the left is a c-commanding NP.[43] She cites the awkwardness or downright ungrammaticality of sentences like (7.96a–f) with the contracted forms as evidence of this need to mention the NP character of the host in the rules.

(7.96)

a. *Never's he been known to do such a thing.
b. *Not only's Louis smart, he's also a great guy.
c. *Speaking tonight's our star reporter.
d. *More important's been her insistence on candor.
e. *Under this slab's buried Joan of Arc.
f. *That the world is round's obvious.

Though we are not in a position to pursue this idea here, it seems not unlikely that the ungrammaticality or lesser acceptability of the contractions in these sentences may have more to do with the prosody of the sentences than with the fact that an NP does not precede the auxiliary. Sentences with preposed phrases such as these are certainly not the same in terms of their intonational structure and timing as sentences whose subject NP is in its normal place, and the fact that Aux Contraction already has a prosodic condition leads us to suspect that the entire matter is to be understood in prosodic terms. The question, in our opinion, is whether rule (7.94) must be amplified in prosodic terms, or whether it should be written to include a factorization into the syntactic terms NP followed by *is/has/had/would*. At stake is whether or not a rule of restructuring (encliticization) with rhythmic conditions also has the power to mention the syntactic category of the host. General considerations about the nature of grammar lead us to think not, and to expect that a deeper examination of the problem will show that these facts about the subtleties of auxiliary contraction have a nonsyntactic explanation.

Chapter 8
The Syntax-Phonology Mapping

8.1 Modularity in the Mapping

In the preceding chapters we have sought to answer (or partially answer) a single question: What is the relation between syntax and phonology? While we have preserved in our answer the standard theory conception that phonology interprets the syntax—i.e., that syntax may influence phonology and not vice versa—we have developed a theory of the phonological interpretation of syntactic structure that departs significantly from the standard theory conception. The standard theory viewed surface syntactic representation and underlying phonological representation as entities nearly identical in character, and held that the mapping from syntax to phonology (the "readjustment") consisted simply of making a few alterations in surface structure and adding the boundary elements that were to represent the junctural properties relevant to certain phonological rules. Significant changes in the theory of phonological representation and particularly the recognition that the phonological representation has a hierarchical organization all its own, have required a fundamental rethinking of the relation between syntax and phonology. The conception of the syntax-phonology mapping that we have developed here involves a two-stage *construction* of phonological representation on the basis of syntactic representation. In the first stage, syntactic structure is mapped into an intonated surface structure, i.e., a surface structure with an associated intonational structure. That intonational structure includes the intonational phrasing of the sentence, the pitch contour(s) of the intonational phrase(s), and the assignment of individual pitch accents to constituents of type Word or smaller. In the second stage of the mapping, a metrical grid alignment (stress pattern) is constructed for the sentence on the basis of the intonated surface structure. Several subcomponents of rules are involved, which apply in cyclic fashion. The output of the second stage is said to be the underlying phonological representation of the sentence, i.e., the input to the phonological component of sentence grammar.

Implied in this theory of the syntax-phonology mapping is a strict separation of the grammar into components and subcomponents that are ordered in an obvious way with respect to each other and consist of rules and principles making appeal to limited sorts of information about the representation they define at their respective stages in the derivation. We take the syntactic surface structure to be defined by rules of a syntactic component that make no appeal whatsoever to aspects of phonological representation. (The challenge to this separation of syntax from phonology presented by Bresnan 1971a, 1972 and Bierwisch 1968 has been answered in chapter 5.) The focus structure of a sentence (an annotation of the syntactic constituents) may be assigned in the syntactic derivation, and it may influence rules of deletion and the like. But those aspects of sentence prosody relevant to focus structure—the pitch accent assignment (and possibly also the intonational phrasing)—are attributed to the sentence only in the mapping from surface structure into a "postsyntactic" *intonated surface structure*.

Three sorts of conditions govern the mapping from syntactic surface structure to intonated surface structure. They are conditions on the well-formedness of that intonated surface structure itself: (i) pitch accents must be assigned to constituents of type Word or smaller, (ii) the (matrix) sentence must consist of a sequence of one or more intonational phrases, and (iii) each intonational phrase must form a sense unit. (Condition (iii) will require that the intonated surface structure be put into direct relation with the semantic representation of the sentence, unless the semantic properties it appeals to are represented in surface syntactic structure; the fact that the choice of intonational contour may also require semantic interpretation reinforces this view of a direct relation between the partly phonologized representation and the semantic component of the grammar.) It is significant that the syntax of a sentence in no way determines its intonational structure. Intonational structure is freely assigned, submitted to well-formedness conditions, and interpreted. It is this freedom in assignment that accounts for the important fact that there is a one-to-many relation between the syntactic representation of a sentence and its phonological representation.

Its intonational structure having been assigned, the sentence is interpreted as a rhythmated structure by several types of rules or principles, which apply in cyclic fashion. Rules making crucial appeal to all aspects of the intonated surface structure—the syntactic structure itself, its intonational phrasing, the association of pitch accents with syllables, and the structure of the syllables themselves—impose the central pattern of rhythmic prominences. (These are what we have called the text-to-grid alignment rules.) They are seconded in their task of creating a rhythmic structure with an appropriately unfolding alternation in strong and weak beats by rules giving rhythmic order to the metrical grid: the rules of grid euphony. These rules themselves appeal not to syntactic structure but rather to the metrical grid so far established in the mapping. Rules of destressing, which have syntactic domains and appeal to syllable structure, may further alter the rhythmic patterns produced. The junctural properties of the sentence are understood to be rhythmic in character and are defined by a set of rules introducing silent grid positions on the basis of the syntactic structure of the utterance (Silent Demibeat Addition, SDA). Further junctural readjustment may be accomplished by rules of rhythmic encliticization. The output of this cyclic grid construction is a complete phonological representation, a sentence fully defined in terms of prosodic structure (intonational phrasing and syllable structure), rhythmic structure (the metrical grid alignment), and intonational contour.

We are assuming that this complete (underlying) phonological representation of the sentence is mapped into a surface phonological or phonetic representation by rules of the phonological component (i.e., phonological rules) of sentence grammar. For the moment we define phonological rules as any rules that in some way modify the segments or syllables of phonological representation, though this definition may require revision. Our hypothesis is that phonological rules make no direct reference to syntactic structure, their application being governed only by the phonological representation itself (which includes the representation of (degrees of) rhythmic disjuncture and the parsing of the utterance into syllables and intonational phrases). We also claim that phonological rules, defined in this way, do not apply in cyclic fashion. In other words, we are saying that the phonological component of the sentence is syntax-free, or that phonology, defined in this way, is "postcyclic." Assuming these claims about the lack of direct dependence of phonological rules on syntax to be true, it seems that the output of the syntax-phonology mapping can be considered to be the phonological representation alone, without an accompanying syntactic representation.

It is the rules of the syntax-phonology mapping, and in particular the rules for defining the rhythmic structure of the sentence, that are unalterably syntax-dependent. Stress rules like the NSR have explicit syntactic domains (these are the End Rules of the grid theory, as defined by Prince 1983), as do the rules of SDA that create rhythmic disjuncture. It is in this grid construction subcomponent that the terms of syntactic and phonological representation are most often intermixed. The rules look at syntax and build phonology. And it is the rules accomplishing this syntax-dependent construction of phonological representation that apply in cyclic fashion.

It is reasonable to ask whether the rules of metrical grid construction share any abstract properties, and in particular whether it is possible to characterize generally what sorts of information about syntactic structure they appeal to. The answer to both questions seems to be yes. The rules of the syntax-phonology maping that we have proposed refer at most to the syntactic category of the constituent domain α on which they apply and to at most one daughter, β, of that constituent, as illustrated below:

(8.1)

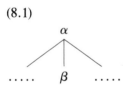

We will call this the *Single Daughter Principle*. Moreover, with the exception of one rule of SDA requiring that α be the S, constituents α and β have been specified (if at all) only for category type (i.e., X^r (Root), X^0 (Word), X^n, where $n \geq 1$ (Phrase)). Call this the *Nameless Domain Principle*. These are striking generalizations. If borne out on further investigation, they indicate that the manner in which syntactic structure may be reflected in phonological representation is very limited indeed.

To sum up, then, we are arguing for a model of the organization of the grammar in which the syntax and the phonology are entirely autonomous coinponents, the rules of syntax making no appeal to phonology and vice versa. Mediating between these components, however, are two others that define the relation between the syntactic and phonological representations of a sentence. The principles of these components have a mixed vocabulary. They appeal to certain limited aspects of syntactic representation in constructing the hierarchies of phonological representation.

8.2 The Syntax-Phonology Cycle

The division of the grammar into components has obvious consequences for the order in which the different sorts of grammatical processes take place in the derivation of a sentence. So it is that syntactic encliticization precedes the attribution of a stress pattern in the syntax-phonology mapping, and this in turn precedes the application of phonological rules (like vowel reduction) appealing to the stressed or stressless character of a syllable. The various subcomponents within a single component are also ordered with respect to each other. In the grid construction component of the syntax-phonology mapping, text-to-grid alignment rules such as the NSR precede (or, more precisely, take precedence over) the rhythm-ensuring rules of grid euphony. And together these rules precede both the SDA rule of syntactic timing and the rules of destressing.

Aside from the ordering implied in our theory of the organization of the grammar into components, another principle of ordering is at work that has very important effects on the derivation of phonological representation from syntactic representation: the principle of the cycle. In our theory, this principle governs not the rules of the phonology, but instead the rules that create phonological representation, specifically, those creating rhythmic structure. These rules are (for the most part) sensitive to syntactic structure, and the cycle is a theory of how they apply to that structure. We will say of the grid construction component that it is a *cyclic component,* which is to say that on each successive cyclic domain the subcomponents of rules apply in the order given above. But, given the cycle, application of a rule from an "earlier" subcomponent may follow application of a rule from a "later" subcomponent, when the latter has taken place on a lower cyclic domain.

The evidence for viewing grid construction in cyclic terms comes from a variety of sources. In our analysis of the basic rhythmic patterns of words and phrases we showed that assuming the cyclicity of TGA rules and GE rules permitted the statement of an important generalization about the interaction of these two subcomponents, the Textual Prominence Preservation Condition (TPPC). The TPPC says essentially that the requirements of a TGA rule applying on a particular syntactic domain must take precedence over any other prominences introduced in the derivation within that domain. This condition is not "surface true." But assuming that it is true on every successive cyclic domain guarantees that exactly the desired range of stress patterns is generated, through a judicious interaction of text-to-grid alignment and grid euphony.

A second argument for the cycle comes from the interaction of phrasal destressing and Beat Movement. We have shown that phrasal destressing "bleeds" Beat Movement. This ordering of destressing before grid euphony is apparently anomalous. Given our general understanding of the organization of the subcomponents, TGA and GE rules that generate the basic stress pattern apply before rules that destress. In fact, this ordering still holds up in the face of the data from phrasal destressing and Beat Movement if the principle of the cycle is assumed.

A third argument for cyclicity in the syntax-phonology mapping comes from the destressing of constituent-final syllables. We have shown that syllables at the end of "real" words (whether these words are generated by rules of word syntax or by syntactic encliticization transformations) may destress regardless of the position of the word in the sentence, though syllables that are not "real"-word-final, but phrase-final, may be blocked from destressing. This difference is explained if destressing and the rules inserting silent demibeats are understood to apply cyclically. SDA does not apply until a supra-Word domain is reached, and there it would block the destressing of any domain-final syllables. But if destressing is allowed to apply earlier, on the Word domain, then word-final destressing may take place.

For these reasons, then, we believe there is a cycle in the syntax-phonology mapping. It allows the theory to express important generalizations without being committed to the claim that they are all "surface true" and thus demonstrates the need for a certain degree of "abstractness" in the grammar.

8.3 Word and Sentence

The primary emphasis of this book has been on the phonological properties of the sentence, as they are defined in the mapping of surface syntactic structure into the (underlying) phonological representation of the sentence via the assignment of intonational structure and the construction of a metrical grid alignment. No progress could have been made toward understanding these aspects of sentence phonology without certain assumptions about the relevant aspects of word phonology, and in particular about the stress patterns of words and the dependence of these patterns on word-internal constituent structure. Within the sentence, function words behave differently from "real" words. Characterizing that difference, and the unique properties of function words, has required an understanding of the properties of "real" words. Moreover, there exist words that are derived by syntactic transformation, and it has been important to ascertain whether transformationally derived words share the phonological properties of words generated by the rules of the word syntax component (morphology) of the grammar.

Perhaps the most important reason for raising the question of word phonology in a book on the relation between phonology and syntax is that words themselves have an internal syntactic constituent structure. Do the same general principles of phonological interpretation—the same principles for mapping syntactic structure into phonological representation—obtain in the word as in the sentence? We believe they do. In this we agree with Chomsky and Halle in *The Sound Pattern of English,* but differ from Liberman and Prince 1977, Kiparsky 1982a, and others who see sentence and word in quite a different light. However, we think the case has not been made for construing the phonological interpretation of word structure and sentence structure in a fundamentally different way, and we therefore continue to entertain a unitary conception of the relation between sound and structure, at whatever level.

The issue revolves, we believe, around the relation between the syntactic constituent structure of an utterance and its "stress pattern." We divide the issue into three parts concerning (i) the nature of the syntactic object interpreted, (ii) the nature of the representation of "stress" and of the "stress rules" interpreting syntactic objects, and (iii) the manner in which "stress rules" apply to syntactic objects. In SPE, words and sentences are represented syntactically as a labeled tree (or bracketing). Stress is represented as an n-ary feature. It is assigned by rules that have explicit syntactic domains and are governed by a variety of conventions (e.g., the Stress Subordination Convention). The rules apply in cyclic fashion, within words and then on the sentence. Liberman and Prince 1977 assume the same sort of syntactic "input" to phonological interpretation. Stress patterns are represented in terms of an s/w-labeled binary-branching (metrical) tree and the feature [±stress]. Standard SPE-like rules assign the feature [±stress], and the metrical tree of a word is constructed as a concomitant of the rule assigning [±stress]. The tree of the sentence stress pattern, however, is claimed to be given by the syntax. Rules for labeling the nodes of trees *s* or *w* are sensitive to syntactic structure (and distinguish between words and phrases), but as far as the sentence stress pattern is concerned, Liberman and Prince point out, the cycle is unnecessary, for the rules labeling syntactic nodes could apply in any order and still produce the same result. Liberman and Prince, Kiparsky 1979, and Hayes 1980, 1982 do show, however, that the construction and labeling of word stress trees must proceed in cyclic fashion or in some way apply to successively higher domains. Given the metrical tree theory of stress, then, the stress patterns of words and the stress patterns of sentences are not derived in the same way with respect to syntactic structure. However, the theory of stress patterns as the alignment of syllables with a metrical grid, which, with Prince 1983, we argue should supplant the metrical tree theory of stress, has meant a return to a unitary theory of the phonological interpretation of syntactic structure—whether of the word or of the sentence. With SPE and Liberman and Prince, we view the structure of words and sentences as a labeled bracketing that is submitted to rules of interpretation (the syntax-phonology mapping). Constructing the stress pattern of words and sentences is a set of rules, some of which have particular syntactic domains (the domain-end prominence rules) and some of which do not (the Heavy Syllable Basic Beat Rule, the Pitch Accent Prominence Rule, and the various rules of grid euphony). We have claimed that these rules apply cyclically, on the word and on the sentence.

Kiparsky 1982a and others have claimed that the cycle can, and should, be eliminated as a principle governing the phonological interpretation of words. Kiparsky advocates a model of word formation based on Siegel's 1974 and M. Allen's 1978 theory that rules of word formation and rules of phonology (including stress rules and, according to Kiparsky, other rules of phonological interpretation) may be ordered with respect to each other, that they may in effect mingle in the "derivation" of a word. As Pesetsky 1979 points out, a theory of word formation and word phonology such as this permits eliminating the cycle. To be precise, such a theory would permit the elimination of the cycle if there is not a "derivation" of a phonologically interpreted word where a phonological rule has any more than one domain of constituent structure to apply to; in other words, phonological rules must necessarily apply after each "addition" of an affix, or after each "formation" of a compound.

In the context of a metrical tree theory of stress, this cycle-less model of word formation and word phonology might be appealing, precisely because it restores a certain unity to the theory of phonological interpretation: there isn't any cycle anywhere. But this seeming uniformity in phonology is bought at the expense of uniformity in syntactic description. According to Kiparsky and his predecessors, sentence structure and word structure must be generated in radically different fashion.

As we have said in chapter 3 and in Selkirk 1982, we see no theoretical or empirical advantage to the Siegel-Allen-Kiparsky theory of word formation as a characterization of the syntax of words. We have argued instead for characterizing word structure exactly as sentence structure is characterized—by a set of context-free rewriting rules. This means of course that the cycle cannot be eliminated in principle in words, for rewriting rules cannot be ordered and thus cannot be interspersed with rules of phonological interpretation. Rather, they generate full-fledged embedded structures, which are available for interpretation only once they have been generated, and to those structures the rules of phonological interpretation could of course in principle apply cyclically. Indeed, they would have to apply cyclically, if the theory is to accommodate the facts of English word stress discussed in section 3.4. Considering that the metrical grid theory of stress requires us to view the phonological interpretation of sentence structures in cyclic terms, it is not a disagreeable result that, given our theory of word syntax, word structures must be interpreted cyclically as well. Thus, if it does in fact turn out that our theory of word formation and cyclic word phonology can handle all the generalizations treated by Kiparsky's model—and we think it can—then we find that the desired unity in the theory of grammar can be restored. Words and sentences can be generated by the same sorts of rules and can be phonologically interpreted by the same general principles of the syntax-phonology mapping.

Notes

Chapter 1

1. But see the discussion of intonation in chapter 5, which takes into account the relation between focus structure (Jackendoff 1972) and prosody, on the one hand, and focus structure and logical form, on the other.

2. On the distinction between surface structure and S-structure (Chomsky 1981), see below.

3. Stowell 1981 has claimed that the set of rewriting rules can be eliminated from the grammar, except insofar as they specify the $\bar{\text{X}}$ category labels of syntactic structure. Since this theory does not impinge on the question of representation in surface structure, still a labeled tree, we will ignore it here.

4. Work in morphology in the last decade has shown that such "spell-out" rules have no place in the grammar. Of particular importance is the demonstration that inflectional morphology is not introduced in the transformational derivation, but is instead generated by rules of word formation, in a separate component. See Lapointe 1980, 1981, Lieber 1980, Williams 1981a,b, Selkirk 1982.

5. In the more recent generative tradition, see Kahn 1976, Selkirk 1978b,c, Kiparsky 1979, McCarthy 1977, 1979a, Halle and Vergnaud 1979, 1980, Clements and Keyser 1981, Cairns and Feinstein 1982, and Harris 1982, among others, on the syllable as a suprasegmental, internally structured entity. In the earlier literature, see, for example, Pike and Pike 1947, Kuryłowicz 1948, Fudge 1969, and others.

6. The works in autosegmental phonology are by now too numerous to cite exhaustively. See, for example, Goldsmith 1976a,b, Williams 1976, Leben 1973, 1978, Clements 1976, Clements and Ford 1979, Haraguchi 1977, McCarthy 1979b, 1981a, Halle and Vergnaud 1980.

7. This is a conception of the syntax-phonology relation not unlike that put forth, but not made explicit, in chapter 15 of Pike 1967.

8. With this conception of syntactic surface structure as having (a sequence of) phonological representations that are already (partially) derived, the notion "underlying phonological representation," if it is to be retained, will require

some elucidation. In fact, the notion must be different for word grammar and for sentence grammar. The underlying phonological representation of word grammar may be thought of as the concatenation of the lexical (most basic) representations of the individual morphemes making up words. This corresponds most closely to the use of the term in SPE. Here we sometimes also use the term *underlying phonological representation* to refer to the level of representation that is the output of the syntax-phonology mapping of sentence grammar and the input to the phonological rules of sentence grammar, i.e., the input to the postcyclic rules of the sentence.

9. Though perhaps not too much should hang on this distinction. The essential claim is that rules that appeal directly to syntactic structure are *only* cyclic, and that in the unmarked case those that don't (our "phonological rules") are not. (See chapter 8.)

10. Actually, Cooper and Meyer draw a distinction between rhythm and meter, which they characterize as inextricably interrelated or interdependent, and they allow that both meter and rhythm involve hierarchically ("architectonically") structured patterns. Indeed, the statement quoted above would also be true (for them) if the words *meter* or *metrical* were substituted for all instances of the words *rhythm* and *rhythmical*. It is Cooper and Meyer's notion of "meter" that corresponds to the notion of "rhythm" that is commonly used with regard to speech. The quotation is apt, nonetheless, as we shall see.

11. It is perhaps regrettable to proliferate the uses of the term *level* in linguistics. But its application here in denoting vertically arranged horizontal lines within a single plane is so apt that to avoid it might jeopardize clarity.

12. In discussing the speech rhythm represented by the metrical grid, Liberman 1975:278 quotes Donington 1974:427–428, who says of a musical rhythm that "It must be shaped to a pattern which the mind can grasp."

13. See Liberman 1975:272; Sweet 1875–76:480–481, to whom we owe the term *principle of alternation*; and Dell (to appear).

14. Liberman 1975:313 advances the hypothesis that all temporally ordered behavior is metrically organized and thus that language is in this respect just like other kinds of human behavior. It remains to be seen, though, to what extent the particulars of the patterns are the same from one sort of behavior to the other.

15. We will use acute accents to denote "greater stress" and grave accents to denote "lesser stress." When, as in this example, degrees of stress within the same word are being represented, no distinction will be made between the degrees of stress of the most prominent syllable of each word in the sequence, so in such instances the acute accent will be used simply to indicate the locus of main word stress. On other occasions, when the relative stress of words in a sequence is at issue, the grave accent may be used to indicate a main stress that is lesser in degree than some other main word stress in the sequence. In *thìrteen*

mén and *thirtèen mén,* then, the grave accents denote different loci of main word stress in *thirteen* and indicate its subordination to the main word stress of *mén.*

16. Note that the term is not being used here in the way Cooper and Meyer have used it.

17. Precursors in this characterization of prominence patterns via metrical trees are Fischer-Jørgensen 1948 and Rischel 1964.

18. In the work in the metrical tradition since Liberman and Prince 1977, only Dell (to appear) has pursued the investigation of the tree-grid relation.

19. There are certain obvious problems with the theory as Liberman and Prince put it, notably the assumption that metrical trees are binary-branching. To maintain this assumption, they must admit a wholesale readjustment of syntactic trees, converting any nonbinary structure into a binary one before "conversion" into metrical trees. Given the lack of independent motivation for such readjustments, this is clearly an undesirable consequence of the theory.

20. The particular choices of branching and *s/w* assignment exhibited here are consequences of Liberman and Prince's particular analysis of English word stress; they are not motivated on general grounds.

21. In Selkirk 1978c, 1980b these levels of prosodic constituent structure were referred to as *prosodic categories.*

22. This use of the notion "foot" is thus not the same as Abercrombie's. Abercrombie 1964 defines feet in terms of stress; stress patterns therefore have some prior, independent existence. In the theory of Selkirk 1980b, Halle and Vergnaud 1979, and Hayes 1980, for example, "stress" has no existence independent of feet. Patterns of stress are simply patterns of feet, the strongest syllable of the foot being the one that might be called the "stressed syllable."

23. Prince presented these ideas in several talks during the academic year 1980–81, including one at the Sloan-sponsored Trilateral Conference on Formal Phonology at the University of Texas, April 13, 1981, and at a University of Massachusetts Linguistics Colloquium, May 15, 1981. The notion that the metrical grid has a direct role to play in the phonology and essentially supplants other representations of stress has also been discussed by Liberman (personal communication). Prince 1983 was unfortunately not available to us when a major part of this work was written. Because of this, the reader will note certain differences between the metrical grid theories of prominence patterns described here and in Prince 1983, and a lack of discussion of the differences.

24. We will argue (chapters 2 through 4) that stress is not simply relational and thus that "main word stress" is to be given a representation different from that of "[+stress]," as a beat on the next higher metrical level at the least.

25. Giegerich 1981a attempts to account for this inherent word prominence in terms of an *s/w*-labeled metrical tree. He proposes to ascribe a "zero syllable" as a weak sister to every lexical item in the metrical tree. The assumption is that

such zero syllables will automatically provide their sisters with the appropriate metrical strength. But the problem, we think, is not to ensure that a word stress is more prominent than a weak syllable, but to ensure that it is more prominent than other stressed syllables without main word stress.

26. However, attempts were made within the standard framework to characterize possible patterns. See especially the work of Vergnaud 1974 and Halle and Vergnaud 1976.

27. On the status of syllable-timed languages, where there is no alternating pattern at the basic beat level, see chapter 2 and Selkirk (in preparation). On the status of stress-timed languages lacking regular alternation at this level, see chapter 2 and Prince 1983.

28. The grid here is only partial, in the sense that it includes the contribution of TGA rules and the rules of syntactic timing that introduce silent demibeats, but not the contribution of GE rules, which would introduce additional alternating beats.

29. Various nongenerative theories of phonology have recognized the syllable as a unit of linguistic analysis; indeed, more than not. See Fischer-Jørgensen's 1975 useful survey and the references cited therein.

30. See McCarthy 1979b, 1981, Halle and Vergnaud 1980, Clements and Keyser 1981, Leben 1980, Ingria 1980, Chierchia 1982a,c, 1983b, Prince 1984, Selkirk 1984, and Steriade 1982.

31. See Chierchia 1982a,c, 1983b, Prince 1984, and Selkirk 1984 for an outline of a theory of phonotactics within an autosegmental theory of the syllable.

32. The classic works on interword juncture in English, among them D. Jones 1931, 1956 and Lehiste 1960, suggest very strongly that there is no resyllabification between words in English, contra Kiparsky 1979.

33. We have excluded the *utterance* from this list, because we believe there is little motivation for it, and because it engenders little debate. The *prosodic word* may be viewed as equivalent to Liberman and Prince's *mot*.
   In the work of Halliday 1967a and Catford 1966 this hierarchy is proposed: tone group (= intonational phrase?), foot, syllable, phoneme. For reasons that will become clear here and in chapter 2, the foot (the Abercrombian foot) does not belong in this hierarchy, but in a distinct rhythmic hierarchy. This amounts to saying that, for Halliday and Catford, no units intervene between the intonational phrase and the syllable.

34. Following recent work on head-argument relations in syntax (e.g., Bresnan 1982, Chomsky 1981), we will assume that an indication of whether two (or more) constituents bear a head-argument relation to each other is in some sense "retrievable" from the (surface) syntactic representation. Conceivably head-modifier relations could find their representation there too (as well as in logical form), perhaps via a system of coindexing.

35. See, for example, Harris 1968 and Kahane and Beym 1948 on the domain of external sandhi in Spanish. See Selkirk 1981a on external sandhi in Sanskrit.

36. The term *major category* refers to the "lexical categories" Noun, Verb, Adjective, and perhaps Adverb (Chomsky 1965). All others are classed as *minor categories,* sometimes referred to as *function words*.

37. See Trubetzkoy 1939, many works in the American structuralist tradition, and Chomsky and Halle 1968, to name just a few.

38. This is true of the rules governing the allophonic variation of voiceless stops in English, for example (Selkirk 1978b).

39. Pierrehumbert 1980, for example, argues that there exist rules of English grammar taking as input a phonological representation of intonational contours in terms of the abstract tonal elements H and L and giving as output the F_0 contour of the utterance. (See chapter 5.)

Chapter 2

1. Steele 1775, Sweet 1875–76, D. Jones 1964, Classe 1939, Jassem 1949, 1952, W. Allen 1954, Kingdon 1958a,b, Abercrombie 1964, 1967, 1968, Catford 1966, 1977, Halliday 1967a, Gimson 1970, Pike 1945, Bolinger 1965b, G. Allen 1972, 1975, Lehiste 1980 (and references cited therein), and Thompson 1980 are to be cited as among the more notable who have worked on problems of speech rhythm in English.

2. A variety of experimental studies have failed to show an exact isochrony of stressed syllables in speech production (Classe 1939, Bolinger 1965b, Uldall 1971, 1972, Lehiste 1973b, 1975a, Lea 1974), though most show a tendency toward isochrony. See Thompson 1980 for a recent study disputing the presence of isochrony in production.

3. There is a fair amount of evidence favoring the psychological reality of isochrony as a perceptual phenomenon (e.g., G. Allen 1972, 1973, 1975, Lehiste 1979a, Donovan and Darwin 1979).

4. In Selkirk 1978a and Selkirk (in preparation) we have argued that French is not entirely syllable-timed, in that syllables containing schwa are not associated with a beat in the initial alignment of syllables with basic beats.

5. Most research has concerned itself with the isochrony of stresed (vs. stressless) syllables. See Lehiste 1980 for discussion.

6. Catford 1966 and Halliday 1967a, for example, posit a hierarchy of units of the phonological organization of the utterance in which the foot has a place: tone group, foot, syllable, phoneme. But since the elements of any given level in the hierarchy are not recursive, this proposal implies that just one level of grouping intervenes between the syllable and the tone group (intonational phrase).

   In fact, it is a mistake to view the foot as a constitutive unit of phonological representation arranged hierarchically between syllables and phrases. It can be shown that the latter form part of a hierarchy that is qualitatively distinct from the hierarchy involved in rhythmic organization. On this point, see section 1.2.

7. Actually, Catford 1966:612 acknowledges the existence of something like Trager-Smith degrees of stress, and claims that the sort of representation he proposes is enough to convey the distinctions, in conjunction with other independently required notions. His proposals concerning degrees of nonnuclear stress are somewhat programmatic, but apparently do not rely on a *rhythmic* characterization of these stresses; hence, they strike us as not making possible a unified treatment of stress and rhythm, as the metrical grid does.

8. Assigning a higher F_0 target level within the current pitch range to an H pitch accent on a syllable with higher stress gives very successful results in synthesizing the intonation of neutral declarative contours (Pierrehumbert 1981).

9. In speaking of relative pitch height here, we assume Pierrehumbert's theory, according to which values for height must be calculated relative to a (declining) F_0 baseline (see Pierrehumbert 1979, 1980).

10. In what follows we will have reason to modify some of the particulars of the metrical grid alignment illustrated in figure 2.2, though the relative prominences, which are at issue here, will remain the same. See chapter 4 on the Nuclear Stress Rule.

11. D. Jones 1964:§931, Kingdon 1958:164ff., and Gimson 1970:§11.03 discuss this stress shift phenomenon as well.

12. Proposals have been made for characterizing stress clash in terms of metrical trees, e.g., Kiparsky 1979 and Selkirk 1978c. We will see in chapter 4 why there is nothing to be gained by this approach.

13. In discussing the same sentence, Pierrehumbert 1980 allows for an even greater variety of metrical grid arrangements, but these, we submit, would only be available either under conditions of nonneutral intonation, where some pretonic word bore a pitch accent as well, or under conditions where the contributions of syntactic timing introduced lengthening or pausing. We will defend this interpretation of the facts in chapters 4 and 5.

14. Logically speaking, another alternative would be to specify that at least one weak *precede* every strong. We have no overriding reason for choosing one alternative over the other here.

15. It is reasonable to ask whether some of the particulars of these rules do not follow from more general principles of grammar and thus whether it might be possible to factor some of these particulars out. Might it not be, for example, that some quite general principle ensures that, of two clashing beats, only the weaker deletes or moves? Such a principle would permit the elimination of two of the rules of Beat Deletion, and would permit Beat Movement to be simplified. Thus it would seem to embody a significant generalization, and we are inclined to incorporate it in the theory. For the sake of explicitness, however, we will leave the rules as they are formulated in the text.

16. Beat Addition is the analogue in this system to Prince's 1983 Perfect Grid Construction (PG). The choices of left- or right-dominant addition correspond

to the parameter "peak vs. trough" that is part of the specification of PG in Prince's system.

Beat Movement is the analogue of Prince's 1983 rule Move x.

17. Though Prince 1983 suggests, and he may very well be right, that in the so-called mora-counting languages, each mora is aligned with the first level of the metrical grid, which is to say that a syllable in such cases would be aligned with two positions. (No syllable counts for more than two morae.)

18. Prince 1983 suggests, for example, that some languages may require that a syllable of a certain compositional type t align with a basic beat and a following demibeat. In our terms, this would mean that, while Demibeat Alignment gives rise to (ii) on the basis of (i), the given language's basic beat rule would give rise to (iii) on the basis of (ii), which is to say that the basic beat rule is adding positions at the lowest level:

$$
\text{(i)} \quad \overset{\text{DBA}}{\Rightarrow} \quad \text{(ii)} \;
\begin{array}{cccc} \text{x} & \text{x} & \text{x} & \text{x} \\ | & | & | & | \\ \sigma_t & \sigma & \sigma_t & \sigma \end{array}
\quad \overset{\text{BBR}}{\Rightarrow} \quad \text{(iii)} \;
\begin{array}{cccc} & \text{x} & & \text{x} \\ \text{xx} & \text{x} & \text{xx} & \text{x} \\ \text{V} & | & \text{V} & | \\ \sigma & \sigma_t & \sigma_t & \sigma \end{array}
$$

(with $\sigma_t\ \sigma\ \sigma_t\ \sigma$ under (i))

19. On syllable geometry and its relation to tree geometry, see Halle and Vergnaud 1979, McCarthy 1979a, Hayes 1980.

20. Syllable type distinctions involving quantity are found in English (Selkirk 1980b, 1981a, Hayes 1980, 1982), Cairene Arabic (McCarthy 1979a), Estonian (Prince 1980), Creek (Haas 1977), and numerous other languages (see Halle and Vergnaud 1979 and Hayes 1980). Distinctions involving vowel quantity are found in French (Selkirk 1978a, Selkirk (in preparation), Dell (to appear)), Passamaquoddy (Stowell 1979), Mountain Cheremis (Ramstedt 1902), Komi (Itkonen 1955), and Eastern Cheremis (Itkonen 1955). Those involving tonal specifications are found in Mixtec (Yip 1982), Proto-Indo-European (Halle and Kiparsky 1981), Fore (Nicholson and Nicholson 1962), and Golin (Bunn and Bunn 1970) (the latter two cited in Hayes 1980).

21. Prince suggests that rime quantity distinctions may be explained in terms of the following sort of rime sonority hierarchy,

(i)
VV
VN   (N = nasal)
VR   (R = liquid)
VO   (O = obstruent)
V

and that languages select a cut-off point in this hierarchy—one above which all syllables would be aligned with basic beats and below which they would not. Note that the notion of sonority hierarchy extends naturally to the vowel quality and tone cases. The schwa of French and Passamaquoddy is presumably less sonorous than all of its fellow vowels, and high tone, which in those languages determines the alignment of a syllable with a basic beat, is presumably more sonorous than low tone.

22. The case of domain-initial position is represented by English, with its "initial stress" rule (Halle 1973b, Selkirk 1980b, and chapter 3 of this volume), German, with its stem-initial stress (Kiparsky 1966), and possibly Eastern Cheremis, Huasteco, Koya, and other such languages discussed by Hayes 1980. Domain-final position is found in Tübatulabal (Voegelin 1935, Howard 1972), Weri (Boxwell and Boxwell 1966), Komi (Itkonen 1955), and other languages cited by Hayes 1980. The case of position before main word stress is represented by Russian (Karčevskij 1931) and perhaps by Hebrew (Prince 1975, McCarthy 1979b, 1981b), where there is pretonic strengthening.

23. These would presumably be the cases of languages with "unbounded feet"; see Halle and Vergnaud 1979 and Hayes 1980.

24. As for main word stress, McCarthy's analysis is that it falls on the final foot (i.e., beat) of the word. In grid terms, the rule would be cast as one that added (aligned) a beat on the third metrical level with the last (second-level) basic beat of the word. McCarthy's rule system thus predicts exactly the loci of the most prominent syllables reported by Mitchell:

(i)

```
    x           x                       x
 x  x        x  x              x    x   x
 x  x  x  x  x  x  x           x    x x x  x
kaa ta ba  in ka sa ra  ?ad wi ya tu hu
```

25. This is in fact our analysis of English function words (i.e., minor category words). See chapter 7.

26. Cases of main stress in second-to-initial position are rare (Hyman 1977), but attested, and they can also be derived under the present analysis. Their rarity is to be attributed to the rarity of right-dominant Beat Addition and of extrametricality on the left (Hayes 1982).

27. *End Rule* is the name given in Prince 1983 to a prominence rule assigning end prominence in a particular domain. (2.36) is one of this class, assigning "main word stress."

28. It would be instructive to consider what it means for Beat Addition to be obligatory when there are two (adjacent) positions to which it could apply but to which, apparently, it applies only once. Italian secondary stress is a case in point. Recall that Italian is a syllable-timed language, one whose every syllable is aligned with a basic beat. In long enough words, such as *generativa* or *contemporaneo,* there are therefore long rhythmic lapses to which Beat Addition may apply. From *generatíva* either *genèratíva* or *gèneratíva* is produced, but not **gènèratíva.* To maintain the notion of obligatoriness that has been assumed up to this point, which says that an obligatory rule applies when and where its structural description is met, we must adopt one of two approaches to deriving the two pronunciations of *generativa.* The first, which I prefer, is to say that Beat Addition does apply twice, and that Beat Deletion follows on its heels to delete one of the adjacent added beats. This solution maintains the notion of obligatoriness and involves no rule or principle not already necessary for inde-

pendent reasons. Note that this solution requires that the PRA *not* be a filter on rule application. The other approach would be to introduce a convention on rule application, reminiscent of conventions proposed in the standard theory, according to which, whenever a single rule encounters "overlapping" environments it applies in only one of them (S. Anderson 1971, 1974, Johnson 1973, Howard 1972, Halle and Vergnaud 1976, Vergnaud 1974). Such an approach allows for limited exceptions to obligatory rules. I am inclined not to take this approach, however, insofar as the proposed theory already has the machinery, in the form of Beat Deletion, to deal with these cases.

29. Note that this condition does not rule out the possibility that one domain-specific TGA rule may override another. This is in fact what happens in English (and in Italian) when Stress Retraction (a word-domain-specific rule) overrides the MSR (see chapter 3). In this case, what ensures that Stress Retraction prevails over the MSR is the more general principle of grammar, proposed by Kiparsky 1973, that the more specific rule prevail over the more general.

Chapter 3

1. The *type* of a category corresponds to its number of "bars" in an $\overline{X}$ theory of categories; see Jackendoff 1977.

2. See Chomsky 1970, Bresnan 1976, Jackendoff 1977, for example.

3. For reasons explained in Selkirk 1982, we dispense with a category type *Stem* for English morphology.

4. Following Williams 1981a, we assume that the syntactic features [±Verb] and [±Noun] are ascribed to affixes; thus a "Verb affix" is an affix with verbal features, not an affix that attaches to a verb.

5. See Siegel 1974 and Hayes 1980, 1982 on Greek compounds in English and their phonological attributes.

6. The notion "level" employed by Pesetsky 1979, following M. Allen 1978, is not that of a category level, or type, of constituent structure, but rather one of a subcomponent of rules in the morphology of a grammar. This notion of level translates fairly straightforwardly into a description in constituent structure terms, as shown in Selkirk 1982.

7. An obvious question is whether there is any systematic relation between the choice of a domain for rules of grid construction and the choice of a domain in syntactic-prosodic correspondences. At this point in our investigation, it is not possible to answer this question.

8. Trisyllabic Laxing accounts for the alternations in pairs like *divine* ~ *divinity, serene* ~ *serenity*. Velar Softening is proposed to account for the k ~ s alternation in *medical* ~ *medicine*, for example. Coronal Assibilation gives z or s from d or t: *permit* ~ *permission, deride* ~ *derision*, etc. Sonorant Syllabification is said to account for the syllabicity of final sonorants that alternate with nonsyllabic sonorants: *hinder* ~ *hindrance*.

9. Actually, the SPE analysis could only ensure that the word stress rules would *not* apply to words containing #-affixes by imposing, ad hoc, the condition that the variables that the rule mentioned *not* contain # (see SPE, chapter 8).

10. There are certain stressless tense vowels on the surface, which we analyze as underlyingly lax, as for example the ones in final position (*happy*) or in prevocalic position (*Canadian*). In this we follow SPE and Hayes 1980, 1982. See Bolinger 1981 for some criticism of this position. Unfortunately, we obtained this study too late to take some of his points into account.

11. The fact that initial syllables are not always stressed is to be explained by the operation of Monosyllabic Destressing (section 3.3).

12. See the discussion of Monosyllabic Destressing, which makes stressed CVC laxed, in section 3.3.3.

13. Final stressless CVC may also be underlyingly stressless, when the final C is extrametrical. See section 3.2.3.

14. In a more precise statement of the rule, the disjunction "CVC or CVV" will be eliminated, in favor of specifying a cutoff point in a ranking of syllable types according to the sonority hierarchy (chapter 2, note 21).

15. In Selkirk 1980b we declared that English stress assignment is not directional. Hayes 1980, 1982 has shown this position to be wrong.

16. Hayes 1980, 1982 actually treats *Mississippi* and *vanilla* differently. We state his position, and argue against it, in section 3.2.3.

17. Recall that neither Beat Movement nor Beat Deletion applies on the second metrical level (cf. chapter 2). This is due to the Principle of Basic Beat Level Integrity (chapter 4).

18. Nanni 1977 suggests that the entire morpheme *-ative* is extrametrical, and Hayes 1980, 1982 adopts this suggestion. But an alternative analysis is possible according to which the *-at-* undergoes a special destressing. See section 3.3.

19. It might be worth considering the possibility of an extrametrical vowel as well, which could explain the absence of stress on the CVV of *happy,* for example. But see note 10.

20. See Harris 1982 and Hayes 1982, who argue that a Peripherality Condition automatically ensures the elimination of domain-internal extrametricality. The approach taken here has the same effect.

21. As Hayes points out, a certain number of words that end in stressless CVCC have an unpredictable stressed CV in penultimate position: *lieutenant, quintessence, inclement, adolescent, discrepant, senescent, pubescent, pubescence.* These can only have been derived if the final *cluster,* but not the final syllable, is extrametrical. Since we do not take this possibility into account here, they remain inexplicable exceptions.

22. Note that in Hayes's analysis, the fact that final CVV(C) syllables are always stressed, but are nonetheless potentially extrametrical with respect to the MSR, is accounted for by extrinsically ordering the rule of his analysis that builds a foot over long vowels (Long Vowel Stressing) and the one that assigns extrametricality to final syllables in certain cases. Long Vowel Stressing precedes the "extrametricality rule." But Hayes could just as well adopt the more restrictive interpretation of extrametricality suggested here, and thereby avoid crucially relying on the existence of rules that assign the property of extrametricality (in the course of the syntax-phonology mapping) and are extrinsically ordered with respect to stress rules. Under Hayes's theory, Long Vowel Stressing is not directional and therefore does not care about the location of the limits of the cyclic domain; consequently, even under his account, Long Vowel Stressing could be taken to apply to extrametrical syllables.

23. CVC syllables are "footed" only at the right extreme of a word in Hayes's analysis—i.e., in final position when the last syllable is not extrametrical, and in penultimate position when it is. CVC syllables earlier in the word are *not* stressed. We take issue with this position in our analysis, according to which all CVC syllables are basically stressed (basic-beat-aligned).

24. Note that this is not the position taken in Selkirk 1980b, where there was no notion of extrametricality and the stress patterns of words were taken to be idiosyncratically lexically given and then submitted to "stress rules" that were in effect redundancy rules.

25. The +H diacritic was abandoned in the 1981 Indiana University Linguistics Club version of Hayes 1980. For what replaces it, see pages 146–147 of the revised version.

26. Hayes offers a handful of counterexamples to the claim made in Selkirk 1980b and here, that a stressed CV syllable must be followed by a weak. They include *inspissate, Achilles,* and *Ulysses.* (The presence of the long vowel in the final syllable is assumed to indicate that the syllable is stressed.) These do not seem to us very telling. In the latter two words, the tensing of the vowel may be somehow attributable to the voicing of the final fricative; and the first is in our pronunciation [ɪnspɪsət].

27. Individual speakers may be expected to give different analyses of the same words, and this ultimately might lead to subtle differences in pronunciation. For a speaker who only haphazardly applies CVC destressing and for whom a final C is not extrametrical in *Wachusett,* we would expect variations in the stressing of the last syllable, whereas a speaker for whom the final C is extrametrical would never pronounce it stressed.

28. There is a well-known set of cases that do not fall under this generalization: *Abernathy, alligator, Aristotle, salamander.* These words have either final *i* or a final syllabic sonorant. With Liberman and Prince 1977 and Hayes, we will consider them to have had one less syllable at the point where main stress is assigned.

29. Kiparsky's 1979 account of the two patterns for *Ticonderoga* involved the claim that the metrical tree for the word (above the feet) could be either right- or left-branching. This, along with the appropriate *s/w* labeling convention and the assumption that the Rhythm Rule applies word-internally (except where impeded by the *Montana* Filter), allows the full array of patterns to be generated.

30. See Giegerich 1981a for an attempt to treat the nonrelational character of main word stress in strictly *s/w* tree terms.

31. Trager and Bloch 1941 and Trager and Smith 1951 observe that the rhythmic patterns of the following pairs are not the same, and thus call for a distinction between stress and word stress: $\overset{2\ \ 0}{\textit{ei}}\overset{1\ \ 0}{\textit{ther nation}}$ vs. $\overset{3\ \ 0}{\textit{emen}}\overset{1\ \ 0}{\textit{dation}}, \overset{1\ \ 2}{\textit{tin tax}}$ vs. $\overset{1\ \ 3}{\textit{syntax}}, \overset{1\ \ 2}{\textit{red cap}}$ vs. $\overset{1\ \ 3}{\textit{contents}}$. Bolinger 1981 (and references therein) denies that this could be the case.

32. As we will show, *-al* does indeed have to be underlyingly stressless (lacking a basic beat), and its consonant therefore extrametrical. Otherwise it would provide the environment for the stress retraction found with stressed suffixes. For example, *paréntal* contrasts with *hélminthòid* in this regard.

33. All prefixes on the root or word domain are either CVV or CVC syllables, so in fact it cannot be ascertained whether the IBR applies with prefixes. They will independently be stressed by the HBR. This means that any differences in the surface stressing of prefixes must be a fact about their behavior with respect to destressing (cf. section 3.3.3). An interesting consequence is that the negative prefixes *in-, un-, non-* must all have the same place in the basic stress patterns, contrary to what has been claimed by M. Allen 1978, for example. There does seem to be a tendency to realize the full (unreduced) form of the transparently negative *un-* and *non-*, more so than with *in-*. This can be attributed in part to the likelihood that they might bear pitch accents and thus remain prominent (see section 5.3.3).

34. Note that the Anti-Lapse Filter may nonetheless be overridden by the *Montana* Filter. According to our account, there is one pronunciation of *Ticonderoga* that contains a lapse. Cf. the discussion above.

35. Actually, not all generalizations reached in earlier accounts are expressed in the present one. For example, we now treat CVC as always being stressed (basic-beat-aligned) in the basic patterns. Neither Selkirk 1980b nor Hayes 1980, 1982 agrees with this position.

36. Hayes 1980 would include *Nèbuchădnézzar, pàraphĕrnália,* and *Kìlimăn-járo* in this list. By our analysis, however, these words are not in the same class as *abracadabra.* Rather, their pre-main-stressed CVC would be stressed by the HBR and then destressed by Monosyllabic Destressing. They thus have the same underlying shape as *Halicarnassus.*

37. Note that if *bíbbity-bóbbity-bóo* is monomorphemic, no amount of magic by rule (3.51) will allow its sequence of ternary feet to be derived.

38. Recall that the difference between the *Ticonderoga* cases and the *Monongahela* cases is that the former have an initial heavy syllable. Therefore, the *Montana* Filter is not absolute, and Beat Addition may produce initial secondary stress, or it may not. In the latter case, the pattern would be like that of *Monongahela* (though the initial heavy syllable is not destressed, resulting in a small superficial difference between this case and *Monongahela*).

39. Rule (3.51) says only that CV may be destressed, not CVV. We know of no cases where destressing of CVV by the Abracadabra Rule must be allowed.

40. In Liberman and Prince's framework, Stray Syllable Adjunction is required in order that extrametrical syllables be incorporated into the tree.

41. By *optimal* we mean a pattern that would be generated as a "normal" case by the basic stress rules, i.e., not including an initial stressed CV followed by a stressed syllable. In this case, on Hayes's theory, the initial CV is stressed because of the requirement that all syllables be included in feet, not because the basic foot rules say that CV can be "stressed" on its own.

42. There is a class of counterexamples to Hayes's claim about the nonexistence of basic ternary feet and their derivation by a rule such as the one suggested. It includes *cátamaràn, húllabalòo, rígamaròle,* and so on. See Hayes's 1980, 1982 discussion of these forms.

43. However, we do not believe this rule is responsible for the laxing of certain underlying CVV syllables in the derivation of surface stress patterns, which instead appear to be produced by some version of so-called Trisyllabic Laxing. (See below.)

44. See Hayes 1980, 1982 for recent articulations of these rules, which were part of earlier analyses such as Ross 1972, Halle 1973b, Liberman and Prince 1977, and Selkirk 1980b, among others.

45. Though, as Liberman and Prince 1977 point out, in designated prefixes even CVV can be destressed. These include *re-, de-,* and others.

46. Consider the derivation of *hòspǐtǎlǐzátǐon*.

(i)

```
                         [[[hospital] iz_em] ation]
Cycle 1
                         x
                         x
DBA, IBR, MSR            x   x x
Cycle 2
                         x
                         x        x
DBA, HBR                 x   x x   x
Cycle 3
                         x
                         x        x
Trisyllabic Laxing       x   x x   x
                                  IZ_em
                         x
                         x        x   x
DBA, HBR                 x   x x   x   x x
                                      x
                         x            x
                         x        x   x
MSR                      x   x x   x   x x
Postcycle
                         x            x
                         x            x
Monosyllabic Destressing x   x x   x   x x
                         hospital iz  ation
```

Note that in this derivation, a permissible one, Monosyllabic Destressing has created a lapse. Thus it would be incorrect to posit a generalized anti-lapse filter instead of the Alternation Maintenance Condition. What makes (i) a possible derivation, apparently, is that it does not eradicate a $\overset{x}{x}$ x configuration. This is what is expressed in the Alternation Maintenance Condition.

47. Ray Jackendoff (personal communication) reports that both *bàssóon* and *bǎssóon* are accepted pronunciations.

48. Among natives of the state, the first syllable is often pronounced stressless, with a reduced vowel: [wɔ̃.skan.sn̩].

49. A few counterexamples still remain (as under Hayes's analysis), words with medial stressless CVC flanked by stressed syllables: *anecdote, designate*. We have no way of deriving these.

50. We are in effect disputing Kiparsky's and Hayes's claim that the stress pattern of *ǐnfírmǎry* and similar words (*percéntǐte, ceméntǐte*, etc.) reflects anything about the cyclicity of the rules involved here. (And here we may be quite wrong.) On our account, *infirmary* (for example) is simply an exception: it should have undergone Sonorant Retraction, and its surface pattern is not explained in terms of the final stressing of *infirm*. If our noncyclic approach to

these cases is correct, this exceptionality has some other explanation (or none at all).

51. Strictly speaking, nothing hinges here on considering Trisyllabic Laxing to be a rule of allomorphy, or morphologically sensitive. An account following the general lines of Kiparsky 1982 and making appeal to the Elsewhere Condition and a judicious use of underlying lexical representation could presumably do just as well. There is no inconsistency in appealing to the cycle, as we do here, and adopting this particular solution to the abstractness problem.

52. The derivation reflects the last-stage effects of "minimalizing," i.e., eliminating excess verticality.

Chapter 4

1. For example, Halle and Vergnaud 1979, Kiparsky 1979, Prince 1980, Selkirk 1980b, Hayes 1980. See especially the work of Dell (to appear), who explicitly discusses the phrasal prominences of French, in a tree-plus-grid framework.

2. Generally, those of the *nucleus* of the contour. (See for example Liberman 1975.) We show in chapter 5 that not only the nucleus but also all other pitch accents of the contour (see Pierrehumbert 1980) must be put into relation with rhythmic prominences.

3. Actually, Bolinger 1958b, 1981 disputes the contention that rhythm plays any role in describing the suprasegmentals of the phrase. For him, prominence above the syllable level is entirely a matter of the presence of pitch accents. We will discuss his position in sections 4.3.2 and 5.3.

4. The *focus structure* of a sentence is the "marking" of which constituents of the sentence have the property of Focus; see Chomsky 1971, Jackendoff 1972, and chapter 5.

5. Except for the theory proposed by Bresnan 1971a, 1972, according to which the NSR applies in the transformational cycle. For some remarks on the untenability of this approach, see chapter 5.

6. This approach was suggested by Prince in Prince 1981 and in class lectures. It would involve stating the NSR in a slightly different way, by substituting *is* or *must be* for *is made*.

7. These are not exactly the examples Schmerling uses, nor exactly the discourse situations she describes, though what she says in general is consistent with what we have said here. Note that Schmerling considers the placement of nuclear stress to be related to the different discourse conditions. Our position, stated in chapter 5, is that it is a matter of pitch accent assignment.

8. Vanderslice and Ladefoged 1972 offer a theory of stress and its relation to intonation that may also seem to resemble the one proposed here. With their set of binary suprasegmental features, they represent the differences stressed vs. stressless ([±heavy]), primary word stress vs. nonprimary word stress ([±accent]) and nucleus-bearing primary stress ([±intonation]). The feature

[+intonation] is assigned to the last [+accent]-bearing syllable in the sentence. Since all words contain a syllable with [+accent], by their rule all sentences will receive the feature [+intonation] (i.e., the intonational nucleus) on their last word. Like the system of SPE, Vanderslice and Ladefoged's system wrongly predicts that there is a "normal" location of nuclear prominence in the sentence—in final position. Indeed, their system is quite like SPE's in considering the distribution of the basic suprasegmental features for stress and intonation (mentioned above) to be entirely predicted on the basis of the syllable content and syntactic structure of the sentence. In other words, their [+accent] is not the analogue of our pitch accent or Newman's heavy stress.

Hirst 1980a makes a proposal somewhat similar to ours that involves assigning a feature [+accent] to any Word (but not necessarily all words) in the sentence, as an operation prior to and somehow determining the stress patterns of the sentence.

9. It should be said that this "standard claim" concerning the presence of nonnuclear final prominences within phrases embedded in the sentence is based on impressionistic and often unsystematic observations. We for the most part concur with the conclusion drawn from these observations—that there must be a linguistic representation of these felt prominences (SPE, Lieberman 1965). In so doing, we ignore the objection that no reliable measurable phonetic correlate of these lesser "degrees of stress" has so far been isolated (Lehiste 1970, Vanderslice and Ladefoged 1972).

10. The claim that when both members of a compound have pitch accents the left-hand member is prominent is false, for reasons explained in section 5.3.

11. The point that every rule has a domain, in this sense, is made in SPE (appendix to chapter 8). On prosodic structure constituents as domains, see, for example, Selkirk 1980b.

12. Of course, why this should be the case is itself an interesting question. We believe the answer is straightforward. In our theory, "stress rules" are rules for building a phonological representation on the basis of a syntactic representation. They form part of the component of grammar that maps syntax into phonology. This is why "stress rules" have syntactic domains. Now we could entertain the hypothesis that rules that were not involved in mapping syntactic structure into phonological structure, but only one phonological structure (including the terminal string) into another, had no access to syntactic information and themselves applied only once a full phonological representation (section 1.3) was established. These rules—the rules of the phonology per se—would therefore not be cyclic.

13. On the nonisomorphism of morphological structure and metrical tree structure, see Liberman and Prince 1977, Kiparsky 1979, Dell (to appear), Selkirk 1980b, Hayes 1980.

14. On this problem, Bierwisch 1968:175 remarks, "What is obviously necessary is a general principle of blocking the operation of the [phrase stress] rules at a certain stage . . ." But he avows that it cannot be formulated in terms

(then) allowed for by the grammar: ". . . the desired condition must depend somehow on the length of the constituent or on the number of accented segments within it." And he leaves the problem open.

15. Provided, of course, that either all the words bear pitch accents, or none but the last does. Otherwise the (unequal) distribution of pitch accents would determine on its own the rhythmic prominence of the sentence, and any emergent pattern would only be accidental.

16. See Liberman and Prince 1977:259, 316, where they explicitly reject an algorithm for interpreting the tree that would faithfully replicate the standard theory stress levels.

17. Dell (to appear) assumes Liberman and Prince's theory according to which the tree is "translated" into a grid, but argues that, for French, a convention different from the RPPR governs the tree-grid relation. For reasons that we will not go into here, Dell argues that the convention is that *s* is stronger than *w or the same* (on the grid).

18. We hasten to point out that the rule is doubtless restricted to apply on sequences contained within the same intonational phrase (IP). (This is a point made about the "Rhythm Rule" in French by Dell (to appear).) But whether this is because IP is a *domain* for the rule, or simply because there are silent beats at the ends of the IP is a question we cannot answer.

19. Recall that destressing rules, which are "postcyclic" (but see chapter 7), are *not* rules of grid euphony and thus are not subject to this principle of BBI. Indeed, the function of destressing rules is to demote syllables that are aligned with (only) a basic beat (and no higher one), so that they are unstressed at the surface (see section 3.3).

20. This pattern of prominence is predicted by our NSR, but not by the Compound Rule. On this matter, see note 10 and section 5.3.

21. The compounds (4.54a,b,e) normally have right-hand prominence when pitch accents are assigned (cf. section 5.2.5 and Kingdon 1958a).

22. The secondary stress of the entire phrase is marked with a grave accent. No other nonprimary stresses are noted here.

23. Of course Dell's (to appear) formulation of the French analogue to the RPPR encounters no such problems, allowing for evenness. See also Liberman 1975, where the interpretation "*s* is no weaker than *w*" is also proposed.

24. This fact has been noted in the literature on speech timing (see, for example, Coker, Umeda, and Browman 1973). Bolinger 1981 has pointed it out as well.

25. Note that this is not the explanation for the lack of Beat Movement in *Marcel proved* . . . that we offered in Selkirk 1978c, where we argued that the difference between that expression and *Marcel Proust* lay in their organization into phonological phrases. The "Rhythm Rule" was taken to have the phonological phrase as its domain, and each word of *Marcel proved* was said to be a

phonological phrase, so that the "Rhythm Rule" could not apply. For reasons given in chapter 6, we now believe that the syntactic timing (silent grid position) approach, first hinted at by Liberman 1975, is far superior.

26. Bolinger 1981 makes a proposal that has the same stress-timing flavor but is not formulated in terms of a rhythmic structure such as the grid. His proposal is that a "long" [stressed] syllable becomes "extra long" before another "long" (p. 17). He points to extra length in the last syllable in *réprobàte jùstificátion,* but not in *sénsitive jùstificátion.*

27. An alternative to a "stress-timing" account of this lengthening would be one of the sort proposed by Liberman 1975, who allows for a "late-level" addition of clash-eliminating silent demibeats and beats to the metrical grid alignment of the sentence. We have resisted adopting this approach so far, restricting the system in such a way that demibeats (and the beats added on top of them) come into existence only through (a) universal Demibeat Addition, which aligns syllables with the grid, or (b) Silent Demibeat Addition, which produces syntactic timing. The idea behind this restriction is that unconstrained introduction of clash-eliminating demibeats probably allows more descriptive latitude than is desirable. But perhaps recourse to such additions will have to be made, if a stress-timing account of lengthening is found to be incorrect.

28. The reader is invited to ignore the fact that *Montana* is on its own reluctant to undergo Beat Movement. In this respect, *Montana* and *good-looking* should be quite comparable.

29. This explanation would seem to contradict Dell's (to appear) "primat des niveaux inférieurs," according to which there is a stronger tendency to attain grid euphony at lower levels than at higher ones, and which would therefore predict a lesser incidence of Beat Movement in cases like *good-looking cowboy.* The fact is that in English clashes appear to be more tolerable at lower levels of the grid than at higher ones.

30. The word *research* has another pronunciation, *résèarch,* with primary stress on the first syllable. Note that the Beat Movement possible in *phònological résearch* is also problematic, since the presence of a silent demibeat after -*ical* would induce Beat Addition on the basic beat level and thereby eliminate the clash.

31. Halliday 1967b:208 points out that *He teaches classics* pronounced with a pitch accent (tone, or whatever) on both *teaches* and *classics* is rhythmically distinct from *He teaches classics* pronounced with no tone on *teaches.* In the first case *teaches* is longer, as would follow from ascribing it a greater grid prominence in view of its pitch accent assignment.

32. It is also possible that Beat Movement can apply here because, in some cases, Beat Addition fails to apply. Beat Addition is by no means obligatory, though it usually applies at the lower levels. In fast speech, however, its application may be suspended, even at the lower levels.

Chapter 5

1. Pierrehumbert 1980 borrows the notion "boundary tone" from Liberman 1975 and the notion "phrase accent" from Bruce 1977.

2. The literature on the expressive meaning of intonation is quite extensive. See Ladd 1980 for a review and references.

3. To say this is in effect to deny that the presence of the high rise at the end of a yes-no question in English (an "expressive" feature in that *high* "means" something different from *low* in this position) is systematically related to the presence of any particular grammatical feature in the sentence. We believe this to be the case—that the choice of intonational contour and the choice of grammatical structure (subject-auxiliary inversion) are independent, though they may converge on the same sentence, having as they do an overlap in discourse function.

4. We will give reasons below for not identifying *focus structure* with what Chomsky and Jackendoff might call *focus-presupposition structure,* where the presupposition structure in some sense contains the focus or foci of a sentence.

5. In other languages it is conceivable that intonational structure is irrelevant to focus, or that intonational structure is only one of several grammatical features related to focus, including word order, the presence of particles, and so on.

6. We draw no distinction here between surface structure and S-structure (Chomsky 1981). What we are calling *surface syntactic structure* is that which is mapped into logical form, on the one hand, and into phonological representation, on the other.

7. See Guéron 1980 on the need for representing focus in logical form, as well as Reinhart 1976 for arguments to this conclusion based on coreference.

8. In the generative tradition, these include the theories of Chomsky 1971, Jackendoff 1972, Bing 1979a,b, Ladd 1980, Williams 1980b, and even Schmerling 1976. In some respects our proposal will seem most similar to Schmerling's; but there are essential differences, as we will show in section 5.2.

9. We should point out that Williams's 1980b theory of focus is explicitly based on the assumption, which we take to be erroneous, that there are no embedded foci.

10. This formulation is not the one given in Chomsky 1971, for it relies on the notion of embedded foci, not countenanced in Chomsky's proposal. Chomsky's focus rule says that a constituent may be a focus if it contains the intonational center of the sentence, the location of the intonational center being determined by principles such as the NSR and Compound Rule of SPE.

11. Nomi Erteschik-Shir (personal communication) observes that focus of the postverbal indirect object in English is necessarily narrow, at least for some speakers. In (i), then, the VP cannot be focused:

(i) She offered PETE the recipes.

This observation, if true, would support the idea that the focus of a higher constituent is determined by the "place" of a focused constituent contained within it in the argument structure of the phrase. It would suggest, too, that the Phrasal Focus Rule should be refined to attend to differences in the *types* of arguments contained within the higher constituent.

12. (5.18a,b) are discussed by Berman and Szamosi 1972, Bresnan 1972, Bolinger 1972a, and Schmerling 1976, for example. See Guéron 1980 for some important insights regarding the logical form and focus properties of such sentences.

(5.18c) is discussed by Bolinger 1965b and Ladd 1980.

13. All of this is doubtless related to the notion of "topic," which we ignore here but will have to contend with at some point. On "topic" vs. "focus," see Halliday 1967b.

14. These examples are drawn from Halliday 1967b, though our interpretation of them differs somewhat from Halliday's.

15. We will assume that in both cases *hill* is the head of the NP, and thus that its focus is the one that guarantees NP focus. When the geographic term *lake* precedes, it may or may not be focused, perhaps because it is in some sense redundant. *Lake HILL* (or *Lake ERIE*) may be in some way comparable to locutions of the type *my sister/SISTER ANDREA*. As for *LAKE HILL* (*NOB HILL*), the first element is perhaps preferentially focused because of its status as a proper name itself.

16. We owe this example to Stephanie Shattuck-Hufnagel.

17. We will assume that each word either capitalized or annotated with an integer for "stress" bears a focus-relevant prosodic prominence, i.e., a pitch accent. Our version of the NSR will guarantee the relative degree of prominence of the pitch-accent-bearing syllables (cf. section 5.3.4).

18. A further problem for a surface structure application of the NSR pointed out by Bierwisch is posed by the contrast between (i) and (ii):

(i)

a. $\overset{2}{\text{Pe}}$ter betra$\overset{1}{\text{c}}$htet das B$\overset{3}{\text{u}}$ch.

b. $\overset{2}{\text{Pe}}$ter hat das B$\overset{3}{\text{u}}$ch betra$\overset{1}{\text{c}}$htet.

(ii)

a. $\overset{2}{\text{Pe}}$ter sch$\overset{3}{\text{a}}$ut das B$\overset{3}{\text{u}}$ch $\overset{1}{\text{a}}$n.

b. $\overset{2}{\text{Pe}}$ter hat das B$\overset{3}{\text{u}}$ch ange$\overset{1}{\text{s}}$chaut.

In all these sentences the NPs are "accentless" and constitute old information. The problem is to explain why the "default accent" in such cases falls on the verb *betrachtet* in (ia) but on the separable prefix *an* in (iia). Bierwisch suggests that the accent falls on *an* instead of the main verb in (iia) for the same reason that it does in (iib), and allows for the possibility that this greater stress on *an* in (iia) is assigned *prior* to the verb's moving into second position. An analysis of this general type is not available in our system (for reasons explained in section

5.2.3 in our discussion of a not dissimilar proposal by Bresnan 1971, 1972). However, at the moment we do not have an explanation for these facts. Probably they result from the status of *an* as some sort of argument of the verb, one receiving focus in preference to the verb itself.

19. The fact that substituting *woman* or *child* for *man* in (5.59a) would require focus on the NP, as in (5.60a–c), shows quite well that "redundancy" is not entirely a matter of sentence-internal semantics, but requires some implicit reference to (possibly) shared assumptions about the nature of the world at large.

20. This is in fact not Newman's transcription. He writes the examples as follows:

(i)
a. ...instrúctions to lèave...
b. ...instrúctions to léave...

(ii)
a. ...pláns to wrìte...
b. ...pláns to wríte...

Still, our transcription preserves his intent. The "heavy stresses" indicated by his acute accents are our capitalized (focus-relevant) prosodic prominences.

21. Here we coincide with Bolinger 1981, D. Jones 1964, and others, who point out that in cases of "semantic fusion" the (Germanic) left-prominence rule is at play.

22. We repeat here Kingdon's 1958a caution not to assume that the basic pattern of compounds such as these is left prominence. As Kingdon points out, such compounds are often prenominal, and in that position regularly undergo a leftward shift in prominence (our Beat Movement), so that statistically speaking they may appear most often with left prominence. But their right prominence in non–stress shift environments reveals their true character.

23. Recall the discussion of "semantically rich heads" in German. See Bolinger 1972a for more examples of compounds of this kind.

24. See Ladd 1980 for a discussion of the *Madison Avenue/Madison Street* contrast, which, in our framework, could be seen as resulting from the operation of the Redundant Focus Rule.

25. See also Hirst 1980b, 1983 for a very interesting approach to the characterization of phonetic rules realizing F_0 contours of English on the basis of a string of tonal segments, which are the phonological representation of the intonational contour.

26. Clements 1981b and Huang 1979 have argued for a metrical tree approach to the representation of tone as an account of downstep and downdrift, for example, and Gårding 1982 argues for "global" features of contours.

27. Both sentences have a pitch accent on *legumes,* which is to say that *legumes* is focused. It happens to be the only focus of the sentences. The H boundary tones could be interpreted as indicating a question.

28. Pierrehumbert 1980 remarks that (5.90c) would be an appropriate answer to the question "What's this?", that (5.90d) might "convey judiciousness," and that the pattern (5.90e) is "often used to convey surprise, or to imply that the speaker is repeating something he really should not have to repeat." Patterns (5.90a) and (5.90b) are typical questions.

29. Pierrehumbert proposes a finite state grammar like the one in the figure below a model of the "syntax" of the English intonational contour.

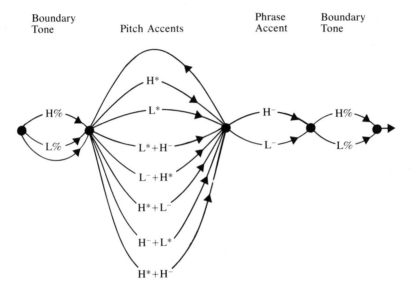

30. But see Bing 1979a, according to whom certain aspects of the contour are predictable on the basis of others. Dell (to appear) also suggests this for French. These cases need renewed investigation.

31. Actually, the claim is a bit too strong, for under certain conditions more than one pitch accent may be assigned to a single word. This does not change the focus structure of the sentence, however. That is, the word is not doubly focused, and the focus properties of the sentence are the same as they would be if the word had one pitch accent. (See examples below in the text.)

Chapter 6

1. The work of Cooper and his colleagues is especially noteworthy. Cooper and Paccia-Cooper 1980 draws together work from earlier studies, e.g., Cooper, Paccia, and Lapointe 1978, Cooper, Lapointe, and Paccia 1977, Cooper 1976a,b. Also bearing directly on this issue are Klatt 1975, 1976, Lehiste 1973a, Lea 1974. See Lehiste 1980 for a useful review. For work of a nonexperimental nature on this topic, see D. Jones 1964, Abercrombie 1967, 1968, Catford 1966, Gimson 1970, Pike 1945.

2. Most of the data on pausing and final lengthening comes from research on speech production; see note 1.

3. This example and its counterpart in (6.2) are discussed in Cooper et al. 1978 and Cooper and Paccia-Cooper 1980.

4. The restriction to final syllables is demonstrated in Nakatani, O'Connor, and Aston 1981.

5. The number and nature of segments in a syllable, the number of syllables in the word, and other factors combine to determine the actual duration of syllables. See Klatt 1976 for a useful review of the various influences on duration.

6. But see Scott 1982 for evidence suggesting the existence of the predicted negative correlation between lengthening and pausing.

7. In the literature on duration, it is often pointed out that final lengthening and pausing seem to appear in the same sorts of syntactic contexts (cf. Pike 1945, Klatt 1975). While this is of course just what we would expect, given our theory, this observation is too vague to be decisive. It would also be consistent with a theory according to which pausing and final lengthening were independent processes, but tended to apply in the same sorts of syntactic contexts. The important and very specific prediction that our theory makes is that for any syntactic context the overall contribution of pausing and final lengthening to duration is fixed, and that within that overall duration there is a negative correlation between the two.

8. But this *ritardando* effect is found only at the end of the sentence (Nakatani, O'Connor, and Aston 1981, Klatt 1976).

9. The asymmetry may not be complete. There is some indication of a degree of pausing before clause boundaries (Cooper 1976a,b), but the effect has not been fully substantiated.

10. The greater likelihood that pitch accents will appear on nouns than on verbs, for example, may explain some slight durational differences in the length of noun- and verb-final syllables noted by Cooper and Paccia-Cooper 1980, who did not control for F_0 in their study.

11. The data concerning this example are from a spectrogram brought to my attention by Victor Zue.

12. There is no substantial pitch movement on *is* here, so its length cannot be attributed to F_0 factors.

13. It is unfortunate that in studying syntactic influences on timing, Cooper and his colleagues did not control for any of these well-known aspects of phonological representation and their effect on final lengthening and pausing (see, for example, Cooper and Paccia-Cooper 1980).

14. Note that because the presence or absence of a vowel before the inflectional ending *'s* affects the number of syllables in the phrase (and hence the metrical grid alignment and the possibility of Beat Movement), the rules deter-

mining whether the ending will have a syllabic or nonsyllabic form must apply *before* Beat Movement.

15. The work of Cooper, Lapointe, and Paccia 1977 confirms the effect. In virtually all the syntactic contexts they examined, with artfully chosen minimal pairs, a stressed syllable preceding a stressless one was longer when the stressless syllable belonged to a following word than when it belonged to the same word (and was word-final in it).

16. Catford speaks of this difference as being optional. Since, on our theory, none of the rules of SDA is optional, we must conclude that the impression of an (optional) lack of rhythmic disjuncture must be attributed to some other factor, perhaps to a faster rate of speech.

17. In her work on the effects of syntax on timing, Lehiste 1973a, 1980 points to the existence of a greater length of time between the main stresses flanking a constituent break when that break is more substantial. She does not localize the contribution to greater length. Examining the same sorts of sentences employed by Lehiste, Macdonald 1976 shows that the greater length is indeed localized on the final syllable of the left-hand constituent at the break.

18. Goldhor 1976, reported in Klatt 1976, finds the N at the end of a subject NP to be longer when the NP branches into A+N than when it consists of N alone.

19. Recall that it is because SDA is asymmetrical, applying at the (right) ends of words and phrases, that it is disjuncture from the right (or following) sister phrase that is important.

20. Cheng cites one pronunciation of sentence (6.33) that does not at all follow from our theory of disjuncture, and for which we ourselves will not hazard an explanation. The sentence is this:

(i)
lau li mai siau pi
2   2   3   2   3

Here, the change of tone on the subject is apparently being "caused" by the tone 3 on the verb, yet the verb is itself unaffected by a following tone 3 at this rate of speech. Cheng discusses this puzzling case, a pronunciation that appears at a rather slow rate of speech, and ultimately opts for what one might call a "phonological solution" of this problem over a simple syntactic account of the phenomenon. The solution involves certain assumptions about the mode of application of his Tone Sandhi Rule and the nature of intermediate tonal representations. We will not investigate it here.

21. See, for example, Camilli 1911, 1941, 1963, Norman 1937, Bianchi 1948, Fiorelli 1958, Leone 1962, Pratelli 1970, Saltarelli 1970, Nespor 1977, Vogel 1977, Rotenberg 1978, Napoli and Nespor 1979, Nespor and Vogel 1979, 1982, Chierchia 1982a,b,c.

22. Chierchia 1982b discusses apparent exceptions to this generalization.

23. They weaken the claim in the case where C = Sentence, and thus where the left-hand phrase would be NP. A subject NP can branch, they assert, and still RS may take place between its last word and the first word of the following phrase. Our account would give no such privileged status to a subject NP, for example. Perhaps in Italian no special weight is given to being a daughter of S, as SDA (6.13) would predict. But even if clause (d) were eliminated from SDA in Italian, we could still not explain why branching counts less with daughters of S than with other constituents, as Napoli and Nespor's account would imply. Clearly, the facts bear further examination.

24. Chierchia also points out that there is *no* RS in environments where the weakened version of the Left Branch Condition, discussed in note 23, predicts it should appear. This is shown by examples (6.38) and (6.39).

25. See Basbøll 1975, 1978 for some very interesting further work on French liaison and the characterization of the junctural properties of the sentence.

Chapter 7

1. For details of the phonology of function words in English, see, for example, Zwicky 1970 and Selkirk 1972.

2. In (7.1) the reduction to [ə] or [ɪ], the loss of [ə] or [ɪ] and accompanying syllabification of sonorant consonants, and the deletion of /h/ all testify to the stressless status of the function words here.

The strong form of *a,* [ej], might well be considered a suppletive variant.

3. See Abercrombie 1964, who argues that, rhythmically speaking, a stressless object pronoun must be part of a word with (enclitic to) a preceding verb, as in *feel it.* Jassem 1949, 1952 underlines the rhythmically proclitic character of the other examples here.

4. Rotenberg 1978 has undertaken to describe some of the phenomena we will be (re)treating here in terms of junctural relations defined strictly on the basis of syntactic structure. For the reasons given in chapter 6, we think a syntactic theory of juncture is inadequate, being unable to come to terms with all the facts.

5. In Selkirk 1972 we argue against the position taken in Bresnan 1971b that stressless function words like those in (7.1) and (7.6) are syntactically proclitic to what follows.

6. On *to*-contraction, see the references in Postal and Pullum 1982; on *not*-contraction, see Zwicky and Pullum 1982.

7. We adopt Kaisse's 1981b position that there is a rule of Aux Contraction, but not the analysis she provides of it.

8. See Piera 1978 for an interesting treatment of the stress level of function words in the framework of Liberman and Prince 1977.

9. *Must* might qualify as a CVC, rather than CVCC, if *st* in general qualifies as a single C, an idea pursued in Selkirk 1978b.

10. See section 7.1.3 for some discussion of why *too* does not destress.

11. Kiparsky 1979 explicitly adopts this position.

12. A third alternative would be to view cyclic rules as being divided into two sets, rules for the word and rules for the sentence, the former of course preceding the latter. Monosyllabic Destressing could be thought of as a sentence cycle rule, beginning to apply on the lowest constituent of the syntax, the word, and proceeding "upward." This conception does not make the ordering of Monosyllabic Destressing after the cyclic word stress rules crucially depend on the Word-Root distinction, available in English but perhaps not in other languages.

13. We are not able to show that one instance of destressing on a lower phrasal domain crucially precedes an instance on a higher phrasal domain, which would provide an additional argument for cyclicity. This sort of argument is not available partly because destressing is only optional; see section 7.1.3.

14. Recall, though, that SDA does not precede destressing within the word domain (section 6.2.1). If it did, no word-final syllable would be able to destress. We ensure that SDA will not block word-final destressing by requiring it to wait to add a word-final silent demibeat until the next higher domain.

15. Note, though, that true diphthongs like [aw], [aj], and [ɔj) are always stressed.

16. The pronunciation [ej] for *a* may only be available when under pitch accent. *A(n)* is a sandhi form, as is [ðij] for *the*, which is also an "emphatic" form of the article.

17. The regular presence of a pitch accent on question words like *how, when,* and *who* may be what blocks a reduction of *who* to [hʊ] in initial position. See Kaisse (1981a) for a different view of the phenomenon.

18. The presence of a pitch accent on *is* in locutions like *the fact is, the point is* will explain the lack of destressing in (i) and (ii), but why that pitch accent should be there we cannot say.

(i)

$$pa$$
$$|$$

The fact is that I can't answer the question.

(ii)

$$pa$$
$$|$$

The point is that nothing can be done about it.

19. Rhythmic alternations in the appearance of the weak forms of function words like those cited here were analyzed by Giegerich 1978, who, following Jespersen 1909, 1962, saw them as reflecting the essentially rhythmic character of speech. Giegerich's analysis is an attempt to couch these insights in a standard SPE format by a rule (optionally) introducing the feature [+stress] on

what are assumed to be basically stressless function words. Clearly Beat Addition on the second metrical level is the analogue in our framework of a rule such as Giegerich's. Aside from the differences in framework, and in assumptions about the generality of this alternating pattern in English, there is one aspect of Giegerich's analysis that we take issue with. Giegerich establishes a "hierarchy of stressability" among function words in order to explain why the "preferred result" of his stressing rule is, for example, (ia) rather than (ib), or (iia) rather than (iib).

(i)
a. | those who are | here   b. *those | who are | here
(ii)
a. | whom will you | meet   b. *whom | will you | meet

Those and *whom* are said to be higher in the hierarchy than *who* and *will,* respectively, and the rule itself is understood to be sensitive to this hierarchy. However, we think that it wrongly characterizes the facts to view the preferred rhythmic patterns of (i) and (ii) as resulting from a hierarchy-respecting application of the alternating stress rule. In both (i) and (ii) the function word that is rhythmically prominent also bears a pitch accent, and it is focused. In our system this means that Beat Addition, or Giegerich's analogue to it, is not at all responsible for the rhythmic prominence here, and that in and of themselves, as bearers of a pitch accent, these function words merit rhythmic prominence. We submit that virtually all of Giegerich's cases of function words appearing higher in a putative hierarchy of stressability are simply cases of sentences where those function words naturally receive pitch accents (hence, focus) and thus greater stress.

20. There is a line from a popular song that plays on the ungrammaticality of this final *'m:*
    . . . I'm biding my time
    'Cause that's the kind of guy I'm.

21. These examples are due to Hirst 1977b.

22. Note that *who* is a personal pronoun and behaves like one. See section 7.1.2.

23. This is in a sense Gazdar's solution. Indeed, he claims (for quite different reasons) that there is in fact no trace in this position.

24. See Selkirk 1972 for arguments against Bresnan's own particular proposal.

25. Note example (i), culled from a newspaper advertisement for a fancy game.
(i)
Looks as good as it's fun to play.

26. Rather than deletion, of course, there may simply be "dummy" categories in the place of the ellipses. Which of these ways of characterizing phenomena like gapping or "VP Deletion" is correct is not important to the point at hand, however.

27. These examples are not so easy to construct. One "function" of placing parentheticals after an item is often enough to make a focus on the preceding word quite natural.

28. See Rotenberg 1978 on a very interesting approach to parentheticals as syntactic objects.

29. We ignore here the issue of the "liberal dialects" discussed by Postal and Pullum 1982. Perhaps speakers of these dialects have a rhythm-based *To* Contraction applying anywhere.

30. It is sometimes said that *it* cannot bear an "emphatic stress" or be focused. Examples we have found show that, if there is some restriction on *it*, it is not the one mentioned:

(i)
The fact that NP_i is ... is indicated by the arc between IT_i and ...

(ii)
IT, too, is something of a problem.

(iii)
That seems to be IT!

(iv)
If you HAVE this, why don't you just use IT to get ...

31. Wasow 1975 uses the supposed sensitivity of rules like Dative Movement and Particle Movement to the pronominal status of an NP to argue that pronouns are base-generated. While we agree with Wasow's conclusion, we do not accept the argument based on these transformations.

32. Note that pronouns in deep structure second position in double object constructions have the same sort of acceptability as pronouns supposedly moved to second position transformationally:

(i)
a. We called John it (that bad name).
b. She envied Mary him.
c. I promised the folks her.

Acceptability is improved when both objects are pronouns, as in the Dative Movement case:

(ii)
a. We call him it.
b. She envied her him.
c. I promised them her.

33. Though it must be said that when both objects are pronouns the result is better. See note 32.

34. Note that contrary to popular belief (cf. Stillings 1975), much more than a string of verbs can be gapped:

(i)
a. MARY was counting on it for a RAISE, and HELEN ___ for a PRO-MOTION.
b. MCGRAW-HILL sent it to her in APRIL, and HARCOURT BRACE ___ in MAY.
c. SOME people looked at it for HOURS, and OTHERS ___ for days on END.

We suggest a very tentative analysis of gapping here, in the form of the following rule:

(ii)
Gapping
A constituent C_n in a sentence S_j may delete if:
a. it is not a focus;
b. it is identical to a constituent C_m in the preceding sentence S_i (i.e., if it is retrievable); and
c. if for every focus F_i in S_i there is a corresponding (paired) focus F'_i in S_j.

The rule says, essentially, that an identical constituent may delete if it is embedded in an appropriate parallel focus structure. There is doubtless more to the rule than this, but it seems worth offering in order to put its focus-related conditions up for discussion.

35. Note that if Pronoun Encliticization were cyclic, it would produce the wrong results in Verb Second constructions, which postpose a subject NP only if the verb has no complement:

(i)
*John the woods $_V$[pushed them]$_V$ John

(ii)
*Away $_V$[drove it]$_V$ Mary

36. Postal 1974 argues that there is a clausemate condition on Pronoun Encliticization, but the facts supporting this position are subtle and somewhat variable ones relating to segmental phonology, so we prefer not to explore them here.

37. As a last comment on the syntactic status of the rule, we should point out that it is not sensitive to the presence of NP-trace in surface structure. A passive sentence whose (derived) subject was originally in first NP object position may show encliticization of the second NP object pronoun:

(i)
a. Bill was given it for the last time.
b. No interpretation was assigned them [m], and I know why.

But because *Wh* Movement is not possible out of that first object position, we have no information about what is a potential contrast; thus it is not clear what interpretation is warranted by the facts of (i).

38. A failure to control for the presence of pitch accent led to a rather inadequate presentation of the relevant facts in Selkirk 1972.

39. Some aspects of Auxiliary Deletion are regular, some are rather particular (Zwicky 1970), and one might be tempted to view some contractions as suppletive variants of the parent weak form. However, the fact that they may be suppletions does not require us to view Aux Contraction as a syntactic rule, as Kaisse 1981b suggests. The important fact about contraction suppletion is that it does not refer to the morphemic or categorial status of the elements in its immediate environment, permitting us to see it as at least a rule of the syntax-phonology mapping, if not a rule of the phonology.

40. Zwicky 1970 has a good discussion of the relevant facts.

41. With a certain amount of formal legerdemain, we managed in Selkirk 1972 to describe the facts of Aux Deletion without assuming an encliticization.

42. We assume that the rules that give the *'s* of *has* and *is* the same surface form as the inflectional endings *-s* will operate after Aux Contraction and Aux Deletion, giving [z] and its variants in close juncture to what precedes.

43. Kaisse formulates the rule as follows:

NP Aux X
 1   2   3 $\Rightarrow$ 1 # 2, 3

Where 1 c-commands 2 and 3 followed 2 at NP-Structure and where if 1 is a (monosyllabic) non-lexical item it need not be an NP and X must merely not mark a movement or deletion site.

The condition on factor 3, a resuscitation of Lakoff's 1970 global condition on *be* contraction, says virtually nothing more than that the Aux cannot be followed by a *wh*-trace or a parenthetical. On the notion NP-structure, see Van Riemsdijk and Williams 1980.

References

Abercrombie, D. 1964. Syllable quantity and enclitics in English. In D. Abercrombie, D. Fry, P. MacCarthy, N. Scott, and J. Trim, eds., *In Honour of Daniel Jones: Papers Contributed on the Occasion of His Eightieth Birthday, 12 Sept. 1961*. London: Longmans.

Abercrombie, D. 1967. *Elements of General Phonetics*. Edinburgh: Edinburgh University Press.

Abercrombie, D. 1968. Some functions of silent stress. *Work in Progress* 2, 1–10. Department of Phonetics and Linguistics, University of Edinburgh.

Adams, V. 1973. *An Introduction to Modern English Word Formation*. London: Longmans.

Allen, G. 1972. The location of rhythmic stress beats in English: An experimental study II. *Language and Speech* 15, 179–195.

Allen, G. 1973. Segmental timing control in speech production. *Journal of Phonetics* 1, 219–237.

Allen, G. 1975. Speech rhythm: Its relation to performance universals and articulatory timing. *Journal of Phonetics* 3, 75–86.

Allen, M. 1978. Morphological investigations. Doctoral dissertation, University of Connecticut.

Allen, W. 1954. *Living English Speech: Stress and Intonation Practice for the Foreign Student*. London: Longmans.

Anderson, J., and C. Jones. 1974. Three theses concerning phonological representations. *Journal of Linguistics* 10, 1–26.

Anderson, S. 1971. On algorithms for applying phonological rules. *Quarterly Progress Report* 103, 159–164. Research Laboratory of Electronics, Massachusetts Institute of Technology.

Anderson, S. 1974. *The Organization of Phonology*. New York: Academic Press.

Bach, E. 1983. On the relationship between word-grammar and phrase-grammar. *Natural Language and Linguistic Theory* 1.1.

Baker, C., and M. Brame. 1972. Global rules: A rejoinder. *Language* 48, 51–75.

Basbøll, H. 1975. Grammatical boundaries in phonology. *Annual Report of the Institute of Phonetics of the University of Copenhagen* 9, 109–135.

Basbøll, H. 1978. Boundaries and ranking rules in French phonology. In B. de Cornulier and F. Dell, eds., *Etudes de phonologie française*. Paris: Editions du Centre National de la Recherche Scientifique.

Bell, A., and J. Hooper., eds. 1978. *Syllables and Segments*. Amsterdam: North Holland.

Berman, A., and M. Szamosi. 1972. Observations on sentential stress. *Language* 48, 304–325.

Bianchi, E. 1948. Alcune osservazioni sul rafforzamento consonantico nel parlar fiorentino. *Lingua Nostra* 9, 76–77.

Bierwisch, M. 1966. Regeln für die Intonation deutscher Sätze. *Studia Grammatica 7: Untersuchungen über Akzent und Intonation im Deutschen*, 99–201. Berlin: Akademie-Verlag.

Bierwisch, M. 1968. Two critical problems in accent rules. *Journal of Linguistics* 4, 173–178.

Bing, J. 1979a. Aspects of English prosody. Doctoral dissertation, University of Massachusetts at Amherst.

Bing, J. 1979b. A reanalysis of obligatory "comma" pause in English. *University of Massachusetts Occasional Papers in Linguistics* 5, 1–23.

Bloch, B., and G. Trager. 1942. *Outline of Linguistic Analysis*. (Linguistic Society of America: Special Publication) Baltimore: Waverly Press.

Bloomfield, L. 1933. *Language*. New York: Holt, Rinehart and Winston.

Bolinger, D. 1958a. Stress and information. *American Speech* 33, 5–20.

Bolinger, D. 1958b. A theory of pitch accent in English. *Word* 14, 109–149.

Bolinger, D. 1961. Contrastive accent and contrastive stress. *Language* 37, 83–96.

Bolinger, D. 1965a. *Forms of English: Accent, Morpheme, Order*. Cambridge, Mass.: Harvard University Press.

Bolinger, D. 1965b. Pitch accents and sentence rhythm. In D. Bolinger 1965a.

Bolinger, D. 1971. *The Phrasal Verb in English*. Cambridge, Mass.: Harvard University Press.

Bolinger, D. 1972a. Accent is predictable (if you're a mind reader). *Language* 48, 633–644.

Bolinger, D., ed. 1972b. *Intonation: Selected Readings*. London: Penguin.

Bolinger, D. 1981. Two kinds of vowels, two kinds of rhythm. Available from the Indiana University Linguistics Club, Bloomington. To appear in *Language*.

Bolinger, D., and L. Gerstman. 1957. Disjuncture as a cue to constructs. *Word* 13, 246–255.

Boxwell, H., and M. Boxwell. 1966. Weri phonemes. In S. Wurm, ed., *Papers in New Guinea Linguistics, No. 5*, 77–93. Australian National University at Canberra.

Bradley, D. 1978. Computational distinctions of vocabulary type. Doctoral dissertation, Massachusetts Institute of Technology.

Bresnan, J. 1971a. Sentence stress and syntactic transformations. *Language* 47, 257–281.

Bresnan, J. 1971b. Contraction and the transformational cycle in English. Ms., Massachusetts Institute of Technology. Available from the Indiana University Linguistics Club, Bloomington.

Bresnan, J. 1972. Stress and syntax: A reply. *Language* 48, 326–342.

Bresnan, J. 1976. On the form and functioning of transformations. *Linguistic Inquiry* 7, 3–40.

Bresnan, J. ed. 1982. *The Mental Representation of Grammatical Relations*. Cambridge, Mass.: The MIT Press.

Bruce, G. 1977. *Swedish Word Accents in Sentence Perspective*. Gleerup: Lund.

Bunn, G., and R. Bunn. 1970. *Golin Phonology*. Pacific Linguistics Monograph Series A, No. 23, 1–7. Australian National University at Canberra.

Cairns, C., and M. Feinstein. 1982. Markedness and the theory of syllable structure. *Linguistic Inquiry* 13, 193–226.

Camilli, A. 1911. Ancora dei rafforzamenti iniziali in italiano. *Le Maître Phonétique*.

Camilli, A. 1941. I rafforzamenti iniziali. *Lingua Nostra* 3, 170–174.

Camilli, A. 1963. *Pronuncia e grafia dell'italiano*. Florence: Sansoni.

Carlson, L. 1978. Word stress in Finnish. Ms., Massachusetts Institute of Technology.

Carlson, L. 1982. Dialogue games: An approach to discourse analysis. Doctoral dissertation, Massachusetts Institute of Technology.

Carlson, R., B. Granström, and D. Klatt. 1979. Some notes on the perception of temporal patterns in speech. *Proceedings of the Ninth International Congress of Phonetic Sciences*, Copenhagen, Vol. 2, 260–267.

Catford, J. 1966. English phonology and the teaching of pronunciation. *College English* 27, 605–613.

Catford, J. 1977. *Fundamental Problems in Phonetics*. Bloomington: Indiana University Press.

Chafe, W. 1976. Givenness, contrastiveness, definiteness, subjects, topics and points of view. In C. Li, ed., *Subject and Topic*, 22–55. New York: Academic Press.

Cheng, C. 1968. Mandarin phonology. Doctoral dissertation, University of Illinois at Urbana.

Chierchia, G. 1982a. An autosegmental theory of radoppiamento. In J. Pustejovsky and P. Sells, eds., *Proceedings of the Twelfth Annual Meeting of NELS*, Massachusetts Institute of Technology.

Chierchia, G. 1982b. Syntactic conditions on external sandhi in Italian and the metrical grid. Ms., Department of Linguistics, University of Massachusetts at Amherst.

Chierchia, G. 1982c. Length in Italian and the autosegmental framework. Ms., Department of Linguistics, University of Massachusetts at Amherst.

Chomsky, N. 1957. *Syntactic Structures*. The Hague: Mouton.

Chomsky, N. 1965. *Aspects of the Theory of Syntax*. Cambridge, Mass.: The MIT Press.

Chomsky, N. 1970. Remarks on nominalization. In R. Jacobs and P. Rosenbaum, eds., *Readings in English Transformational Grammar*, 184–221. Waltham, Mass.: Ginn. Reprinted in Chomsky 1972b.

Chomsky, N. 1971. Deep structure, surface structure and semantic interpretation. In D. Steinberg and L. Jakobovits, eds., *Semantics: An Interdisciplinary Reader in Philosophy, Linguistics and Psychology*, 183–216. Cambridge: Cambridge University Press. Reprinted in Chomsky 1972b.

Chomsky, N. 1972a. Some empirical issues in the theory of transformational grammar. In S. Peters, ed., *The Goals of Linguistic Theory*. Englewood Cliffs, N.J.: Prentice-Hall. Reprinted in Chomsky 1972b.

Chomsky, N. 1972b. *Studies in Generative Grammar*. The Hague: Mouton.

Chomsky, N. 1973. Conditions on transformations. In S. Anderson and P. Kiparsky, eds., *A Festschrift for Morris Halle*, 232–286. New York: Holt, Rinehart and Winston.

Chomsky, N. 1980. On binding. *Linguistic Inquiry* 11, 1–46.

Chomsky, N. 1981. *Lectures on Government and Binding*. Dordrecht: Foris.

Chomsky, N., and M. Halle. 1968. *The Sound Pattern of English*. New York: Harper and Row.

Chomsky, N., M. Halle, and F. Lukoff. 1956. On accent and juncture in English. In M. Halle, H. Lunt, and H. MacLean, eds., *For Roman Jakobson*, 65–80. The Hague: Mouton.

Chomsky, N., and H. Lasnik. 1977. Filters and control. *Linguistic Inquiry* 8, 425–504.

Clark, M. 1978. A dynamic treatment of tone with special attention to the tonal system of Igbo. Doctoral dissertation, University of Massachusetts at Amherst.

Classe, A. (1939). *The Rhythm of English Prose*. Oxford: Basil Blackwell.

Clements, G. 1976. The autosegmental treatment of vowel harmony. In W. U. Dressler and O. E. Pfeiffer, eds., *Phonologica 1976*. Innsbrucker Beiträge zur Sprachwissenschaft. Innsbruck: Institut für Sprachwissenschaft der Universität Innsbruck (1977).

Clements, G. 1977. Tone and syntax in Ewe. In D. Napoli, ed., *Elements of Tone, Stress and Intonation*, 21–99. Washington, D.C.: Georgetown University Press.

Clements, G. 1981a. Akan vowel harmony: A nonlinear analysis. In G. Clements, ed., *Harvard Studies in Phonology*, Vol. 2.

Clements, G. 1981b. The hierarchical representation of tone features. In G. Clements, ed., *Harvard Studies in Phonology*, Vol. 2, 50–107.

Clements, G., and K. Ford. 1979. Kikuyu tone shift and its synchronic consequences. *Linguistic Inquiry* 10, 179–210.

Clements, G., and S. Keyser. 1981. A three-tiered theory of the syllable. Occasional Paper #19, Center for Cognitive Science, Massachusetts Institute of Technology.

Coker, C., N. Umeda, and C. Browman. 1973. Automatic synthesis from ordinary English text. *IEEE Transactions on Audio and Electroacoustics* AU–21, 293–297.

Cooper, G., and L. Meyer. 1960. *The Rhythmic Structure of Music*. Chicago: The University of Chicago Press.

Cooper, W. 1976a. Syntactic control of timing in speech production. Doctoral dissertation, Massachusetts Institute of Technology.

Cooper, W. 1976b. Syntactic control of timing in speech production: A study of complement structures. *Journal of Phonetics* 4, 151–171.

Cooper, W., and M. Danly. 1981. Segmental and temporal aspects of utterance-final lengthening. *Phonetica* 38, 106–115.

Cooper, W., C. Egido, and J. Paccia. 1978. Grammatical control of a phonological rule: Palatalization. *Journal of Experimental Psychology: Human Perception and Performance* 4, 264–272.

Cooper, W., S. Lapointe, and J. Paccia. 1977. Syntactic blocking of phonological rules in speech production. *Journal of the Acoustical Society of America* 61, 1314–1320.

Cooper, W., J. Paccia, and S. Lapointe. 1978. Hierarchical coding in speech timing. *Cognitive Psychology* 10, 154–177.

Cooper, W., and J. Paccia-Cooper. 1980. *Syntax and Speech*. Cambridge, Mass.: Harvard University Press.

Cooper, W., and J. Sorensen. 1981. *Fundamental Frequency in Sentence Production*. New York, Heidelberg, Berlin: Springer-Verlag.

Cooper, W., J. Sorensen, and J. Paccia. 1977. Correlations of duration for nonadjacent segments in speech: Aspects of grammatical coding. *Journal of the Acoustical Society of America* 61, 1046–1050.

Crompton, A. 1978. Generation of intonation and contours from a syntactically specified input. *Nottingham Linguistic Circular* 7, 59–112.

Crystal, D. 1969. *Prosodic Systems and Intonation in English*. Cambridge: Cambridge University Press.

Culicover, P., and M. Rochemont. 1981. Stress and focus in English. *Studies in Cognitive Science* 1, University of California at Irvine.

Danes, F. 1960. Sentence intonation from a functional point of view. *Word* 16, 34–54.

Delattre, P. 1940. Le mot est-il une entité phonétique en français? *Le Français Moderne* 8, 47–56. Also in Delattre 1966.

Delattre, P. 1961. La leçon d'intonation de Simone de Beauvoir. Etude d'intonation déclarative comparée. *The French Review* XXXV, 59–67. Also in Delattre 1966.

Delattre, P. 1966. *Studies in French and Comparative Linguistics*. Janua Linguarum Series Major XVIII. The Hague: Mouton.

Dell, F. To appear. L'accentuation dans les phrases en français. In F. Dell, J.-R. Vergnaud, and D. Hirst, eds., *Les représentations en phonologie*. Paris: Hermann.

Dell, F., and E. Selkirk. 1978. On a morphologically governed vowel alternation in French. In S. J. Keyser, ed., *Recent Transformational Studies in European Linguistics*. Linguistic Inquiry Monograph 2. Cambridge, Mass.: The MIT Press.

Donington, R. 1974. *The Interpretation of Early Music, New Version*. New York: St. Martin's Press.

Donovan, A., and C. Darwin. 1979. The perceived rhythm of speech. *Proceedings of the Ninth International Congress of Phonetic Sciences*, Copenhagen, Vol. 2, 268–274.

Downing, B. 1970. Syntactic structure and phonological phrasing in English. Doctoral dissertation, University of Texas at Austin.

Downing, B. 1973. Parenthesization rules and obligatory phrasing. *Papers in Linguistics* 6, 108–128.

Downing, P. 1977. On the creation and use of English compound nouns. *Language* 53, 810–842.

Egido, C., and W. Cooper. 1980. Blocking of alveolar flapping in speech production: The role of syntactic boundaries and deletion sites. *Journal of Phonetics* 8, 175–184.

Emonds, J. 1971. Evidence that indirect object movement is a structure preserving rule. *Foundations of Language* 8, 546–561.

Emonds, J. 1976. *A Transformational Approach to English Syntax.* New York: Academic Press.

Erteschik-Shir, N., and S. Lappin. To appear. Under stress: Functional explanation of English sentence stress. *Journal of Linguistics.*

Faure, G., D. Hirst, and M. Chafcouloff. 1980. Rhythm, isochronism, pitch, and perceived stress. In L. Waugh and C. van Schooneveld, eds., *The Melody of Language,* 71–80. Baltimore: Park Press.

Fiorelli, P. 1958. Del raddappiamento da parola a parola. *Lingua Nostra* 19, 122–127.

Fischer-Jørgensen, E. 1948. Some remarks on the function of stress with special reference to the Germanic languages. Third International Congress of Anthropological and Ethnological Sciences. Brussels: Tervuren.

Fischer-Jørgensen, E. 1975. *Trends in Phonological Theory: A Historical Introduction.* Copenhagen: Akademisk Forlag.

Fromkin, V., ed. 1978. *Tone: A Linguistic Survey.* New York: Academic Press.

Fudge, E. C. 1969. Syllables. *Journal of Linguistics* 5, 253–286.

Gårding, E. 1982. Prosodic expressions and pragmatic categories. *Lund Working Papers* 22.

Gazdar, G. 1981. Unbounded dependencies and coordinate structure. *Linguistic Inquiry* 12, 155–184.

Gee, J. P., and F. Grosjean. 1981. Performance structures: A psycholinguistic and linguistic appraisal. Ms., Northeastern University.

Giegerich, H. 1978. On the rhythmic stressing of function words: A modest proposal. *Work in Progress* 11, 42–51. Department of Linguistics, Edinburgh University.

Giegerich, H. 1980. On stress-timing in English phonology. *Lingua* 51, 187–221.

Giegerich, H. 1981a. Zero syllables in metrical theory. In W. U. Dressler, O. E. Pfeiffer, and J. R. Rennison, eds., *Phonologica 1980,* Proceedings of the 4th International Conference on Phonology, Vienna. Innsbruck.

Giegerich, H. 1981b. On the nature and scope of metrical structure. Available from the Indiana University Linguistics Club, Bloomington.

Gimson, A. 1970. *An Introduction to the Pronunciation of English*. 2nd ed. London: Edward Arnold.

Goldhor, R. 1976. Sentential determinants of duration in speech. Master's thesis, Massachusetts Institute of Technology.

Goldman-Eisler, F. 1972. Pauses, clauses, sentences. *Language and Speech* 15, 103–113.

Goldsmith, J. 1976a. Autosegmental phonology. Doctoral dissertation, Massachusetts Institute of Technology. Available from the Indiana University Linguistics Club, Bloomington.

Goldsmith, J. 1976b. An overview of autosegmental phonology. *Linguistic Analysis* 2, 23–68.

Grammont, M. 1914. *Traité pratique de pronunciation française*. 9th ed. Paris: Delagrave.

Grammont, M. 1933. *Traité de phonétique*. Paris: Delagrave.

Green, M. M., and G. E. Igwe. 1963. *A Descriptive Grammar of Igbo*. Oxford: Oxford University Press.

Guéron, J. 1980. On the syntax and semantics of PP extraposition. *Linguistic Inquiry* 11, 637–677.

Haas, M. 1977. Tonal accent in Creek. In L. Hyman, ed. 1977b.

Hale, K., and J. White Eagle. 1980. A preliminary account of Winnebago accent. *International Journal of American Linguistics* 46, 117–132.

Halle, M. 1971. Word boundaries as environments in rules. *Linguistic Inquiry* 2, 540–541.

Halle, M. 1973a. The accentuation of Russian words. *Language* 49, 312–348.

Halle, M. 1973b. Stress rules in English: A new version. *Linguistic Inquiry* 4, 451–464.

Halle, M., and S. J. Keyser. 1971. *English Stress: Its Form, Its Growth, and Its Role in Verse*. New York: Harper and Row.

Halle, M., and P. Kiparsky. 1981. Review of P. Garde, *Histoire de l'accentuation slave*. *Language* 57, 150–181.

Halle, M., and J.-R. Vergnaud. 1976. Formal phonology. Ms., Massachusetts Institute of Technology.

Halle, M., and J.-R. Vergnaud. 1979. Metrical structures in phonology. Ms., Massachusetts Institute of Technology.

Halle, M., and J.-R. Vergnaud. 1980. Three dimensional phonology. *Journal of Linguistic Research* 1, 83–105.

Halle, M., and J.-R. Vergnaud. In preparation. *Three Dimensional Phonology*. Massachusetts Institute of Technology.

Halliday, M. A. K. 1967a. *Intonation and Grammar in British English*. The Hague: Mouton.

Halliday, M. A. K. 1967b. Notes on transitivity and theme in English, Part II. *Journal of Linguistics* 3, 199–244.

Hankamer, J. 1973. Unacceptable ambiguity. *Linguistic Inquiry* 4, 17–68.

Hankamer, J., and J. Aissen. 1974. The sonority hierarchy. In A. Bruck, R. A. Fox, and M. W. LaGaly, eds., *Papers from the Parasession on Natural Phonology*, 131–145. Chicago Linguistic Society, University of Chicago.

Haraguchi, S. 1977. *The Tone Pattern of Japanese: An Autosegmental Theory of Tonology*. Tokyo: Kaitakusha.

Harris, J. 1968. *Spanish Phonology*. Cambridge, Mass.: The MIT Press.

Harris, J. 1982. *Syllable Structure and Stress in Spanish: A Nonlinear Analysis*. Linguistic Inquiry Monograph 8. Cambridge, Mass.: The MIT Press.

Haugen, E. 1956. The syllable in linguistic description. In M. Halle, H. Lunt, and H. MacLean, eds., *For Roman Jakobson*, 213–221. The Hague: Mouton.

Hayes, B. 1980. A metrical theory of stress rules. Doctoral dissertation, Massachusetts Institute of Technology.

Hayes, B. 1982. Extrametricality and English stress. *Linguistic Inquiry* 13, 227–276.

Hirst, D. J. 1976. Syntactic ambiguity and intonative features: A syntactic approach to English intonation. *Travaux de l'Institut de Phonétique d'Aix* 3, 463–493.

Hirst, D. J. 1977a. Emphatic intonation in generative grammar. In F. Carton, D. Hirst, A. Marchal, and A. Seguinot, eds., *L'Accent d'insistence/Emphatic Stress. Studia Phonetica* 12, 123–136. Paris, Montreal, Brussels: Didier.

Hirst, D. J. 1977b. *Intonative Features*. The Hague: Mouton.

Hirst, D. J. 1977c. Phonology of Intonation. *Sigma* (Revue Annuelle, 1977, No. 2). Publication du Centre d'Etudes Linguistiques. Université Paul Valéry, Montpellier.

Hirst, D. J. 1980a. Intonation et interprétation sémantique. In M. Rossi, et al. 1981.

Hirst, D. J. 1980b. Un modèle de production de l'intonation. *Travaux de l'Institut de Phonétique d'Aix* 7, 297–315.

Hirst, D. J. 1983. Structures and categories in prosodic representations. In A. Cutler and D. R. Ladd, eds., *Prosody: Models and Measurements*, 93–109. Berlin, Heidelberg, New York: Springer.

Hoard, J. 1966. Juncture and syllable structure in English. *Phonetica* 15, 96–109.

Hoard, J. 1971. Aspiration, tenseness and syllabicization in English. *Language* 47, 133–140.

Hoard, J. 1978. Remarks on the nature of syllabic stops and affricates. In A. Bell and J. Hooper, eds., 1978.

Hockett, C. F. 1955. *A Manual of Phonology*. Indiana University Publications in Anthropology and Linguistics 11. *International Journal of American Linguistics* 21.4, Part 1.

Hooper, J. 1972. The syllable in generative phonology. *Language* 48, 525–541.

Hooper, J. 1976. *An Introduction to Natural Generative Phonology*. New York: Academic Press.

Howard, I. 1972. A directional theory of rule application. Doctoral dissertation, Massachusetts Institute of Technology.

Huang, J. 1979. The metrical structure of terraced level tones. Ms., Massachusetts Institute of Technology.

Huggins, A. W. F. 1972. On the perception of temporal phenomena in speech. *Journal of the Acoustical Society of America* 51, 1279–1289.

Huggins, A. W. F. 1974. An effect of syntax in syllable timing. *Quarterly Progress Report* 114, 179–185. Research Laboratory of Electronics, Massachusetts Institute of Technology.

Huggins, A. W. F. 1975. On isochrony and syntax. In G. Fant and M. A. A. Tatham, eds., *Auditory Analysis and Perception of Speech*. New York: Academic Press.

Hyman, L. 1977a. On the nature of linguistic stress. In L. Hyman, ed. 1977b.

Hyman, L., ed. 1977b. *Studies in Stress and Accent*. Southern California Occasional Papers in Linguistics 4. University of Southern California, Los Angeles.

Ingria, R. 1980. Compensatory lengthening as a metrical phenomenon. *Linguistic Inquiry* 11, 465–497.

Itkonen, E. 1955. Über die Betonungsverhältnisse in den finnisch-ugrischen Sprachen. *Acta Linguistica Academiae Scientarium Hungaricae* 5, 21–34.

Itkonen, E. 1966. *Kieli ja sen tutkimus*. Helsinki: WSOY.

Ivič, P., and I. Lehiste. 1973. Interaction between tone and quantity in Serbo-Croatian. *Phonetica* 28, 182–190.

Jackendoff, R. 1972. *Semantic Interpretation in Generative Grammar*. Cambridge, Mass.: The MIT Press.

Jackendoff, R. 1977. $\bar{X}$ *Syntax: A Study of Phrase Structure*. Linguistic Inquiry Monograph 2. Cambridge, Mass.: The MIT Press.

Jackendoff, R., and F. Lerdahl. 1982. A grammatical parallel between music and language. In M. Clynes, ed., *Music, Mind, and Brain*. New York: Plenum.

Jaeggli, O. 1980. Remarks on *to* contraction. *Linguistic Inquiry* 11, 239–246.

Jassem, W. 1949. Indication of speech rhythm of educated Southern English. *Le Maître Phonétique* 92, 22–24.

Jassem, W. 1952. *Intonation of Conversational English*. Wroclaw.

Jespersen, O. 1909. *A Modern English Grammar on Historical Principles. Part I: Sounds and Spellings*. Heidelberg: Winter.

Jespersen, O. 1962. Notes on metre. *Selected Writings of Otto Jespersen*. London: Allen & Unwin.

Johnson, C. D. 1973. *Formal Aspects of Phonological Description*. The Hague: Mouton.

Jones, C. 1976. Some constraints on medial consonant clusters. *Language* 52, 121–130.

Jones, D. 1931. The "word" as a phonetic entity. *Le Maître Phonétique*, 3rd series, No. 36. Reprinted in W. E. Jones and J. Laver, eds., *Phonetics in Linguistics: A book of Readings*. London: Longmans.

Jones, D. 1956. The hyphen as a phonetic sign: A contribution to the theory of syllable division and juncture. *Zeitschrift für Phonetik und allgemeine Sprachwissenschaft*, Band 9, Heft 2, 99–107.

Jones, D. 1964. *Outline of English Phonetics*. 9th ed. Cambridge: Heffer.

Kahane, H., and R. Beym. 1948. Syntactical juncture in colloquial Mexican Spanish. *Language* 24, 388–396.

Kahn, D. 1976. Syllable-based generalizations in English phonology. Doctoral dissertation, Massachusetts Institute of Technology.

Kahn, D. 1980. Syllable-structure specifications in phonological rules. In M. Aronoff and M.-L. Kean, eds., *Juncture*, 91–106. Saratoga, Calif.: Anma Libri.

Kaisse, E. 1977. Hiatus in modern Greek. Doctoral dissertation, Harvard University.

Kaisse, E. 1978. On the syntactic environment of a phonological rule. In W. A. Beach, S. E. Fox, and S. Philosoph, eds., *Papers from the 13th Regional Meeting of the Chicago Linguistic Society*, 173–185. Chicago Linguistic Society, University of Chicago.

Kaisse, E. 1981a. Appositive relatives and the cliticization of *who*. In K. A. Hendrick, C. S. Mosek, and M. F. Miller, eds., *Papers from the 17th Regional Meeting of the Chicago Linguistic Society*. Chicago Linguistic Society, University of Chicago.

Kaisse, E. 1981b. The syntax of auxiliary reduction in English. Ms., University of Washington.

Karčevskij, S. 1931. Sur la phonologie de la phrase. *Travaux du Cercle Linguistique de Prague* IV, 188–228.

Katz, J., and P. Postal. 1964. *An Integrated Theory of Linguistic Descriptions.* Cambridge, Mass.: The MIT Press.

Kenyon, J. S. 1966. *American Pronunciation.* 10th ed. Ann Arbor, Mich.: Wahr.

King, H. V. 1970. On blocking the rules for contraction in English. *Linguistic Inquiry* 1, 134–136.

Kingdon, R. 1958a. *The Groundwork of English Stress.* London: Longmans, Green & Co., Ltd.

Kingdon, R. 1958b. *The Groundwork of English Intonation.* London: Longmans.

Kiparsky, P. 1966. Über den deutschen Akzent. *Studia Grammatica* 7. Berlin: Akademie Verlag.

Kiparsky, P. 1973. Elsewhere in phonology. In S. R. Anderson and P. Kiparsky, eds., *A Festschrift for Morris Halle.* New York: Holt, Rinehart and Winston.

Kiparsky, P. 1978. Issues in phonological theory. In J. Weinstock, ed., *The Nordic Languages and Modern Linguistics.* Vol. 3. Austin, Tex.: University of Texas Press.

Kiparsky, P. 1979. Metrical structure assignment is cyclic. *Linguistic Inquiry* 10, 421–442.

Kiparsky, P. 1981. Remarks on the metrical structure of the syllable. In W. U. Dressler, O. E. Pfeiffer, and J. R. Rennison, eds., *Phonologica 1980,* Proceedings of the 4th International Conference on Phonology, Vienna. Innsbruck.

Kiparsky, P. 1982a. Lexical morphology and phonology. In *Linguistics in the Morning Calm,* 3–91. Seoul: Hanshin.

Kiparsky, P. 1982b. From cyclic phonology to lexical phonology. In H. van der Hulst and N. Smith, eds., *The Structure of Phonological Representations (Part I),* 131–177. Dordrecht: Foris.

Kiparsky, P. 1983a. Lexical levels in analogical change: The case of Icelandic. Ms., Massachusetts Institute of Technology.

Kiparsky, P. 1983b. Word-formation and the lexicon. Ms., Massachusetts Institute of Technology.

Kiparsky, P. 1983c. Some consequences of lexical phonology. Ms., Massachusetts Institute of Technology.

Kisseberth, C., and M. I. Abasheikh. 1974. Vowel length in Chi Mwi:ni: A case study of the role of grammar in phonology. In A. Bruck, R. A. Fox, and M. W. LaGaly, eds., *Papers from the Parasession on Natural Phonology,* 193–209. Chicago Linguistic Society, University of Chicago.

Klatt, D. H. 1975. Vowel lengthening is syntactically determined in a connected discourse. *Journal of Phonetics* 3, 129–140.

Klatt, D. H. 1976. Linguistic uses of segmental duration in English: Acoustic and perceptual evidence. *Journal of the Acoustical Society of America* 59, 1208–1221.

Klatt, D. H. To appear. Synthesis by rule of segmental durations in English sentences. In B. Lindblom and S. Ohman, eds., *Frontiers of Speech Communication Research*. New York: Academic Press.

Klima, E. 1964. Negation in English. In J. Fodor and J. Katz, eds., *The Structure of Language*. Englewood Cliffs, N.J.: Prentice-Hall.

Kuno, S. 1972. Functional sentence perspective. *Linguistic Inquiry* 3, 269–320.

Kuryłowicz, J. 1948. Contribution à la théorie de la syllabe. *Biuletyn polskiego towarzystwa jezykoznawczego* 8, 80–114.

Ladd, D. R. 1980. *The Structure of Intonational Meaning*. Bloomington: Indiana University Press.

Ladd, D. R. 1981. English compound stress. In V. Burke and J. Pustejovsky, eds., *Proceedings of the Eleventh Annual Meeting of NELS*. Graduate Linguistic Student Association, University of Massachusetts at Amherst.

Ladd, D. R. To appear. Phonological features of intonational peaks. *Language*.

Lakoff, G. 1970. Global rules. *Language* 46, 627–639.

Lakoff, G. 1972a. The arbitrary basis of transformational grammar. *Language* 48, 76–87.

Lakoff, G. 1972b. The global nature of the nuclear stress rule. *Language* 48, 285–303.

Langendoen, D. T. 1975. Finite-state parsing of phrase-structure languages and the status of readjustment rules in the grammar. *Linguistic Inquiry* 6, 533–554.

Lapointe, S. 1980. A theory of grammatical agreement. Doctoral dissertation, University of Massachusetts at Amherst.

Lapointe, S. 1981. The representation of inflectional morphology within the lexicon. In V. Burke and J. Pustejovsky, eds., *Proceedings of the Eleventh Annual Meeting of NELS*. Graduate Linguistic Student Association, University of Massachusetts at Amherst.

Lea, W. 1974. Prosodic aids to speech recognition: IV. A general strategy for prosodically guided speech understanding. *Univac Report* No. PX 10791. St. Paul, Minn.: Sperry Univac.

Lea, W. 1975. Prosodic aids to speech recognition: VII. Experiments on detecting and locating phrase boundaries. *Univac Report* No. PX 11534. St. Paul, Minn.: Sperry Univac.

Lea, W. 1977. Acoustic correlates of stress and juncture. In L. Hyman, ed. 1977b.

Lea, W., and D. R. Kloker. 1975. Prosodic aids to speech recognition; VI. Timing cues to linguistic structure and improved computer programs for prosodic analysis. *Univac Report* No. PX 11239. St. Paul, Minn.: Sperry Univac.

Leben, W. 1973. Suprasegmental phonology. Doctoral dissertation, Massachusetts Institute of Technology.

Leben, W. 1978. The representation of tone. In V. Fromkin, ed. 1978.

Leben, W. 1980. A metrical analysis of length. *Linguistic Inquiry* 11, 497–511.

Lehiste, I. 1960. An acoustic phonetic study of internal open juncture. Supplement to *Phonetica* 5. Basel, New York: S. Karger.

Lehiste, I. 1970. *Suprasegmentals*. Cambridge, Mass.: The MIT Press.

Lehiste, I. 1971a. Temporal organization of spoken language. In L. L. Hammerich, R. Jakobson, and E. Zwirner, eds., *Form and Substance: Phonetic and Linguistic Papers Presented to Eli Fischer-Jørgensen*. Copenhagen: Akademisk Forlag.

Lehiste, I. 1971b. The timing of utterances and linguistic boundaries. *Journal of the Acoustical Society of America* 51, 2018–2024.

Lehiste, I. 1973a. Phonetic disambiguation of syntactic ambiguity. *Glossa* 7, 197–222.

Lehiste, I. 1973b. Rhythmic units and syntactic units in production and perception. *Journal of the Acoustical Society of America* 54, 1228–1234.

Lehiste, I. 1975a. The role of temporal factors in the establishment of linguistic units and boundaries. In W. U. Dressler and F. V. Mares, eds., *Phonologica 1972*. Munich, Salzburg: Wilhelm Fink Verlag.

Lehiste, I. 1975b. Some factors affecting the duration of syllable nuclei in English. *Salzburger Beiträge zur Linguistik* 1, 81–104.

Lehiste, I. 1977. Isochrony reconsidered. *Journal of Phonetics* 5, 253–263.

Lehiste, I. 1979a. The perception of duration within sequences of four intervals. *Journal of Phonetics* 7, 313–316.

Lehiste, I. 1979b. Perception of sentence and paragraph boundaries. In B. Lindblom and S. Ohman, eds., *Frontiers of Speech Research*. New York: Academic Press.

Lehiste, I. 1980. Phonetic manifestation of syntactic structure in English. *Annual Bulletin,* No. 14, 1–27. Research Institute of Logopedics and Phoniatrics, University of Tokyo.

Lehiste, I., J. P. Olive, and L. A. Streeter. 1976. Role of duration in disambiguating syntactically ambiguous sentences. *Journal of the Acoustical Society of America* 60, 1119–1202.

Lehiste, I., and G. E. Peterson. 1960. Duration of syllable nuclei in English. *Journal of the Acoustical Society of America* 32, 693–703.

Leone, A. 1962. A proposito del raddoppiamento sintattico. *Bolletino del centro di Studii Filogici e Linguistici Siciliani* 7, 163–170.

Levi, J. 1978. *The Syntax and Semantics of Complex Nominals*. New York: Academic Press.

Liberman, M. 1975. The intonational system of English. Doctoral dissertation, Massachusetts Institute of Technology.

Liberman, M. 1978. Modelling of duration patterns in reiterant speech. In D. Sankoff, ed., *Linguistic Variation: Models and Methods*. New York: Academic Press.

Liberman, M., and J. Pierrehumbert. 1984. Intonational invariance under changes in pitch range and length. In M. Aronoff, R. Oehrle, B. Wilker, and F. Kelley, eds., *Language Sound Structure*. Cambridge, Mass.: The MIT Press.

Liberman, M., and A. S. Prince. 1977. On stress and linguistic rhythm. *Linguistic Inquiry* 8, 249–336.

Liberman, M., and I. Sag. 1974. Prosodic form and discourse function. In M. W. LaGaly, R. Fox, and A. Bruck, eds., *Papers from the 10th Regional Meeting of the Chicago Linguistic Society*, 416–427. Chicago Linguistic Society, University of Chicago.

Lieber, R. 1980. On the organization of the lexicon. Doctoral dissertation, Massachusetts Institute of Technology.

Lieberman, P. 1965. On the acoustic basis of the perception of intonation by linguists. *Word* 21, 40–54.

Lindblom, B. 1968. Temporal organization of syllable production. *Quarterly Progress and Status Report 2–3*, 1–5. Speech Transmission Laboratory, Royal Institute of Technology, Stockholm.

Lindblom, B., and K. Rapp. 1973. Some temporal regularities of spoken Swedish. Papers from the Institute of Linguistics, University of Stockholm, Publication 21.

Lyberg, B. 1979. Final lengthening—partly a consequence of restrictions on the speech of fundamental frequency change? *Journal of Phonetics* 7, 187–196.

McCarthy, J. 1977. On hierarchical structure within syllables. Ms., Massachusetts Institute of Technology.

McCarthy, J. 1979a. On stress and syllabification. *Linguistic Inquiry* 10, 443–466.

McCarthy, J. 1979b. Formal problems in Semitic phonology and morphology. Doctoral dissertation, Massachusetts Institute of Technology.

McCarthy, J. 1981a. A prosodic theory of nonconcatenative morphology. *Linguistic Inquiry* 12, 373–418.

McCarthy, J. 1981b. Syllable weight, stress, and pretonic strengthening in Tiberian Hebrew. In H. Borer and J. Aoun, eds., *Theoretical Issues in the Grammar of Semitic Languages*. MIT Working Papers in Linguistics 3.

McCarthy, J. 1982. Prosodic structure and expletive infixation. *Language* 58, 574–590.

McCawley, J. 1968. *The Phonological Component of a Grammar of Japanese*. The Hague: Mouton.

McCawley, J. 1969. Length and voicing in Tübatulabal. In R. I. Binnick, A. Davison, G. Green, and J. Morgan, eds., *Papers from the 5th Regional Meeting of the Chicago Linguistic Society*, 407–415. Chicago Linguistic Society, University of Chicago.

Macdonald, N. 1976. Duration as a syntactic boundary cue in ambiguous sentences. Presented at IEEE International Conference on Acoustics, Speech and Signal Processing, Philadelphia, 1976.

Malagoli, G. 1946. *L'accentazione italiana*. Florence: Sansoni.

Martin, J. G. 1970a. On judging pauses in spontaneous speech. *Journal of Verbal Learning and Verbal Behavior* 9, 75–78.

Martin, J. G. 1970b. Rhythm-induced judgements of word stress in sentences. *Journal of Verbal Learning and Verbal Behavior* 9, 627–633.

Martin, J. G. 1972. Rhythmic (hierarchical) versus serial structure in speech and other behavior. *Psychological Review* 79, 487–509.

Mitchell, T. F. 1960. Prominence and syllabication in Arabic. *Bulletin of the Society of Oriental and African Studies* XXIII/2. Reprinted in T. F. Mitchell, *Principles of Firthian Linguistics*, 75–98. London: Longmans.

Mohanan, K. P. 1982. Lexical phonology. Doctoral dissertation, Massachusetts Institute of Technology.

Nakatani, L., and J. A. Schaeffer. 1978. Hearing "words" without words: Prosodic cues for word perception. *Journal of the Acoustical Society of America* 63, 234–245.

Nakatani, L., K. O'Connor, and C. Aston. 1981. Prosodic aspects of American English speech rhythm. *Phonetica* 38, 84–106.

Nanni, D. 1977. Stressing words in *-ative*. *Linguistic Inquiry* 8, 752–761.

Napoli, D. J., and M. Nespor. 1979. The syntax of word-initial consonant gemination in Italian. *Language* 55, 812–841.

Neidle, C., and B. Schein. No date. Sundry remarks on comparatives, contraction, and dialect variation. Ms., Massachusetts Institute of Technology.

Nespor, M. 1977. Some syntactic structures of Italian and their relationship to the phenomenon of raddoppiamento sintattico. Doctoral dissertation, University of North Carolina at Chapel Hill.

Nespor, M., and I. Vogel. 1979. Clash avoidance in Italian. *Linguistic Inquiry* 10, 467–482.

Nespor, M., and I. Vogel. 1982. Prosodic domains of external sandhi rules. In H. van der Hulst and N. Smith, eds., *The Structure of Phonological Representations (Part I)*, 225–256. Dordrecht: Foris.

Nespor, M., and I. Vogel. 1983. Prosodic levels above the word and ambiguity. In A. Cutler and D. R. Ladd, eds., *Prosody: Models and Measurements*, Berlin, Heidelberg, New York: Springer.

Newman, S. S. 1946. On the stress system of English. *Word* 2, 171–187.

Newman, S. S. 1948. English suffixation: A descriptive approach. *Word* 4, 24–36.

Nicholson, R., and R. Nicholson. 1962. Fore phonemes and their interpretation. *Oceanic Linguistic Monographs*, No. 6, University of Sydney.

Norman, H. 1937. Reduplication of consonants in Italian pronunciation. *Italica* 14, 57–63.

O'Connor, J. D., and J. L. M. Trim. 1953. Vowel, consonant, syllable: A phonological definition. *Word* 9, 103–122.

Ohman, S. 1967. Word and sentence intonation: A quantitative model. *Quarterly Progress and Status Report 2–3*, 20–54. Speech Transmission Laboratory, Royal Institute of Technology, Stockholm.

Oller, D. K. 1973. The effect of position in utterance on speech segment duration in English. *Journal of the Acoustical Society of America* 54, 1235–1247.

O'Malley, M. H., D. R. Kloker, and B. Dara-Abrams. 1973. Recovering parenthesis from spoken algebraic expressions. *IEEE Transactions on Audio and Electroacoustics* AU–21, 217–220.

Osborn, H. 1916. Warao I. Phonology and morphophonemics. *International Journal of American Linguistics* 32, 108–123.

Pesetsky, D. 1979. Russian morphology and lexical theory. Ms., Massachusetts Institute of Technology.

Piera, C. 1978. A class of clitics and a class of phonological filters. Ms., Cornell University.

Pierrehumbert, J. 1979. The perception of fundamental frequency declination. *Journal of the Acoustical Society of America* 66, 363–369.

Pierrehumbert, J. 1980. The phonology and phonetics of English intonation. Doctoral dissertation, Massachusetts Institute of Technology.

Pierrehumbert, J. 1981. Synthesizing intonation. *Journal of the Acoustical Society of America* 70, 985–995.

Pierrehumbert, J., and M. Liberman. 1982. Modeling the fundamental frequency of the voice. Review of W. E. Cooper and J. M. Sorensen, *Fundamental Frequency in Sentence Production*. *Contemporary Psychology* 27.9.

Pike, K. 1945. *The Intonation of American English*. Ann Arbor, Mich.: University of Michigan Press.

Pike, K. 1947. Grammatical prerequisites to phonemic analysis. *Word* 3, 155–172.

Pike, K. 1967. *Language in Relation to a Unified Theory of the Structure of Human Behavior*. 2nd ed. The Hague: Mouton.

Pike, K., and E. Pike. 1947. Immediate constituents of Mazateco syllables. *International Journal of American Linguistics* 13, 78–91.

Postal, P. 1974. *On Raising*. Cambridge, Mass.: The MIT Press.

Postal, P., and G. K. Pullum. 1978. Traces and the description of English complementizer contraction. *Linguistic Inquiry* 9, 1–29.

Postal, P., and G. K. Pullum. 1982. The contraction debate. *Linguistic Inquiry* 13, 122–138.

Pratelli, R. 1970. Le renforcement syntactique des consonnes en Italien. *La Linguistique* 6, 39–50.

Prince, A. 1975. The phonology and morphology of Tiberian Hebrew. Doctoral dissertation, Massachusetts Institute of Technology.

Prince, A. 1976. Stress. Ms., University of Massachusetts at Amherst.

Prince, A. 1980. A metrical theory for Estonian quantity. *Linguistic Inquiry* 11, 511–562.

Prince, A. 1981. Pertaining to the grid. Talk presented at the Trilateral Conference on Formal Phonology, University of Texas at Austin, April 1981.

Prince, A. 1983. Relating to the grid. *Linguistic Inquiry* 14, 19–100.

Prince, A. 1984. Phonology with tiers. In M. Aronoff, R. Oehrle, B. Wilker, and F. Kelley, eds., *Language Sound Structure*. Cambridge, Mass.: The MIT Press.

Pulgram, E. 1970. *Syllable, Word, Nexus, Cursus*. The Hague: Mouton.

Pullum, G. K., and P. M. Postal. 1979. On an inadequate defense of "trace theory," *Linguistic Inquiry* 10, 689–706.

Pyle, C. 1972. On eliminating BM's. In P. Peranteau, J. Levi, and G. Phares, eds., *Papers from the 8th Regional Meeting of the Chicago Linguistic Society*, 516–532. Chicago Linguistic Society, University of Chicago.

Ramstedt, G. J. 1902. Bergtscheremissische Sprachstudien. *Mémoires de la société finno-ugrienne*, 17. Helsinki.

Raphael, L. J., M. F. Dorman, F. Freeman, and C. Tobin. 1975. Vowels and nasal duration as cues to voicing in word-final stop consonants: Spectrographic and perceptual studies. *Journal of Speech and Hearing Research* 18, 389–400.

Rapp, K. 1971. A study of syllable timing. *Quarterly Progress and Status Report*, 14–19. Speech Transmission Laboratory, Royal Institute of Technology, Stockholm.

Rees, M. 1975. The domain of isochrony. *Work in Progress* 8, 14–28. Department of Linguistics, Edinburgh University.

Reinhart, T. 1976. The syntactic domain of anaphora. Doctoral dissertation, Massachusetts Institute of Technology.

Riemsdijk, H. van, and E. Williams. 1980. NP structure. *Linguistic Review* 1.2.

Rischel, J. 1964. Stress, juncture, and syllabification in phonemic description. *Proceedings of the 9th International Congress of Linguists, Cambridge, Mass., 1962*. The Hague: Mouton.

Rischel, J. 1972. Compound stress in Danish without a cycle. *Annual Report of the Institute of Phonetics of the University of Copenhagen* 6, 211–228.

Rosetti, A. 1962. La syllabe phonologique. *Proceedings of the 4th International Congress of Phonetic Sciences*, 490–499.

Ross, J. R. 1967. Constraints on variables in syntax. Doctoral dissertation, Massachusetts Institute of Technology.

Ross, J. R. 1972. A reanalysis of English word stress, Part I. In M. K. Brame, ed., *Contributions to Generative Phonology*. Austin, Tex.: University of Texas Press.

Ross, J. R. 1973. Leftward, ho! In S. Anderson and P. Kiparsky, eds., *A Festschrift for Morris Halle*. New York: Holt, Rinehart and Winston.

Ross, J. R., and W. E. Cooper. 1979. *Like* syntax. In W. E. Cooper and E. C. T. Walker, eds., *Sentence Processing: Psycholinguistic Studies Presented to Merrill Garrett*. Hillsdale, N.J.: Lawrence Erlbaum Associates.

Rossi, M., A. di Cristo, D. J. Hirst, P. Martin, and Y. Nishinuma. 1981. *L'intonation: De l'acoustique à la sémantique*. Paris: Klincksieck.

Rotenberg, J. 1978. The syntax of phonology. Doctoral dissertation, Massachusetts Institute of Technology.

Safir, K., ed. 1979. *Papers on Syllable Structure, Metrical Structure, and Harmony Processes. MIT Working Papers in Linguistics* 1.

Saltarelli, M. 1970. *A Phonology of Italian in a Generative Framework*. The Hague: Mouton.

Schane, S. A. 1978. L'emploi des frontières de mot en français. In B. de Cornulier and F. Dell, eds., *Etudes de phonologie française*, 133–147. Paris: Editions du Centre National de la Recherche Scientifique.

Schauber, E. 1977. Focus and presupposition: A comparison of English intonation and Navajo particle placement. In D. J. Napoli, ed., *Elements of Tone, Stress, and Intonation*. Washington, D.C.: Georgetown University Press.

Schmerling, S. 1976. *Aspects of English Sentence Stress*. Austin, Tex.: University of Texas Press.

Schmerling, S. 1980. The proper treatment of the relationship between syntax and phonology. Paper presented at the 55th annual meeting of the Linguistic Society of America, December 1980, San Antonio.

Scott, D. 1982. Duration as a cue to the perception of a phrase boundary. *Journal of the Acoustical Society of America* 71, 996–1007.

Selkirk, E. O. 1972. The phrase phonology of English and French. Doctoral dissertation, Massachusetts Institute of Technology. New York: Garland.

Selkirk, E. O. 1974. French liaison and the X̄-notation. *Linguistic Inquiry* 5, 573–590.

Selkirk, E. O. 1978a. The French foot: On the status of "mute" e. *Studies in French Linguistics* 1, 141–150.

Selkirk, E. O. 1978b. The syllable. To appear in H. van der Hulst and N. Smith, eds., *The Structure of Phonological Representations (Part II)*. Dordrecht: Foris.

Selkirk, E. O. 1978c. On prosodic structure and its relation to syntactic structure. In T. Fretheim, ed., *Nordic Prosody II*. Trondheim: TAPIR.

Selkirk, E. O. 1979. The prosodic structure of French. Paper presented at the 9th Annual Linguistic Symposium on Romance Languages, Georgetown University, March 1979.

Selkirk, E. O. 1980a. Prosodic domains in phonology: Sanskrit revisited. In M. Aronoff and M.-L. Kean, eds., *Juncture*. Saratoga, Calif.: Anma Libri.

Selkirk, E. O. 1980b. The role of prosodic categories in English word stress. *Linguistic Inquiry* 11, 563–605.

Selkirk, E. O. 1981a. On the nature of phonological representation. In J. Anderson, J. Laver, and T. Meyers, eds., *The Cognitive Representation of Speech*. Amsterdam: North Holland.

Selkirk, E. O. 1981b. English compounding and the theory of word structure. In T. Hoekstra, H. van der Hulst, and M. Moortgat, eds., *The Scope of Lexical Rules*. Dordrecht: Foris.

Selkirk, E. O. 1981c. Epenthesis and degenerate syllables in Cairene Arabic. In H. Borer and J. Aoun, eds., *Theoretical Issues in the Grammar of Semitic Languages*. MIT Working Papers in Linguistics 3.

Selkirk, E. O. 1982. *The Syntax of Words*. Linguistic Inquiry Monograph 7. Cambridge, Mass.: The MIT Press.

Selkirk, E. O. 1984. On the major class features and syllable theory. In M. Aronoff, R. Oehrle, B. Wilker, and F. Kelley, eds., *Language Sound Structure*. Cambridge, Mass.: The MIT Press.

Selkirk, E. O. In preparation. Stress in syllable-timed languages. Ms., University of Massachusetts at Amherst.

Severynse, M. 1977. Irregular stress patterning in lexical compounds. *Harvard Studies in Phonology* 1, 369–389.

Siegel, D. 1974. Topics in English morphology. Doctoral dissertation, Massachusetts Institute of Technology. New York: Garland.

Sorensen, J. M., W. E. Cooper, and J. M. Paccia. 1978. Speech timing of grammatical categories. *Cognition* 6, 135–153.

Stanley, R. 1973. Boundaries in phonology. In S. Anderson and P. Kiparsky, eds., *A Festschrift for Morris Halle*. New York: Holt, Rinehart and Winston.

Steele, J. 1775. *An Essay towards Establishing the Melody and Measure of Speech*. Facsimile edition, Scholar Press, 1969.

Steriade, D. 1982. Greek prosodies and the nature of syllabification. Doctoral dissertation, Massachusetts Institute of Technology.

Stillings, J. 1975. The formulation of gapping in English as evidence for variable types in syntactic transformations. *Linguistic Analysis* 1, 247–274.

Stowell, T. 1979. Stress systems of the world, unite! In K. Safir, ed. 1979.

Stowell, T. 1981. Origins of phrase structure. Doctoral dissertation, Massachusetts Institute of Technology.

Strauss, S. 1979a. Against boundary distinctions in English morphology. *Linguistic Analysis* 5, 387–419.

Strauss, S. 1979b. Some principles of word structure in English and German. Doctoral dissertation, CUNY Graduate Center.

Streeter, L. 1978. Acoustic determinants of phrase boundary perception. *Journal of the Acoustical Society of America* 64, 1582–1592.

Suiko, M. 1977. Strong and weak forms in English. In M. Ukaji, T. Nakao, and M. Kajita, *Studies Presented to Professor Akira Ota on His Sixtieth Birthday*. Studies in English Linguistics 5. Tokyo: Asaki Press.

Suiko, M. 1978a. Strong forms of auxiliary before ##. Ms., Yamaguchi University.

Suiko, M. 1978b. A phonological analysis of *Wanna* formation. Ms., Yamaguchi University.

Swadesh, M. 1947. On the analysis of English syllabics. *Language* 23, 137–150.

Swadesh, M., and C. F. Voegelin. 1939. A problem in phonological alternation. In M. Joos, ed., *Readings in Linguistics,* Vol. 1, 4th ed., 1966. Chicago: The University of Chicago Press.

Sweet, H. 1875–76. Words, logic, and grammar. *Transactions of the Philological Society, 1875–1876,* 470–503. (In *Collected Papers of Henry Sweet,* Oxford, 1913.)

Sweet, H. 1891. *A Handbook of Phonetics.* Oxford: Henry Frowde.

Sweet, H. 1908. *The Sounds of English—An Introduction to Phonetics.* Oxford: Clarendon Press.

Thiersch, C. 1977. Topics in German syntax. Doctoral dissertation, Massachusetts Institute of Technology.

Thompson, H. S. 1980. *Stress and Salience in English: Theory and Practice.* Palo Alto, Calif.: Xerox Palo Alto Research Center.

Trager, G. L. 1942. The phoneme "t": A study in theory and method. *American Speech* 17, 144–148.

Trager, G. L., and B. Bloch. 1941. The syllabic phonemes of English. *Language* 17, 223–246.

Trager, G. L., and H. L. Smith, Jr. 1951. *An Outline of English Structure.* Studies in Linguistics: Occasional Papers No. 3. Norman, Okla.: Battenberg Press.

Trubetzkoy, N. S. 1939. *Grundzüge der Phonologie.* Translated into French as *Principes de Phonologie,* by J. Cantineau. Paris: Klincksieck, 1949.

Tryon, D. T. 1970. *An Introduction to Maranungku.* Pacific Linguistics Monograph Series B, No. 14. Australian National University at Canberra.

Uldall, E. T. 1971. Isochronous stresses in R.P. In L. L. Hammerich, R. Jakobson, and E. Zwirner, eds., *Form and Substance: Phonetic and Linguistic Papers Presented to Eli Fischer-Jørgensen.* Copenhagen: Akademisk Forlag.

Uldall, E. T. 1972. Relative durations of syllables in two-syllable rhythmic feet in R.P. in connected speech. *Work in Progress* 5, 110–111. Department of Linguistics, Edinburgh University.

Umeda, N. 1975. Vowel duration in American English. *Journal of the Acoustical Society of America* 58, 434–445.

Vanderslice, R., and P. Ladefoged. 1972. Binary suprasegmental features and transformational word-accentuation rules. *Language* 48, 819–838.

Vennemann, T. 1972. On the theory of syllabic phonology. *Linguistische Berichte* 18, 1–18.

Vergnaud, J.-R. 1974. Quelques règles phonologiques du français. Thèse de troisième cycle, Université de Paris VII.

Vergnaud, J.-R. 1977. Formal properties of phonological rules. In R. Butts and J. Hintikka, eds., *Basic Problems in Methodology and Linguistics*, 299–317. Dordrecht: D. Reidel.

Voegelin, C. F. 1935. Tübatulabal grammar. *University of California Publications in American Archaeology and Ethnology* 34, 55–190.

Vogel, I. 1977. The syllable in phonological theory; with special reference to Italian. Doctoral dissertation, Stanford University.

Vogel, I., and M. Nespor. 1979. An interaction between stress and length in Italian. Paper presented at the winter meeting of the Linguistic Society of America, 1979.

Vogel, I., and S. Scalise. 1982. Secondary stress in Italian. Ms., University of Nijmegen, University of Venice.

Wasow, T. 1975. Anaphoric pronouns and bound variables. *Language* 51, 368–383.

Wheeler, D. 1981. Aspects of a categorial theory of phonology. Doctoral dissertation, University of Massachusetts at Amherst.

Whorf, B. L. 1940. Linguistics as an exact science. In J. B. Carroll, ed., *Language, Thought, and Reality*. Cambridge, Mass.: The MIT Press.

Williams, E. 1976. Underlying tone in Margi and Igbo. *Linguistic Inquiry* 7, 463–484.

Williams, E. 1980a. Predication. *Linguistic Inquiry* 11, 203–238.

Williams, E. 1980b. Remarks on stress and anaphora. *Journal of Linguistic Research* 1, 1–16.

Williams, E. 1981a. On the notions "lexically related" and "head of a word." *Linguistic Inquiry* 12, 245–274.

Williams, E. 1981b. Argument structure and morphology. *Linguistic Review* 1.1.

Yip, M. 1982. The interaction of tone and stress in Molinos Mixtec. Ms., Massachusetts Institute of Technology.

Zwicky, A. M. 1970. Auxiliary reduction in English. *Linguistic Inquiry* 1, 323–336.

Zwicky, A. M. 1975. Settling on an underlying form: The English inflectional endings. In D. Cohen and J. R. Wirth, eds., *Testing Linguistic Hypotheses*. New York: Wiley.

Zwicky, A. M. 1977. On clitics. Paper presented at the 3rd International Phonologie-Tagung at the University of Vienna, 1976. Available from the Indiana University Linguistics Club, Bloomington.

Zwicky, A. M. 1982a. An expanded view of morphology in the syntax-phonology interface. Proceedings of the 11th International Congress of Linguists, Tokyo, August 1982.

Zwicky, A. M. 1982b. Stranded *to* and phonological phrasing in English. Ms., Ohio State University.

Zwicky, A. M., and G. K. Pullum. 1982. Cliticization vs. inflection: English *n't**. Available from the Indiana University Linguistics Club, Bloomington.

Index